To Boldly Go

Ron Palmer

PNEUMA SPRINGS PUBLISHING UK

First Published in 2011 by:
Pneuma Springs Publishing

To Boldly Go

Pneuma Springs

British Library Cataloguing in Publication Data

Palmer, Ron.
To boldly go : where so many have gone before.
1. Palmer, Ron. 2. Palmer, Ron--Travel. 3. Voyages and travels. 4. Seafaring life. 5. Ship captains--Great Britain--Biography.
I. Title
910.4'5'092-dc22

ISBN-13: 9781907728150

Pneuma Springs Publishing
A Subsidiary of Pneuma Springs Ltd.
7 Groveherst Road, Dartford Kent, DA1 5JD.
E: admin@pneumasprings.co.uk

W: www.pneumasprings.co.uk

To Boldly Go

Where so many have gone before

PROLOGUE

Retirement even the thought of such can be for some people a daunting experience especially if they are unprepared. Fortunately, for my part I had an aptitude for DIY which was to come into my, shall I say afterlife, a life after working for someone else for 35 years that is. As it turned out I retired early in my mid fifties, and took the opportunity to move to British Columbia a place I've had a desire to be since being on a ship trading between there and the West Indies, timber one way and sulphur for the paper mills the other, this being in the mid 1950s. Vancouver was my first sojourn after retirement to stay in that wonderful part of the world until Pender Island beckoned to me, a small island of some 2000 souls, a friendly laid back island and one of the Southern Gulf islands in the Strait of Georgia. This as it turned out was a fortunate choice as apart from the laid back character that suited my new outlook on life it gave opportunities for my skills that would be hard to put into practice in a city the size of Vancouver. After building a house for my then girlfriend and myself I branched out into doing handy-man jobs which progressed from minor repair jobs to erecting 100 sq ft cabins on lots that off island folks owned and needed a roof over their heads and a place to camp out when visiting the island. These items proved to be quite popular to the point that my then neighbour at that time bequeathed me with the sobriquet Ronnie Two Sheds which was quite amusing but inadequate as by this time there were quite a few more than two of these sheds if you like dotted around the island. This size incidentally was convenient; a structure of 100 foot floor space didn't require planning permission. It has always been my contention that in North America generally and in Canada in particular, as was the case in this instance, if a person can read and has a practical aptitude one can do whatever one wishes to do as long as they stay with-in the regulations, it is all written down in easy to understand books. And should you go wrong there is always the Building Inspector to put you back on track. So it was then that I progressed to building houses and unbeknown to me at that time, a forty-foot sloop. But more of that experience later.

The relationship that I was in became quite intolerable in time and I soon moved out to live on my own. This bachelor status lasted for some three or four months then such is life on Pender one drifts towards another kindred soul and off we go again. By this time I was established as a reliable turn up on time worker and the jobs kept coming in. My present partner was a keen boater having secured a 'Skippers ticket' for small sailboats. So it was then, against my initial protests, as having spent thirty-five years at sea, and was not quite enamoured with putting out onto the waters again. But then, what is life but a compromise and so we were soon proud owners of a 27ft Tanza sloop called 'Knotty Girl' seized by the bank from the owner due to none payment of debt and offered to the highest bid.

We took possession of said 'Knotty Girl' in a boatyard in North Vancouver and brought it over to Pender, not without some anxious moments I must add as coming under Lions Gate Bridge, which connects Vancouver with the North Shore, the engine promptly cut out and we drifted out into English Bay with the outgoing tide. In which that direction was a plus, rather than being pushed back towards our starting point. In this unfamiliar situation, being strangers to the boat, I managed to get the sails up which due to the poor wind speed had our movement a little better than without any wind at all. However, after letting the engine cool down it fired again on the first attempt and so we chugged along at engine revolutions that wouldn't overheat the engine again across the Strait of Georgia and into Active Pass, between the islands of Galiano and Mayne, by evening twilight. Not a good time of day for visibility but by keeping to the starboard side of the Pass we managed to get through without running into or being run down by one of the frequent ferries plying between Vancouver Island and the Mainland.

The engine a petrol model continued to behave and in due course we arrived at Otter Bay Marina, our destination. This is where a feature that had particularly pleased me, a searchlight mounted on the bow, came into play as the dock became brilliantly illuminated as we approached eliminating any chance of making a violent contact with the said dock in the dark. So it was that the first adventure with our new toy came to a satisfactory conclusion.

From then on we had many interesting jaunts in the boat, sometimes with friends, but most of the outings were by ourselves, even venturing further afield to what became a favourite spot - the Marine Park at Wallace Island. By this time I had got over my reservations about being a boat owner and settled down to being a responsible and proud small boat sailor by making improvements where necessary and the general upkeep, in particular. Of course it wasn't all a bed of roses and one particular incident occurred which I think had my partner, Jan, starting to lose interest in the joys of boating. This happened on one particular summer evening after I had come home from work. On my suggestion we had gone down to the boat with a bottle of wine and went out to try our luck at salmon fishing. Chugging along nicely at a decent trolling speed we got as far as the entrance to Navy Channel, the channel between Pender and the Mayne the next island north. When the fishing line fouled with the result that in attempting to retrieve it resulted in losing the whole tackle, it was getting towards dark anyway so we started back to the Marina. But, such is life, the engine packed in, just quit and as any attempt to start it again only produced an ominous sound from the solenoid suggesting a dead battery and that no way was this lump of old iron going to spring into life. A most puzzling situation as with the engine running one would expect the battery to be fully charged. In due course at a later date this phenomenon became apparent. The switch for the searchlight, that wonderful and useful addition to the boat's equipment, is located in the cockpit at the same height and position of my right leg, the two had obviously made contact and the light was switched on unnoticed at the time due to the brightness of the evening. Well, as they say one can live and learn. All was not lost though as there was a small breeze blowing landwards so it was just a case of hoisting the sails and away we would go. Right, now it was time for the sail to misbehave and made it impossible to hoist even the main or the jib due to the downhaul fouling near the top of the mast. By this time the boat was drifting towards the rocks, which would not do at all and giving me visions of having to explain to the insurance people an embarrassing situation. So down went the anchor in time to stop the shoreward drift.

Fortunately the mast was equipped with steps so it was no problem to get up to clear the fouled line. It should be mentioned here that Pender Island is by-passed by large ferries plying between Swartz Bay on Vancouver Island and Tsawwassen on the mainland, with the bow waves from these vessels coming ashore on the island. While I was up the mast clearing the obstruction the boat was hit by a mini tsunami from a passing ferry which caused the boat to roll heavily with me clinging to the mast for dear life swinging through a violent arc of the surrounding atmosphere like a manic metronome, and to observe the winch handle slither across the deck and disappear over the side. Lesson two; don't leave the winch handle on deck there are pockets for such items.

Once everything had settled down and I had descended to the deck, quite shaken I might add, with the breeze filling the sails, it was up anchor to continue on our way. In due course we were off the home marina just as the wind died only to be carried past on the outgoing tide. This state of events brought the boat to the next marina along the shore a welcome haven called *Thieves Bay* and a private marina. Not that this designation troubled me, any port in a storm as they say to misquote a saying. It was with judicious manipulation mainly with swinging the rudder back and fro and the inset of tide into the bay that we came up against the breakwater extension, a fortunate bundle of pilings rather than the shelving side of the breakwater proper. It was from this position that we could hand the boat into the marina and tie up to the first dock. A most fortunate occurrence as had this tidal indraught not brought us into a safe berth who knows where we would have drifted off to. With the battery flat there was no communication with the VHF either. All was not a disaster though as this particular marina is a short uphill 20 minute walk home to which much wearied we arrived just after midnight. It never rains but it pours they do say and this occasion proved the point as someone had entered the house and walked off with the radio. Now this was indeed odd as it was the only item taken when there were other more valuable items; to whit a camera and a video camera also. Entering the house uninvited was quite an easy matter, but not usually a problem as not many people lock their doors on Pender it being that kind of community minded place. In this instant however our house was open due to major renovations being carried out and access was therefore much easier, and on subsequent occasions when we were out of the premises other objects were taken. These incidents were reported to the police and an investigation carried out, although the items in question were not recovered it was strongly suspected that the next door neighbour on being interviewed was a prime suspect, a person who carried a chip on his shoulder with a miserable and anti-social demeanour to boot. However, the thefts stopped after this interview and the items were replaced through the insurance. From that time on though precautions were taken to deter thieves from entering, not without leaving the bitter taste of resentment against this particular neighbour, at creating a distrust towards the island in general, until he and his wife eventual left the island and the trust in ones fellow man returned.

So it was then that we continued to use the boat until the time came to move on to a bigger and more roomy vessel, this being strongly suggested by my partner, whom I must add I generally agreed with seeing the advantages suggested in this move. So it was then that we were on the look-out for a hull that I could fit out to our requirements. In the course of this search we acquired a catalogue of one hundred hulls and plans thereof. It didn't take long for us to choose the type of boat we would like, it was a case of thumbing through the choices and both saying together without any hesitation, that one, a van de Stadt Norman. A forty foot sloop with an all round view from the saloon section, we both appreciated the social aspect of such a vessel, particularly as one didn't descend into a dark interior, plus two berths and spacious bathroom with stand up shower on the port side and roomy galley on the starboard, a truly perfect choice for our needs. All that remained was to order such a hull and this is were the first hiccup occurred in the original plan, on making inquiries I was advised that contrary to the assumed statement in advertising one hundred hulls they didn't provide the hulls, rather a prospective buyer would purchase the drawings and commission their own boat builder. Such an enterprise would require a builder from off island as Pender just didn't have such an animal so further elevating the cost. After a little soul searching it was decided that I would build the boat myself, a foolhardy decision of overconfidence one might surmise, but given a good set of drawings and Mylar plans that eliminate the need for lofting it didn't appear to me to be an overwhelming negative prospect. Then the next glitch raised its ugly head; the plans called for either a steel or aluminium construction neither of which I have the skills for, welding not being my forte. No problem as it turned out, on contacting the designers in Holland and advising I wished to use a foam core method of construction they very kindly sent another set of drawings for a fibreglass lay-up which would be needed for the construction method I proposed.

So it was then that the conception was put into being and progressed with great confidence and ease to the launching just short of three years later with the only part of the construction for which I needed professional help was with the fibreglass lay-up, for this a professional was engaged, and with my assistance I learned a lot on the art to the point I was able to complete the interior and other areas on my own. All in all a most wonderful experience which occupied all my waking hours six days a week, taking Sunday off, to rest and recuperate and prepare myself for the coming week. All in all the happiest period of my life, I would say. There were also breaks taken in the routine to go on holidays and six weeks to build a handicraft studio for my partner. The only downside to this boat building project was when it was completed I had an overwhelming desire to build another boat, not an unusual emotion I believe from what I've been made to understand. However, I managed to cure this prohibitively expensive notion by writing a book on the subject: Titled; *Building a Foam Cored Boat*, which satisfactorily laid this ghost to rest. During the course of construction I was asked many times if my plan was to sail around the world an idea that seems to fascinate armchair sailors. My response was always, 'I have spent all my working life staring at the ocean and that I was disinclined to repeat the experience, though I must admit to a germ of an idea being planted in my subconscious by these notions.

So followed some years of pleasurable and comfortable boating ranging further afield than with the Knotty Girl, experiences which once or twice transited the Strait of Georgia to Vancouver, it was on one of these jaunts that put my partner in a non-boating- ever-again frame of mind. The occasion being when we went to Vancouver to take a group of schoolteachers and their protégées to escort the replica of Captain Cook's Endeavour on it's way after being in museum mode at the Maritime Museum. All went well until the return trip motoring across the Strait when it started to blow quite strong lifting the sea to a lumpy and spume blown condition. I was prepared to hoist a sail to steady the boat in this seaway even though I didn't consider the situation to be particularly alarming, certainly not for myself, nor would I have thought a licensed small boat skipper, just to make things more comfortable but I was shouted down. And that was that, reduced to boating by myself as the dog had already refused to sail again, which in her case I could empathise as she had been violently seasick. So it was then that another phase of retirement enjoyment passed into history. And so it was that the glue that held our relationship together started to lose its adhesion. Not eminently noticeable at first but in this odd situation with one partner originally reluctant to have a boat and the other keen on doing so the roles had reversed. For my part I wanted to use this wonderful means of transportation I had created across the waters to the utmost and with my working life finally over I saw no reason to move backwards. I had this renewed desire to go, and go I did, which brings the reader to the first of my retirement nautical adventures, to circumnavigate Vancouver Island.

Part One

TRAVELS WITH MYSELF

Starting out on an adventure with a hangover is not the best state to be in. Although one functions well enough physically in familiar surroundings, the brain seems to prefer being in a state of repose. Which can lead to a marked difference between what is fact and what is fiction.

Over the years I have experienced enough hangovers to understand the routine. First thing on rising from one's bed, drink a couple of mugs of tea to counteract dehydration, get something to eat and get on with the day doing what one normally does, with the resolve never to drink so much ever again, ever, at least not until the next time, by noon the dull ache in the brain area has usually subsided, and the thought comes to mind that a good night's sleep without benefit of alcohol will solve everything.

Jan, now my wife, and I had visited friends the previous evening, a sort of bon voyage occasion, 'have a nice trip' sort of gathering. Well saying farewell without a drink, or two, (or three or more) isn't really wishing a person bon voyage. Now is it? Hence the ubiquitous hangover that was to dog me until the nights repose.

The plan was to get an early start from the berth at Thieves Bay, Pender Island, where other friends were to see me off with a glass of Champagne, to cheer me on my way, or that was the plan. Fortunately, or not, this plan was abandoned due to fact that on coming home the previous evening the car had suffered a puncture, and the time it took to change the wheel put the time of departure out of whack, and with the subsequent knock on effect the waiting friends had decided to give the send off a miss.

The reason for deciding to take off alone for a circumnavigation of Vancouver Island was varied and complex, Primarily, I couldn't persuade anyone to come with me. There might be a message there, not even my dog would come along having been seasick on that previous jaunt, the same goes for car journeys where she had to be tricked into getting in the car. Being with me was OK for her as long as it didn't involve any form of vehicular travel, now going for walks that were an entirely different ball of wax, so I didn't take this to be a personal affront. Just that she didn't like boats or cars. And in these respects she was asserting her privileges. Having said that, although the company would have been welcome to talk to of an evening stopover and for someone to help out with handling the boat and taking a turn with the cooking the lack of company proved to be no big deal at all, in fact I came to realise by this forthcoming experience that I much preferred my own company. And talking to oneself is not so bad as long as I didn't keep saying 'pardon' there would not be any need to repeat what I had said. Or for that matter there would not be any concern about my sanity.

In recent years, well in the last twenty or so since moving to Canada I have met people who in their rudeness cut across a conversation and interrupting as though what the speaker is saying is of no importance and starting their own conversation with someone else in the group. I find this most frustrating as I cannot understand why this should be necessary. Is it to do with modern living? Is it how people are brought up? I have noticed, come to think of it, that parents do not remonstrate with their off-spring when they interrupt a conversation as when in my childhood we would be reminded most sharply to wait until a person had finished speaking before offering a comment.

However, this impolite attitude would not occur on this trip as I would be talking to myself almost exclusively, and as things turned out I managed quite well without interruptions. At stopovers I met some very nice interesting people who were well mannered enough to listen without interrupting or being interrupted by the present company. These interludes with the unexpected company I met on the way very nicely filled in the gaps between my solo conversations.

Of course even though for whatever reason people turned down the offer of a sojourn on the briny and the experience of circumnavigating Vancouver Island without exception were always ready with advice, particularly on which way round one should travel. The uncontested favourite being counter-clockwise due to the prevailing winds was the given reason. Being of a naturally perverse nature and expecting reasonable weather at the time of year I opted to proceed clockwise. My reason being, and knowing myself quite well, that once I had rounded Cape Scott at the top end of the island and started downhill so to speak I would be like the old horse that could smell its stable and make a dash for home. All the places of interest that I wished to see were all on the west coast so it made sense to me to travel in the clockwise direction. As things turned out it was the right decision, though not for the reason given here.

As for being on my own the thought didn't bother me at all as I had had good grounding in this mental state. In my younger days during the summer holidays from school during my thirteenth and fourteenth years I took off on Danish fishing boats from my home town to Esbjerg in Denmark which fished in the North Sea until a worthwhile catch had been harvested. This would take about ten days out as fish was most plentiful at that time in the years after the Second World War the stocks having recuperated during this period of no fishing. I would stay in Esbjerg for a couple of weeks then return to the UK. One can well imagine that being in the company of a group of people who do not speak one's own language for any length of time that one tends to be alone within oneself. Not lonely, but being alone with one's own thoughts by being effectively shut out of any conversations. So in that situation I was given good training for future adventures.

Over the years, and particularly during my career in the Merchant Navy, I spent a great deal of time in my own company. This may have been because of the special circumstances one finds in such a profession. Standing a watch on the bridge of a ship with your own thoughts for company, particularly in the wee small hours of the middle watch, does not make for companionable conversation. And of course the saying, 'Board of Trade mates', is very true. You sail with someone more probably than not of a different background and interests with little in common, although a friendly relationship may crop up between you at the end of the voyage you go your separate ways. More likely than not never to cross paths again.

No matter, my boat and my thoughts were to be my companions. And at age sixty-five no big deal. After all it wasn't to be a circumnavigation of the world with the prospect of a vast ocean to be alone on, should the need be I could pop in to the nearest place of refuge on this particular jaunt. My boat too had been built by myself and thus knowing it inside out gave much comfort and a sense of well being to give confidence on the undertaking, so no worries there.

My boat had been named by my partner in respect of my abiding interest of all things Cook, James, explorer and scientific navigator that is. And I thought that 'Ron's Endeavour' to be appropriate and flattering in a sense although I hold no aspirations to be in the shadow even of that great man. It did come in handy though when meeting people on my travels as invariably any greeting was bound to include, "You must be Ron." Relieving the situation of one side of any introduction.

This then was the situation and the means by which I was to be transported around Vancouver Island. A voyage that was planned to be of four weeks duration, only took eighteen days. Bringing to light another quirk of my character, i.e. come on get a move on, chop-chop don't hang about. Well, we have to live with our selves, don't we?

It was a very comfortable boat and also a good sea boat with a large forward sleeping cabin sporting a dresser and hanging closet. A full size bathroom with stand up shower stall. The galley is large too with deep double sink, a four burner propane cook top and full size oven. A chest type freezer and a fridge. The lounge area comprises a large banquette with table around which six adults can comfortably be seated. This section is raised to give an all round view through the spacious windows of the great outdoors, a definite must when watching the world go by in inclement weather. The adjacent navigation position is in the same general area but on a lower level and close to the inside control console. Aft of this area and beneath the cockpit is another spacious berth roomy enough for two adults. All in all a well appointed boat and what more could a man asks for messing about on the ocean.

There are steering and engine controls from either the cockpit pedestal or from the inside console. Both positions have the necessary instruments for establishing wind speed and direction, depth of water and boat speed. The Auto pilot control is mounted on the cockpit pedestal for easy access. The Radar is mounted above the wheel at the inside steering position. The GPS readout is located above the chart table in the navigation section. Both radar and GPS being comforting features for navigating in fog. All these displays giving confidence and a feeling of wellbeing, a get up and go state of mind.

Strange though it may seem, no matter what the weather I much prefer being outside. Especially in fog when other traffic, or logs and kelp rafts lurking out there to trap the unwary can be seen before running into them. Radar is not always reliable in picking up echoes of small targets even in still conditions and almost impossible when the weather is boisterous, even large targets may well be hidden in the clutter. For avoiding hitting large land masses though it is very useful.

During the duration of the first leg of this enterprise the winds were expected to be from the southwest and on the port beam and good sailing aspect. As it turned out the wind was either totally absent being replaced by thick fog or, from right ahead blowing at a brisk rate of knots. Consequently these conditions lent themselves to motoring almost exclusively between stopovers.

So much for forward planning.

DAY ONE

Freedom alone substitutes from time to time for the love of material comfort

At 0900 I slipped the moorings at Thieves Bay, Pender Island and headed directly into a south-westerly wind of 21 knots. The wind blowing hard against the ebb tide created a short standing sea and the forward movement of the boat soon brought spray over the bow. The fact that the sky was overcast and a continuous drizzle had set in didn't make for an auspicious start to this grand adventure. By noon though the wind had died a little and the sun came out, so my spirits lifted a little. Not the spirits consumed the previous evening, fortunately. The effect of those was still lurking in the darkest corners of my brain.

It was my intention to head off down the Haro Strait and make for Sooke, the planned first port of call. This would have been an ideal stopover prior to the run to Bamfield on the second day. As it turned out, due to not paying sufficient attention when passing Moresby Island I found that I had inadvertently made for the San Juan Islands a definite left hand down a bit situation, as it turned out this *faux pas* worked to my advantage.

The interesting thing about passing through these islands was that I found myself dwelling on how these islands were transferred from a joint British and American administration to become solely American territory and why the border between the United States and Canada took such an illogical turn to cut off Point Roberts on the mainland so that the bottom four square miles of this peninsula that is attached to Canada became American territory, and everything above remained Canadian instead of continuing the border on the 49th parallel through Point Roberts into the empty void of the Strait of Georgia before turning south, surely it would have made more sense to turn south in Boundary Bay to meet up with the border line where it now turns south to the east of Saturna Island. I guess we can only wonder about that one, most likely it due to ignorance of geography on the part of the Treaty Commission.

The San Juan deal is more clearly defined though, and it is an interesting piece of history for this part of the world.

In 1494 Spain and Portugal with the blessing of the Catholic Church whose Pope Alexander V1 (who happened to be a Spaniard) had, in the Treaty of Tordesillas exercised his divine right to divide the known world, or in the case of the Pacific rim, unknown world, between these two nations for their own spheres of influence. There being no place in this new world order for the likes of France or England, the Pacific coast, and by definition the country behind, from Cape Horn to the Bering Sea falling to the Spanish.

After negotiating what was to be referred to as the Nootka Sound Convention on the 28th October 1790 between Britain and Spain the land north of Cape Mendocino in California was ceded to Britain for the right to trade. Not that Spain had any valid claim to it in the first place as there were no settlements north of San Francisco, and had shown very little in the way of propriety rights anyway until Captain James Cook landed at Nootka Sound in 1779.

The area from California to the Strait of Juan de Fuca became known in time as the Oregon Territory and at first even though jointly occupied from 1818 for ten years by the United States and Britain it came under the influence of the Hudson Bay Company for their fur trade.

In 1842 American settlers were flooding into the Oregon Territory and as the population increased, the Hudson Bay Company whose interests relied on the fur trade could not withstand the pressure of settlement retreated to the north. Oregon, in 1848 then became territory of the United States.

James Douglas, assistant to the Chief Factor of the Company at Fort Vancouver on the Columbia River, was sent to find a suitable site for the new west coast headquarters, preferably to the north of the 49th parallel. Douglas however disagreed with Vancouver Island being partitioned to become partly American territory and chose a site with two good harbours on the southern tip of the island. It was here that Douglas built Fort Victoria. The population slowly grew around the fort and as a result of this growth Douglas successfully petitioned the British Government and Vancouver Island became a colony of Britain and Douglas was appointed Governor of this new colony in addition to being Chief Factor of the Hudson Bay Company at Fort Victoria.

The earlier retreat from the Oregon territory was an experience that Douglas would never forget and he was determined that no further encroachments by the Americans would happen, insisting that the border would be determined by the Columbia River. This would have placed most of what is now Washington State in Canada. By 1860 however he had to accept another retreat.

The Treaty of Washington to determine the border between Canada and the United States was signed by both parties in 1871. They agreed that the border would run on the 49th parallel of latitude from the Great Lakes until it reached the Pacific coast, the border would then turn south and follow the centre of the navigation waters between the mainland and Vancouver Island, then westwards through the Strait of Juan de Fuca to the Pacific proper. However, the exact location of the border had not been set down in these areas.

There are many islands in the Strait of Georgia and the closest to Victoria and largest was the San Juan group which was settled by both Americans and people whose allegiance was to Britain. The main trading post being operated by the Hudson Bay Company.

In due course no doubt due to the difference in cultures cracks began to appear in the community structure. This came to a head when a pig belonging to the manager of the trading post strayed onto an American farmers land and commenced uprooting the farmer's crop of potatoes. The farmer incensed at this intrusion shot the pig. Rather a high handed overkill sort of thing to do one would think. But when there is a strain in relations in a community this act is not really surprising, even though the owner of the pig was the most powerful person on the islands.

When Douglas heard of this incident he too was incensed and was determined to put a stop to the nonsense taking hold of the community. He therefore sent a Royal Navy gunboat to settle the affair. Rather a big stick to find an amicable settlement but then that was the arrogance prevalent at the time with powerful people. So, surprise, surprise, the Americans retaliated with a gunboat of their own and also landed troops. Douglas in turn also landed troops escalating the conflict. This is how the situation remained for some months in what became known as the Pig War. The situation now looked menacing with neighbour set against neighbour along national lines. Fortunately, the commanders of he two military contingents being professional soldiers and not emotionally involved in the situation decided to set up their respective camps at opposite ends of the island, which incidentally did not preclude the entertaining of each others garrisons.

Obviously this state of affairs could not continue, communication between London and Washington failed to resolve the issue, it was therefore decided to ask Kaiser Wilhelm of Germany to arbitrate on the fate of the San Juan islands. Who, much to the chagrin of the British population decided in favour of the Americans claim.

Therefore, in 1868 the San Juan Islands became American Territory.

The passage through the San Juan Islands provided a magnificent view of Mount Baker, an extinct volcano in Washington State. So named for Joseph Baker, 3rd lieutenant of the Discovery by Captain George Vancouver on the occasion of the surveying and charting of the Pacific North-west in 1792. Baker was credited with being the first European to sight this most spectacular mountain. At this time year, during the advanced summer Mount Baker has mostly lost its mantle of snow and bald patches of the underlying rock have appeared. No matter though, come winter this impressive mountain will once again be shrouded to restore its natural splendour to the delight of all the skiing fraternity and those who only want to admire the raw beauty of nature's work of art.

Rounding Cattle Point at the south end of San Juan Island and passing through Middle Channel I directed my course towards The Strait of Juan de Fuca and the Pacific coast of Vancouver Island. I wasn't too far across Haro Strait when I came to realise I would not make Sooke on this day. The choice of where to spend the night was either Victoria or Oak Bay Marina. It soon became clear that this would be Hobson Choice as I was getting dangerously low on fuel. So Oak Bay it was, a good choice it was too for no sooner had I reached the bay than the wind picked up. Such is fortune, had I not diverted through the San Juan Islands I would have been caught in open waters with this boisterous weather.

On the approach to the Marina breakwater there are one or two hazards which must be avoided and thankfully well marked. Inside though, if one is a first time visitor, it can be a little confusing looking for the fuel dock as this lies at the far side of the marina, and one must skirt the mooring slips until the fuel dock comes into view.

The fuel dock was almost totally occupied when I arrived but with the wind in the direction it happened to be I was blown on to a berth just ahead of two skidoos. Much to the Dock Jocks annoyance.

"Why didn't you wait for instructions?" he demanded. With I thought a little more asperity than the occasion seemed to warrant especially to a prospective customer.

"In this wind?" I pointed out, "there wasn't a great deal of choice."

"You could have stayed well clear."

"Sure," I said, and then reasonably, I thought nodding to another boat lined up behind me, "then he would have slipped in ahead of me." As he was showing signs of being reasonable with this statement of the obvious, I challenged the premise further. "Besides what is that monstrosity doing at a fuel dock taking up most of the space?" The object in question was being some sort of float with racks for kayaks and no visible means of propulsion.

The young man probably in his late teens glanced at the object in question and sounding miffed at being ill-used, "He said he wasn't going to be long, just had to use the toilets, that was half an hour ago."

"Such is the call of nature," I offered. And as I was alongside, albeit with my bow sticking out over the end of the dock, I had no intention of moving until I had refuelled and assigned a berth for the night. So I figured a more conciliatory approach would be the order of the day, and changed the subject back to the weather.

"The wind seems to be getting up," I commented.

Probably thinking it was not the done thing to be annoyed at paying customers and happy at the change of subject he brightened somewhat and became more friendly.

"Yes. I haven't heard the weather forecast for an hour or two but I can get it for you. Will you be requiring a slip?"

"Indeed I will," I said, "I've no intention of venturing out into the Strait in this wind. But I'll fuel up first if you don't mind."

How situations can change for the better when one adopts a reasonable tone with people who feel the need to assert their limited power. After refuelling and with the help of the Dock Jock holding the boat off from banging against the dock I settled down into the assigned berth.

After tying off the mooring lines and seeming to be unaware that the next boat had taken my place at the fuel dock. "I'll see if I can get the weather forecast for you."

I didn't have the heart to tell him I could get the forecast myself on the VHF radio, "That's very kind of you thank you."

"If you would like to go up to the office and check in I'll have it for you by the time you get back."

As the day was young I put the kettle on for a brew, and found time to put my feet up and relax. There was plenty of time to go to the office and pay my dues later, at this moment in time for that ever relaxing elixir, a cup of tea, was the order of the day.

While thus relaxing the weather report arrived courtesy of the young man, presumably he had VHF in the little cubby-hole by the fuel pumps as he had returned from that direction and the boat that had been waiting behind me had moved off again no doubt also fuelled up.

The weather report was favourable for the next day, the wind reaching 27 knots during the next few hours then easing over night to 10 knots by morning, which seemed fine to me as I wouldn't be leaving before morning anyway.

In due course I stirred my stumps went to office and paid my moorage for the night, then taking advantage of there being fresh water at the berth I filled in the time until dinner by washing down the decks and paintwork, this chore produced much wonderment at how dirty the boat had become even in the pristine air of Pender. We do have airplanes over flying between Vancouver and Victoria and it is not beyond the realms of probability for the microscopic nuclei pollution fallout from the exhaust from these flights to descend onto the unsuspecting boating public's pride and joy, and everything else for that matter.

Another mistake in the scheme of things became evident as I had forgotten to take anything out of the freezer for dinner. On lifting the lid off the freezer I was pleasantly surprised to see that Jan, bless her had packed the chest to the gunwales with frozen food. Heavens, I thought how long does she expect me to stay away there must be enough food in there to last six weeks. But fortune smiled, lying on the top of treasure trove lay a packet of kippers, my favourite repast in an emergency. I didn't doubt for a moment that, Jan, that thoughtful lady, anticipating my propensity to forget to prepare for meals had placed them where they would not be missed. So all was well with my little world, the kippers were soon thawed out, and with mashed potatoes, peas and carrots all from our garden I was soon tucking in with a glass or two of our homemade wine to a sumptuous feast. And the inner man soon became satisfied and replete.

The evening was quite warm, regardless of the rising wind so after washing the pots and disposing of the kipper bones I brought out a cushion and relaxed with the rest of the wine in the cockpit and listened to the cacophony of slapping halyards against the masts of other boats. Rather smugly I congratulated myself on having my halyards inside the mast. There was quite a parade of pedestrian traffic along the dock, mainly from the returning whale watching boats, although some were obviously other strollers who were just enjoying the evening and viewing boats in the marina. For me the enjoyment was from the interest shown by covetous glances directed towards my boat with some of those passing by enquiring as to what design the boat was.

As the sun went down the air became cooler and time to move inside. After reading for a while with one eye on the wind gauge as the wind was getting up to the predicted 27 knots it was time for bed, a contented man and thankful not to have been caught out in the Straight on such a wild night. On future cruising junkets there were situations with much stronger winds but let's say that would be in the future and this was a learning curve of sorts.

DAY TWO

The fog comes on little cat…. sits on silent haunches and then moves on

Carl Sandburg 1878-1967

I am an early riser because once I wake up I can see no sense staying in bed. This has its disadvantages in the summer months with it getting light early and that is when I come awake. Wintertime though I invariably lie in until 7 o'clock. When home our cat knows this because it is at this time he comes in through the open bedroom window, jumps on the bed and proceeds to walk all over me as much to say, "get up you lazy bum, I want my breakfast."

It matters not a whit what time I go to bed I always come awake at the dawn of day, and it has been like that most of my adult life. The down side to this inability to sleep during daylight hours has its aggravations as when in my career during the captaincy phase on occasions having been on the bridge all night I found it impossible to sleep during the daylight hours. This phenomenon proved to be a considerable nuisance on one particular occasion, due to the particular circumstance at the time the ship was programmed to arrive and leave several different ports in Northwest Europe during night times all within a space of eleven days. Apart from one night in Hamburg the rest required my presence on the bridge. But, such is life in the fast lane, and I am digressing shamefully.

The second day of this particular adventure was to be no different, Sam the cat or not. The routine was the same: out of bed, empty the bladder, put the kettle on, and over a couple of cups of tea, that life awakening elixir, contemplate the programme for the forthcoming day. This morning ritual is followed by a breakfast of cereals then potty time. A shave, clean the dentures and run a comb through my hair having myself ready for the day ahead. At this time of year we are ready to start the day at 0630.

But, to quote the Ayrshire lad, 'The best laid plans of mice and men aftimes gang aglae.' This morning plans were no exception, nothing major I'm pleased to say. Just that I had the key to the dock security gate for which there was the return of a $25 deposit due and the office didn't open until 0730, and for the sake of an hour I was not about to keep the key and forfeiting the deposit and as it was a relatively short run to Port Renfrew I occupied my time in tidying up and washing the previous days pots and checking the engine oil. Which I was surprised to see was quite low so I made a mental note to check this on a regular and frequent basis. With generally pottering about I managed to kill time until the office opened.

During the period of this trip around the island and after each day's run the engine oil had to be topped up which I found to be unusually odd for the engine was relatively new with only one hundred hours on the clock. This was a matter that should be taken up with the engine supplier when I returned home. The result of this inquiry short of taking the engine out of the boat and being stripped down, proved inconclusive, just keep a close watch on the levels and maybe the problem will resolve itself in time, was the advice to which I had to be satisfied.

When the time came to take my leave the same young man from the day before was on hand to assist my departure, and give me the latest weather report and very helpful he was too in holding the boat off the dock while I gunned the engine to clear into the channel as the wind although eased was still quite strong and holding the boat onto the dock. On clearing the slip with the stern pointing in the direction of the way I wished to go, an unavoidable situation as due to the limited space between the wharves I had been obliged to dock stern first. The same limitations existed when leaving, there not being enough room to turn the boat in the channel as a forty foot boat requires some space for these manoeuvres. Steering with a stern way on a boat is not the best situation as a boat needs to be moving without the benefit of the engine before steerage is possible otherwise the transverse thrust created by the propeller on the rudder makes a mockery of the guiding hand on the wheel. However, a little judicious manipulation of the engine to get some way on the boat managed to get us moving and all would have been well except that the wind blew us onto the propeller of an outboard motor which was sticking out into the channel and had me cursing the inconsiderate clown who had parked his boat in such a position. A few scratches and a slight gouge on the port bow found us clear of the channel and on our merry way with another item on the mental to do list. Telling me that these things happen and sure as eggs are eggs it won't be the last.

By 0745 we were clear of the breakwater and heading into a 19 knot wind from the south which suited my purpose favourably for it was just a short run to the Trial Islands which when rounded would put the wind on the port beam with a chance to put up the sails and do some sailing. This then was the favourable situation but, best laid plans etc. one should never anticipate favourable situations, certainly not with the weather and certainly not in British Columbia as they are almost certain to make a liar out of you as the vagaries of the wind hereabouts can be quite frustrating. I had the Genoa hoisted and filled with the wind for maybe about ten minutes before it was flapping about uselessly with not enough wind to keep it filled and moving the boat through the water. So it was back to motoring.

The morning was warm in the sunshine so there was pleasure in cruising along in the calm waters entertained by pleasant thoughts of what was in store during this time of solitude. However, on the Washington side of the Strait a thick white bank of fog had formed and was inexorably creeping towards the Canadian side. This threat interrupted the serenity of the morning and prompted thoughts towards a cup of coffee while the going was good before being socked in by this unwelcome hiccup to my plans. The radar was also activated in the anticipation of the probable meeting with another boat or solid object in the reduced visibility.

By 0930 Race Rocks were abeam to port as this course took us between the rocks and the Vancouver Island. The thought at this time came to mind how different it was that a vessel the size of 'Ron's Endeavour' drawing a mere five feet could pass without danger of grounding, compared to ships the size of which I had been accustomed during my career at sea. It was a strange feeling to realise one could do this even though the situation were markedly different. Old training is still with us I guess to consider the two very different situations in the light of putting oneself in the way of danger. Doubts do enter one's mind and linger though as to whether a passage can be traversed through a narrow channel especially as they appear much narrower on the chart than what they actually are. But I'm here to discover myself and a relationship with the boat. So go for it was the order of the day, and go I did.

After clearing Race Passage the fog came in, patchy at first then by 1030 off Sooke it lifted. Not for long though, it soon settled in again thick as a hedge.

It was during the gap in the fog that on checking the radar the heading line was about forty-five degrees out of line. This anomaly became obvious as according to the heading line we would eventually run into Vancouver Island while with visual observations and GPS positions this could not be. One more item for the job list and I made a mental note to consult with those that know, in the meantime I set the electronic bearing marker as an indicator to where we should be heading.

Now fog is definitely not my favourite weather condition, I could never feel happy with the restricted visibility and the niggling thought that there may be something out there in the murk to run into. After a while though I realised that my attitude as with the concern in navigating Race Passage was a big ship mentality, with only thirty-five feet of boat in front of me and an instant response capability from the engine controls and the helm there was little chance of running into an unresisting object. With this revelation I brought up the high stool from the inside steering position and made myself comfortable in the cockpit close to the cabin entrance with my feet on the coaming where I could keep an eye on the radar. In this position I could observe any approaching large object on the radar, any smaller objects like logs or kelp rafts would be sighted visually through the swirling fog and with the engine controls to hand avoiding action could be taken in good time.

The radar worked well when picking up large objects. A Fisheries and Oceans vessel of the stern trawler design presented itself well before a visual sighting, so all was well with the world in this respect. The only objects to be concerned about were the logs and kelp rafts which needed to be avoided as both could cause damage to the boat, logs being considered the worst offender especially those what are known as a dead head, these hazards float vertically being not quite totally waterlogged and for the most part barely visible, when hit by a vessel they are knocked under water then rising again to possibly hit the spinning propeller of the craft with obvious dire results. Kelp too although not as dangerous as logs due to the softer nature can foul a propeller and bring the boat to a sickening stop in one tangled mess, better to be safe than sorry by ensuring due diligence. By this time the wind had died completely and the fog just hung like a blanket in the surrounding air giving an ethereal feeling to the whole surroundings, not however without enhancing the thought processes in pondering as we were now in the Strait of Juan de Fuca how that name came to be so called.

*****

Juan de Fuca an old Greek pilot in the employ of Spain alleged discovery of the Strait in 1592. Alleged, because these claims to his discoveries were treated with scepticism by his employers, and in light of subsequent proof to the contrary his claims really were farfetched.

According to the story, Juan de Fuca was sent by the Viceroy of Mexico in search of the fabled Strait of Anian the passage which would enable a more direct and quicker route to the Orient from Europe. The Northwest Passage if you will.

And I quote: 'In 1592, beyond California, between latitudes 47 degrees and 48 degrees, he found a broad inlet into which he entered, sailing for more than twenty days passing by islands and landing at divers places seeing people clad in beasts skins. A fruitful place it was, rich in gold, silver, pearl and other things. In due course he arrived at the Atlantic Ocean and sailed back again through his passage to Acapulco.'

He received neither reward nor gratitude from his masters, which in the light of things is not surprising. We now know in this modern day that this claim is blatant fantasy. But, even then that such a passage to the Atlantic could not be true because the English had given all their voyages over to the search for a Northwest Passage, and as the Hudson Bay was so well charted, and the only ice free possibility, there could not be such an easy passage from the Atlantic to the Pacific. Juan de Fuca was dismissed, his services no longer required.

James Cook on his third voyage in 1778 with instructions from the Admiralty to search for a passage from the Pacific side sighted and named Cape Flattery, being as he said flattered to think there would be a safe harbour there to repair his ships, on the south side of the Strait just before nightfall. During the night his ships were blown off the coast by gale force winds only to regain landfall at Nootka Sound. So missing the opportunity of exploring this inlet, and with Cook's acumen for exploration, an opportunity continued to be sadly missed to recognise the true worth of this waterway.

It remained for Captain C.W.Barkley, a fur trader in his ship the Imperial Eagle in July 1787 to honour Juan de Fuca. Captain Barkley immediately recognised the Strait as the one mentioned in that pilot's account and so named it after him.

*****

The fog for the most part of this trip stayed as thick as a hedge and my whereabouts and the safety from other vessels and objects of flotsam and jetsam continued to be established by GPS and radar. However at times the fog thinned and it was possible to see the occasional fishing skiff. Usually with two or three people hanging out the fishing lines totally engrossed in their activity as they didn't seem to notice my passing by, at least there was no recognition of this.

If one cares to look at a chart of this part of Vancouver Island it will be noted that from Sooke to Cape Beale it is a continuous unbroken coastline with the exception of Port San Juan where Port Renfrew lies, in fact one might think that land when first formed, if given to a flight of fantasy, that some giant had pushed his thumb into the yet to be solidified molten mass. And created this pronounced indentation as this is the only such feature on the whole length of this section of coast. Before the reader condemns me for some kind of nut, remember, I am on my own and I do have an imagination and what better way to pass the time in thinking up these odd fantasies to which I make no excuse.

It was in the fog then that I approached Port San Juan and established the red and white buoy at the entrance then set a course that would take me up to the top of the bay and a safe anchorage. All the while on this course I kept a watchful eye on the soundings until the water depth shelved to fifteen feet to where I anchored still not having seen the shore, God bless modern technology. Anyway I had arrived safely without an anxious moment thanks to science, the anchor was down and holding, time for a beer. Three in the afternoon is not usually considered to be a time when the sun is below the yardarm and the time to be imbibing in alcohol but, what the heck I was chuffed with myself in surviving this fog shrouded day.

I hadn't been long into a glass of beer when a Coastguard inflatable pulled up alongside with three officers aboard looking impressively large in their survival suits. Wondering if they were checking for illegal immigrants or contraband even I went up on deck to see what was what.

"Afternoon," I said

"Afternoon," one replied, "are you OK here?"

Well as I didn't quite know where here might be I could only reply, "I hope so, the anchor is holding alright."

The same guy nodded with what I took to be look of doubt.

"Thank you for your concern though," I said politely under the blank non-committal stares of all three officers. The spokesman nodded again and gunned the engine promptly disappearing into the murk.

The visit had left me curious as to why they should show such concern and went back to my beer with the thought that they probably were just checking to see that I was a bone fide boater enjoying an outing in the fog. It was while mulling over these thoughts that I realised that once again I had forgotten to take something out of the freezer for dinner. Which dispelled the visit from my mind with this more important event, and what to do for dinner? Kippers again? I think not, sausages then? They wouldn't take long to thaw out just put them in cold water for an hour and a meal ready to be cooked. With mashed potatoes onion gravy and some peas and carrots a repast fit for a king.

I took this opportunity while I remembered and before I forgot to check the engine oil, which was low again, something was amiss here as to my mind the engine should not be burning oil a definite case of bringing the matter up with the people who supplied the engine. After all with only a hundred hours on the clock this could not be right. I also checked the days run and was pleasantly surprised to learn I had covered fifty-seven miles during this section of the trip at an average speed of 7.86 knots. As the tide had been favourable it seemed that the timing for this odyssey was right on. And as the trip progressed with the tides mostly in my favour I felt quite chuffed at me at getting something right, putting the anti-clockwise school of thought out of whack. In fact I became convinced that somebody up there was looking after my interests. Such is the imagination.

Later on after these chores I cooked and ate the evening meal of sausages, new potatoes, peas and carrots and a glass or two of homemade wine. Then going up on deck the concern of the coastguard chappie became apparent as the fog had lifted sufficiently to see the beach was quite close, maybe a hundred yards away. There didn't seem any cause for concern though as the anchor was well set with plenty of water under the keel, so I decided to stay where I was. A further lifting of the fog revealed a number of yachts at anchor over towards Port Renfrew.

"So that was the anchorage?"

Well I was settled and I couldn't see any sense in picking up and anchoring again to be with a bunch of strangers. On reflection it occurred to me I was enjoying my own company. Was I becoming a recluse? Not a bad thought really in the scheme of things, at this moment in time I knew I didn't want company.

*****

Port Renfrew lies on the south side of Port San Juan, so named by Manual Quimper, in command of the Princesa Real while exploring the Strait of Juan de Fuca in 1790. This vessel has an interesting history because it was originally named Princess Royal a vessel belonging to Captain James Colnett. This vessel with two others was seized by the Spanish at Nootka Sound and their crews imprisoned at San Blas the Spanish naval station in Mexico. The Spaniards claiming that these British ships were in Spanish Territory illegally. A situation that nearly had Britain and Spain going to war over the right to trade on this coast. The return of the ships and their crews became part of the negotiations which became known as the Nootka Sound Convention which was to be negotiated by George Vancouver and Quadra at Nootka in 1792, but more of that later.

Of course the port originally carried the Spanish spelling of Puerto de San Juan but was eventually anglicised to the present spelling. This eventually led to some confusion with regard to mail deliveries, more often than not the mail was sent to the San Juan Islands. In 1895 the settlers decided to change the name to Port Renfrew in honour of Lord Renfrew who had planned to settle Scottish crofters in the area.

*****

After the evening meal and the washing up I took up my favourite position standing in the hatchway and leaning on the cabin top. In this position I spent a pleasant hour observing the different groups of people on shore. With camper vans parked on the berme above the beach I surmised that this was a holiday spot within reach of people with the right sort of transport to get here and camp. With all the kids running around I took this inspired observation to be a dead giveaway. From what I could gather some of these groups were trying to catch fish, but what type of fish was beyond me as they didn't appear to catch anything. Just throwing a net into the water and immediately pulling it in again seemed to me was not going to meet with success. However, maybe it was fun for them.

One or two small open boats passed by and disappeared into the San Juan River at the head of the bay, presumably after a days fishing and could even be the boats I had passed in the fog earlier in the day some way along the coast. At the time of passing earlier it crossed my mind how they would find their way home in the fog as there was no apparent signs of radar on so small a vessel. But then, they could quite well have had a hand held GPS units and a compass, these items could aid a body home especially if you were local, as they no doubt were, and familiar with the area. However, no assistance was requested from me as I passed by so one only assumes they knew what they were up to.

The fog had finally cleared away completely which allowed for a fine view of the bay. The beaches were littered with tree stumps and logs which is not an unusual sight on the BC coast. Logs break away from their rafts when being towed to the sawmills and eventually get washed up on a beach somewhere. Port San Juan has gentle shelving beaches which provide an excellent reception point for logs to ground on when driven into the bay by the winter gales.

On some beaches the local councils arrange these logs for sun worshippers to lie behind and take shelter from the wind. One is more likely to see this arrangement though in the bigger cities like Vancouver rather than the isolated communities like Port Renfrew.

The evening was wearing on and the air becoming chilly so time to go below and batten down the hatches. The anchor was holding nicely, with plenty of water under the keel and no wind, so all was well with my little world promising a comfortable and quiet night. But first see about the heading marker on the radar and wonders upon wonders the old adage; if all else fails, read the instructions, rang true, and it turned out to be quite a simple procedure to have, ‘ship’s head up’ mode.

After contemplating the events of the day over a glass or two of wine I read for a while then turned in pleasantly tired from being out in the sea air.

DAY THREE

His risings fogs prevail upon the day

MacFlecknoe (1682)

I woke up at 0530 cursing under my breath, as I'm on my own there is no point to saying it out loud, to a beautiful day of thick fog. Thick as a hedge again, with visibility down to almost nil, no matter as by now I was beginning to accept that I wasn't going to have much in the way of sightseeing on this trip. So I decided to first have breakfast, do my chores then push off in the hope that the fog would eventually clear. With the GPS and the now fully operational radar there should be no problem feeling my way to Bamfield.

Regardless of my concerns about the fog I did remember to take something out of the freezer for the evening meal. A nice Forfar Bridie would do very nicely, garnished with mashed potato and the ubiquitous peas and carrots, a dollop of HP sauce would go nicely too, just to give the meal that extra bit of zest. And a little smearing of margarine on the veggies rather than gravy to smooth the way just for a change, after all one needs variety to enhance the enjoyment of a meal. Which, the reader might ask, 'why peas and carrots' with every meal? Well, carrots are, or the carotene they contain are well known to be an anti cancer element. And as for peas, don't they go with carrots? Like love and marriage, bacon and eggs, that sort of thing one might say. Once again a meal fit for a king. While on the subject of food I decided to make a sandwich for lunch just in case the fog situation prevented so doing at the appointed hour, seems as though my memory was improving to remember all these tasks.

At 0715 up came the anchor and off we set into the swirling fog with a quiet prayer that the instruments would not fail and leave me blind. With this thought a film I had seen many years previously came to mind, the title of which evades me. However, this American millionaire was being transported with his goods and chattels to his private island off the west coast of Scotland by a Clyde puffer, which is a small cargo steamer that plied its trade in that part of the world. During the journey they ran into thick fog, the American of course became quite alarmed as to their safety anxious that they would run into one of the island and be wrecked. The skipper assured him that there was no danger as they would know where they were by radar. Looking around the wheelhouse the American pointed out that they didn't have radar. To which the skipper drew his attention to the galley boy going forward carrying a bucket of coal. That's our radar going forward now the lad will heave a lump of coal into the fog and if it splashes we are fine, and if it clunks we know we are too close to the land. 'Works like a charm it does, sir.'

Maybe I should think to bring a bucket of coal on these journeys into the fog just in case the radar packs in. On sighting the entrance buoy at the entrance to Port San Juan the fog had lifted a little the visibility clearing to maybe half a mile, not perfect but promising. The fog soon closed in again with wisps of the stuff curling around the stem, so I took up my position as of yesterday, feet on coaming and seated on the high stool.

While progressing along the coast several fish boats loomed out of the fog which had been large enough to be picked up on the radar so their appearance was anticipated without my being shocked at a large unyielding object suddenly appearing out of the gloom. The manifestation of these objects if unexpected suddenly appearing out of no-where, can, if ones nerves are wound up from peering into a wall of cotton wool could give one a very anxious moment, alarm even.

As though trying to compensate for these miserable conditions nature chose to bring out the sun and as it was astern of the boat a beautiful rainbow appeared ahead so tantalisingly close it was as though we would run into it and be so close to the legendary pot of gold. Fat chance, one has a better, though very slim chance of winning the lottery. Nice thought though. Maybe I should keep a look-out for Leprechauns and claim the pot of gold.

Somewhere along this coast, approximately half way to Bamfield probably, the Pacific swell started to gently lift the boat unseen in the thick fog giving a strange ethereal sensation, an out of world feeling in the damp blanket surrounding my immediate world. This swell was to stay with me for all the way to Cape Scott at the top of Vancouver Island thankfully causing no discomfort, just a gentle rise with approach of the wave and an almost imperceptible slide down the other side, soothing almost. About this time the wind started to pick up to blow at 7 knots. So out with the Genoa again to assist my passage, to be sure this situation lasted about ten minutes before dying away again making the Genoa a limp flapping nonentity to be hauled in again. Although British Columbia has one of the most perfect boating areas in the world at times the often erratic winds can be most frustrating.

The fog finally dispersed on approaching Cape Beale to reveal a beautiful clear sunny day, the sort of day that one should expect in BC as we like to say, 'it is always like this in BC' when the sun shines. The run up Barkley Sound, (native name Nitinat), to Bamfield became one of the most pleasurable legs of this odyssey.

*****

Captain Charles William Barkley, mentioned earlier of the British Trading vessel, Imperial Eagle, discovered and named this beautiful sound in 1787, with its many rocky islands after himself, as with most colonising Europeans the local indigenes were quite often ignored. And on reflection Barkley Sound does have certain melodic appeal, Nitinat to my mind seems to grate somewhat. On this particular voyage he had with him his seventeen year old bride, Francis, who could claim the honour, for what it is worth, of being the first white woman to visit British Columbia.

*****

Bamfield is a small fishing village which lies in its own little inlet on the south side of Barkley Sound four and a half miles from Cape Beale. And if my memory serves me correctly from those far distant schooldays, this was where the undersea telegraph cable came ashore from Australia the Pacific section linking the British Empire in a world wide communications network. This cable link is probably not used anymore as the advance in technological knowledge would no doubt have made this system obsolete. This would have to be investigated during my stay here as a matter of interest and the large building on the opposite bluff looked promising as the type of building which would serve as a communications building. Seeking wisdom and truth was all part of this journey and as I was in no hurry to disappear into the fog again I would be content enough to explore the possibilities of this settlement.

Part of the Pacific Rim National Park is just a few miles to the south, and the West Coast Trail a forty-seven kilometre hike from Port Renfrew ends at Pachana Bay close by between Bamfield and Cape Beale. No doubt a welcome sight to those hardy souls having hiked the distance, (no pun intended) although the soles of their feet would be ready for a hot mustard bath after such a distance. There is a shuttle bus operating from Bamfield, Port Alberni, Nanaimo and Victoria to each end of the trail during the hiking season. The trail was original created by rescue services to access the many vessels driven ashore and wrecked on this coast as previously it was well nigh impossible to get through the dense forest to render assistance.

The village of Bamfield is split into two parts by the inlet to form East and West Bamfield. Both parts have an array of quaint buildings, stores, bed and breakfast establishments and private homes. Most of the docks near the entrance and on each side of the inlet carried the legend, ‘Private Dock’. So obviously there would be no point in tying up at one of those. As the predominance of buildings were on the west or right hand and not having been here before I decided to direct my search to this side of town. The General Store dock, mooring time limited to twenty minutes seemed to be a good place to park as I needed engine oil and it would be a good place to inquire for the whereabouts of a dock I could stay at over night.

The engine oil was not forthcoming as I required a 4 litre container which they did not stock. Well, as I still had some oil left over I decided to wait until the next stop if none could be purchased in the quantity I required here in Bamfield. The store clerk was kind enough to direct me to the Government dock towards the south of the town as the best place to moor for the night, so I directed my course to that dock. While proceeding in this direction further into the inlet. I noticed that a walkway followed the shoreline for its full length from the customs dock to, as it turned out to where I was to moor. This aroused my curiosity and I made a mental note to investigate after settling in.

The dock proved to be ideal as this early in the day there were no other boats tied up and I had the choice of any position along the outer length of the moorings. However, there were groups of boys spaced at different positions along the full length all apparently fishing as I felt my need to be paramount I called out to one group that I was coming alongside and to watch their lines, more for my well being than theirs as monofilament fishing lines can foul up a propeller before you can say piscatorial artist. Boaters and quite often anyone who happened to be around usually help a boat coming alongside to moor. In this instance I had to hop onto the dock and take my own lines as apart from the aforementioned boys fishing there wasn't anyone around and they didn't seem to be inclined to perform the task, probably due to being busy getting their lines out of the water.

"Sorry, lads, but I needed to moor here," I offered ever polite.

"That's alright," said the eldest. "We can move to the other side."

With that they gathered up their tackle and moved.

Later on, after having a late lunch I decided to explore the town on this side of the inlet.

But first maybe I could get some information from the lads who were now fishing on the other side of the dock.

"Do you lads live in Bamfield?" I asked.

They all looked up at me but, again it was the one I took to be the eldest who answered.

"No." he said, "We're on vacation with our parents."

"You wouldn't know how Bamfield got its name then?"

"No." He shook his head and looked at the other boys. They also indicated a negative response to the question.

"No matter," I said. "I'll ask up the road."

As I walked away there was a general whispered conversation amongst my piscatorial friends. Probably asking each other why some old nut would ask such a dumb question.

Close by the general store I had noticed on the way in a Visitors Information centre, so what better place to find out the answer to the question and satisfy my curiosity and to maybe find out a little of the history of Bamfield.

While out walking I'm not a person who cares to backtrack over a route but rather to proceed in one direction and take another view on the return seems to me the most sensible way to view the surrounding country, therefore I decided to go along behind the waterfront buildings and return by way of the boardwalk. So on leaving the dock I made my way up the back road called the Cape Beale Trail, incidentally this route runs parallel to the waterfront and gave no indication of going in the Cape Beale direction or nowhere near to this landmark, nor did the map give any help either. This particular section of town was interesting anyway as much of it was a dirt track between two rows of residential properties. It struck me as interesting because I was wondering what it would be like in the rainy season as the road must become a quagmire, and to take my deliberations a step further, so to speak, I had thoughts of the populace squelching their way in muddy boots. However, only an academic thought as I would not be here to see such a spectacle.

This Cape Beale Trail was well signposted at the intersections which indicated which turnoff led where, to get back to the waterfront I took one to the right indicating I was now on Broughton Road which ended at a flight of steps that led down to and brought me right to the Visitors Information Centre.

This building gave the impression that due to the sagging nature and the signs of rot on the lower parts of the siding suggested the structure was quite old. The window frames also added to the impression with their wooden frames and single glazing something one doesn't see much of these days, more for the thirties or forties period or even the last century, another question to ask inside to satisfy my curiosity.

The inside of the building was quite spacious suggesting a onetime warehouse or maybe a fish processing plant after all in days passed this community would have been in close proximity to the abundant salmon runs in the heydays of yore, before over fishing had decimated the stocks. One more question to ask and be answered by the young lady attending the counter.

The far end of the room seemed to be devoted to displays of handicrafts and souvenirs, and as I'm not into collecting mementos and the young lady was attending to another customer I interested myself in a display of old photographs on the back wall.

'H.S.M. Tusker (sic) at Nootka Sound.'

'H.S.M.? H.M.S. Surely?'

'Where Cape Cook visited in 1778.'

'Cape Cook? Captain Cook surely,' they have to be typo errors.

The other customer was going out of the door so I approached the information desk loaded with my many questions that were begging answers.

"Excuse me could you tell me how Bamfield got its name?"

"I'm sorry," she said. "I don't know."

My surprise at this negative response must have shown in my face. Justified surprise I might add as one would expect people working in an Information Centre to be informed on such matters. However, she did try to make amends and suggested that I might find what I was looking for among the photographs, pointing to the collection I had just been perusing.

"I have just been looking at those without any luck I'm afraid. And there seem to be one or two errors anyway."

"You could try the Library, they would most likely know," still trying to be helpful.

I perked up at this suggestion, of course why didn't I think of that?

"Yes I said that might be the best course of action where might that be?

"It's over in East Bamfield next to the Research Station. You will have to take the ferry over to the other side then it is about twenty minutes walking from the ferry dock."

All the other questions I wanted to ask had suddenly lost their importance in the uselessness of the situation so I thanked the young lady for her help and left, somewhat disappointed with the waste of time and resolved to research other sources for the Bamfield question. After all this is a learning trip and just not a whiz around Vancouver Island.

The boardwalk along the waterfront had a particularly interesting story attached to it having been built from lumber that had been delivered to Bamfield by mistake. The supplier apparently was loath to pay the cost of handling and shipping the lumber back to Port Alberni so it was just abandoned. The enterprising locals stepped in taking over the abandoned supply not missing an opportunity of such an unexpected gift to construct this waterfront thoroughfare.

At first I believed it to be a means of getting from one part of the town to the other, and so it was in a sense but, it was also a delightful attraction were one could stroll taking in the sights across the water to East Bamfield, or to look inland at the neat houses as one passes by. There are one or two sights that come to mind while writing this.

One being the hospital, more so because seeing this building is so unexpected. In a community the size of Bamfield one doesn't expect to see a hospital and I realise I may be being presumptuous in saying this, so shall I just say it surprised me. A clinic maybe but a hospital? Set in its own garden, delightful though it was I couldn't but feel that it was unnecessary in such a small community. On the water side of the boardwalk there was the hospital dock complete with helicopter pad so obviously there was a means to evacuate patients to a larger hospital. Apart from considering the functional aspects of getting patients to better medical facilities the setting was pretty being as it was on a float on the inlet.

Two other sights I found to be interesting more so because they were unexpected. One being a coffee bar of the same design as one meets with in warmer climes. That is to say, a central serving area with an open covered deck with chairs and tables for the customers to sit and enjoy their refreshments with views across and along the inlet. In warmer climes one would be sitting under a canopy of palapa leaves. Here though a corrugated transparent plastic covering sufficed to keep off inclement weather that might chance by, after all in these northern latitudes any sunshine should be enjoyed. The deck was built over the water so it was pleasant to sit and watch the traffic on the inlet.

While taking advantage of these pleasant surroundings and enjoying a cup of coffee a ship of about 500 tons and about 100 feet in length, named 'Lady Rose', sailed past and was seen to proceed further up the inlet where it tied up on the far side in East Bamfield. On making inquires of the girl attending the coffee counter I was informed that this vessel plied its trade between Port Alberni and Bamfield, dropping off supplies at the villages and other communities along Alberni Inlet and the Barkley Sound shore. On approaching a community that was expecting supplies a blast on the ships whistle brought out the recipients of the expected delivery in their boats to receive the 'Lady's' bounty. In Bamfield though the 'Lady Rose' came alongside to off load her cargo. I was made to understand that a resident of Bamfield could phone in a grocery order to a store in Port Alberni, the order would be put on board the 'Lady Rose' free of charge, and for a nominal fee the ship-owner transported the goods to the consignee at Bamfield, who was required to be at the wharf when the ship docked. What a wonderful old world community spirit this conjured up, something we don't see a great deal of these days.

Next to the coffee bar there is a small hexagonal building calling itself the Trading Post although it didn't seem to be large enough to hold more than one person at a time, in fact it wasn't much bigger than a telephone kiosk. The owner must have had a sense of the ridiculous or a fan of the Beatles for the path leading up to this 'establishment' was strewn with pennies with a plaque advertising it as 'Penny Lane'. A variation of the wishing well theme maybe? Outside of the 'Trading Post' there is a signpost with arrows pointing to and indicating directions to different parts of Bamfield. One of these directions gave me cause to blink in surprise at the boldness of the statement as it was labelled,

'Dogshit Lane'. Not a sign particularly loaded with finesse but then why not at least it didn't leave dog owners in any doubt as to where they should take their dogs for their calls of nature.

There are several signpost along the boardwalk of a more sedate nature that give directions to different parts of West Bamfield, one which caused me some confusion as it was on several posts all giving directions to the fish dock except the signs pointed away from the inlet to the west and no-one I asked could give me a logical reason for this as there was no fish-dock in that direction anyway. I was beginning to wonder about this place.

The only way to get from one side of the inlet to the other is by 'water taxi', a misnomer if there ever was one, and there doesn't seem to be any organisation to this service either. If one desires to use the service one must stand on the dock, and if the ferry happens to be on the far side, then hope you will be noticed by looking as if one wishes to cross to the other side. Either that or the lady in the coffee shop will call on the VHF and hopefully the driver will be listening, then the wait isn't so long before the boat appears. For three dollars and a five minute ride and passengers are deposited on the far side. This conveyance proved to be a fibreglass boat of the run-about type, propelled by an outboard motor. Not what one would consider a ferry but no doubt suitable for crossing the Inlet? And no doubt a nice little earner for the operator.

The young man operating the ferry proved to be quite chatty and expounded on the theory that there was gold in the hills behind Bamfield. To support this theory he showed me photographs he had taken on a certain day during the previous year which had a golden glow in the centre of each photograph. I was assured that the image could only be seen when the sun was at a certain declination on a specific day of the year. When being asked of which day that would be he became non-committal and returned the photographs to his pocket. Being of an imaginative turn of mind I began to wonder if this wasn't some ploy to get me interested in staking him for a search for this Eldorado. As it was the subject never came up for we had arrived at the dock in East Bamfield, not without an inward sigh of relief on my part as I'm loath to being suckered and any attempt along these lines brings out a short sharp remonstration along the lines of, 'sex and travel.' On settling the fee I inquired if he would be on hand for the return journey to West Bamfield to this he assured me that he would.

My reason for making this trip across the inlet was to satisfy my curiosity about the Telegraph Station. Or should I say the Marine Research Station as it now is. After being without any appreciable exercise over the last two days the twenty minute hike would be most welcome.

The first building I came to within the station grounds was the Cafeteria and what a welcome sight that was after trudging up the hill on such a warm day. A cup of tea would be most appreciated.

On entering the cafeteria I noticed a group of people sitting around a table with refreshments and deep in conversation but, there was no-one behind the serving counter to dispense the goodies. Odd I thought; how does one get a cup of tea around here as I tried to get some attention.

Standing there peering into the kitchen behind the counter trying to catch sight of someone I was approached by one of the men from the table.

“Can I help you?” he asked.

I turned to the voice expectantly, “I came in for a cup of tea but there doesn’t seem to be anyone around.”

“This is the university cafeteria, and not for the general public,” he said by way of explanation.

“Oh! Sorry, I didn’t realise,” and turned to leave.

“I’m sure we can treat you to a cup of tea.”

“Are you sure? I didn’t mean to intrude.”

“It’s no problem. Here are the teabags, hot water, and the milk is over there.” He nodded comfortingly and smiled, then moved away to rejoin his group of what I now took to be Academics from the Research Station.

‘What a pleasant person not to make me feel uncomfortable by asking me to leave.’

Taking my tea I went and sat by the window and, so as not to appear intrusive any more sat with my back to the group.

Across the grounds from the cafeteria and on a lower level is the Marine Research Centre, which to my great satisfaction proved to be the original building of the Cable Station now defunct in that capacity. Now it was funded by five western universities for research in the marine environment. After finishing my tea I took myself down to further increase my knowledge on the history of British Empire communication. The history of the Cable Station is well represented by photographs and printed narrative in the entrance lobby and it was here that I spent a pleasant half an hour boning up on the history all the while wondering how it was that I could still remember the basic facts of this place from over fifty years previously when I had a job remembering what I did on the previous day.

*****

In 1902 an undersea telegraph cable had been laid between, Auckland, New Zealand, Sydney, Australia, Fiji and Fanning Island to Bamfield. It continued overland across Canada and across the Atlantic to London. Thus connecting the Commonwealth countries with a secure means of communication between these countries respective Governments. Bamfield was chosen because it was the closest point on the Canadian Pacific coast, terminating four thousand miles of undersea cable. One can only wonder at a commitment for such an undertaking, especially in light of what today would be considered to be primitive technology. There were problems though due to the length of the cable which was caused by the resistance in the wires even for slow speed transmission of 135 words a minute. This resulted in distortion in the reception of the message making it difficult to interpret. A much improved cable was later laid, and yet another, and due to improved technology the cables by-passed Bamfield and continued on to Port Alberni making the station here at Bamfield redundant.

*****

Much satisfied at resolving my curiosity on this matter I retraced my tracks to the ferry pleased that this journey was downhill.

From the layout of East Bamfield with the streets going off to each side of the main road with residential as well as business premises it would appear that this is the most populated side of town. The fact that there was a pub on this side suggested that this observation was probably quite correct.

It crossed my mind to sample the delights of what this watering hole offered as it was a warm afternoon and a cold beer would have gone down nicely. However, on reflection though I abandoned the idea, drinking alone in a strange place didn't particularly appeal to me at this time. Besides to sit in a gloomy pub at this early hour would be an offence to such a glorious day. On such a warm balmy afternoon as this I would barmy to even consider the thought, so on to the dock then.

For crossing over to West Bamfield as it turned out there was to be no delay as the ferry was already waiting on this side.

On the return trip across the inlet the ferry operator didn't bring up his pet topic again and I had no intention of doing so either thinking that a change of subject would be more appropriate.

"You have quite a neat little operation here," I ventured. "Does it provide a living for you or just a hobby?"

"It is not my operation; I'm just standing in for the regular guy who's indisposed."

I didn't make comment to this statement as I expected with his chatty demeanour he would most likely fill in the blanks without any prompting from me. Not a bad assumption either.

"Yes! he is having problems with the licensing people."

He became quiet for a moment probably wondering if he should say more. Then looked apologetic, and said, "Well you shouldn't drink and drive a car, should you?"

"Ah." I said, nodding understandingly. "Quite right."

"Well the same goes for a boat. So I'm running the boat while he is sorting things out."

As though enough had been said on the subject the boat bumped against the dock announcing our journeys end.

The boys who had been fishing had left when I walked towards my boat. There was several more pleasure craft moored up at this time. Both powerboats and sail, no doubt the arrival of these craft had put an end to the lad's peaceful pastime.

On coming back on board and reflecting that I had missed out on liquid refreshment at the pub I decided to have a beer of my own while mulling over the events of the day so far.

After this welcome refreshment, restless and curious to know what boats had arrived during my absence I soon took to taking a stroll along the dock. It was during this walk that I had occasion to help a couple of boats moor. The first, an American boat approached the dock and a crew person being a female passed me a bow line, which I secured for her, she thanked me and looked away a little self consciously I thought. I then moved towards the man at the stern who ignoring my offer jumped down onto the dock and tied the stern line himself. Suit yourself I thought refusing an offer made in good faith in such a discourteous manner. But then, 'there's now't as queer as folk,' as we say in Yorkshire. Probably city folk whom I have noticed seldom look a person in the eye when spoken to. And a smile also seems to be alien to their nature by the look of this guy.

Now the next boat was as different as chalk is to cheese as the manner of this couple was to the other extreme. Not only did they look me in the eye while offering thanks they actually came ashore after mooring to introduce themselves.

"John Humphries," said the man, "This is my wife Helen."

Shaking hands I also introduced myself. "Do I detect a Belfast accent," I asked.

The sense of well-being just took off from that point and it soon became evident why this camaraderie was so evident. During the ensuing conversation it transpired that John and me had both been in the same line of work. Although John had left the British Merchant Navy before completing his penance, so to speak, to become a supercargo here in British Columbia we had both been in tankers. Although different companies, he with Esso and me with Shell and both deck officers.

It is in the nature of life's happenings and it goes without saying that people with common interests soon find plenty to talk about and we were soon deep in conversation, and I must confess at this juncture that although I wished to know as much as possible about the people and places I was to meet with on this circumnavigation I found in this particular instance I was hogging the conversation and talking about myself, something I don't do very often so put it down to being starved of human contact these past few days which caused me to run off at the mouth, in retrospect I consider myself a listener rather than a talker.

John and Helen had spent the previous eighteen months living on their boat mostly moored in Victoria, taking the odd junket when the mood stirred them as they had no ties to hold them and their house rented out. What a wonderful way to live, not that it would do for me at this particular time as one should have a companion to share the pleasures. Now that was a lovely thought though to be foot loose and fancy free with a compatible companion.

After a short visit to my boat, a glass of wine and a look around my new found friends returned to their boat with an invitation for me to come over for dinner. My protests that I had a meat pie waiting to be consumed were summarily dismissed with instructions to put the thing in the fridge for the morrow and present myself at six o'clock. What a wonderful meal it was too, John had barbequed chicken, Helen the salad and spiced beans which were out of his world, the wine being my contribution.

I couldn't help noticing while aboard the 'Star Tracker', A steel boat built by Waterline Yachts of Sidney, how neat and tidy everything was in the cabin and how different to the casual tidiness of my boat. Definitely a woman's touch makes all the difference.

Shortly after this excellent meal with delightful company the wharfinger did his rounds collecting the moorage fees. Taking this opportunity of yet again seeking wisdom and truth on the subject of Bamfield as the lack of information was still niggling my need to know. I brought up the subject as to where the name came from with the dues collector, if I had thought on at the time I could have asked at the Research Station if other matters hadn't been uppermost. Or for that matter from the ferryman but, there the time was short and the subject matter already decided.

"You wouldn't happen to know where Bamfield got its name, would you," I asked half expecting a negative response.

Looking up from making out the receipt he gave me the answer that made my day. "Bamfield is a corruption of Banfield. William Eddy Banfield came to the West Coast on H.M.S. Constance in 1846. He was the first white man to settle here, later becoming Indian Agent and trader. In 1862 he was drowned in a canoe accident that some hereabouts suspecting foul play, murdered in fact, nothing proven of course." As though to bring finality to his discourse the wharfinger with a flourish ripped off the receipt from the pad and handed it to me. "Twenty dollars, please."

I handed the man his twenty with many reflective thanks for the enlightenment on the subject of Bamfield. With the thought that he would be an asset to the Information Centre.

One of the questions that were asked of me by just about everyone I met, and the Humphries were no exception was, 'Why are you going clockwise around the island?' Of course I had no real perception as to why I was doing it this way travelling in the opposite direction to what seemed to be the accepted procedure to everyone else. But then I tend to follow my own judgement and not rely on another man's compass so to speak, and instinct and my reasoning told me to go clockwise, and clockwise I'm going. Not to say that was an answer so I just settled for, "Just perverse I suppose." And to give a little more clarification offered the horse and stable theory, which sometimes raised a smile, of pity probably, if nothing else.

Maybe I should have asked why they were going the opposite way, but didn't and no doubt missed the chance to learn something to my advantage. Maybe next time just to see what the difference would be.

Also, and this I didn't impart to anyone for my reason for this contrary direction I'm a great admirer of Captain James Cook. And although he didn't circum-navigate Vancouver Island he did cover this section of the island north from Cape Flattery on his quest to prove, or destroy a myth of there being a passage over the top of the North American continent from the Pacific side. This admiration for Cook could well have influenced my thinking.

As things turned out it was the counter-clockers that would have all the adverse weather conditions.

John expressed his desire for an early start on the morrow probably about five, so not wishing to overstay my welcome I thanked them for a most pleasant evening and a wonderful meal, and bidding them a good passage south to Port Renfrew I took my leave.

The evening air was so still and peaceful on returning to my boat so I decided to sit outside in the cockpit with a book and a glass of wine before turning in reflecting on a most enjoyable and productive day.

DAY FOUR

Look, stranger, at this island now....and silent be (Auden)

Turning out of bed at six o'clock I put the kettle on then checked to see if the Humphries had left. Their berth was deserted so I silently wished them bon voyage, a safe and fog free passage south to their next port of call.

The morning promised a pleasant day and I took a deep breath of the morning air in anticipation of this day's run to Tofino via Ucluelet to fuel up and hopefully replenish the propane.

Half a dozen of these deep breaths and the kettle were calling for attention, so below I went for morning tea and the other ceremonies of the morning ritual.

By 0700 I was cast off from the Bamfield dock on my way to Ucluelet. I could easily have topped up the diesel at Bamfield, but the propane would have meant crossing over to East Bamfield then lugging the tank half a mile up the road to have it filled then return with a much heavier tank. At least the arrangement at Ucluelet provided propane right at the dock it pays to do one's homework, nez pas. This information kindly provided by John Humphries, another plus for going the opposite way around to the people whose brains I could pick for services ahead of me, which deserved a mental pat on the back for being such a clever fellow.

As the morning progressed the sky became overcast with light airs thankfully the dreaded fog kept away, what a blessing that was for one must thread a course through a maze of islands that litter Barkley Sound. From Bamfield it is just a short run through Satellite Passage in the Deer group of islands. Then across Imperial Eagle channel to the Broken Island group, and then the short run to Ucluelet. Obviously, this rock dodging section of the passage is best done in clear visibility when one can see what obstacles lie ahead, and all around also for that matter.

Although there are many channels to choose from in this particular group of islands the Satellite Passage and Coaster Channel are the widest and being unfamiliar with the area I considered it prudent to take the more circuitous route and use the wider channels. Had there been the thick fog experience during the previous days run I should have considered it more sense to have avoided this area all together and retraced my steps to Cape Beale then headed in open water to Ucluelet. But then that was as maybe, but these islands are part of the Pacific Rim National Park and should not be left out if possible on such an adventure as this, so here we were rock dodging and enjoying the scenery. Considering this situation; had I not embarked on a circumnavigation of Vancouver Island and this resolve firmly in my brain I might well have taken the time to explore Barkley Sound in its entirety or much more than I was so doing. As a matter of fact judging by the number of boats anchored in the numerous bays it would appear to be a most popular attraction for the boating community. Maybe I'll make a point of coming here one day for an extended stay and bring someone who could tip the scales and say, 'let's stop here or let's explore this or that.' Someone who could change my mind set of, 'come on get a move on, you won't get around the Island by dawdling.' Maybe even a run up Alberni Canal to Port Alberni? Now that would be pleasant.

On a journey such as this when a body travels alone, apart from talking to oneself, the mind also becomes stimulated by thinking up the most ridiculous scenarios. Take for example what went through my mind on the way across Barkley Sound: How did Ucluelet get its name? Could it be that the first white travellers in this area looking for somewhere to land, one says to the other, 'have you any idea as to where we are' Other person; 'No do you have a clue yet?'

Much more of this and I'll soon be saying, pardon.

That one will definitely not be in my Bumper Fun book. But, with thoughts like these the days just fly by. And, as the saying goes; 'You don't have to be mad but it helps.'

Actually Ucluelet is a Nootka Indian word which means, 'people of a sheltered bay.' And sheltered it certainly is, the inlet is narrow and four and a half miles in length lying in a northwest/southeast direction with the entrance at the southeast end, and protected from winds from all directions except southeast.

The distance from Bamfield to Ucluelet is only about twenty miles as the crow flies and once again it was a motoring passage. By 1030 we were off the fuel dock but, as often happen it was hurry up and wait situation. In this instance there were fish boats jockeying for position to get alongside so it was a case of hold off and wait. Fortunately there was a sail boat alongside refuelling and assuming that a fish boat wouldn't risk damaging this vessel by pushing in I manoeuvred to take his place as soon as he left, but, the boat occupying the berth was in no hurry.

Even though it was a man and wife team and elderly one would expect them to be in accord through experience with what should be done to expedite an undertaking, in this instance the coordination of watering and refuelling operations. Fat chance, first the fuel, go to the office and pay then come back and he then takes on water with the man controlling the procedure and the woman watching. Two tasks, two people, one task each would have been the order of the day, as it was this non division of labour took all of twenty minutes while everyone else was hanging about waiting to get alongside. As they moved off a fish boat was showing signs of pushing in so as I considered I was next slipped in ahead of him. And why not a sailboat takes much less time to refuel than an enormous fish boat? Ten minutes later refuelled and with a recharged propane tank I was off on my way to Tofino.

Between Tofino and Ucluelet lies an extension of the Pacific Rim National Park. In which Long Beach is a part. By world standards this is not all that long just about five and a half miles. But when one considers that British Columbia was carved out by glaciers during the Ice Age making for high mountains and deep inlets and valleys, to have a beach at all should be considered a phenomenon and in that respect the appellation, Long Beach is justified.

As I travelled along parallel to the beach rising and falling with the Pacific swell and watching these same waves crashing onto the beach I reflected on what this section of coast must be like in the winter when storms hit the coast, exposed as it is to the open expanse of the Pacific the waves having travelled for hundreds, nay thousands of miles to crash violently onto this unprotected shore.

Just as long as one is wrapped up safe and warm watching such a spectacle from on shore then it would maybe be a magnificent experience, but from out here in constant danger of being driven ashore and wrecked I shudder to think on the horrors.

One other matter of interest and this was an actual fact and not one of my fantasies. What I first thought to be a small log that necessitated a slight diversion of course. Became on becoming closer not a log but an otter floating peacefully on its back with front legs folded apparently asleep. On coming abeam of this creature it was only about two feet away and totally unaware of my presence up to that moment it then slowly opened its eyes which then shot open with apparent alarm and away he went quick as a wink. I could empathise with him as it is not a nice feeling to be rudely awoken. However, I must admit to a smile at his obvious surprise and thankful too that I had made the course alteration otherwise bumping into him would really have put the wind up the little fellow.

By two o'clock in the afternoon I arrived in Tofino with the familiar feeling of where to tie up for the night. No matter, the same situation arose that was the rule at Bamfield and I found the visitors' berths were well into the inlet and I tied up at the one remaining berth at the Government dock. A rickety structure it was too and showing its age with rotten boards and drooping to one side as though the floatation was derelict, but beggars can't be choosers and as I only wished to moor here for the night and not buy the place why should I care.

*****

Tofino, so named in 1792 by the Spanish Captains Dionisio Galiano and Caytano Valdez out of respect for that great Spanish hydrographer Don Vincente Tofino de San Miguel.

These captains were surveying and charting the coast of what is now British Columbia on behalf of the Spanish Government at the same time that Captain George Vancouver was charting more extensively the same coastline for the British Government. This was a period of history when Britain wanted the right to trade in this part of the world to which Spain was vehemently opposed, claiming exclusive rights under the Treaty of Tordesillas. Eventually, under the terms of the Nootka Sound Agreement Spain backed down and the coast was opened up to all comers, fur traders in particular as sea otter fur was the most sought after commodity.

*****

The fishing and tourist town of Tofino is situated at the north end of the coastline that Long Beach is a part, with Ucluelet to the south and located in a sheltered inlet from the prevailing winds from the southwest. One could almost say that these two towns were a matching pair of fishing communities. Although there is little of the commercial fishing being followed these days, both communities now rely on tourism and sport fishing. Tofino though has the advantage over Ucluelet however as it is well placed to operate fast boats into Hot Spring Cove a little to the north. Also this is the western end of the Trans Canada Highway which terminates right at Tofino First Street Dock.

Having settled in to the berth I decided to take a walk into town and pay the moorage dues on the way. Also, now I was in civilisation I could do my E.T. bit and phone home which proved to be a non sequitor and also proved to be most frustrating as after two hours of trying and several attempts through the operator all I got was the answering machine. No matter, try again later after the evening meal.

Tofino is well supplied with retail outlets and in this respect outshone Bamfield. Taking advantage of this situation I looked around for a Liquor Store with the intention of replenishing my beer supply. Would you believe there was a signpost giving directions to different places of interest including directions to where I wanted to be, i.e. the Liquor Store.

After a fruitless search in the direction indicated I gave in and asked directions of a passer-by, much to my chagrin the sign, as in Bamfield, pointed away from the place indicated, makes one wonder whether the local authorities are trying to tell strangers to this town something, or is it part of the west coast culture to confuse visitors.

After another fruitless attempt to phone home I decided to return to the boat for a beer. On coming down to the dock a group of men presumably sports fishermen had landed their catch, and a fine array of seafood it was too, lingcod, halibut, (my favourite) a salmon and a very plump snapper. I was tempted to ask if I could buy a fish from them, just a small one maybe, but at that juncture they started to discuss who should have what. One member of the group became quite querulous over his portion, 'I'm not having that rubbish,' he said pointing at the salmon. To which the others totally ignored him as he whinged on in the same vein.

What an odd bunch, I reflected; no-one had suggested that he was to have the salmon anyway.

There wasn't any point in hanging about listening to these guys argue over whom should have what, and the proposed mental offer to buy a fish seemed to be inappropriate then, so I made my way regretfully back to the boat, the snapper with potatoes, peas and carrots with a glass or two of white wine would have made a very tasty repast indeed.

Unlike Bamfield there was no coming and going of boats to the dock that I was moored to so the possibility of socialising was discounted. Rather all the boats that were there gave the impression of being long term residents and for the most part presented a look of neglect and abandonment, some even derelict. Could I be in the wrong berth I wondered? But then the wharfinger made no comment when I paid my moorage dues and I had explained where I was tied up. It was just the general air of neglect that got to me I guess. The dark looming clouds threatening rain didn't improve my mood either.

Whatever, there was tomorrow's plan of action to consider, and for the immediate future I would prefer to catch up with some reading. I had brought two excellent books with me: Between Silk and Cyanide, written by a man, who when in his early twenties during the Second World War defined his exploits at Code making. Leo Marks, considered to be a cryptographer of genius. Incidentally, he was the son of Benjamin Marks the owner of legendary bookshop at 84, Charing Cross Road. The reader may recall the film of the same name with Anthony Hopkins.

The other book titled, Soldier Sahibs deals with the men who as District Commissioners in India during early days of the British Raj before and during the Sepoy Mutiny, their trials and tribulations there dealing with the turbulent tribes of the North West Frontier provinces. Both books, to my mind, excellent reading matter for one who likes to read history and as the reader may have realised by now, with the many references in this book to the early happenings on this coast that I have an interest in history. In point of fact I read very little else for entertainment for to my thinking if one doesn't improve their knowledge then there is little point in reading at all. For me to read a novel that stems from the authors imagination, and unfortunately, as so often happens includes misguided facts and half truths then I consider it a sheer waste of time. Far too often novelists trot out what they pass to the reader as fact when the opposite is the case. One only has to take the rubbish that Hollywood is passing out as historical fact to understand my point. And let's face it, 'if it ain't right it's wrong.'

The book that I was reading during this junket, Soldier Sahibs, was about men who were recruited by the East India Company to administer areas of India up to and during the Sepoy Mutiny or as it is more commonly referred to as the Indian Mutiny. This choice of reading matter arose from a book I read some fifty odd years ago that dealt with the career of one of these men. His name was John Nicholson and his administration was so effective that a cult, formed by members of the Pathan tribes, sprung up around him. This cult became known as 'Nickel-Seyns' and was so loyal that when an assassin came up to a group of his followers demanding to know who was John Nicholson one of the followers declared that they were all Nicholson here and was promptly shot by the assassin for his pains.

It should be mentioned that Nicholson heartily disapproved of this following and would only suffer their presence in his tent providing they kept quiet and didn't prostrate themselves and make abeyances. Failure to do so would earn them a flogging a penalty which never varied: three dozen lashes on the bare back which apparently they didn't mind but on the contrary rejoiced in their punishment as having been noticed by their master.

Another anecdote from his life worth a mention is the one were he walked into the officers mess tent and apologised for the lateness of their lunch as he had been hanging the cooks. Nicholson's spies had reported that the cooks had poisoned the soup. When confronted the cooks heartily denied the accusation but would not taste the soup on religious grounds. An unfortunate monkey was therefore fed some soup and died in agony shortly afterwards. In the context of the time there was nothing outrageous about what Nicholson did, the cooks had attempted murder and were duly punished according to the law rough and ready though it may be. History should not be recast in a more congenial form just to suit modern day sensibilities. They were rough days on the Northwest Frontier of India full of treachery and deceit, yet these young men that were instilled with Victorian ethics and with an almost religious sense of duty ruled vast territories putting down unrest and keeping the peace. Dispensing justice with an even hand to the benefit of all, they were incorruptible.

John Nicholson was mortally wounded at the storming of the Kashmir Gate in Dehli during the Sepoy Mutiny. He died four days later at age 35 and his last words were, 'Tell my mother I died doing my duty.' She lost three sons in the service of the East India Company.

How differently we look at life these days, and with how little respect we treat each other, the values that the young men of Nicholson's ilk would today be treated with contempt when they got in the way of looking after number one as these values have sadly become redundant.

It would not surprise me in the least if some politically correct individual demanded an apology for Britain's involvement in India, conveniently forgetting what a stabilising influence their presence was on the sub-continent. Well, we must wait and see after all if they can apologise for the Irish Potato Famine, distressing though that was, when they had no involvement personally and when there is a consensus of opinion that the Government of the time was not responsible anyway. But then playing to the crowd is de-rigour in modern day political thinking.

During this interlude of reflection the plan for tomorrow was decided upon. I would take the route behind Flores Island and emerge close to the entrance to Hot Springs Cove. By taking this route I would avoid the Pacific swell and the possibility of fog and hopefully be able to enjoy some scenery. With this plan of action decided upon I settled down to preparing dinner of the meat pie postponed from the previous evening, some mashed potato, peas and carrots. All to be washed down and the palate cleaned with a glass or two of red wine. Excellent stuff for the digestion.

When the evening ritual was over, and as it was still reasonably early I took a walk ashore to the phone. Again with no connection. The walk to the phone took about ten minutes and obviously ten minutes to return but with one exception; I didn't walk on the return I ran as quickly as these old bones could bear the strain as the heavens had opened up and the rain came down in torrents drenching me to the skin in minutes. Back on board I was to realise that I was wearing the one pair of trousers I had with me and as they were soaked a problem arose. There is a propane heater on the boat but, as propane heat gives out moisture it is no good for drying clothes. Sitting around in my underwear pondering the problem and wondering why I could have been so remiss in the wardrobe department. Not the end of the world though there was a solution which could take care of the situation on the morrow. So, after another couple of glasses of wine I turned in.

DAY FIVE

That fall upon it out the wind

Waking at the usual time to an overcast sky with light rain, the wind from the south east, the speed of which was indeterminate due to the sheltered position, eyeing the weather, for no apparent reason I abandoned my plans to travel the inside route and opted for the open ocean. With the overcast sky and the rain the inner passage didn't seem too appetising anyway. And with the wind from the south east maybe I could get the sails up and do what I came to do and sail. Ah! How hopeful we mere mortals can be.

The hour was early, and as I couldn't yet get underway I pottered about getting breakfast and the rest of the morning ritual, cleaned up and tidied things away. As it was still too early for the shops to open where I could buy a pair of jeans, I read some more.

Come nine o'clock and still raining, my trousers still sodden I donned my oilskin trouser, sea boots and floatation jacket. And with the hood up I made my way ashore.

Without trousers to create the necessary friction the oilskin trouser kept slipping so I had to resort to hoicking them up and clutching the thigh area firmly with both hands. Reminiscent, I thought of Vanna White from the Wheel of Fortune, lifting the skirts of her evening gown to mount the steps to the letter board. It was thus that I proceeded to the men's wear shop.

Of course with my luck they didn't open until some ten minutes after I arrived. No matter, quite a group had gathered probably with the same misconception of opening time. And it was interesting listening to their comments. What did strike me as odd while waiting for the doors to open was a woman who was crossing the street? Remember it was raining and quite cool. This woman though had the flimsiest of blouse or shirt, or whatever. But what struck me as out of place was the shortest of mini skirts. Come on now, these went out of fashion decades ago. The long bare legs ending in high heels made me wonder if she was just coming home from a party. Later I reassessed my thinking to whether she was advertising something. But, on a rainy day in Tofino, at this hour? “Get real.” I muttered.

Once inside the shop I was prepared to buy a pair of jeans in my size and leave, but the saleslady insisted that I try them on. This I know is the usual routine, but it is quite awkward stripping off sea boots and oilskin trousers in a small booth. But then I really did not have a choice. As it turned out, although the waist size and the leg length were what suited me, in this case the waist was a little too tight. I understand this is normal with different brands having different inch measurements. Anyway I ended up with a pair of jeans, which the saleslady insisted would be more comfortable around the waist (even if a little slack), and the leg could be shortened at a later date. Who am I to argue? I just wanted to be on my way. So clutching my purchase under my arm, and with a little difficulty, hoicked up my oilskin trousers again, and returned to the boat and cast off and proceeded to the fuel dock.

Refuelling didn't take long for the fuel consumption from Ucluelet to Tofino was only a few litres. It is wise though to top up whenever possible just in case.

The 'Bismarck' didn't, and look what happened to her.

Still wearing my original morning outfit I went into the office to settle the bill.

"Turned out nice again," said I. Dripping water on his floor, and indicating my sodden floatation jacket. "Are these things supposed to be waterproof?"

Looking me over with a whimsical smile, "The new ones are."

I had noticed the survival suits and floatation jackets hanging up when I came in and was half a mind to give in and buy one, but rejected the idea on the grounds that the amount of sailing that I do such an expense would not be justified. I appreciated the hint though.

"You are a born salesman, sir." said I with a smile, and took my leave.

Back on board I took the hint, and replaced my old floatation jacket with the top half of the oilskin ensemble.

By ten o'clock I was on my way again and out into the Pacific heading towards Hot Spring Cove. On such a miserable day that named place warmed the cockles of my heart, and it was full ahead on the engine. The wind increased in its intensity as I progressed. By eleven thirty it was up to twenty knots with a driving rain. Fortunately with the wind in the south east the rain was lashing my back, so I could more or less be thankful I wasn't travelling south. And I can't resist saying, going in the direction that the counter-clockwise exponents advised. Even so, as the day advanced the sea started to get up, and with the Pacific swell more or less on the beam, and the seas building up from astern the boat started to gyrate and constant steering was called for, meeting and counteracting the push of the waves on the hull, the autopilot being useless in these seas. Whenever a wave banged into the hull the circuit breaker would pop, and around in circles we would go, something else to investigate.

With the constant beating of the wind and rain on my back I started to feel cold to the point of shivering. Not the sort of situation one expects to find on a July day. This wouldn't do at all of course. Fortunately the canvas wheel cover was within reach so with this draped around my shoulders life became a little more pleasant.

Maybe I should have bought a survival suit after all. I must remember to put that on my wish list, should I ever embark on another journey such as this. With these thoughts we progressed with the aim of getting the boat into harbour and me into a hot shower.

By the time of arrival at the entrance to the cove the sea had built up to the point where the boat was surfing. Once again I blessed whoever it was up there that was keeping an eye out for me and prompted the decision to come the way I had, for had I taken the inside route it would have been calm around Flores Island, but coming down the last four miles towards Hot Spring Cove I would have been battering head on into these same seas.

Hot Spring Cove is a narrow inlet two miles in length with the hot springs at the seaward end on the east side. The Parks' jetty is well sheltered about half way into the inlet on the same side as the spring. Approaching the jetty I was fortunate to come alongside with plenty of room to spare in the one remaining space, and with the help of the wharfinger tied up between a motor sailor and two fish boats rafted up together astern.

"Rough out there, is it?" asked the wharfinger.

"It is that, and cold too," I replied with a shiver. "It's a hot shower for me. So I can thaw out."

"Yeah! You look a bit peaked."

With that he moved off, and I went below for that welcome shower. The sunscreen applied this morning in anticipation of a pleasant sunny day would also have to come off unused. That's how it goes sometimes. When you don't expect to get sunburn, you do. And when you do expect to be burned, you don't.

Having the engine heat the domestic hot water is certainly a blessing. Even with the short run of only three and a half hours from Tofino there was more than enough hot water for a long relaxing shower.

Shortly after, while having a late lunch an inflatable high speed boat came into the cove loaded with tourists for the hot spring. The sight of these people made me smile. They were all dressed alike in red survival suits and yellow peaked rain gear jackets. All that was showing of the red survival suits was their legs. As all these people were bunched up together they reminded me of a box of day old chicks. Albeit, chicks that had had a soaking.

Anyway they all disembarked, removed their heavy weather gear and trooped off to the spring. I'm not partial to crowds so I made a mental note to wait until they returned before making my investigation of the hot springs. I had a job to do anyway.

Quite recently the fuel gauge on the main tank had been replaced with a new one. Unfortunately, the holding screws would not tighten the plate down hard enough and diesel had been forced through the seal when refuelling. These screws had to be replaced with the original bolts. Sod's Law of course dictated that this particular job was in the most awkward position and had to be carried out while lying down and with arms stretched out to reach this almost impossible location. It was a fiddly and tiring position to be in so it was a case of replacing these fasteners one at a time with an extended break in between, a time consuming task. In this weather I wasn't going anywhere so time was not a pressing consideration.

Another problem that had cropped up while struggling with the nuts was an annoying drip over the bed in the forward berth. With the boat now lying head to wind the rain was being driven under the flange on the chimney cowl. At least that is what I assumed to be the most likely cause. This ingress of water was obviously making its way along and inside the foam deck head and coming out in way of the skylight. Fortunately this leak was located before the bedding became soaked, so it was only a matter of moving the bedding to the after berth, turning up the forward berth cushions and place pans in strategic positions.

Sealant doesn't stick to wet surfaces so this repair would have to wait until a more auspicious time, when the area had dried out, or at least it had stopped raining.

As the afternoon wore on, and another nut replaced, the tourists started to drift back to the dock and prepared to leave. It was therefore time for me to visit these hot springs. As it was still raining and blowing hard I decided that today I would just view the situation with the intention of taking the plunge into the springs in the morning, early, before the tourist boats arrived.

So donning oilskins and 'wellies' over my new jeans, I set out.

The pools that are fed by the hot springs are a mile away from the jetty and close to the end of the peninsula. The walk is made easy because of the boardwalk put there by the Parks people. And what an excellent piece of workmanship it is, all gradients are made easy for walking either by gentle slopes or by means of steps. When a change of direction occurs the decking is radiused by wedge shaped planking. The whole structure is a work of art. Heaven only knows what one would have done without this boardwalk. Only the hardy would attempt the trek across the forest floor and clamber over fallen trees etc. Even so, it was quite a trudge hampered as I was with sea boots and oilskins.

Of course the visiting boaters have to leave their mark, and there are numerous boards with a boats name carved into it. It must be admitted though that these carvings have been very neatly done, and do credit to both the carver and the boardwalk. Should I ever return here to Hot Spring Cove, I must remember to bring a mallet and a chisel, and engrave my boats name for posterity? Probably though by that time there won't be any space left to carve 'Ron's Endeavour'. But a nice thought though never-the-less.

I passed the odd tourists straggling back to the dock but by the time I reached the springs the place was empty of people. Most likely, if I had arrived when people were still there I could have found the pools more easily by observing a body or two wallowing in the water. Whether I was expecting something more substantial than the small shallow pools that were there, I don't know. What I did know was that they took some finding and disappointingly small. That is what occurs, I suppose when one anticipates what isn't there. The plans for the morrow were therefore abandoned. What would be the point of coming all this way to get into hot water? I manage to do that quite easily and with less effort in the normal course of living. Besides, it is raining. How would one keep their clothes dry? The area did not run changing rooms.

This lack of enthusiasm for what the native people refer to as, 'Smoking Water' is not really surprising after all as I don’t get enthusiastic about very much at all these days, and haven't for many years, a bit long in the tooth for that sort of thing. Although that is not strictly true, I can get enthusiastic about a subject when listening to someone relating an experience that they impart with enthusiasm. That is what happened here I suppose in Bamfield both John and Helen really got me interested in Hot Spring Cove just by how they told of their visit. No doubt the weather, hopefully, when they were here would have been better than this persistent wind and cold miserable rain. Which, in these circumstances, doesn’t sharpen ones sense of enjoyment?

On arriving back at the jetty I passed a boy and a girl, probably in their late teens heading towards the camp ground. Both inadequately dressed for the weather, lank wet hair, and generally soaked. Still they resolutely headed off into the woods bowed under the weight of their back packs. Ah! Youth. What challenges there are in life to surmount? For me I'll settle for a cosy cabin, a beer and a good book. Then dinner.

Blast! I didn't take anything out of the freezer, what a dingledorf am I for forgetting yet again.

Time to think, should I take something out now and try a rapid defrost? Looking into the freezer didn't bring any enthusiasm or inspiration. All was not lost though. As I can seldom be bothered with cooking breakfast of a morning, rather I take the easy route with a bowl of cereals. So why not a change to routine and have bacon and eggs this evening? They would go well with potatoes, peas, and carrots. And a couple of glasses of wine to wash it all down wouldn't go amiss either.

The plan of action was adopted, and what a good wholesome meal it was too. Cooking in the particular frying pan that is on the boat, for some reason made the bacon taste absolutely delicious, it was the same Ayrshire bacon I always buy from the Scottish butcher in Brentwood Bay, but for some inexplicable reason this time it tasted absolutely fabulous. A promise was made to me to partake in this meal again before getting home. Being out in the wind and the rain all day probably put an edge to my appetite also, sharpening up the taste buds so to speak. Crikey, I'm beginning to drool, thinking about this feast.

As the evening wore on the dock soon became deserted of any human form. The tour boat had left some time ago. The wharfinger had retreated across the inlet. The only sign of life was from the boat across the dock, through the window I could see the owners in apparent prayer. As for the other boats nothing. What with the wind picking up and rain driving, it was no wonder. Anyone with any sense would be battened down. Thankful that I was not out in this storm, but secure in my cosy boat I read for a while then took to my bed. Or should I say my other bed.

DAY SIX

Good company and good discourse are the very sinews of virtue
The Compleat Angler Isaac Walton

During the night heavy rain and gusting winds made for a restless sleep. Getting out of bed earlier than my usual time I tried to estimate the wind speed but being in a sheltered position this was not possible to any degree of accuracy. The barometer was reading 29.8 inches, which was lower than the previous evening, which didn't indicate an early improvement in the weather. No matter, no-one, least of all me would be going anywhere today. So a pot of tea, and considering how to pass the day took up some time, and of course take out something for this evening's dinner. I wasn't about to forget again. One of my wife's delicious turkey pot pies, I would think, would make for a delightful repast.

By eight o'clock the weather still hadn't eased. The wharfinger though was out and about checking out the dock and boats, suitably kitted out for the weather in shorts, oilskins jacket, and bare feet. I did think to ask him aboard for tea and conversation, but by the time I had got to the hatch he was hopping aboard the boat moored across the dock from me. This type of boat one would describe as being, with the long deck aft of the wheelhouse, a fish boat that had been converted to a live aboard.

The owner and the wharfinger obviously knew each other as they were soon deep in conversation. I later learned that the gentleman on this particular boat would be taking over as relief wharfinger for a few days.

I decided, before tackling the fuel gauge again, to pull out the radar manual and see if I could find out how to line up the heading marker. This didn't get me anywhere though as there wasn't any instruction that I could find on how to fix this particular problem. At least before I was diverted by the need to make coffee, then it didn't seem all that important. The electronic bearing marker was serving the purpose of heading line admirably.

Much later, after returning home, the company that initially supplied the radar explained the procedure, by the simple expedient of directing me to a particular page in the Owners Manual. As they say, 'If all else fails, read the instructions.' Properly.

As the morning progressed there wasn't any sign of life on the dock. I caught glimpses of people moving about on the fish boats moored astern. And the running up of generators reminded me there was life around. Of course the tourists in their high speed inflatable were conspicuous by their absence. Small wonder really. It would have to be a most irresponsible tour guide to be out in this weather.

In the early afternoon the wharfinger and a boater were overheard discussing the weather. Apparently the boater had been to the Hot Springs where he could look out of the Cove to open ocean and was reporting high winds driving white caps off the waves.

Oh well. The replacing of screws with bolts on the fuel gauge sensor was yet to be finalised. The batteries could be checked, so I had better get on with these chores and get them out of the way.

During the afternoon, after the fuel gauge was secured and the batteries having been topped up, I was enjoying a cup of tea and reading a book when there was a tap on the window. Looking up the wharfinger was beckoning for my attention.

Popping my head out of the hatch, I invited him in for tea.

"No thanks. What I want to ask you is would you like to go across to the other side for dinner this evening?"

"Well, I..." I said doubtfully. A little taken aback by this unusual suggestion.

"The reason I ask is because the Royal Victoria Yacht Club had arranged dinner for sixty people and they can't make it, they are holed up in Friendly Cove with the weather. What I'm doing is rounding up what people I can from the boats here. Sort of making up some numbers."

"Well, Yes, O.K. I guess so."

"Good. We'll all go in my boat. Be ready for six thirty." As a parting shot he said, "It will cost you fifteen dollars."

I nodded agreement.

Fifteen dollars seemed reasonable. If they were accommodating sixty people there must be a sizeable restaurant over the other side. And by definition a good meal.

Happy in the thought of a pleasant and maybe convivial evening I put the turkey pot pie in the fridge and returned to my cup of tea.

And would you believe it had stopped raining, time to seal the leak on the chimney.

Come six thirty, freshly shaved and showered I presented myself at the wharfinger boat. Not only had the rain held off, the wind had died, presenting a calm fresh summer evening. Things looked promising for the morrow.

The other boaters had also emerged from their hidey-holes and presented quite a crowd. Not sixty in number by any means but a good representation. So, in holiday mood we all boarded the wharfinger boat.

“Hi! I'm Jennifer.”

Standing next to me, holding out her hand was this charming young lady. I won't try to guess her age because everyone younger than me appears to be young. But her good looks were certainly easy on the eye.

“Ron Palmer,” I replied, shaking the offered hand. “Which boat are you from?”

Jennifer mentioned the name of the boat, but I must admit I have forgotten. First stages of 'old timers’ I shouldn't wonder.

As it turned out the boat was thirty feet in length, with five people on board. 'Paddy' the owner a lawyer from Victoria, his wife and two children, and Jennifer who was crewing, who were all members of the Royal Victoria Yacht Club and had got ahead of the pack of thirty boats stranded at Friendly Cove in Nootka Sound. Getting into Hot Spring Cove ahead of the weather.

No doubt I would be meeting the residual of this south bound flotilla on my way to Nootka Sound tomorrow. The storm had passed over, so unless another low pressure system sprung up over night, there was every reason to believe this would be so.

Looking at the houses in this village on this the other side of the Cove put in doubt the possibility of a fine restaurant. This doubt was soon realised as we all trooped into a private house comprising two rooms set out with a table and chairs in the one room, and plastic garden furniture in the other. How on earth sixty people would have fitted into this space will forever remain a mystery.

Paddy, Jennifer, Paddy's young son, and yours truly, seated ourselves at one of the garden tables.

I don't wish to be too critical of the meal because I know my short comings where food is concerned. Green salad I'm not partial to, and tend to give it a miss. Salmon falls in the same category, unless it is moist and lightly cooked. Baked potatoes I like fine when they can be eaten, but the ones served here defied the efforts of my dentures to penetrate their case hardened exterior. Looking around at the other diners, deep in conversation and tucking in to the meal like true trenchermen and women, didn't strike me as there being any concerns with the food there. Or maybe the party mood was a result of being let out of close confinement.

So, wistfully thinking of my delicious turkey pot pie, peas and carrots, I did my best with what lay before me.

When the apple pie came though the disappointment at the rest of the meal was pushed to the back of my mind, this pie was delicious. A great pity that I couldn't have filled up with several helpings of this.

The alacrity with which the invitation to take away what food one desired was met with, only reinforced the premise that either my taste buds were different. Or my wife's food had spoiled me for rougher fare. Maybe what was missing was the wine.

However, on our return to the far side the evening had taken on that feeling that there had never been a gale passing through here. It was a gorgeous warm summer evening, as much to say, 'Who me?" I know not of any bad weather.' A portend for good weather for the next section of the circum-navigation.

While we had been dining a sailboat of about fifty feet had come into the cove and rafted up to me. Overlapping each end and boxing me in on the inside against the wharf. It was crewed by a Belgium couple who had sailed down from Prince Rupert heading for San Francisco. I expressed the concern that I hoped they were early risers, because I would be leaving about eight.

Paddy, family and crew came aboard the 'Endeavour' for a glass or two of wine and a visit to round off the evening. And once again I met interesting people with stories to tell.

The one story that Paddy told filled me with both amusement and concern. Concern because he made it sound so easy to have a boat flop over, and I must say here that others since then have related their experiences of being knocked down.

Jennifer, in particular related her experience of turning turtle with relish. The fact that the boat comes upright immediately does not make me breathe any easier at the prospect that this experience might happen to my boat. I made a mental note to keep the hatch battened down in boisterous weather. Just in case.

On the occasion that Paddy related, his boat had come up on a wave to the point that the rudder came out of the water. The boat then broached to and over it went. The casual way that this experience was related made me wonder if this wasn't a normal happening for him.

What made me smile though was that since then the children had to wear lifejackets and their cycling helmets, and are sent to play in the 'V' berth, while daddy did his sailing thing. Sounds like fun.

Another point that came up in discussion was the best time to cross Nahwitti Bar. This is a shallow stretch of water by Hope Island, the first island of any note after rounding Cape Scott, and the entrance to Goleta's Channel.

At certain times, when the North-westerly winds were blowing with any appreciable strength and meeting with an out going tide, standing waves can occur creating dangerous conditions for small craft and a rough ride for bigger vessels. Obviously it is desirable to cross at slack water. But when and where was this slack water? I hadn't been able to find anything in the tide tables. The present company had crossed the Bar without any trouble, but couldn't supply the relevant information. This problem became a nagging bug. If I couldn't get this information from the boaters I met with then I was resolved to contact the coastguard. Most likely place would be from Winter Harbour or failing that, then to call up the lighthouse on the VHF on Cape Scott.

Pondering this problem, after the company had left, and as the leak from the skylight had stopped, I took myself to bed in the forward berth again.

DAY SEVEN

For solitude sometimes is best society

Paradise Lost

At five in the morning I was awake and out of bed ready to face the coming day's adventure. And what a day for adventure it was. The sky was cloudless and without a breath of wind. It would mean motoring again, but it would be nice to get away and make progress to Friendly Cove, a place that had such historical meaning, a place where both Captain James Cook and Captain George Vancouver were to leave their marks. This Cove was to be the highlights of the whole trip. A place that I had long wanted to visit. I had toured the north of Yorkshire visiting everywhere that Cook was associated with in his youth. The Fortress of Louisburg in Cape Breton where Cook met Samuel Holland, a Military Surveyor from whom Cook learned surveying skills, and the Bay of Kealakakua in Hawaii, where Cook was killed. Friendly Cove was to be yet another place of deep historical meaning for me. What a cruel joke that would turn out to be.

It was still early after finishing my morning ritual and as I was loath to disturb my neighbours who had boxed me in. I took a stroll towards the camp ground, a place that I had yet to see. My goodness, what enterprises we think up to pass the time. As it turned out I never got that far anyway. On passing the boat moored ahead of me I noticed people activity. These people were part of the flotilla circum-navigating Vancouver Island in the opposite direction to me, so, as the problem was still unresolved, maybe they would know the time of low water at Nahwitti Bar. I abandoned the campground quest and returned to the dock.

"Good morning." I said to the elderly man leaning out of the wheelhouse door.

"Ya! Going to be a nice day, I think."

Sounds foreign. Possibly German?

"You are with the Yacht Club, are you?" I asked.

"Ya,"

"Did you have any problems coming across Nahwitti Bar?"

"Nein. No"

"I'm trying to find out the time of slack water at the Bar on the 30th. You wouldn't know what time that would be would you?"

After all, I reasoned, if all these boats had crossed the bar then surely someone would know where to find this information.

"Sure" he said, "Come inside." He moved aside to let me pass.

Then I stood out of the way to let who I presumed to be his wife pass. She was busy with her early morning cleaning chores and it doesn't do to get in the way of this female industry. She dragged a rug out on to the dock and started shaking and brushing it.

In the meantime my saviour had pulled out a laptop computer. My heart sank as he brought up a tide program at least that is what I deduced it to be, computers and I don't get along too well. A word processor I can manage in the very basic mode. But, the vision before my eyes, in my ignorance of all things technical, was an instrument of the devil.

I began to wish that I hadn't asked, but good manners dictated that my presence should not be terminated just yet.

While he was doing the calculations a head belonging to yet another elderly gentleman rose into view from the accommodation below. He didn't speak, but scowled nicely. I nodded a greeting and his scowl deepened.

In due course the lap top produced the desired results, and the information written on a piece of paper. Looking at the times handed to me caused some doubt, not so much that they were incorrect, but rather that they were based on Campbell River, which is way down the east coast of Vancouver Island. Surely, Alert Bay which is much closer would have been the reference port. Still, with computers? Maybe it was programmed to refer every tide around the coast based on Campbell River. And who am I to doubt?

However, with the information received we chatted a little about what routes to follow, what weather conditions we had met, just the usual subjects that arise on such occasions. Time was pressing though, and as I was anxious to be on my way, I thanked him for the information and returned to my boat in preparation of leaving.

The fish boats had left, so that would give me space to slip astern and out from between the dock and the fifty footer. There were enough people on the dock to help with this operation, and the activity aroused those on board the other boat, so it was only a matter of letting go from the dock and passing his lines ashore for me to be free and clear, and on my way.

Paddy and crew were also leaving, so with calls of, 'good luck', 'bon voyage', and other calls of good natured banter we parted company,

When clear of the dock I took the opportunity to hoist the mainsail, this would help steady the boat against the ever present Pacific swells. Being on my own I find it expedient and sensible to go forward to perform tasks out of the cockpit when close to shore. Then, should it be my great misfortune to fall overboard at least I can swim to shore before succumbing to hypothermia.

Quite recently there was a case of a boat being wrecked on the coast and the body of, presumably the lone sailor, attached to the boat with a life line. It was assumed that he had fallen overboard and could not get back on board again, and so drowned. A most tragic accident, but I could take some comfort from this knowing that it wouldn't happen to me, after all I don't wear a lifeline. Having said that, it will be considered along with the survival suit for any future adventure.

By 0730 I was clear of the Cove and heading towards Nootka Sound. The fish boats were out, but soon hidden by the fog rolling in from the open ocean. Oh! Dearie me, here we go again. How many of the remaining Royal Victoria Yacht Club boats will loom out of this murk.

Between Hot Spring Cove and Nootka Sound lies Hesquiat Harbour. John and Helen Humphries had strongly recommended a stop here at Boat Basin which is at the top of the bay. This was the place where Annie Ada Rae-Arthur created her world famous garden out of the wilderness, virtually by her own labours. At the same time bearing eight of her eleven children. She also, by her shooting skills, earned the title of Cougar Annie.

Although neighbours did the heavy labour of felling the trees, the clearing and burning of the stumps, the actual creation of five acres of garden was left to this resourceful and tough lady. By all accounts her husband, being of poor health, was not given to heavy manual labour so the brunt of the work fell to the determined and dedicated Annie.

Of course in situations such as existed at Boat Basin all sorts of myths and legends grow up around the principal character, and Annie was no exception. The facts remain though, that she did clear the land for her garden. Although the word garden could be misconstrued to mean something that one would have behind the house to grow vegetables for ones own consumption. The actual garden that Annie created amounted to some five acres. The produce grown here, and the nursery plants, eventually were shipped all across Canada and the world.

Livestock, in the form of pigs and goats, etc were also part of this enterprise. Of course those domesticated animals had to be protected from wild animals. Hence the title Cougar Annie.

Over the years Ada Annie Rae-Arthur opened a general store and a post office.

Although I would have loved to spend some time here I had wasted a day at Hot Spring Cove and was anxious to get on with my travels. And I was beginning to suspect a growing urge to get home.

While proceeding towards Estevan Point, boats from what I presumed to be from the flotilla appeared one by one out of the fog. Although there should have been something like twenty-seven or so, only six appeared on my course. No doubt they would be well spread out by the time I came across them and for the most part invisible in the fog.

On sighting Estevan Point Lighthouse I started to reflect on how difficult it must have been approaching this coast in the days of the sailing ships. These vessels relied on the wind for propulsion, and if there was no wind and close to the shore, then boats would have to tow them into a sheltered anchorage. How easy it is these days with modern charts and motors to get about.

*****

Nootka Sound gave the first sighting of land for Cook since Cape Flattery. He was desperately in need of a safe harbour to carry out repairs to his ships. Parts of the foremast called trestles which supported the upper mast on the Resolution were rotting and had to be replaced.

With what relief he viewed this Sound can only be imagined. There were no charts for him to consult for this coast. The Spaniards had been here some years before in 1774, but what charts they had made were not available to Cook. In fact the Spanish Government had sent out an expedition with orders to arrest Cook's expedition, should they be sighted. So it was hardly likely that they would make the charts available.

Cook named the southeast entrance to the Sound, Point Breakers due to the number of sunken rocks here, on which the swells break continuously. Of course he was unaware that Commander Juan Perez of the Santiago had named this point of land after his second lieutenant Estevan Jose Martinez, the first place in British Columbia to be named for a white man. One can't help wondering what sort of relationship these two had, a cousin maybe? After all, would it not be more appropriate to name the first point of importance on their cruise with an appellation of a more illustrious personage. Say, the king of Spain, rather than the first name of the second mate.

Making their way into the Sound, mainly by being towed by the ships boats due to the absence of wind, the ships first anchored in Resolution Cove on what is now Bligh Island. The next day the ships boats found a more appropriate cove on Nootka Island proper, where the ships could be moored to the shore. Although Cook didn't give a name to this harbour it later became named in 1786, Friendly Cove.

This cove was also the meeting place of Juan Francisco de Bodega y Quadra, and Captain George Vancouver in 1792. These two gentlemen had been sent by their respective governments to determine the boundaries under the dictates of the Nootka Sound Convention.

It will be remembered that the dispute between Britain and Spain came about over this territory due to the seizure of British trading vessels by the Spanish, and the claim of John Meares, a fur trader that he had land here gifted to him by Maquinna the local native chief. And as British subjects had actually started a settlement here then this fact established a valid title to the land.

An agreement was not forthcoming though. Quadra had arrived in April expecting to meet Vancouver. However, Vancouver was busily exploring and charting the other side of the island and didn't arrive until four months later. During this interlude it had been difficult to establish clear evidence of these buildings and tracts of land involved. This complicated matters for Vancouver. The matter therefore was left for the British and Spanish governments to resolve.

Vancouver, however, with his charting of that island which was to bear his name, claimed to be the first European to circum-navigate the island and establish its insularity. Although on this particular voyage he had only charted from Cape Flattery around to Nootka Sound. He had, as a midshipman with Cook also sailed from Cape Flattery to Nootka, thus in effect being able to claim to be the first European.

*****

Once again, coming into an inlet the fog lifted to reveal a bright sunny day. I found this would happen every time I approach an inlet. It was incredible really, almost as if there was an invisible barrier denying the fog entrance. The fog didn't thin gradually, but just seem to evaporate in one go.

However, here I was approaching a place I had dreamed of visiting for years, motoring along towards Friendly Cove. When a most peculiar thing happened, a voice, in my head said, 'Don't go in', it seemed almost a shouted command. And without any hesitation I didn't. I just carried on towards Tahsis. I was at a loss as to why this happened, but there was no gainsaying this, the voice was so positive it just had to be obeyed. Weird, I might be going nuts, but at least it isn't Alzheimer's disease. Most of my life while performing a particular task, I've had on occasion a little voice in my sub-conscience saying, or should I say a feeling, that what I was doing was not the right way to do it. Sometimes if the voice was ignored then I would have to do the job over again, or undo what turned out to be wrong. Needless to say I started taking notice of these sub-conscience warnings. But for this occasion to be almost a shout I cannot for the life of me explain. And now I'll never know what the warning was about. I just contented myself with a glance over my shoulder while passing. With the thought that it was such a small cove to hold two ships each of a hundred feet in length.

Not much thought was given to why Friendly Cove was missed out on the passage to Tahsis. That is what happened, and there was no going back now. It wasn't until after this trip was over that I would wonder about the reason why these voices happen. The only answer I can come up with, and this is an assumption, there must be some sort of sixth sense buried somewhere deep in my brain. Well, that's my answer and I'm sticking to it.

It was a beautifully warm summer's day, and the waters of the inlet calm. After the periods of the fog and cold winds and driving rain, this was a time to relax and enjoy. Not for long though. My attention to the scenery and soaking up the sun was soon dispelled with the banging on the hull.

Thud, thud, thud.

Damn! I'd run into a raft of kelp and a piece, or pieces of this had caught up in the propeller. Bang, bang, bang, against the hull with every turn of the screw. Fortunately being close to the controls the engine was stopped and then after a moment of thought put in reverse. This action cleared the kelp, and with a sigh of relief that no damage had been done, we proceeded on to Tahsis now with much more attention keeping a sharp look-out for these nuisance obstructions.

Wouldn't it be nice if someone decided to harvest these navigation hazards and process them into Kombu, that exceedingly nutritious sea vegetable which the Orientals are so fond of eating? If nothing else it would do away with the need to import this product.

Was it my imagination, or do I detect a vibration. If so then that would be one more thing to worry about. But as nothing could be done about a possible shaft re-alignment until the boat was hauled, and as I was far from such an event, keeping my fingers crossed was the best course to follow. And a reduction of revolutions did seem to solve the problem. What a worry wart I had become. I decided to talk to myself on different subject and dissolve these imaginary problems.

At least it wasn't a deadhead. That thought kept me alert from then on as it would not do to become immobilized in a windless inlet

Deadheads are partially submerged logs that have become waterlogged to the point they float vertically in the water. At this point they are particularly dangerous, for if a vessel hits one they tend to sink and then come up again in slow motion, usually in way of a propeller. One can imagine what effect that would have on ones progress.

Arrived at Tahsis fuel dock at 13.45, due to the breakwater protecting the dock and my angle of approach with a wind being from the direction it now was, it took two attempts to get alongside. The newness and neatness of the dock and marina were a pleasant surprise after the fuel docks previously visited. Two young Dock-Jocks eagerly took the lines, and smartly dressed they were too. Presentation is always a winner in my book. While fuelling, the conversation turned to the Royal Victoria Yacht Club again.

"Did you come across the flotilla from Royal Victoria Yacht Club?" asked the attendant, a pretty girl in her early twenties. She seemed to be in charge of the other two young people, and directing them in tying of the mooring lines.

"Yes. I did. Well some of them anyway, the fog was quite thick outside. Two boats made it to Hot Spring Cove before the bad weather came in. The rest were at Friendly Cove, and shut in there."

"It was blowing pretty hard here too. They were here a couple of days ago. Thirty boats." She seemed quite proud.

And so she should. To accommodate so many boats over and above the permanent residents must have been quite an achievement.

But blowing hard here in this sheltered place? Twenty miles from the open ocean. Then why not, the inlet would probably act as a funnel when the wind is from a particular direction.'

"The people I met at Hot Springs were very enthusiastic about the welcome they got here. Banners greeting them and everything" I said. "Very appreciative they were."

She smiled, "Yes?"

I nodded. "Yes, very." And smiled in return.

"Will you be requiring moorage tonight?"

"Sorry, no. I want to get down to Rolling Roads, or thereabouts. This will give me a good start for Winter Harbour tomorrow."

What was the matter with me? Being held over for a day at Hot Spring Cove seems to have instilled a will to get going as fast as possible. Not taking time out to smell the flowers seems to be a normal way of life with me. Been there, done that. What's next? Attitude. A pity really. What I should have done is persuaded someone of a more sedentary nature to have come along on this trip. Then, I would have had someone else to consider and slowed down, spending more time visiting more places. Maybe next year? Yeah, maybe?

The fuelling completed, I topped up the water tanks. Then after another fruitless attempt to phone home, paid the bill and took off.

Just a short distance down the Tahsis channel there is a turn off into the Esperanza Inlet which passes by the north and west side of Nootka Island. It was this route that I took with the intention of finding a resting place for the night and a good jumping off spot for tomorrows run. The anchorage behind Catala Island, in what is called the Rolling Roadstead was the first consideration. No doubt the rolling would be acceptable if not too intense and the distance to Winter Harbour would be lessened for the run on the morrow, after all a Roadstead is a place where ships anchor, but then. “Guess what?” As I reached the end of Esperanza Inlet, surprise, surprise, the fog shut in thick as a hedge again.

Now followed an anxious half an hour or maybe a little less, I wasn't watching the clock. Of course the original plan had to be abandoned and plan 'B' put in hand. This was to try and get into Queen Cove without running into the numerous rocks scattered around the entrance. Although the normal emotion for these situations should have been fear, and possibly a strong smell of an unpleasant nature, but this wasn't so. At least I wasn't aware of this emotion, only a terrible dryness in my mouth. In fact it was impossible to get any saliva working at all.

So, with the chart in one hand and the other hand gripping firmly on the wheel, I watched the rocks looming out of the murk just feet away on the starboard bow, feeling my way by instinct more than anything else. In this manner I made my way around the corner into Birthday Channel. It must have been my birthday for the fog lifted again to reveal the open bay and an especially beautiful evening. I think it would be unnecessary to explain why under the circumstances this time the evening was especially beautiful.

Making my way into Queen Cove I vowed that if the fog was there in the morning I would not leave until it had cleared. There was no way I would repeat this evening’s rock dodging performance.

Queen Cove is a snug little cove totally land locked except for a narrow entrance accessed to the west of Queens Cove village which lies on an Indian Reserve immediately to the southeast. The anchorage in here is well protected from the elements, which gave me a strong sense of security.

Not so long ago there was a flourishing community on the east side, the remains of which are now hard to locate. This decline is now a feature of this coast, the fish stocks these communities thrived on have been depleted over the years, and most of the inhabitants have moved on giving their habitations back to nature.

On anchoring in this calm little backwater the first thing I did was to have a beer, then as I was still a little up tight from my experience and the dryness in my throat still lingering from entering this calm little backwater, I had another beer. This sorted out my fog fried brain considerably, and brought the saliva back to my arid mouth. I was then in the mood for the passed over meal of yesterday evening.

Now into the seventh day of my trip I had settled down and began enjoying my own cooking, and, of course my own company. I'm convinced that for me anyway this is the only way to travel, by oneself with no television, no one else to interrupt one's thoughts. (They do say that television is ruining the art of conversation. So without television as well this was a double bonus). Maybe by the end of this circumnavigation I will have made up my mind whether I want company or not.

And most importantly, especially if a companion is without sailing experience, then there would be the added responsibility for another body that might do something naive and possibly dangerous. Mind you having said that, for somebody to make and hand up a coffee and a muffin on a long cold haul would be nice. There was only once though this need occurred, and that was on the run from Winter Harbour to Cape Scott. An experience that could, if I'd thought about it, have been circumvented by preparing a flask and having muffins within handy reach while at the wheel. But then isn't hind sight, 20/20?

However these shake down cruises are what this is all about, i.e. preparing for the next trip.

The fact that radio reception was nil most of the time didn't bother me. This I found surprising for at home I'm avid for the news of the outside world. Listening to the CBC news broadcasts during the day, and watching the BBC during the afternoon is, or should I say was, a part of my daily bread. I don't doubt that on my return home the same routine will be picked up on again, as though I had never been away. Quite likely, in the first while, I would be paying little attention, as I would most likely will be thinking of this trip and the planning of a subsequent junket.

DAY EIGHT

It was beautiful and simple as all great vistas are.

Getting up early and after doing my leisurely morning routine saw me on my way by 0630, and no fog. What a blessing.

What I had noticed while shaving was that I had managed to get rather a red nose from too much sun the day before. Typically me, and shutting the stable door after the horse has flown, so to speak, I applied generous amounts of sun block to all exposed areas of skin especially to this forward facing appendage after the damage had been done.

Remembering to wear a hat I went forward and lifted the anchor, and motored out of Queens Cove into a beautiful summer's morning.

After clearing the Gillam Channel I set a course for Solander Island off Cape Cook, the northwest corner of Brook Peninsula. This put the wind right astern again but with little velocity. So once again it was to be a motoring passage to Winter Harbour. Although Solander Island was thirty-five miles away it stood out against the horizon bold and clear. What a blessing this amazing visibility was after all the fog and miserable rain so far experienced.

Having such a wonderful day to enjoy, put me into a light hearted mood. This prompted a little ditty to pop into my head, and to the tune of 'I'd like to get you on a slow boat to China.' I started to sing;

'Out on the briny, with a nose red and shiny.'

'All by myself alone.'

'Rolling and heaving, on these swells ever more.'

'Pitching and rolling,'

'Heading for that far away shore.'

A little disjointed maybe, and out of tune, but so what, it's a wonderful day. Why shouldn't I immortalise this trip in song?

This perpetual ocean swell that rolls in from the Pacific gives little discomfort to the traveller, at least under these calm conditions, with just a gentle lifting when the wave passes under the boat to settle down again as the wave has gone by.

When driven by high wind though a different tale would be told, then life could be uncomfortable with the possibility of spray, or seas breaking over the deck. Pitching and yawing like an out of control bucking horse.

But not on this day, this day was to become a pleasant reward for putting up with those miserable days of fog. When there was little time to relax from constantly peering into the reduced visibility, uptight and anticipating an unresisting object to suddenly appear.

These swells have an advantage for the traveller though. When they reach the shore they break against the rocks, even the hidden rocks are revealed with swirling water. What better indication could one have of the hidden dangers lurking beneath the surface, the message is, beware, and keep clear.

For the first time on this circumnavigation the full vista of Vancouver Island became apparent. This was the first day I could relax and view the stark beauty of the West Coast of Vancouver Island. The whole aspect of this rugged coast, and back into the mountains, for as far as the eye could see was laid out before me. The mountains and hills all carpeted with millions of trees, coming right down to the waters edge. With the odd bare patch where clear cutting of the forest had occurred.

Beautiful from this safe distance, but heavens, what a dilemma to be wrecked on this hostile shore. Even if one survived such a tragedy there would be the unpopulated wilderness to contend with. Possibly where no human eye has ever set foot. Not to mention the wildlife. Crashing through the undergrowth looking for a human habitation would soon lead to disorientation and to being hopelessly lost.

Viewing all this from a distance had me at a loss as to how one could describe the appearance of Vancouver Island. After much pondering it came to me, and I likened what I was looking at as a large green cloth with threadbare patches, thrown down, and then bunched up into a higgledy-di-piggledy mass of mounds. The area of the cloth that had become high would be pinched and pulled into random round or pointed peaks. The sunken parts of the cloth would be the valleys. The colour green would represent the trees and the threadbare patches the clear cut forest. After discussing this with myself, we decided that it was a fair representation of Vancouver Island. And, just in case these observations would be grounds for a visit from the men in white coats, and for me to be locked up, I should be careful to keep this view of Vancouver Island to myself.

Vancouver Island of course was named for Captain George Vancouver. But not originally. When Vancouver met with Juan Francisco de la Bodega y Quadra at Nootka Sound in August 1792 to settle the details of the Nootka Sound Convention. Quadra had asked Vancouver to name this Island that he had recently circumnavigated. Vancouver, in respect for Quadra, and the friendship that had developed between them, named it Quadra and Vancouver's Island. Early Admiralty charts show the island with this name, which the Hudson Bay traders later shortened to Vancouver's Island. By the mid eighteen hundreds, however, the 's was dropped and thus became as we know it today, Vancouver Island.

Quadra, however, did have an island named for him on the east side which forms the east side of Discovery Passage and Seymour Narrows. Not as big as the big island, but then losers can't be choosers.

Lost in these revelries the trip passed quickly enough and by noon I was opposite Solander Island. A large cone shaped rock sticking up three hundred and ten feet above the ocean. And lying just a mile from Cape Cook, the point of land on the northeast of Brooks Peninsula. That large rectangular lump of land that sticks out from Vancouver Island into the Pacific.

Where the name Solander came from I know not. There was a gentleman, Dr. Carl Solander, who was with Joseph Banks' party on Cook's voyage on the Endeavour. I would like to think that this little island was his namesake, for he was very well liked by Cook and his officers. One day maybe all will be revealed.

*****

James Cook was not responsible for naming this cape after himself and those places that he did either were already named by a previous explorer or later changed. In fact he gave very few names to this island coastline. In the Nootka Sound area he bestowed names to islands, peninsulas, coves and channels, in favour of his ships and officers. Bligh Island being one in particular.

Contrary to Hollywood's abuse of history, Bligh was an extremely capable seaman and navigator. With the most important of ranks, at twenty-one years of age. Sailing Master, on this, Cook's third voyage of discovery. He was noted for his bluntness in manner and speech, and in his dealings with people, but non-the-less worthy of recognition by having Cook name an island after him.

Other examples of place names given by Cook in this inlet of Nootka Sound are Gore Island, Clerke Peninsula on Bligh Island named for the Charles Clerke in command of the Discovery, the companion ship on this expedition. King Passage and Williamson Passage, both officers of these ships.

The point of land we know today as Cape Cook was originally named Woody Point by Captain Cook, but in 1860 it was renamed in honour of that greatest of all navigators by Captain G.H. Richards, R.N

*****

The run to Winter Harbour entrance from Solander Island is just twenty miles, this distance being covered in just under four hours. The low speed being caused no doubt by an adverse current.

During the afternoon a brisk breeze of around ten knots had sprung up, but as this was right astern, and, with my disinclination to leave the cockpit without a safety harness, which, needless to say I had failed to bring with me. I was loath to put up the mainsail. The Genoa of course could be operated from the cockpit, but by this time I was happy just motoring. Suspecting that no sooner had I put up the Genoa, the wind would drop away, and the sail would flap around like a drying shirt on the wash line. So that was it, the situation remained as is.

Over on the starboard quarter, a boat that had motored by heading in the opposite direction, was attempting to put up his foresail. The difficulty he seemed to be having in this exercise with the boat bucking and tossing in the swell was an added reason for me to carry on in the present mode.

Entering Winter Harbour Inlet put me for a moment in doubt as whether I was in the correct place. Compared to the chart the actual visual aspect is quite different. In fact one gets the impression of entering a blind bay. It isn't until approaching nearly to the top of this 'illusionary' bay that the inlet turns sharply right to reveal a waterway stretching further inland. Shortly after this right hand turn there is another sharp turn to the left, when the village of Winter Cove is revealed. At one time a busy and prosperous fishing port, sadly, no more and yet another victim to the depletion of the fish resource.

During the passage of the first part of the approach I witnessed a scene that was quite unusual, something that I had never seen before. Flying in and out of the trees there were four seagulls swooping and harassing an eagle. I found this happening difficult to accept after all an eagle is a more powerful bird than a seagull. Why didn't it retaliate? As I pondered this a thought came to me which made me wonder if my mind was going. If an eagle is a bird of prey. Why didn't it take sanctuary in the nearest church?

Since this happening and on this voyage of learning I have learnt many things. One being that eagles are quite often attacked by groups of other birds. Another is that to prevent these attacks an eagle will perch in a tree underneath foliage. Every day we learn something new don't we?

It was my intention to fuel up before mooring for the night, so as to get an early start for the run up to Cape Scott, and then to Nahwatti Bar. As yet I had no information as to the time of slack water at the bar, but was hopeful of this problem being resolved here at Winter Harbour. The information received from the German chappie didn't give me any confidence in its validity. If necessary I would phone the Coast Guard.

On approaching the fuel dock I was pleasantly surprised to see two young ladies, maybe in their thirties, hurrying down the dock, presumably to take my lines.

My, I thought, they have lovely wharfies here.

As it turned out they did take my lines.

“Are you the Wharfinger,” I asked.

“Good heavens no,” one of the girls replied, “We saw you coming in while we were doing our laundry, and came down to help you moor.”

“That was most kind of you. Thank you.”

One of the girls had turned and left, but the one I took to be the youngest introduced herself.

“I'm Diane, my friend and I are moored further along the dock. There is space there if you are planning to stay the night.”

“I am thank you. I'll move over after I've refuelled.”

“See you there then.” she answered and moved off. Presumably back to the laundry.

As I watched her go I thought what a charming person. I bet she isn't one of those city dwellers who are afraid to speak to, or even look a stranger in the eye.

With that I hopped off and went looking for the fuel attendant, who was conspicuous by his absence. On asking as to his whereabouts, from two sports fishermen who were cleaning their catch, I was instructed that he was to be found up in the store, which he ran in conjunction with the fuel dock. Sure enough, that is where he was, and with me in tow returned to the fuelling station.

As we proceeded back along the dock I couldn't help thinking how alike this place was, in attitude anyway, to the island I live on. He didn't lock the store when he left it. If there was someone else there or not, I didn't see them.

This trust that rural communities have in their fellow humans is a blessed thing, but fragile in its naivety. More and more this trust is being abused by those who feel they can take what is not theirs, just by the fact that an article of easy acquisition is there and not being guarded. A sad reflection on the state of modern society. We must become more aware of locking things up I suppose, the car, the house, and anything else that isn't nailed down. Otherwise, quite possibly they won't be there when needed.

On a lighter note though, and this joke I heard recently. Which I found, in light of what I have just said quite amusing.

This chap had parked his car, a convertible, and was quite a way down the road when he realized that the car was unlocked with the top down. In alarm he hurried back hoping that his bagpipes which were on the back seat hadn't been stolen. Not only were the bagpipes still there but someone had thrown another set of bagpipes in.

As we approached the boat the fuel guy exercised an obvious wisdom.

"You must be Ron?" he said, looking at the name on the side of my boat. "My name's Ron also."

"A dead giveaway isn't it," I said with a smile. "My last name isn't Endeavour though."

As he busied himself unlocking the shed door and switching on the pumps I corrected my previous observation about not locking things up, and assumed there must have been someone else in the store. Either that or maybe the locals could be trusted but not the visiting boaters. Who knows there are all sorts of possibilities? It could be that I was the first boat to fuel up since the previous day. When locking up over night would be a sensible requirement. I was about to raise this subject when he pre-empted me with a question of his own.

"You haven't been here before." This was a statement.

"No, I haven't."

"Thought so, I know every boat that has been here for the last nine years."

Either this Ron had an incredible memory, or he was pulling my leg.

"That's incredible." I said "You must have a terrific memory."

"Yup." he said looking pleased.

"This boat is only two years old anyway, so you wouldn't have had to stretch your memory too far back, had I been here before." I made this statement hoping for a favourable comment on my pride and joy. But then pride has a way of back firing. Or to quote my old Granny, "Pride always comes before a fall."

In this case there was no response.

By this time the fuel tanks had been topped up. So I settled the bill and moved further into the harbour to the Government Dock and moored up behind two other boats. Which I assumed were the boats belonging to Diane's party.

I settled in, and had a late afternoon cup of tea; it was still only around five o'clock. Having been prompted by Diane to the fact that there were laundry facilities, I gathered up my dirty laundry and proceeded there.

The girls were still there when I arrived, folding and packing their laundry. Quite a job it was too.

"Crikey, you must have been out a long time." I said, indicating the clothes.

"Coming around Cape Scott the engine broke down and we got swamped." said Diane. Who seemed to be the more forthcoming of the two?

"Good heavens," I said.

“Yes it was really awful. Everything got soaked. It was terribly rough weather. Ian, that's my husband, managed to fix the problem. But not before we had been thrown around all over the place. And our friends,” nodding towards her companion, “stayed close.”

“A good job you were travelling together.” I said wondering what would be in store for me on the morrow.

Diane nodded. “Yes, it was awful. On top of everything else, we had just caught a fish. There was no way we could deal with that, so Ian just cut the line.”

“You had crossed the Nahwitti Bar then,” I asked, “You wouldn't know what time slack water is tomorrow evening.”

“No, but Ill ask Ian, he'll know.”

And so they left. They with their laundry, and me with my anxious thoughts on the run to Cape Scott on the morrow.

While the laundry was under way, I took a stroll around the settlement. I say settlement for it is really just a collection of buildings that must have grown up with the once prosperous fishing industry. There was the obligatory fish processing plant, now closed. The ever present walkway fronting the houses. Of those a few were brightly painted and with an appearance of being well maintained. Sporting the announcement that they were Bed and Breakfast establishments. These no doubt catering for the sports fishermen. For the rest there was a sad scene of dereliction and abandonment, overgrown gardens fronting buildings that are well on the way to collapse. How sad it all is that Winter Harbour has come to this. At one time, at the height of the west coast fishing industry, it must have been a quaint and picturesque little village, vibrant and bustling with activity. There is one charm that is still evident though and that is the friendliness of the people. They still have a smile, and look one in the eye and a, “Hello,” for strangers.

When I asked Ron, of the fuel dock and general store, about the isolation of Winter Harbour, I was assured that it wasn't really a problem for any major shopping Port Hardy was only fifty miles away. Albeit along dirt roads, where it was wise to travel with a four wheel drive vehicle, especially in the winter.

When asked if he would consider moving to somewhere like Port Hardy, rather than this isolated place. In no uncertain terms, I was informed that Winter Harbour had its advantages. Particularly the neighbourliness of his fellow, shall we say isolationists. And the city is for city folk. This is a sentiment I well recognized, for it used to be like that at first on the island I moved to in the eighties. Before the influx of city folk bringing their city ways with them, rather than adapting to the rural community they came to.

Maybe I should move to Winter Harbour and regain all that has been lost to me. A deep sense of belonging, with good people. But then it would be a case of starting all over again. And at my age? I don't think so.

These thoughts put me in a nostalgic mood, so I decided to do my ET bit and phone home. For once I got through on the first attempt. It perked me up no end to talk to my wife and to know all was well. And for a bonus a friend, Anne, was over visiting with her kids.

This friend had at one time been with the Department of Fisheries and knew Winter Harbour well, having been here on a number of occasions. So we discussed the place on familiar grounds. Sharing the same ideas of how quaint Winter Harbour was.

Although the time lapse between our respective visits must have marred the picturesque outlook. For Anne remembering a thriving community, and for myself seeing the onset of decay.

It was with these thoughts that I collected the laundry and returned to my boat, to hang up the washing and cook dinner. Guess what? I hadn't taken anything out. No problem. Remembering the succulent feast concocted the last time dinner was not taken out. I fried up some bacon and eggs, complimented with peas, carrots, and potato. Yum! Not forgetting the wine of course. I have often wondered what it was like to have wine for breakfast. I suppose it is stretching it a bit by having breakfast in the evening. But, no matter. I highly recommend the practice.

After washing up I returned to the dock with the intention of taking another look around when I ran into the girls again and was introduced to their husbands. During the ensuing conversation it transpired that Ian and Dianne's friends were from Oregon, and the high desert. A place that I had visited once or twice, and I was curious to know why it was called a desert. It seemed quite the opposite to me, who always pictured a desert to be something like the Sahara. But the high desert of Oregon even had cattle grazing on it. Craig, that is, who was from these parts, blanched at the mention of cattle.

"Don't mention cattle to Craig." said his wife.

"Why is that?" I asked.

After a moments pause and some interjected conversation from the others that I did not pick up on. I gathered he must be a vet or maybe a government inspector that dealt with cattle. Because apparently after being in contact with these high desert cattle a person had to wash their every body opening with alcohol, as a prevention against E-Coli infection. A grim thought in anyone's book if you ask me. No wonder Craig looked miffed at the suggestion of cattle.

At that moment Ian returned with some crab he had cooked. To which I learned something else this day.

In the fishing port I was brought up in we always ate crab meat with the yellow part mixed in as this gave an added flavour. But those days were long before the seas became polluted. Over the years, whenever crab was dressed by me, I always included the yellow part as well. Call it traditional, if you like. According to Ian, and I don't doubt his knowledge on the subject, the yellow is the pancreas of a crab and thus contains trace elements filtered out of the polluted sea. Well, you live and learn. Out goes the yellow.

It was my intention to ask them aboard for a glass or two of wine, but that invitation seemed to have been bypassed, and we all trooped aboard Craig's boat, for my part anyway to have a look around. The boat was very roomy, and professionally finished and well appointed. With all the bells and whistles. A comfortable boat, no doubt, but for me in my stiff old age, difficult to get into over the high entrance coaming. This seems to be a feature with the boats I've been on. Presumably to keep water out of the cabin should the cockpit be swamped? For me, I'll stay with the easy access where I can hop in and out. Should there be a threat of being swamped then I hope I have had the presence of mind to shut the doors and close the hatch before that happens.

Craig had only recently bought the boat and was still familiarizing himself with all the details. The previous owners must have been off-shore or intended doing so as there was a distress beacon mounted on the bulkhead, and an inflatable life raft securely caged to the rail. Which, if this method of securing the life raft was how it looked, i.e. A permanent fixture. Then if the boat sank in a hurry the life raft would probably sink with it. These inflatable are usually secured with a hydrostatic release. Then if the boat sinks before the raft can be thrown overboard, it will release itself. A comforting sight I would think to anyone in the water having a life raft pop up close by.

After the tour a glass of wine was proffered, and sitting comfortably in the cockpit a lively all round conversation took place that lasted for at least an hour. Towards the end of this time frame a particular subject cropped up that I would care to mention here because it was one of those coincidences that one meets from time to time.

Up until that moment I hadn't been introduced to Craig's wife. So I ventured to ask.

“Carol.” she said. “My mother thought it appropriate, as I was born on Christmas Day.”

“I didn't know that,” said Dianne, somewhat surprised.

“My brother was born on Christmas Eve, so he was called Chris.” Carol added.

"Well that is a coincidence," I said, "I've a friend who was born on Christmas Day, and she is called Carol also."

By this time I sensed that the conversation was waning. With three fifths of the company becoming restless. Small wonder really as I understood they had not yet had dinner. I decided that I had overstayed my welcome, and so wishing them all a pleasant trip south, I took my leave.

On returning to my boat I consulted the tide tables to where Ian had directed. Slack water at Nahwitti Bar was at seven in the evening the next day, which gave me ample time to get there by leaving Winter Harbour by mid morning.

Why I hadn't found the reference to Nahwitti Bar myself after perusing the tide tables on numerous occasions beats me. This is one occasion where, 'If all else fails, read the instructions' didn't apply. Maybe it should be, 'If all else fails, read the instructions thoroughly.' The best I can say for my inattention is that more than once I've been accused of looking with my nose.

A burst of laughter came from Craig's boat. An appropriate punctuation to my feeling of foolishness.

No matter, no-one is perfect. It had been a most pleasant day and once again with the company of good people. With this feeling of euphoria I read for a while, and then went to bed.

DAY NINE

And weariness treads on desire

(Roman satirist)

The day woke to clear skies, and from what I could judge in this sheltered harbour, with little wind.

As there was no great need to get under way, I took a leisurely approach to the morning routine. This left me with time to take a walk ashore. This walk was more to stretch my legs than for my other reason. Although, taking a different path revealed another aspect of the place. There is a hiking trail off the back road, through Botel Park. This would be of interest to hikers, I suppose, but for me a person of more sedentary pastimes, decided to give it a miss. What with the sports fishing, camping and hiking, Winter Harbour isn't without its attractions.

Back at the dock there was no sign of life emanating from the other boats. A pity really. I would have liked to have said cheerio. Earlier I had noticed Ian jump onto the dock then back on board. So one would gather that there was life there.

Although it was still quite early, around eight o'clock, I decided to take my leave. There was little point in hanging around, better to leave now and hurry up and wait. Who knows what delays may occur on the way to Cape Scott and Nahwitti Bar.

On the way out of the harbour I took the opportunity to hoist the mainsail. This would help steady the boat against the swell on the run up to Cape Scott. Yeah, right. 'Best laid plans of mice and men, etc.'

A number of early birds were fishing off the entrance as I passed by and out into the Pacific. Setting a westerly course would take me on a short run of one mile to pass Parkins Rocks before heading northwest for Cape Scott.

Within a few minutes of setting this westerly course the wind increased in intensity from the south to put this on my port beam. Boiling along with the starboard side deck practically awash was not a point of sail that had been planned. So the choice was between coming up into the wind to bring the boat in more of an upright position, or spilling some wind out of the sails to achieve the same effect. Bringing the wind around to the port quarter was out of the question as this would put me on a collision course for Mr. Parkin's rocks.

As it was my intention to go north rather than south the choice became Hobson's choice. Fortunately the sheet release, although in front of the wheel, was slightly to the right on centre of the track. So it was just a matter of reaching around the wheel and pulling the sheet out of the cleat. But like everything else in this world things don't go exactly like we plan.

If it was a case of standing upright and at right angles to the boat then this position would place me away from reaching around the wheel to perform this simple operation. So, bracing myself as best I could with my knees against the coaming, this on the lower side of the boat, and steering with my left hand, I reached around the wheel and grabbed the sheet to give it a mighty pull. Nothing happened. The pressure of the wind on the sail made it impossible to release the sheet with one hand. The reader will appreciate that while all this was going on the boat is barrelling along with the starboard deck lapping up water.

The situation was resolved by bracing my position with my right knee and steering with my left knee. In that manner, I could apply both hands to releasing the sheet and achieve the desired result.

Coming into a more upright position caused the anxiety to lessen somewhat. The whole exercise however had become academic, because the short run had been accomplished while all these contortions were being practised, and it was now time to alter course to the northwest anyway.

As the morning progressed the wind increased to twenty-five knots, and gusting to thirty. Fortunately the wind was from the south which put it astern. Having listened to the trials and tribulations of my recent acquaintances on their trip south in these parts, I couldn't help thinking how fortunate I was travelling in the opposite direction with the wind and seas astern. Was there someone up there looking out for me? I asked myself for the umpteenth time.

All was not a bed or roses though. One must always pay for good fortune. And it was my lot to remain at the wheel for five hours. In conditions such as existed at this time, with the Pacific swells on the beam, and seas that have been built up with the wind coming from right astern, the boat took up a rolling as well as a gyrating motion. Up would go the stern giving a little wriggling motion before settling down again. All this as the swell pushed the boat to starboard and back to port. The autopilot was useless to keep a course, as in anything less than calm weather would flip the breaker, cutting out the power to the system, and off we would go in circles. In these sea conditions, apart from any other consideration, it is best to hand steer as every push of the waves has to be anticipated and counteracted before control is lost. A visit to the instruction book as soon as possible was planned. I had the niggling feeling that a higher rated breaker would be required to solve this problem.

At least it wasn't raining, and the weather was warm. Nor was there any chance of fog. So there were good reasons for counting one's blessings.

This then was the situation on the run up to Cape Scott. Like most things in life one puts up with their lot. My only regret was being muffin-less for this period of time.

In conversation with other travellers, Sea Otter Cove had been recommended as a stopping off place. This cove lies nine miles below Cape Scott, and once inside provides a snug anchorage. A little care would have to be taken when entering due to the numerous rocks littering the entrance, but well worth a visit so I was told. This in itself was probably sound advice under normal conditions, and weary as I was with the continual attention to steering, a pleasant thought. But with Queen Cove experience still fresh in my mind, I wasn't about to repeat the rock dodging exercise again should a fog set in, either arriving or leaving this harbour of repose. Besides, with the wind and this sea running straight into the cove, I decided it would be an act of absolute folly to make the attempt. I wasn't that desperate for a muffin. So I pressed on.

As I rounded Cape Scott, looking up at the lighthouse, I mused on the possibility of the keepers looking down on me wondering what silly bugger would be out in this weather. But there again they probably would have seen enough over the years to accept that this situation is old hat. My other thought was what the conditions would be once the corner had been turned. If the wind continued blowing in the same direction, then surely the land would give a lee for calmer conditions. Fat chance.

Rounding Cape Scott gave a course change of ninety degrees, which should have provided that welcome lee. This was not be to. The wind must have been heading for the same destination as myself, for it came around the corner with me, and blew from north of west with the same intensity. And so we proceeded we two travelling companions, my boat and I and the wind, with the same intention of heading towards Nahwitti Bar.

Well, the wind can do as it wishes, for me I needed a break, and the way to do this was to find a sheltered bay to rest up. There was plenty of time before slack water at Nahwitti Bar so it was not necessary anymore to hurry up and wait. Much better to anchor out of the wind and rest for a couple of hours.

With this thought in mind I took a chance and engaged the autopilot. Watching how the autopilot would react in these sea conditions for a moment, satisfied. I went below to consult the chart. Well, what do you know, the autopilot having a mind of its own, blew to breaker on the panel and away we went in a left hand circle. Having experienced this phenomenon on numerous occasions before I had the presence of mind to re-engage the switch before dashing back on deck to take control again and clutching the chart.

Later, after ten minutes or standing at the wheel, I decided to sit down on the lazarette locker. This is what I had been doing on and off all morning, taking a load off my legs, to sit on a cockpit cushion. Only this time the cushion had disappeared. Taking off, no doubt, with the wind on that violent turn to port. As I was disinclined to go back and search I pressed on to Nissan Bight, with the thought that some deserving person may perform a rescue and earn themselves a cushion.

Nissan Bight is just five miles from Cape Scott so by one thirty I had the anchor down, and tucked nicely under the lee of the land.

The mainsail was then stowed complete with the cover. I had no intention of putting that up again this trip. I could not foresee ever having to need it on the run down Johnstone Straight anyway; if a suitable wind did happen then the Genoa would have to suffice.

After a late lunch I took up a horizontal position in the forward berth and examined the back of my eyelids, feeling the ache slowly leaving my legs. In this manner I contemplated the next stretch of the days run to Bull Harbour on Hope Island. Of course the main consideration was to get over Nahwitti Bar at slack water, or maybe a little before. Low water was at seven o'clock but with the ebb against the wind it would be folly to attempt a crossing much before this time with the strong possibility of standing seas.

*****

Nahwitti Bar lies between Sutil Point on Vancouver Island and Mexicana Point on Hope Island. Both these Points of land were named for the ships of the Spanish survey of these waters by Dionisio Galiano on the Sutil. And Caytano Valdez on the Mexicana in 1792. This survey was carried at the same time as George Vancouver's expedition, and on occasion the two surveys would be conducted jointly.

*****

In the narrowing passage between these two points the sea bed becomes shallow, and in conjunction with a five knot current going out meeting a strong westerly wind coming in, very high, steep waves can be experienced causing extremely dangerous conditions. Certainly I was not about to put this to the test, especially today when the present wind strength predicted a difficult crossing. Rather, wait here in Nissan Bight, rest up, and leave in time for the seven o'clock slack water. So, after resting a while I popped my head out of the hatch to check on the situation only to note that the anchor was dragging. This was not so surprising as kelp, that ever present bane on a boater’s life, doesn't make for a good holding material. Picking up anchor and clearing away the kelp didn't cause any problems, and I was soon heading towards Nahwitti Bar at a greatly reduced speed to cover the thirteen miles left to go.

There was no respite from manning the wheel though. There was still the following sea with its accompanying gyrations. But thankfully the swell had been left behind in the Pacific. And there are compensations in most situations, not everything is always doom and gloom, no less so on this day. The sun was shining. Making for a pleasantly warm afternoon. And as long as I wore a hat and sunscreen, I wouldn't be making up ditties on the morrow about red shiny noses.

So, the afternoon passed. Headway was being maintained at a justifiable pace. Still some distance from Nahwitti Bar a cruiser overtook me heading straight for the Bar. Keeping him in sight he seemed to cross without any adverse effect. So, abandoning the principle of not using another man's compass, I increased speed to check out for myself the conditions. As matters turned out I arrived at the Bar one hour before slack water. The crossing was lumpy, but after the day's outing a doddle.

Come six thirty found me anchored in Bull Harbour on Hope Island. A most peaceful and tranquil interlude after such a boisterous day.

This harbour is strategically placed as a stopover for boats travelling around Vancouver Island, both clockwise and counter clockwise. Not intentionally mind you. The place just happens to be there. The one advantage that the counter clockwise boaters have is that the passage over the Nahwitti Bar, being close by, can be planned much more finely. They just sit in the harbour until it is time to leave. Whereas, in the case of those of my persuasion, we have to hang about in the open ocean. This is no big deal if the weather is favourable, but the pits on cold miserable days. Could this be why people I met thought it odd that I was travelling, in their minds, the wrong way round? An interesting thought and worth pondering for future reference.

Bull Harbour is entered from the south side of Hope Island, and is a mile and a half in length, due north. About half way in the channel is divided by Norman Island, behind which lies the anchorage. There is a public dock here, but while I was there no-one bothered to tie up to it, preferring to anchor.

These anchorages by their very nature bring out a persons individuality. There is no need to walk a dock, taking other boats lines, socializing and being part of a community. One can be alone and observe. The one thing that did impress me while standing in the hatchway observing passing boaters was that no-one appeared to acknowledge any other presence. Whenever a boat came in to the anchorage, which apart from myself, was studiously ignored by the boaters already there, I know because I was taking notice.

After an excellent and most welcome dinner, yes I did remember this time, of Steak and Kidney pie, (created by the hands of my good friend Anne), Potato, peas and carrots. I decided to do what I most like to do when in an anchorage on a warm and pleasant evening. Stand in the hatchway and absorb the peace, and observe my surroundings. As there were several boats in the anchorage there were plenty to occupy my curiosity.

On occasion a head would pop up out of a hatch on another boat, look around to see what was going on, which was nothing of course. Then the head would disappear. In time a head would pop up from another boat, look around, and then disappear. Probably having seen their shadows. It must be something like this living in Gopher country.

Just after nine o'clock the fog came rolling in. So, counting the day's blessings, I battened down the hatches, read for a while, and putting myself around a glass or two of wine, this time for the pleasure of I turned in to sleep the sleep of the just.

DAY TEN

As is my wont, and as daylight approaches, the night's sleep ebbs away and I come awake. It has been like that for most of my adult life. In fact I find it impossible, no matter how long I've been awake and active to sleep during the daylight hours. Having said that, I took the opportunity to have a pee and check on the weather before returning to bed to doze and pass another hour.

The fog was thinning considerably so hopefully it would have dissipated all together by the hour of departure. I was getting used to fog by this time and it wasn't bothering me all that much really. Any obstructions, like other vessels looming out of the gloom can be seen before any hard contact is made, and any evasive action can be taken in sufficient time to avoid a collision. It is just that under these circumstances one must exercise constant alertness with no chance to relax and take in the scenery should there be any. These conditions can be trying and very exhausting if experienced for any length of time.

Taking a leisurely approach to the morning, having breakfast and doing my thing I noticed that the fog had lifted completely. At eight thirty with the prospect of clear weather I picked up anchor and proceeded to the entrance in anticipation of a pleasant run down to Port Hardy.

The other boats in the anchorage appeared devoid of life with no gophers to observe my departure, a pity really as in my happy frame of mind I would have liked to give someone a cheery wave. Maybe it was just as well, for rounding Norman Island revealed a thick fog in Goletas Channel. My euphoria immediately, unlike the fog dissipated. Well nothing ventured nothing gained, and by now I was an experienced fog hound, so into the murk of Goletas Channel with the resolve to keep a sharp lookout. Without a doubt there would be a few fish boats around, or maybe the ferry that serves between Port Hardy and Prince Rupert? To be run down by either one of these monsters would not be to my liking.

*****

Goletas is the Spanish word for schooners and this name was given to the channel by Galiano and Valdez, the two Spanish captains previously mentioned in honour of the schooners under their command, Sutil and Mexicana.

The names of these two gentlemen, and their ships also appear now and again on the British Columbia coast which is an interesting point as both men had an extremely poor opinion of this coast and its inhabitants, and I quote, 'the lonely and barren abodes of the interior of this strait offer no attraction to the trading navigator.' An opinion that both Galiano and Valdez shared, they also found the spectacular scenery of the north-west Coast, 'dreary and inhospitable,' but then in their defence they were only here to do a job away from the fleshpots of the developed world of Spain and in New Spain their base. No doubt though, like most people in their situation, didn't baulk at leaving their names to posterity.

*****

The twenty-one mile run to Port Hardy was completed by noon with the average speed of six knots, quite impressive to my way of thinking. The fog was my constant companion for the whole length of Goletas Channel but, very kindly lifted at the entrance to Port Hardy Bay. By now I was beginning to realise that this is what the fog does, i.e. lift at the entrance to a bay, change of air temperature probably. At the entrance to Port Hardy one must navigate through a narrow channel so the absence of fog was a blessing and made for an easy approach to the fuel dock.

Once again fortune smiled on this miserable sinner, for on approaching the dock an ominous black cloud was sighted to the west accompanied by flashes of lightening and loud claps of thunder. Definitely a rain bearing cloud. Could I make it to the dock before it dumped its load? I asked myself with some trepidation. Not only did I make it to the dock I also managed to top up the fuel tanks. No sooner had the filler caps been replaced than the heavens opened up giving me just enough time to get into the office to shelter. Never have I experienced such a downpour in this part of the world, in the tropics, yes, but in BC one doesn't expect such a torrent? Could this be a result of the Global Warming we hear so much about? I wondered. Timing the flashes to the crack of thunder put the lightening no more than a mile away at its closest. This torrent lasted for only about fifteen minutes and thankful that I hadn't been caught out in it as I would have been soaked to the skin in no time at all, counting my blessings that I didn't have to buy another pair of trousers. The gentleman in charge of the dock very kindly suggested that I stay alongside until the rain had passed. I took up this most welcome offer not wanting to get a soaking.

*****

Port Hardy was named for Vice-Admiral Sir Thomas Masterman Hardy, of kiss me Hardy fame at Nelson's death, or that is what Lord Nelson is purported to have said as Hardy held the dying Nelson in his arms during the Battle of Trafalgar, or was it 'Kismet,' Hardy, he had said?

*****

After the rain had passed on its way I moved around to the Quarterdeck Marina, it was interesting to see so many fish boats tied up and with a definite look of abandonment about them, caught up no doubt in the sad decline of the fishing industry so that they had no employment now? When I was in these parts in 1956 fish boats were wall to wall in the channels, there is no doubt those halcyon days will not return. Technology, mismanagement of the spawning grounds and short term greed has made sure of that.

Settling in to the appointed berth and having paid my moorage dues I phoned my friend Kathy and invited her down to the boat for Happy Hour.

I first met this charming young lady when our volunteer boys were building replacement docks at our marina. Kathy, being the daughter of the project Head Honcho had also been roped in to help out. And what a good help she proved to be, I don't think I've ever seen anyone so efficiently move and stack so much lumber in such a short time. At the risk of being considered a chauvinist pig, I would say that Kathy would make some lucky man a good wife, not only for her ability to shift lumber though, but more for her good natured charm and a sense of humour. And before the reader gets any wrong ideas, I already have a wife.

After resting up for an hour or two I took time out to stretch my legs. Inquiring at the Marina Office I was advised by the lady there that the town was quite a distance away and considered too far to walk. So put out by this information I hung around and watched the sports fishermen land and clean their catches. From the number of fish boats tied up at the dock it would appear that sports fishermen are the only people catching fish these days. Halibut, it would seem, by the number landed was the fish of choice, the top weight for this day's catch weighed in at 110lbs. A nice size in anyone's book, but then they are the fastest growing fish I believe so it wouldn't take very long for them to reach such an impressive weight.

On returning to the boat I considered the idea of preparing and cooking an evening meal on the boat, then shelved the idea until my guest arrived no doubt she would have a car and prefer to eat ashore. Not a bad idea in my estimation as it would be a nice change from my culinary efforts.

On the off chance that Kathy would opt for the former considerations I pulled out my supply of prepared curry and rice that only needed heating, which was a proportion suitable to feed two people. Should this plan be unacceptable and the evening meal taken ashore, then the next two evening meals would covered by the curry, not literally one would hope, besides I might be being a little presumptuous in assuming that Kathy would want a curry. After all choices had been covered the problem became academic anyway.

My agonising and decisions on this earth shattering problem was interrupted by catching sight of Kathy walking along the jetty, getting me to my feet and off the boat to meet and greet.

"Mister Palmer," she said by way of greeting, emphasising the Mister.

"Miss Heslop, How are you?

"Good. How are you?

"I'm well thank you, and much better for seeing you though."

What a charmer you aspire to be Palmer.

With a broad grin Kathy climbed on board and plonked herself down on the settee just inside the entrance, either because it was handy to do so or maybe for a quick escape should that be necessary. There to remain for the rest of the visit, having no desire to inspect the rest of my beautiful boat, and it crossed my mind that this must be a first at such lack of interest until she offered the explanation that she wasn't feeling too well with an upset tummy, a result of having partied long and hard the night before. *'Curry and rice therefore was off the menu,'* was my inspired thought.

After a pleasant half hour catching up on the news, a glass of wine, and subjects of common interest the decision was made to eat ashore.

The Pub at the Quarterdeck Marina had the same ambience as any other pub in any marina anywhere on the coast that I had frequented, they serve drinks of course, and meals which seem to come from a central source as they all have the same offerings, with a difference only in the quality of the preparation, which in the case of this particular establishment on a scale of one to ten I would be obliged to give seven.

The clientele, for the most part have the same characteristics as any other like establishments i.e. wearing a head covering of the ubiquitous baseball cap. 'T' shirts that advertise someone else's products, the wearing of a head covering while eating a meal is something I have never been able to come to terms with. Not ever having seen this phenomenon anywhere but within the North American continent. Maybe I couldn't come to terms with this lack of etiquette because it was such a shock when I first observed this, and I've been in Canada now for eighteen years. Different upbringings, I guess. The one redeeming feature was the waiter didn't follow this particular tradition, at least not while serving.

When the meal was over we didn't hang around as we were both feeling a little tired, Kathy having just returned from her hectic holiday, and myself, well it's not unusual for me to be tired in the late evening especially having ingested so much fresh air and fog. After taking me via the store for milk then dropping me off at the marina we went our separate ways, for my part pleased that we had met up again.

Returning to the boat, I didn't even bother with a nightcap nor reading for a while. I just put the curry back in the freezer and anticipating my usual forgetfulness on matters of meals I took out a Bridie for the following evening, then climbed into bed and went out like a light.

DAY ELEVEN

Having breakfasted and performed the usual morning chores I was on my way out of Port Hardy by seven o'clock accompanied by a flotilla of sport fishermen no doubt to deplete the fish stocks even further. The day promised to be pleasant with light airs, cloudy, but clear of the dreaded fog, the absence of which was particularly welcome for on this leg of the journey to Port Neville there were channels to navigate and obstructions to be avoided that are best dealt with in clear visibility.

Is there someone up there looking out for me? Of that I'm becoming increasingly convinced. Or is it the first signs of paranoia?

These channels etc. would begin after a twelve mile run from rounding Masterman Island at the entrance to Port Hardy Bay up to Malcolm Island and the beginning of Broughton Strait.

*****

This strait was named for Lieutenant William R. Broughton, commanding the armed brig Chatham, companion ship to the Discovery on George Vancouver's expedition to this coast in 1792.

*****

It was at this stage of this circumnavigation that I got to thinking that maybe it would have been better to have travelled counter clockwise around Vancouver Island. Putting the weather situation to one side of my thoughts which had certainly been in my favour. To follow George Vancouver's progress instead of going against it would have put my observations in chronological order with those of this navigator. This is a mute point of course and it was too late at this stage of the odyssey to argue the point and there was nothing else to do but view Vancouver's progress in reverse order to my own. After all I wasn't on a journey of re-discovery but just to see and absorb as best I could what these dedicated men of Vancouver's expedition observed and pay homage to them and their many achievements.

By noon the wind had increased to sixteen knots from the north-west. Taking advantage of this I hauled out the Genoa to get a little extra propulsion. With the wind astern there was little point in shutting off the engine and making a reduced speed under sail only there was still a long way to go before evening and on sail power alone would make for slow progress.

Come to think of it, so far, the wind except for the first day and that brief interlude leaving Winter Harbour had been from no other direction than right astern. If this state of affairs continues I shall probably make the whole trip under motor power.

Not to worry it was a beautiful day. The sun was shining with a lovely cooling wind which, with the progress I was making reduced it to a breeze. So, on with the straw hat and the sun block and just enjoy the scenery.

"Out on the briny with a nose red and shiny".......

Just beyond Alert Bay on Cormorant Island the western end of Johnstone Strait begins, or ends, whichever way one happens to be travelling. This stretch of water of some sixty miles in length and but a mile wide carries on down all the way to Chatham point which is the north end of Discovery Passage. These two geographical points, Chatham and Discovery were named for George Vancouver's ships.

*****

Johnstone Strait however, is the name given by Vancouver to the sailing master of the Chatham. Johnstone was the first European on surveying this channel in the Chatham's cutter to realise that due to the tides flowing through this waterway that Vancouver Island was indeed an island and not part of the mainland enabling Vancouver's expedition to break out into the Pacific. Taking only a week's supply of provisions two of the ship's boat set out from Homfrey Channel just to the north of Desolation Sound where the ships were anchored. With great difficulty and with the help of the local Indians towing them, they passed through Arran Rapids into the channels beyond, taking Welbourne and Sunderland channels into Johnstone Strait, charting and surveying as far as Pine Island some sixteen miles northwest of Hardy Bay. Having established that there was a passage to the Pacific they returned to the ships exhausted and deplete of provisions, their last meal taken the day before. Sadly, during this particular investigation of the coast the boat crews suffered from what has become known as Red Tide, this scourge poisons bi-valve shellfish thus making it inedible for human consumption, as these men were not aware of this and having feasted on mussels became violently ill, with one man dying. These dedicated men having surveyed the above mentioned channels on the outward journey returned by Nodales Channel to make further surveys of a possible alternate route. One can only admire the dedication of these men in pursuit of their duties to take every advantage of promoting this survey regardless of their personal comforts. Anyone who has spent any length of time sitting on a hard wooden bench would well understand their discomfort.

*****

It is amongst this and other relatively narrow channels that kayakers abound, large flotillas of these minor craft are forever present. No sooner is one group avoided than another appears further down the channel and another collision avoidance situation occurs. For some inexplicable reason, to me anyway, they always seem to be crossing the channel and not parallel to the shoreline. I suppose like the chicken crossing the road analogy they want to get to the other side.

My friend Mike a fisherman, Anne's husband, who plies these waters in pursuit of his occupation, refers to kayakers as nautical speed bumps with obvious good reason. For if an inattentive mariner should get in amongst them that is what they would become. Especially as they appear to be totally unaware of the Rules of the Road, seagoing variety that is.

On a sunny day though they are easy to spot, the whirling motion of the wet paddles glinting in the sunlight creates what appears to be a bunch of mini windmills. It does seem to me though that being so low in the water and are therefore difficult to see otherwise these miniscule adventurers are taking dangerous chances with their safety. In fog, snow, heavy rainstorms or any other condition similarly reducing visibility one would hope that they would stay away from the waters used by bigger vessels.

Further down the channel I came up with a small pod of three Killer Whales two adult and a small one travelling northwards, probably on a family outing, going in the same direction as the kayakers. I was again reminded of these chancers by giving free rein to my imagination which I might add is always ready to run amok. Now, should a whale surface immediately underneath one of these speed bumps one could only imagine the terror of the occupant when lifted violently into the air, no doubt the interior of the kayak would soon be converted into a holding tank. Whales harassing kayakers would then possibly become a *cause celebre* for the environmental protesters.

Travelling along the calm waters of Johnstone Strait I found this peaceful interlude conducive to mind wandering on many subjects particularly those that involve contentions between environmentalists and those that they target. This brought me to the next observation; whale harassment.

When coming abeam of this pod I sighted a tug approaching from the opposite direction at full speed with a bone in its teeth, as the saying goes. This tug ran right over the place that the whales had submerged, which had me concerned that they could have been injured and as I don't wish to see any animal hurt. I kept a sharp look out after the tug had passed on to see if there was any indication of this. Nothing, the whales surfaced in the tugs wake some way behind and in unison blew spumes of contemptuous vapour into the air. What is this whale harassment thing we are forever being admonished about? These particular whales didn't seem to care about this close encounter.

It was thus progressing along Johnstone Strait enjoying the warm sunshine of this lovely summer's day occupying my time in wool gathering thoughts I arrived off Port Neville by four o'clock.

It is not certain how Port Neville came to be so named. It has been suggested that Vancouver could have named this, 'snug and commodious port', after Lieutenant of Marines John Neville. But who this person was is a mystery as he doesn't appear on the muster roles of either the Discovery, or the Chatham. But, that is as maybe, a snug and commodious port it certainly is with a Public Dock on the right hand side and just half a mile inside the entrance.

There was a fish boat moored alongside the dock when I approached and although it took up most of the float there was still enough room to moor, albeit with my bow sticking out over the end of the float requiring a spring line rather than a head rope.

At the shore end of the jetty is an old wooden building that at one time was the General Store that is now closed. Close by there is a Post Office which is open for three days a week. Arriving boats can have their mail forwarded here which will be held pending the addressees arrival. An art gallery and a gift shop are close by also, all closed when I arrived. It was difficult to see who might be around to look after these services as no-one seemed to be in residence although it was obvious that someone looked after the place as the lawns behind the old store were in immaculate condition.

Shortly after my arrival the fish boat which had been loading stores left and moved over to the other side of the bay and anchored with other fish boats that were already there. I was later given to understand that fish boats waited at Port Neville for the opening of the fishing season in Johnston Strait, the opening determined by the Department of Fisheries. Sometimes these openings lasted for only a few hours so it made sense to be on hand and ready to go. Such is the sad state of the depleted fisheries on the west coast.

With the fish boat having departed and leaving more room I considered moving back and mooring in a better position. However, this plan was abandoned on sighting another sailboat approaching the dock. This approach was proving to be a little awkward due to the wind and the tightness of the available space. But with a couple of attempts and the assistance of yours truly a successful moor was made possible.

As almost always in these cases were a boater helps another boater securely moor introductions are made and a rapport established. In this case I made the acquaintance of Michael and Beryl, with their boat, 'Sliver'. They were enjoying a boating holiday for a few weeks, but only on this side of Vancouver Island, their home port being Fisherman's Cove in West Vancouver. Now this is remiss of me but, although it was mentioned, I didn't catch their last name which is not surprising with my faulty hearing. If you lovely people ever read this missive please forgive this doddering old fool. What I did remember though was that Michael was an anaesthetist, no doubt the reason for remembering this piece of information could have been that I have difficulty pronouncing the word.

Introductions made I was invited to inspect their boat. Of particular interest was the boomed jib. It was the first time that I had seen such a rig and I was quite impressed by the possibilities this type of rig offered. In a nutshell, a boomed jib acts in the same way as the mainsail does with a track and sheets controlled from the cockpit. However, on boarding the boat and observing how a boomed jib reduces the headroom in the cabin my enthusiasm waned considerably. Of course everything about boating is a trade off one way or another, and in this case for better sailing qualities one has to forego creature comforts. But, each to their own, for me and in light of the events so far when all progress has been made under motor I will settle for comfort.

During the course of our subsequent conversation it was revealed that we would both be heading for Campbell River on the morrow. I expressed my concern about transiting Seymour Narrows on the flood tide and suggested I might wait to get there at slack water, to which Michael gave me some homespun truth on the subject.

"Why wait for slack water? As long as the tide is with you there isn't any problem, you will just be moving with a body of water," he advised.

"When I was out here in nineteen fifty-five all ships waited for slack water before making the transit," once again with the big ship mind set.

"That was before they blew up Ripple Rock, now ships go through all the time with the tide of course."

"Good point that."

*****

It is surprising, considering the hazards relating to Ripple Rock that Vancouver's' ships passed through the Narrows with astonishing ease, Lieutenant Baker remarking in his journals that the ships, 'soon drifted through these Narrows by the strength of the tide.' Vancouver did not detect this notorious Ripple Rock apparently, as no mention was made in either the ship's log or his journals, so it would appear that the ships passed through on the first of the ebb which runs to the north when the rock would have been submerged.

*****

With my mind at ease with the subject of passing through Seymour Narrows we went over to my boat. Beryl I gathered was quite impressed with the layout particularly with the stand-up full size shower, another feature their boat lacked due to the jib rig cramping the space. The galley also met with a glance of admiration. But being a woman it is not surprising these areas meet with approval.

They didn't stay for long, just a quick look around and a chat. Beryl I noticed sat on the banquette just inside the entrance door, which seems to be the favourite seat for visitors, for myself too when under way in calm, clear weather conditions, this being due to the all round view it affords.

It did cross my mind to ask them to stay for the evening meal until I realised that the Bridie rescued from the freezer early wouldn't make much of a meal divided into three. Ah! Well, better planning some other time. As it turned out they soon left for their own boat, and I settled down to read up on Port Neville.

*****

In 1792 when George Vancouver's expedition was engaged in surveying this coast, and after passing through the Narrows, Port Neville was passed by unexamined by Johnstone, proceeding on his survey ahead of the ships as were two other inlets. The discovery of this pleasant harbour was therefore credited to Joseph Whidbey, Sailing Master of the Discovery.

It should be mentioned at this point in the narrative that Sailing Masters were very important personages in this period of history. Although the overall responsibility for the execution of the voyage was Vancouver's the Sailing Masters actually sailed the ships. They were also in charge of the boats that went ahead of the ships, charting and surveying the coast. Due to his recurring illness Vancouver could only on one occasion attend a boat expedition, during the course of this Pacific coastal survey, which incidentally was from Birch Bay and back via what is now Burrard Inlet as far as Squamish, with a diversion along the Sunshine coast to examine Jervis Inlet and Howe Sound a period of ten days at which the men were constantly at the oars during daylight hours and at times well into the night.

While the ships were anchored in the Bight on the opposite shore waiting for the tide in the Strait to turn in their favour, which later became named St. Vincent Bight, Whidbey was sent over to survey the inlet which is now Port Neville.

The entrance to the inlet is a quarter of a mile wide and maintains this width for two and a half miles before opening into a wide bay, well, wider than the entrance, the dimensions being three quarters of a mile by three.

Port Neville was settled in 1916 by the Hansen family of Scandinavian origin. The impressive structure of the General Store, built in 1920 is a monument to the building skills to the father of the late Olaf Hansen.

*****

The store though now closed, is situated at the landward end of the jetty, and as one ascends the ramp from the dock the building gradually comes into view creating an impressive perspective, the sight framed as it is with the jetty railings.

After dinner was over I was enjoying a glass of wine to help the digestion I noticed a large object moving towards the shore. This puzzled me as there wasn't a tide, at least not in that direction, strong enough to move any inanimate object such as a log at such constant speed. My curiosity aroused I went up on deck with binoculars to get a better look. To my surprise the object turned out to be a black bear which appeared to have swum over from the far shore a good quarter of a mile away. On reaching the beach behind the dock, not even bothering to shake the water from its fur, the bear nonchalantly walked up to and disappeared behind the Post Office building. It had been my intention to explore the area beyond the dock but the thought of meeting with a bear, on whose territory it might be, soon had that intention shelved for a later time, maybe on the morrow.

The inlet of Port Neville is an impressive place in as much as it lends itself to investigation by the curious and being of an inquisitive turn of mind I favoured the idea of taking the dinghy and doing a tour. But not on this trip as I was anxious to get on down the Strait to Campbell River and the possible thrill of Seymour Narrows, being on my own although relaxing and the pleasure of meeting interesting people I was feeling the need to be with those close to me. A great pity really as there was so much to see, so maybe next time someone would come with me and share these pleasures.

With my curiosity put on hold I went below to prepare the charts and plan the next day's adventure.

These preparations having been put in hand I read for a while with the wine to hand for that delightful time of day, nightcap time and contentment, then turned in and fell asleep immediately. And why not, peace of mind is a great inducement for sleep.

DAY TWELVE

An' by the whirling rim I've found how the rushing wall goes round.

As there was no great hurry to get under way and depart this pleasant place I took a leisurely approach to breakfast and the usual morning chores. Another chat with Michael and Beryl discussing our separate plans for the day, in which they advised that they intended leaving a little later than myself as for most of the distance to Seymour Narrows the tide would be against us, but being a morning person I had to be up and doing, and what better way of doing than going. We were both heading for Campbell River so it was agreed we would meet there.

Casting off, and with a friendly wave I left the dock clearing the entrance by 0930. The morning was fog-less, thank goodness, with a cloudy sky and the wind out of the north-west at 25 knots. Once again the weather was favourable. However, like Newton's second law of motion for every action there is an equal and opposite reaction. Or, to paraphrase to this particular instance, if good fortune smiles on you it doesn't do to get too complacent because something is bound to happen to dispel this euphoria.

On this particular pleasant morning having entered the strait I slowed the engine and left the cockpit to pull in the fenders, on returning to the cockpit with the sun in my eyes and glare off the water adding to the loss of vision. There was an almighty bang from the fore part of the hull. Good Christ! What was that I thought? My first being that I'd hit a rock but then the boat was still moving through the water, then came the rumbling and scraping sound along the hull, realising then it must have been a log that I'd hit and with an awakened presence of mind caused by the adrenaline rush I immediately cut the engine and waited and mentally crossed my fingers that it wouldn't smash the propeller, then I would have been well up the proverbial creek. With an immense feeling of relief I watched this great bald log breach and leap out of the water like a thing possessed just astern of me. With some trepidation I anxiously eased the engine into gear and slowly increased the revolutions with mounting confidence. All was well.

At times like these when the situation could have been much different I get to wondering what the alternatives could be when faced with disaster. In this particular case had it been a loss of mechanical means of propulsion, with a fair wind and tide in my favour it would have been a matter of up with the sails and get along like that but, that would be fine unless the wind died and the tide changed, and what about the Narrows? I'd hate to think what that situation would promise with no control of the boat hurtling along at sixteen knots. All conjecture anyway and not likely to happen on this trip as no damage had been caused to the propeller. Come to think of it, George Vancouver and subsequent other sailing craft went through and they didn't have engines. I guess I just have an over active imagination and these gloomy thoughts were academic anyway as I still had the use of an engine. To safer realms of speculation I directed my thoughts to wondering what the results would manifest themselves when next hauling the boat?

As a practice piece and to satisfy myself over the possible need to revert what the thoughts had evoked I hoisted the Genoa. This only provided a minimum of mental comfort as the tide was against me for the first part of this passage so progress was not particularly brisk. However, in this manner the journey continued for the best part of an hour before the wind died and the tide turned to the flood.

It was during this pleasant sunny morning that the realisation as to what happens to kayakers when they are not kayaking, and where do they rest after a hard day's paddling came to be realised. On passing West Thurlow Island, just past Vansittart Lighthouse, I observed a cluster of igloo style tents on the shore the type that looks like half a giant multi-coloured Easter egg. Ah! I thought to myself so that is where they go when not paddling the waters of the strait. The fact that there were several kayaks pulled up onto the beach was a definite confirmation to this premise. Also it was a bonus to know that these particular maritime speed bumps would not cause a diversionary measure on my part in the immediate future.

And so the morning and early afternoon passed pleasantly. The Autopilot was behaving itself so to make a coffee for elevenses and a sandwich for lunch was a doddle, and then to sit quietly and watch the forest pass by.

Passing two fish boats which were close to the south shore I was reminded of Michael's admonition to give the outlying buoy a wide berth as between the boat and the buoy would be a gill net suspended quite close to the surface and to run over it could easily foul my propeller not to mention having to deal with irate fishermen, and I did not wish to add such dilemmas to my list of tribulations, apart from these considerations the running over the log and kelp episode were still fresh in my mind, besides there was ample sea room for any diversionary action of the nets to be taken.

From what little I've seen of the BC coast I must admit that I'm at a loss as to why the environmentalists are getting their knickers in such a twist over logging activities. The few areas that I passed that had been logged had young healthy trees growing there, which will no doubt grow into big trees and in the fullness of time be harvestable. If I may make a pun, 'there is far too much big-o-tree around this subject.' So I ask the question, to this sustainable growth why do these varlets protest so much?

A few years ago I was doing a plumbing installation in a house that was built entirely of solid cedar logs, Panabode the design is called. Now the carpenter building this dwelling whose profession this was and who did nothing else for a living, when the building was completed took himself off to the Carmanah Valley to hug trees in protest at the logging. Now I ask is there any logic in these double standards? As long as the logging industries continue to replant the harvested areas and avoid blocking the spawning beds in the salmon streams then there will be no sympathy from me for the efforts of the loony fringe. To be fair though if there were no protesters to make the logging companies sit up and take notice then the forest would then continue to be raped and salmon streams blocked it could be claimed.

I do find it shameful though that these people who have nothing better to do than set up and attend protests feel it their god given right to disrupt whole communities from their livelihoods, and I refer in particular to that event in Ganges, Saltspring Island when a protestor chained herself to a logging truck and created a shutdown in the business district with no traffic able to move thus causing a loss of business to the shopkeepers, honest folk only wanting to earn a living. After the police had released her from the truck she had the unmitigated gall to claim success for her protestations.

By the time I had finished mulling over these ongoing problems between the environmental groups and the logging companies I had rounded Chatham Point and was heading down Discovery Channel. It was time therefore to pay attention to what was the approach to Seymour Narrows and the accelerating body of water. As the Narrows approached I began to have a slight feeling of anxiety, nothing as serious as to give up the attempt and turn around, but rather a fear of what may lie ahead. Some comfort was gained to allay this feeling when observing two high speed inflatable boats whizzing around and as their actions didn't suggest anything foolhardy. Why should I worry in my much larger boat? I asked myself.

Apart from the impression that the land was moving exceedingly quickly the transit had nothing to be concerned about, so, sit back and enjoy the experience was the order of the day, and go with the flow. At least for the moment, for after disgorging out of the Narrows at a high rate of knots into the turbulent waters of Discovery Bay I was faced with a double whirlpool the declivity of which was quite deep, in my alarmed state of mind was some four feet. Each of these whirlpools where turning in opposite directions with maybe four or five feet between them. Nothing for it but to, *close your eyes lad and go for it.*

Well I didn't close my eyes but, went for it and headed for the separating footage. If the reader has ever experienced the push and pulling effect of tiderips on a small boat then the passage between these two whirlpools would have been a profound disappointment, there was nothing to it just the roaring sound of the water as it swirled around the vortex on each side of the boat. Then as the tiderips got hold and ejected the boat into calmer waters so I had an inkling of what a cork must feel like shooting out of a bottle. A little exaggeration here I must admit but a fair description of the situation. As a matter of fact this section was the least bouncy, the tiderips while crossing to Campbell River proved to be much more pushy and pulley. Then into the calm waters of the marina, due to the fast moving tide which threatened to sweep the boat past full throttle on the engine was required to get through the opening in the breakwater, then on to moor at the fuel dock. Once again, as what happened at Port Hardy, the heavens opened up and released a torrent of rain, on this occasion I waited for the downpour to pass before taking on fuel after all it wouldn't do to get water into the fuel tanks.

By four o'clock I had settled into the allotted berth and went to pay the marina dues.

Discovery Harbour Marina was built on native aboriginal land and operated by the local Indian band. It is a very large marina protected from the fast moving tides by a vast breakwater. Every possible amenity to the boater is situated here, apart from the usual showers and garbage disposal which one expects to find in any self respecting marina just about every other service is catered for from a large array of stores. Canadian Tire, Starbucks and the like. I was particularly pleased to find a nautical store where I purchased a chart from which every other store I had visited didn't have, which filled in the gap for the next day's passage to the next port of call.

Possessing a comprehensive set of charts for the areas one intends sailing is an absolute must, if for no other reason than the comfort of knowing that there are no hazards ahead which have to be avoided. I mention this obvious point because even though the waters in BC are very deep even up to the shoreline and any rocks are usually noticed by the water surging around them. However, there are always exceptions to a rule and if one didn't have charts then one wouldn't know where the unsighted rocks lie. A case in point would be Ripple Rock that used to be in Seymour Narrows, 'one of the vilest stretches of water in the world,' according to George Vancouver, contradicting Lieutenant Baker's journal entry. Quite possibly Vancouver must have formed his opinion from another observation. From 1875 to 1958 Ripple rock had claimed 120 vessels and over 110 lives. The rock consisted of two peaks lying just under the surface which was not visible at slack water. When the tide is moving, and can be up to fifteen knots it turns the immediate area into a churning mass of water hiding the location of the highest points of the rock, as well as increasing the danger due to swirling currents. In 1953 the BC government decided to do something about the problem and have Ripple Rock blasted apart. This was an interesting exercise as due to the strong tides it proved impossible to drill down into the rock as the drilling barges either broke away or found it impossible to hold their position so a network of tunnels was dug from Maud Island to the rock and then upwards. The subsequent excavation took 27 months to complete and then packed with 1375 pounds of Nitromex 2H. At 9.31 on the 5th April 1958 Ripple Rock was blasted into history, with 370,000 tons of rock hurling into the air, and declared to be the largest non-nuclear explosion in the world, and never again to claim another ship. To the interested reader a more detailed description of this hazard can be acquired on Google Search, Ripple Rock, and Seymour Narrows.

Meanwhile back at the marina.

During the meandering around the shops I came across a liquor store and what a wonderful opportunity to treat myself. After all I had been journeying now for twelve days on a subsistence of wine and the occasional beer only. Yes, a treat would go down very well indeed. Being a creature of habit I made straight for the Scotch section and to my delight they stocked, to my mind the only blended scotch, due to its smooth texture, worth drinking. And the winner is, 'The Famous Grouse.' I came across this delectable 'water of life' some years ago under rather unusual circumstances. The shipping company I worked for at the time had a policy that only one brand of scotch, likewise rum, gin, etc. should be carried on their ships which made sense because otherwise so many other varieties would accumulate on the whim of different tastes, and unconsumed stocks would accumulate to the detriment of the ship-owner. Anyway, the scotch in question was not the brand usually carried.

I had just joined this particular ship and is my wont within a reasonable time when the bonded store could be opened and the contents inspected along with other storerooms. Imagine my horror when on entering the bonded store to see a wooden case marked The Famous Grouse. Not ever having heard of this beverage before and queried the Chief Steward on the offending article.

"What an earth is that?" I asked. "Wine?"

"No, sir, scotch."

"That isn't the brand normally carried."

"The last captain ordered it."

"And now I'm lumbered with it," I stated with a hint of resentment.

This may sound a bit odd but, I was a dutiful company servant at the time and this situation offended my sense of duty, and in this respect it was agreed that we would have to live with the situation by working our way through this unwelcome addition to the liquid beverage stock by supplying the officers bar and in the meantime I would have a bottle in my cabin. Between these two locations the offending article would be consumed. Later that evening I gritted my teeth with duty on my mind and poured myself a tot of this liquid, closed my eyes and took a sip. Then carefully setting the glass down on the table I picked up the phone and dialled the Chief Steward number.

"Hello, Chief Steward here."

"This is the captain. That Famous Grouse scotch we discussed this morning."

"Yes, sir?"

"Don't put any up in the officer's bar. I'll be drinking it."

From that moment on 'The Famous Grouse' has been my scotch of choice and replaced the previous nominated scotch on every ship I served on.

I mentioned this little anecdote as an example of how fortune can at times favour us by guiding us to those we love best.

On returning to the boat I put this prize to one side and prepared and ate dinner, with wine of course. The scotch was for a nightcap.

After clearing away and washing the dishes I got out the charts and tide tables to prepare for the next day's adventure. Comox, I thought that might be worth a visit, maybe even a night's stopover if timely and suitable.

While mulling over the choices there was a tapping on the window catching my attention, and to my delight it was Michael and Beryl grinning at me. Popping my head out of the hatch I invited them on board with the hope I would be appraised of their passage through the Narrows.

Without any hesitation on entering the cabin Beryl promptly seated herself on the settee just inside the entrance as mentioned previously a choice position for most visitors and indeed certainly for myself also.

"You like that seat, don't you?"

Beryl nodded, grinning her confirmation.

"What was your speed coming through the narrows?" asked Michael.

"Blessed if I know," I answered "I was too attached to the wheel."

"I checked on the GPS. We did fifteen knots."

"Wow! Well with two of you on board these things can be checked. There was no way I was going to hand over the steering to the autopilot, too risky. If that thing had popped off at a critical moment I would have been in a right pickle," which conjured up an image of making rapid progress with the tide while motoring in circles.

"Well it wasn't all fun and games, the Spinnaker carried away on coming down the Strait, a right mess it is too," opined Michael.

Michael seemed to be quite upset over the matter which isn't surprising really, no-one enjoys having problems like that to happen to their boat.

"Anyway, we had best get back. We just wanted to check and see if you got here alright. Come on Beryl."

And so they departed.

I didn't consider it appropriate to go around to their boat this evening to check on their misfortune, and made a mental note to pop around in the morning before I left. Now it was time for that much anticipated nightcap, read for a while, then to bed.

This musing on their problem which being an experienced sailor Michael could well handle progressed to a train of thought on the subject of boating problems which brought to mind a character who was obsessed with the idea of sailing, not that he knew anything about the subject as he set out from his home port in England armed only with a road map, for whatever good he thought that would be. He must have been dedicated to his dream though for within the space of a year he had to be rescued by the lifeboat no less than ten times. The upshot of his failed endeavours was he has since been advised by the authorities that he will have to pay for any subsequent rescues, and is now taking sailing lessons. As is obvious, my mind is free ranging so I make no excuses for this inconsequently observation.

*****

Campbell River was mentioned in George Vancouver's journal as a good source of fresh water for his ships. Of course it wasn't so named at that time it wasn't until the survey period 1857-61 of H.M.S.Plumper that it acquired the name honouring Samuel Campbell surgeon of that ship. Although not proven it seems extremely likely that this was the name given to the river and the town that subsequently grew up around it. Obtaining fresh water for ships in those days was always a worry, although not on this coast one would assume which has an over abundance. The problem of getting it into the ship was the difficulty which meant the empty barrels had to be transported ashore in the ship's boats, filling them, and then bringing them back on board, an arduous and time consuming practice. Vancouver's presence here had come about by chance. Due to Johnstone's advice on the inadvisability of trying to follow the continental shore after his experience at Arran Rapids, Vancouver decided to try for a passage on the west side of Georgia Strait. Chatham's anchor however, fouled a rock and the Discovery left with instructions for them to follow where they would wait on the western side. Quite possibly this change of plan gave Vancouver time to find fresh water and also observe, 'one of the vilest stretches of water in the world.'

DAY THIRTEEN

An unsolicited lecture to ponder

The onset of daylight released me from the arms of Morpheus, and what a beautiful day it promised to be, a clear sky with not a cloud in sight, with the wind out of the north-west at five knots. Being a natural sceptic this sight brought to mind the adage: Sun before seven, rain by eleven. As this is an English saying and usually comes true there, hopefully it didn't apply in British Columbia.

Well, as always it was the usual start to the day; gathering my thoughts and planning over a couple of cups of tea, then breakfast a shave, brush the teeth and get dressed. How pleasant it is in this relaxed age of casual dress. No longer do I have to put on a uniform or depending on the circumstances a suit. Since retiring and living in Canada the order of the day was for jeans and checked shirt, or special occasion's slacks and a loose fitting shirt. As a matter of fact I have a hard time remembering, should the interest strike me, when I last wore a tie. Although come to think of it I wore a suit and tie at my wedding to my second and present wife. But, such is life in the fast lane I have a hard time remembering when that happy day was without looking it up in the marriage certificate. It is odd that I can remember clearly events from my childhood and yet what I did yesterday requires a great deal of thought, catechising to myself the events of the day from when awakening and using the steppingstones of the day's events until reaching a satisfactory conclusion of the day's happenings. But to be truthful, half the time I don't bother if the events of the day had been important enough I'm sure they would have come to mind.

Having started this day in the usual way the time had progressed to seven thirty, remembering my promise I set off to find, 'Sliver', Michael had mentioned in passing which berth they were in so it was no big deal seeking them out, only two docks to the south. We chatted for a while, but there wasn't much to talk about which happens when one is preoccupied with problems. As they still had a few days left of their holiday, and rather than beat back to home base to have the previous day's damage fixed they had decided to stay in this marina to get back into shape again, as there was no need for me to hang about I made for Comox. Michael advised waiting for the tide to slacken off but then I'm not much of a one to hang about needlessly and my itchy feet demanded I get a move on. Besides the tide would only be against me as far as Cape Mudge which was only a couple of miles, then it was the open stretch of Georgia Strait where there would be little strength in the tide to impede my progress. So it was farewell to these nice people with commiserations on their bad luck, and I returned to my boat.

By eight-thirty I had cleared the breakwater and headed south away from Campbell River that sport fisherman's Mecca. Well does it deserve that title of being the best salmon fishing in the world although Port Alberni would pooh-pooh that claim, at one time? Salmon over a hundred pounds were being caught here on a regular basis. Now with the decline in fish stocks the size is also decreasing. I guess they just don't have the time to grow.

The tide was quite strong between Campbell River and Cape Mudge as Michael had said it would be, but my progress was not being retarded significantly to be of any concern and I covered the three miles within a reasonable time.

On occasion bucking against the ebb tide is preferable to moving with the flood in this particular section of Discovery Passage, especially if there are strong winds from the south or southeast. It is just to the south of Cape Mudge that the opposing flood tides meet, this phenomenon being the flood from the north in Discovery Passage flowing south and meeting the flood tide coming from the south in Georgia Strait.

This Cape was named for Zachary Mudge, 1st lieutenant of George Vancouver's ship Discovery. It lies at the promontory at the south extremity of Quadra Island, dividing Discovery Passage from Sutil Channel. It is in this vicinity on the shallow water of Wilby Shoals when the flood tide conditions occur coupled with a strong southerly wind very dangerous seas build up creating a very hazardous situation for small craft, sometimes these seas stretch across the full width of the entrance to Discovery Passage. Fortunately this was not the day to be so indisposed; the wind was gentle and from the northwest and the ebb tide was running.

Coming abeam of Cape Mudge I reduced the revolutions on the engine by a third. Comox wasn't very far away and I didn't want to get there too early, mid afternoon would be fine. Strange though it may seem reducing the engine speed increased the speed over the ground to eight knots by GPS, while the speed through the water indicated five knots. Ridiculous but true, it was unlikely that the tide would have such an effect of the boat's hull form to create a difference of this nature, even though the tide was an hour and a half into the ebb and running south which, though favourable of course but of minimum velocity would not make much of a difference. This rapid advance would bring me to Comox by twelve thirty and much too early to end the day and as Ford Bay on

Hornby Island was only another thirteen miles I decided to press on. That resolve didn't last long either as I was making grand progress. French Creek just past Qualicum Beach looked a likely spot and only another thirteen miles past Hornby, so the course was adjusted to suit this latest decision.

But then yet another change of plan, radical even, looking across the Strait to the mainland it came to mind that rather than making a long day of pushing on from one rejected decision to another pushing ever south until arriving home why not go over to Powell River for the night then take a look at Desolation Sound and see what George was on about in so naming the place. After all I had only been away under two weeks, so give it another few days 'fella' to round out the trip.

Obviously it makes sense to go into the Sound with full fuel tanks and as it wasn't until the morrow this change of plan would be enacted the course was set towards Powell River to fuel up and stay over night. Powell River is a mill town with its own facilities, which no doubt exclude private boats mooring there, or re-fuelling either. These necessities would be found at Westview marina next door to the south of the mill.

The wind picked up during the afternoon from the north and quite brisk, twenty knots plus at times, kicking up white caps and spraying over the boat. The sky remained clear though and the spirits remained high though salt caked.

Progress towards Westview was maintained at a reasonable speed in spite of the gyrating motion caused by the building seas. A place to respect is the Strait of Georgia which can be as peaceful as a sleeping child one minute then up comes the wind and a lop develops making a passage exceedingly boisterous and uncomfortable.

Westview Marina is in two sections with the ferry terminal in between. The ferry connects with Vancouver Island at Comox with the mainland and judging by the size and frequency of the ferries there is quite considerable traffic on this route.

In the early evening I entered the south section of the complex which caters for transient boats and headed for the fuel dock. A youngish looking man was calling out from a dock float as I passed and waving his arms in a frantic manner, what with the noise of the engine I couldn't make out what message he was trying to convey. Obviously by his gestures it must be something of importance, so, cupping my hands around my ears to better receive the message and with many an 'Eh!' I began to imagine myself as an old crone in trying to understand what he was saying and indicating that I would return after having refuelled, to which dock I was now approaching and about to come alongside, and preparing to tie up to this dock which strangely seemed to be abandoned. Odd, I thought surely they wouldn't leave the place unattended after all some dishonest person might just fuel up and leave without paying. While musing over the possibilities I noticed two gentlemen watching me from a fish boat parked nearby.

"Any idea where the attendant might be?" I called out.

"They're out of fuel," one of them offered. "You will have to go Lund."

"Lund?" I asked. "Where is that?"

"About an hour and a half with your boat, towards Desolation," said the second man.

Hoping the word desolation wasn't going to be prophetic and not be able to get fuel there either. The thought also flit across my mind as to how he related time and distance to my boat. Not considering the thought worth pursuing I just thanked them and unmoored and manoeuvring the boat to a position where the previously mentioned young man was waiting to direct me to a berth, he then made off in some haste only to reappear at the dock he had indicated.

More hand signals and calling, as I was near enough heading into the slip to hear him this time.

"You'll have to back in, sir."

Reversing was always a pleasing prospect, at least when it went right. Put the wheel amidships and build up enough sternway then disengage the engine, the boat can then be steered and proceed at a stately pace in a direct line to where I wanted to be then put the wheel over and glide gracefully stern first into the berth without the benefit of the engine, a most impressive sight.

At least that was the plan, having re-entered the main channel and got the boat turned around to point the boat stern first into the approach channel, and this is where the secret of stern navigation begins: The bow must be perfectly still with no movement either to port or starboard, the stern way then commences, at least that is the plan when it works right, not this occasion however to my embarrassment the boat was soon being handed off other boats by the ever attentive dock jock. Not an impressive sight by any means and most damaging to my ego. In due course though the boat was moored up alongside two other boats with a small gap of water between then two more boats rafted up on the next finger, the space between not much bigger than space for a kayak.

Having settled into my new berth with a nice cup of tea, a flickering of light caught my attention with peripheral vision causing me to glance out of the window towards the next boat to see a television programme in full swing. *'God!,' I thought. One of the advantages of boating is to get away from civilisation and all its ballyhoo in general and away from the one eyed monster in particular.* Still each to there own, and as long as I'm not kept awake with the thing, why should I bother?

As a matter of curiosity I observed the best I could from my isolated position if it was a clear picture and if there was anything of interest worth watching, unsuccessfully as it turned out. While taking this academic interest the thing was switched off and a man poked his head out of the hatch and gaining my attention expressed the hope that I wouldn't be leaving too early in the morning.

"What do you call early?" I asked.

"Well, we get up around eight thirty." He offered.

"Crikey! That's half the day gone." I said rather facetiously at an attempt at humour.

At this comment falling on stony ground he looked a little nonplussed but, as I wasn't in any rush to get going in the morning with just a short run to Lund I felt obliged to be magnanimous.

"Not to worry, I have one or two things to do before I leave." I hadn't but then I could wash the salt off the boat to fill in time. Let's hope that wouldn't disturb their repose. Ah! Don't you just love the concern that people have for their creature comforts?

Anyway, I had something to do before the store closed, so I took my leave and went to buy engine oil and a Canadian flag to replace the washed out version hanging off the backstay. This done I prepared and ate the evening meal no explanation offered here as to what delightful repast that entailed in the way of veggies. After washing the pots I went into the cockpit to enjoy the remains of the day and the remains of the wine left over from dinner and take in peace of the dying day.

I wasn't occupied in this pleasant pastime for long before being hailed from the boat on the short stretch of water on the other side. *"Blast, there goes the tranquillity."* As I turned my head towards the voice across the water I was posed a question.

"Where did you get the toe-rail?" This guy asked.

"Sorry? I replied, my thoughts having been interrupted.

"Where did you get the toe-rail?"

"Vancouver." I answered. "A marine store on Powell Street. Can't remember the name of the place though."

"You can't get them anymore," he said with a note of finality.

'*Can't say as I would want to,*' I thought.

"No-body makes extruded toe-rail anymore,"

To this piece of earth shattering news I just nodded as the guy was beginning to irritate. Whether I was supposed to make some comment or not, I don't know as he seemed to be waiting for some sort of response.

The following conversation or should I say lecture was what really niggled me as it brought to mind a captain I had sailed with who would stick out his chin in a pugnacious gesture and ask a pertinent question, say for example how did I decorate a room at home, did I paint or paper the walls? On giving my views on the subject the answer was invariably, "You're wrong, mate. And I'll tell you why." He would then proceed to tell me how he would do the job as if it was the only way, no gainsaying, no alternative method being possible. As a conclusion the lecture would always end with the statement. "It's as simple as that."

Anyway, I digress, back to the chap next door.

"What material is your side deck?"

"Plywood. Three quarter ply."

"Did you fibreglass the underside of the deck before fitting the rail?"

I had to think on this for a moment as it had been some time since that part of the job had been carried out. "No. Just two lay-ups on the top side and over the hull." Wondering why he was so interested in this particular subject of toe-rails and the fixing of such. But, it was soon obvious that he just wanted to voice his opinions and lecture on the subject.

"You have to fibreglass the underside as well," he said. "And I'll tell you why."

'God, No. A blast from the past.'

"You have to first fit the toe-rail and bolt it down, and then remove the bolts and fibreglass under the deck. Then when the fibreglass is set up you re-drill the holes and fasten the toe-rail down."

I could have just nodded and accepted his lecture but, a little peeved at his attitude I thought to wind him up. "I just screwed mine down." I offered.

A definite look of alarm crossed his face. "It has to be bolted down, if you don't the rail can be ripped out." He said making a ripping sound while making a forceful upward gesture with his hand to illustrate the point. "With all the stress forces acting on it." He then indicated in the general direction of his own toe-rail presumably, and of the objects in question. Whatever they might be.

Then as a final parting gesture because I was to take my leave from this arrogant prig, "Well," I said. "The only stress on my rail is the fenders that hang off it and to stop my foot slipping over the side." I then did what I could never have done and got away with from the previously mentioned captain, Got up and left to go below before the, 'It's as simple as that,' announcement.

DAY FOURTEEN

As is my wont I came awake at daylight, but as Lund and Prideaux Haven my next ports of call was not so far there was no rush to leave. So, throwing the sheets over my head to shut out the light an attempt was made to doze off. Fat chance, as soon as I come awake my mind switches on and comes into gear. With this sort of churning going on in my head I may as well get up and ponder the coming day with that life blood of man, a nice cup of tea.

In this leisurely manner, with the inclusion of breakfast and other matters that cried out for attention a couple of hours had passed pleasantly by. Then to the promised wash down.

Eight thirty had not yet arrived but my neighbour appeared fully dressed, which suggested to me that something was amiss. It cannot have been my activities that had disturbed him because he greeted me in a cheery manner, an attitude that is not conducive to being rudely wakened. Of course it is considered rude to enquire on a personal matter what got him out of bed so early, so I just returned the compliment. An explanation was soon forthcoming as just at this moment a young woman appeared helping an elderly gentleman up from below into the cockpit. Then both the woman and the 'good morning' chap both started to help the elderly chap over the rail and onto the dock. This exercise became fraught with difficulty as the fellow was non too spry and once they got him over the rail confusion and bewilderment seemed to possess him making the younger man become somewhat irritable trying to help, with many failed attempts, to get the old chap to place his foot where he was directing it.

"No Dad, no not there, here where I'm putting your foot."

However, in due course, 'Dad' got his foot where it was supposed to be and the exercise was finally completed with the elderly gentleman safely off the boat. With an apologetic smile in my direction from the woman the three of them went off along the dock.

Would this be my fate I wondered should I live so long? Sad really when one gets old and has to rely on others to help you with even the most simplest of tasks. I could only assume that the old fellow had suffered some medical problem, a stroke maybe? On further reflection one can only admire the younger couple who were caring for him as it couldn't be easy for them to look after him on outing in such a small boat. There must have been genuine warmth there to be so close.

The morning was without a breath of wind and promised to be a hot day. By eight forty-five I had cast off and began making my way north to Lund. I was curious as to how they would get the old chap back on board but not nosey enough to wait for them return.

The toe rail chappie didn't appear as I left, so no more un-solicited advice was forthcoming.

Shortly after leaving Westview the Powell River paper mill was abeam. It is a well know fact that certain visual manifestations, or smells, will trigger off thought processes connecting to the past with alarming clarity. The sight of the mill and the accompanying smell of pulp that goes with it and the protective breakwater of sunken World War Two merchant ships was no exception. It was forty-five years ago that I was here as a young third mate of a cargo ship carrying sulphur from Galveston, Texas, for the mill which is an ingredient in the manufacture of news print and tasting my first alcoholic drink. Not an earth shattering experience to relate but just as an example of the point which I was making on the subject of memory triggers. The occasion that came to mind was me sitting in a bar for men only, drinking beer at ten cents a glass, as that is how it was in those days, women with escorts only allowed to drink in a separate bar, archaic laws in today's liberated society. Without a doubt this thought was prompted by the ten cents a glass situation.

There was also the friendliness of the people I remembered who would take visiting seamen under their wing. Invite them into their homes for a most welcome meal, the ship's fare was something less than a delight as I recall, and to watch some television which was still a novelty in the fifties much enjoyed and appreciated.

A conducted tour of the mill to watch the making of newsprint was also a poignant memory. Watching fascinated through a glass window the raw logs being brought up the escalator into the enclosed chamber to have the bark removed by high pressure water jets. The naked log then reduced to wood chips by whirling knives, the power of which was awesome to watch; in minutes a log would be reduced from a tree trunk into a mass of small wood pieces destined to be a newspaper.

These chips would then proceed to the next stage to be turned into pulp then slurry containing ninety percent water, (a figure that could be challenged as I'm relying on ancient memories.) This slurry was then fed over heated rollers into this massive machine drying the slurry until it emerged at the far end as a roll of newsprint, a fascinating process which still has me in awe, especially how the slurry was fed over an open gap before entering the heating process. As I said memories do get triggered by the sight of something in the past even though with time they become somewhat vague, nice to know that the brain is operating on all cylinders though, and with these memories for company I motored on towards Lund arriving there at eleven. Fuelling didn't take up too much time so there was little chance to assess the place, just a quick caste of the eye to get a favourable impression of what appeared to be a holiday destination.

Just after eleven of the clock I was on my way again chugging north through the narrow Thulin Channel and avoiding a deadhead. Two schools of dolphins kept me entertained by keeping pace with the boat crossing over from side to side and occasionally diving underneath to appear further over nearer to the shore. A delightful mammal, the dolphin, they do say that there are two peaks of intelligence on our planet on one stands man on the other the dolphin, I sometimes times wonder whether the dolphin isn't the more intelligent, at least he seems to be content with his lot in this environment, unlike man who forever wants to change the world to suit his needs.

There were many boats going in the opposite direction to the south which would indicate there would be a choice of a place to put the anchor down for the night, and it seemed to me that I was wasting my time trying to indicate to these passing boats that there was a deadhead ahead of them because no-one seemed to acknowledge my signalling, probably thought my gestures were rude. Well good luck to them, keep a sharp lookout.

Rounding Sarah Point, sited at the north end of the Malaspina Peninsula so named by George Vancouver for his sister, with the point on the opposite side of the channel on Cortes Island named for his other sister Mary. Between these two points one then enters Desolation Sound to be met with an awesome sight of stunning magnificence with the mountains at the far end of the sound rising to an incredible height and on this beautifully clear summer's day standing out so distinctly to take one's breath away. No doubt Vancouver was less than impressed by the beauty of the place than I was to so name this stretch of water. In disregard of the scenery he must have been impressed by the lack of facilities for storing his ships. It certainly couldn't have been through the lack of majesty, as the awesome sight of the mountains cannot have been less spectacular then as they are now. The man must have been suffering from his on-going illness to take such a jaundiced view in putting the place down, but then he wasn't in these parts to admire the scenery. If I may quote from his journals, he justifies this appellation thus: 'This Sound afforded not a single prospect that was pleasing to the eye, the smallest recreation on shore, nor animal or vegetable food. Whence the place obtained the name Desolation Sound; where our time would have passed infinitely more heavily, had it not been relieved by the agreeable society of our Spanish friends.' It should be mentioned here that when Vancouver named the sound it covered what is now Homfrey Channel and from Bute Inlet to the two points named for his sisters.

The entrance to Prideaux Haven is narrow but deep so there was no problem entering even for Vancouver's ships, as I had not ever been here before I felt it prudent to keep an eye on the depth sounder as is my wont when entering strange places, a practice that has served me well in the past. Going aground would most embarrassing especially on a falling tide.

At twenty past one on this gloriously hot sunny summer afternoon the anchor went down in a fairly crowded Prideaux Haven. The first order of the day was to put up the awning giving a much needed shade. This awning was home made from rip stop nylon, or would it be better to say custom made to suit this particular boat, whatever, my wife with her infinite skills with the sewing machine stitched the material, and myself with ever present good ideas created the spreaders from half inch PVC pipe with screw fittings to join the two parts and disassemble them for easy stowage. Quite often with good ideas at the time they were conceived don't always work as planned which proved to be the case with the spreader connections. The problem in this case was that the connections couldn't be screwed together fully and kept falling apart. No doubt in their plumbing role a proper connection would be made with use of a special tool of sorts but, it was not to my advantage to create a continuous piping for the flow of water, so, I resorted to reducing the size of the thread for a more satisfactory connection, which served well enough for these circumstances, actually having the two parts drooping on each side of the boom had its advantages also as protection from the lowering sun.

To think that only yesterday beating across the Georgia Strait bundled up against the cold wind and today even stripped down to bare necessities to alleviate the almost unbearable heat. But, that is British Columbia coast for you even in summer the weather can turn miserably cold one day and the next day be almost too hot to bear.

It was here in this haven that Vancouver's officers found a deserted Indian village, deserted by humans but much to their chagrin not by fleas, the place was infested with them attacking the officers so relentlessly that even immersion up to their necks in the water would not relieve the torment, only by boiling their clothes could the fleas be purged. From Vancouver's journals this village I deduced must have been on Eveleigh Island as the journals also describes the defensive works that faced outwards to Homfrey Channel and high up on the cliff, the village was estimated to have contained at least three hundred souls. The thought did cross my mind to row over and take a look but quickly abandoned. It was too hot to row over and doubtful if anything remained of the village, and the fleas if any remained were welcome to the place.

Sitting under the awning I whiled away the afternoon watching people swimming and cavorting in the water which is what I would have been doing had I had the presence of mind to have brought swimming trucks with me. The water temperature was an incredible 66 degrees Fahrenheit or for those of the metric persuasion 18.9C. In BC's glacial and snow fed waters this haven of warm bath water can only be described as incredible. A dog was also swimming with its owner which I recognised as being a Border collie, when the swimmer rested holding onto an anchor line the dog would lay over the guy's legs also taking a breather. They do say that a dog has an owner and a cat a servant but it seems the dog had the servant in this instance. As I also own a Border collie I would willingly attest to that statement.

My dog has an unusual colouring for this breed as it was a predominately brown coat were normally black is the predominate colour with maybe brown in selected areas, the neck and blaze white a distinctive must on all this breed. Only once in my life have I seen a dog with the same colouring as mine and that was in a pub in Devon. Now what do I see swimming around in BC waters but yet another dog exactly the same. Now that I consider my dogs colouring to be most unusual this sighting for the second time I found this manifestation to be nothing less than a most bizarre occurrence. Regretfully, I won't be able to express surprise anymore on sighting a dog with the same markings as it now all seems so commonplace. But this was not to be the only coincidence to be met with on this trip, which will be referred to in its proper place and has nothing to do with dogs.

As evening closed in the air cooled a little and the bodies that had been frolicking in the water returned to their boats and in due course re-emerged on deck suitably clothed, no doubt after a fresh water shower, to fire up the barbeques and dispense the drinks. Being the normal routine, almost a ritual one might say, in the boating world when the sun is well below the yardarm. I couldn't help but wonder if I might have been doing the same thing had I had company. Living together on a small boat one has to be sociable or soon be at each others throats.

As it was there were more important matters to worry about: After motoring for several hours one would expect the batteries to be fully charged but, in the couple of hours that I had been here the house batteries had gone flat. Even with my limited knowledge of things electric I would have thought that three batteries providing thirty-six volts would have lasted a little longer. Fortunately the cranking battery is separate from the house set so these could be charged up again when the engine was running. In a situation such as this, for me anyway who is no whiz at electrics I could only try to find the source by elimination. In this respect everything in the chest freezer was transferred to the fridge and switched off, the freezer that is.

While undertaking this transfer a packet of sausages came to hand, these were completely thawed so the evening meal had been decided upon without any input from me and, considered a plus as I'd forgotten once again to take something out for the meal.

Into the frying pan they went these guys accompanied by a sliced potato all soon sizzling away giving off a mouth watering aroma, with a carrot and a few peas steamed to perfection made for an excellent repast which had me entertaining thoughts of should it ever come to pass I could make out very well on my own. Not a gourmet cook by any stretch of the imagination, but passable to keep starvation at bay. Not being knowledgeable in wine etiquette which wine to serve with sausages I took a stab and brought out a nice Chateauneuf du Pap, which complemented the meal to perfection. As this was the only wine I had anyway the decision was made that much easier. There are certain advantages of being blissfully ignorant on certain subjects. In this respect had I been a wine snob could have suffered the meal without the benefit of a complementary glass of wine. So it was then with the inner man replete and the pots washed I retired to the cockpit with remains of the wine and watched the day close with night creeping into this haven of peace.

Listening to the muted sounds of conversation drifting across the water I resolved that being on ones own was the preferable situation when with ones thoughts, undisturbed by idle chatter, can wander at will to imaginary places and people, and not have to be dutiable and listen, or take part in any mundane conversation. This was a time of day to reflect on the day's events and plan for the morrow and consider how fortunate we are to live in such a beautiful province. The winters are mild if wet, the summers dry and warm, well most of the time anyway, maybe even hot during the day but, cool at night. We are truly blessed to feel at peace with the world in such places as Prideaux Haven. Sitting comfortably in the cockpit sipping this excellent wine to while away the darkness of the late evening watching the reflections of the boats lights on the glass like water. I asked myself. What else could a man ask in this troubled world? Nothing.

Having expounded on the pleasures of relaxing and realising the advantages it affords I should mention here in this happy state that it has up until now been missing in my makeup. All my life I have been active, a get up and go sort of character, restless and wanting to be doing something that gets life moving, relaxation has to be forced on me and in these circumstances the mind is churning over with ideas to fill in the void one might say. During the course of this adventure it has been a case of get going as soon as possible and make for the next port of call. It has been fortunate that there hasn't been any evidence of roses as I wouldn't have made the time to stop and smell them. But now in this tranquil haven relaxation has now entered my lexicon of life.

As the evening wore on the night became black, so black that the shore which was quite close was indistinguishable. The night was also becoming distinctly cool a situation that reminded me that a nice warm bed awaited.

DAY FIFTEEN

Prideaux Haven on this dawn was as still and as quiet as when the previous day ended, with no sign of life from any of the other boats either. Well not everyone is an early riser I guess.

After the usual leisurely morning routine it was up anchor and away, chugging out of this delightful haven by 0720.

There are three choices of channels that one can take to the north, Homfrey Channel being the furthest east which takes the longer route round Redondo Island and follows the continental shore. The other choices were Waddington Channel or Lewis channel which necessitate going back down Desolation Sound. The start of Waddington Channel was just across from Prideaux Haven taking the west side of Redondo and the most obvious choice to the Octopus Islands Marine Park by way of The Hole in the Wall.

Early on this particular morning the water was like glass with not a breath of wind to ripple the surface. The only breeze available was what the boats movement created. Within the hour though this placid existence was shattered, approaching from astern with engines roaring with a bone in its teeth was one of those enormous floating gin palaces that come up from south of the border to cruise Canadian waters each summer. In no time at all, this monster was abeam and passing. Taking a deep breath of anticipation I put the helm over to meet his wake on my port bow and was soon plunging and bucking in his wake taking heavy spray over the bow. I would be less than honest if I didn't say that this provoked a twinge of resentment at his indifference that these boats had in the matter of courtesy towards others.

It is with small wonder that, and I've heard it said many times a resentment some Canadians have towards the Americans who come to Canadian waters, fish and can the salmon they catch then return wither they have come from without contributing anything into the Canadian economy, having brought enough supplies with them from their home ports without any need to replenish here.

But that was of no immediate concern for myself at the moment, once this turmoil had calmed down I engaged the autopilot and went to investigate what I well anticipated and I was not a happy camper at what awaited me. The spray coming over the bow from this cretin that had just recently passed by had come through the partially open hatch above the forward berth and wet the bedding.

Not seriously, fortunately, but in patches that would need to be dried out before bedtime. Well the day promised to be warm and dry, so it was off with the sheets and upending the cushions, as a precaution against another wetting I closed the hatch tightly.

It crossed my mind how calmly I had taken this imposition to my wellbeing, not too long ago I would have been shaking my fist and mouthing all sorts of imprecations towards this disturber of my peace. Could it be that these travels calmed this demon that I previously had in my breast, or just advancing age mellowing me? There is no doubt though that in such peacefully majestic and tranquil coastlines and fiords it is difficult to get angry, a muttered, "Youuuu, bast-aard!!! Would have helped though I'm sure, sotto voce even, just loud enough to prevent the blood boiling before cooling down to normality again.

Just after nine of the clock Dean Point at the narrow neck of the northern end of Waddington Channel was abeam and we were in Pryce Channel heading in a westerly direction towards the Hole in the Wall. At this time a breeze had sprung up on the port beam and as slack water was not until early afternoon I decided to sail for a while. So out went the Genoa and off with the engine. Ten minutes later the wind shifted to right ahead at a brisk eight knots. So, in with the Genoa and on with the engine but motoring at much reduced revolutions. Strange is it not? Whenever the sails go up the wind either dies or shifts to a useless direction. Ah! Well, these things are sent to try us.

One hears many horrendous stories about the many rapids that abound in these parts. The Hole in the Wall in particular, as I had no experience of these particular waters I was not about to ignore the stories of others who had been here, whether the stories had been embellished or not. So on arriving early at the eastern entrance of this narrow channel I decided to bide my time to transit the four miles of channel to the rapids at the western end and catch the last of the ebb, the change in direction to the first of the flood would then have the flow of water to my advantage.

Curiously, there were quite a number of boats coming out of the channel against the ebb. Odd I thought should I take notice of the stories? Or cast caution to the winds and go for it? The boats that were coming through were the fast runabout types with shallow draughts and high speeds, therefore caution prevailed and I waited. After all the stories told that one could hear the roar of water forcing its way through as far away as the Octopus Islands if this were true then it made sense to wait. Anyway it was time for lunch.

Around one o'clock a sailboat was observed making for the Yuculta rapids to the north of my position which according to the chart was more turbulent than the Hole in the Wall specie. The boat in question passed through quite safely clinching my hesitancy and I headed for the hole. Progressing at a leisurely pace brought me to the narrows at the western end at the top of the hour and through I went with Michael's advice on transiting Seymour Narrows Ringing in my ears, 'it's just a moving body of water.' And so this was the case here albeit ejecting into an area of tide rips that had nowhere near the ferocity of Discovery Bay. In fact the Hole in the Wall proved to be a doddle. Another question entered my thoughts at this time. Why Hole in the Wall? It was not even in the broadest stretch of the imagination a hole. To my mind a hole is a hole, i.e. an area of space surrounded by solid. Which in this case would be a hole in the cliff, rather I thought, wouldn't Cleft in the Cliff, or Crack in the Wall. A hole never, still I suppose it does have a romantic ring to it, so why not?

Half an hour later I had crossed over Okisollo Channel and into the Octopus Islands Marine Park. A quiet tranquil place it is too and reminiscent of Prideaux Haven. There were a few boats there already but plenty of space to anchor tucked away in a corner far enough away not to bother anyone or for that matter to be bothered by.

Strange though, no matter how early in the day I arrive at a destination there always seems to be several boats already there occupying the place. Could it be I wondered that they stay for several days in the same place? That is a possibility I suppose as not everyone feels the need to get going, a leisurely approach to life might be a good thing, maybe I'll try it one day.

All the boats here had a line to the shore as well as being anchored which seemed like a good idea and would make for more space when a boat does swing on the anchor and so prevent banging into each other, this gave me an opportunity to use the dinghy and time for it to earn its keep, so far during this trip it had just tagged on behind following like an obedient dog while travelling and acting as an unofficial fender when getting trapped between the boat and the dock. Now it came into its own transporting me to the shore with a suitable line. When one considers the price of an inflatable dinghy against the usage it gets it becomes a disproportionately costly item, but then one needs the item now and again, so what alternative is there?

Although the sun was hot there was an intermittent breeze blowing into the cove keeping things cool. It was because of this breeze I noticed a definite whiff of perfume, a resinous smell something like furniture polish. At least that is how it smelled to my jaded olfactory organ, as mentioned earlier when a familiar smell presents itself a familiar memory is also conjured up. This smell brought back the memory of approaching Ceylon from the west, or should I say Sri Lanka as it now called, during the northwest monsoon season there is a definite smell of spices wafting from the land. This thought came to me now and I wondered if these present resinous smells were coming off the trees. Alas! This romantic notion was short lived for on sighting the immediate area I noticed that a guy on the next boat over was polishing his bright work and the most likely source of this delightful smell.

After settling in to this new berth I made the effort to phone home on my newly acquired mobile phone with negative results. This was a little disappointing as the thing had been bought especially for making contact with home base, as it was not being appreciated that I could sometimes be in the realms of non signals. So I made a cup of tea and sat under the collapsed awning observing the activities around the anchorage. The guy polishing his brass must have a hide like a rhinoceros to be without a shirt slaving away with the hot sun beating on his back. Dedicated to his task too the way he was titivating his boat, surely there are more appropriately cooler times for these activities.

Anyway, a more interesting scene presented itself and I turned my languid attention from the domestic chores of my near neighbour. Also close by and a little astern of the boat that previously had my attention was one of those power boats, trawler I believe they are called and flying an American flag. A dinghy had just come up to the stern of this boat with much excitement from two clucking females when two guys got out of the dinghy onto the swim platform and hauled up a fair sized Ling cod. This developed into an excited photo op with much Oohing and Aahing. Not without justification in my opinion as the creature must have been at least eighteen inches in length.

Later in the afternoon the air started to cool and while I was contemplating the evening meal a dinghy bumped alongside with a couple on board. A man and a woman of middle age, probably in their late fifties or thereabouts. Their arrival brought me to my feet with a greeting.

"Nice boat," the man said.

"Yes," I answered feeling that ever present emotion of pride at any favourable mention of my boat. "Come aboard if you like, have a look around."

To this invitation and with no further persuasion they both promptly climbed over the transom.

Introductions and handshaking followed with the announcement that they were from the boat previously mentioned, the one that required polishing during the heat of the day. This fact could not go unmentioned of course and I was advised that the polishing and general titivation of the boat was an annual event.

Stephanie and Carston were their names they inspected the interior of the cabin in a cursory manner. I find that people tend to do that, look around in a cursory manner as though they were embarrassed at their intrusion. And I have to admit to being the same and not try to look too obvious at their life style. Stephanie, being a woman took more than a cursory glance at the galley. With compliments at how well appointed it was, the bathroom also received her praise particularly for the full size stand up shower. Not an unusual phenomenon I suppose, cooking and bathing seem to be uppermost in a woman's psyche. Anyway they didn't stay long, just a polite chat after refusing a glass of wine. In which Carston mentioned an interesting point about American boats which is worth a mention here. Apparently, the boating laws in the States require a holding tank for their sewage and a pump out facilities at designated stations. It is against the law to discharge sewage into coastal waters. This situation has created a problem when cruising in Canadian waters as pump out stations are not yet mandatory in Canada, and as these sewage tanks are self contained they can't be discharged overboard anyway. The mind boggles at what the Americans must do for relief when the tanks are full.

After these nice people had left I turned my attention to dinner a feast of hamburger patties as they had de-frosted, the veggies were not a problem either as I only had potatoes, peas and carrots anyway. There is great deal to be said about simplicity in the presentation of meals, it certainly cuts out agonising about making a choice. However, the fact that the salt had run out did make for a hiccup in the presentation of this otherwise excellent repast, with a mental note to resolve the salt problem at the next port of call.

And so the day came to an end as it always does with either reading and a glass of wine, or reviewing the events of the day with a glass of wine, or maybe just a glass of wine. Is this civilisation or not?

DAY SIXTEEN

Arranging for departure from the Octopus Islands Marine Park to coincide with the first of the flood at the Hole in the Wall that would carry me through the Yaculta Rapids also at the last of the flood would allow me to leave at a leisurely time of around nine thirty.

My companions of the previous evening left at the same time but heading south, with a cheery wave we parted company and went our separate ways, with me heading out across the Okisollo Channel to the Hole in the Wall.

With the last hour of the flood tide there was still some turbulence in the entrance waters with the bow being pushed from one side to the other in the tide rips. Nothing alarming or dangerous though and it only lasted for about five minutes, too turbulent though for the autopilot which required my manual steering. I did review my opinion of this stretch of water though and wondered what it must be like in full flood. But then I will most probably never know as I have no intention of making the passage at such a time and an observation from the top of the cliffs steep sided as they were would not be viable option either even if I wanted to attempt the climb.

The four miles of the Hole and another four miles to Big Bay to refuel was a reasonably quick passage arriving at eleven to meet with coincidence number two if one counts the swimming dog as coincidence number one. On making the turn to starboard into the Bay to line up for the fuel dock there was a boat approaching from the north which was also directing his course for the fuel dock. I recognise that boat I said to myself, obviously the chap on the other boat also recognised me as he was waving. Bless my cotton socks I muttered to myself that's Jim Rendal and his girlfriend Louise, Jim being the operator of the excavator for the Pender excavating company and well known in the local boating fraternity having ventured far and wide during his summer excursions.

There was a line-up for the fuel dock so we managed to come close enough for a chat and exchange of pleasantries. Both parties wondering at the co-incidence of meeting up in the middle of no-where, they had spent the past three weeks cruising up Bute Inlet and extolled the beauty of this place. It must have been for the scenery as there doesn't seem to be much else of interest if the charts are to be believed. But then Jim does get about in his boat to places that would never occur to me, he even sailed around the Washington Coast and into the Columbia River crossing without incident the treacherous and violent bar at the mouth of this river sailing as far as and into the Snake River, quite an enterprise by anyone's standards.

Bute Inlet was not on my itinerary for this trip and if anything would have to wait for the future. There are so many wonderful places to visit on the British Columbia coast and impossible to take them all in on one excursion. It had been my intention to fuel up and catch the slack water at each of many rapids between there and the Johnstone Strait stopping again at Port Neville for the night. But then the delay waiting for space at the fuel dock could put this plan in jeopardy, so shifting my thinking I decided to stay the night and fuel up in the morning and catch the slack water on the morrow. With this plan decided upon I could walk up to the Arran Rapids to watch the full tide roaring through. Ah! Yes, the best laid plans etc.

These rapids are where George Vancouver's expedition had to turn back and seek another way around Vancouver Island on the west side of Georgia Strait. Having reached Bute Inlet by way of Homfrey Channel they considered an attempt to pass through these rapids far too dangerous. Johnstone the Sailing Master managed to get through in one of the ship's boats but, even with the help of the local Indians towing him through against the tide is was deemed a difficult and dangerous exercise for the ships. Which begs the question: Why not wait for slack water? That could be deemed stated in hindsight as these early explorers had no inclination of what to expect on this coast, it could have been thought that these rapids were actually a river.

On coming into a vacant berth the mooring lines were taken by the young dock jock, a young Australian lad as it turned out I was to learn, (the accent being a dead give-away) who was working his way around the world taking jobs where he could to finance this dream. What wonderful experiences these young people embark on, so different from my day when on leaving school you were expected to get a proper job a career preferably. He assigned me the berth that I was in fortunately as there didn't seem to be any other choice, and I went off to the office to pay the moorage dues and purchase a chart for part of the next leg. Also a packet of salt. Well the chart I wanted they didn't have just about every other chart for this area but not the one I wanted, all was not lost though as they had salt.

On arriving back at the dock I noticed that Jim had got alongside the fuel dock so I went over to have a chat. Then on returning to my boat I was advised that the berth was needed for a seventy foot gin palace, although this phrase was not used. Well it makes sense I suppose a seventy foot boat generates more revenue than a forty foot boat. There was a discussion along the lines of fitting me in at another berth but, on viewing the layout I decided against this offer, and as I had forgotten to pay the moorage anyway felt it best to press on to Port Neville. Funny how these chance incidents can take over and change ones decisions. In this instance I didn't mind too much missing out on the Arran Rapids as I could return on a more convenient spring tide next year when the volume of water passing through should be more impressive. Also the convenience of this change of plan suited the situation as the ebb would be about to start at the first rapids in the Gillard Passage. As I had plenty of fuel, and ignoring the Bismarck anomaly, I set off on the next leg of the odyssey.

Proceeding along the channels towards Johnstone Strait was a pleasant interlude on this warm sunny day taking in the scenery which varied very little, just a mass of trees from the water's edge right up to the peaks of the surrounding high ground. But, conducive to conjuring up many thoughts and imaginings of how the tree fellers managed on such steep slopes, then the most ridiculous thought came to mind, no doubt they would have one leg shorter than the other to compensate. Ridiculous I know but, that is how it goes when on one's own.

Towards evening I entered Johnstone Strait by way of Sunderland Channel and into a full blown gale howling down the strait and right on the nose and against the ebb tide, where else? The boat was pitching heavily in the short steep swell with spray coming over the bow causing me to duck in an evasive action. I had wrapped the wheel cover around me and crouched behind the cabin entrance bulkhead so avoiding a soaking and popping up and down the while keeping a sharp eye out for logs. Fortunately I'd had the foresight to batten down the hatches forward at the first sign of the weather changing, even so the force of the wind had driven salt water to find entry round the galley window seal, just a dribble but enough to spoil a box of cereals. It occurred to me that having bought salt at Big Bay this sprayed salt was an extra I could well do without.

It was only a short run into Port Neville and uncomfortable though it was bouncing up and down it was getting dark so I pressed on rather than turning back to take shelter under the lee of the nearest island.

The entrance to Port Neville seemed to me to be a lot wider than I recalled from the previous visit, no doubt the gloom of late evening and the weather could account for this illusion. Better wider than narrower though I thought inconsequently.

The approach to the dock became the next problem as a much bigger power boat was trying to manoeuvre into the open space of the one remaining berth. A fish boat occupied a space in the middle of the main dock, which if they had moved up a little would have made space for another boat alongside. Anyway, while trying to judge my approach to coincide with the power boat getting alongside I could then go around his stern and get a berth on the inside of the dock, when lo and behold he abandoned the exercise and moved off again. This caused me to take the way off my boat to avoid him and with the wind now pushing me sideways I fell heavily against the fish boat, in the process bending two stanchions which filled me with something less than glee. While I waited alongside the fish boat the power boat came around again for another attempt to moor and again abandoned the exercise. No more Mister Nice Guy showing this dithering amateur the courtesy of waiting off. I waited until he had cleared then slipped into the berth myself. The chap that took my lines remarked that the power boat was wanting this berth to which my comment was, 'Tough,' After ploughing into the bad weather outside in the Strait for the previous couple of hours and then sustaining damage to my boat through the unprofessional antics of this rank amateur, when all he had to do was stop off the berth and the wind would have put him alongside. My mood created little sympathy for his problem. The man looked at me reflectively for a while then probably thinking I wasn't going to expand on this comment became quite chatty, asking my intentions for the morrow and on being informed that I was planning an anti-clockwise circumnavigation he advised that fog was forecast for the strait tomorrow, to which as I had radar that didn't particularly bother me at least the wind wouldn't be the problem. After looking up at the radar antennae he cast his gaze about the general area then took off in great haste along the dock, up the ramp, and along the shore towards what appeared to be a derelict float.

As it appeared the previously mentioned interloper, (if I may be polite on the subject of the dithering power boat operator) after yet more attempts to berth his boat finally ended up moored on this float that lay a little way out towards the entrance from the main dock, and this was where my erstwhile companion had headed to help moor this boat. I can only hope his help was appreciated. If I had waited for this boat to moor I would still be out there, sometimes impatience has its reward.

After pottering about for a while tidying things up and getting the charts sorted out for the next days run another fish boat had arrived and rafted up to the guy astern, Thankfully, not taking up the berth directly across from me on the inside of the dock. This berth was soon occupied by a sailboat which had come down from further up the inlet, no doubt getting away from an anchorage which in this wind could have caused them to drag anchor. This boat had the unusual name of 'Butch Cassidy' a name that no doubt causes curiosity as to why an owner would choose such a name for his boat. All sorts of possibilities spring to mind, but then it was just an idle curiosity on my part and not considered worth pursuing, after all what a person calls his boat is his business, so I returned to my beer and to the book I was currently reading. Not for long though, shortly after there was a tap on the window to attract my attention. Looking up I perceived two smiling faces a man and a woman whom I didn't know indicating that they wished to speak with me. Curious I popped my head out the hatch.

"Hi!" I said in an inquisitive manner.

"Foam core," asked the man, pointing at the hull of my boat.

"Yes," I said curious to know how he would know.

"Airex?"

"Yes," I answered, pleased and impressed at his perception.

"I thought so, with such a nice boat you would only use the best."

Pleased, and thoroughly taken with these nice people. What else could I do but invite them aboard.

"Would you care for a beer?" I asked.

"Thank you, we'll bring our own."

And so it was that my boat became inspected again, and I can only say that I can only feel immense pleasure when an interest is shown by other boaters, or anyone else for that matter, and why not it is my pride and joy and it really is a distinctive vessel.

After the introductions Patrick and Heather who were from Horseshoe Bay and heading for Prince Rupert which is quite a long way up the coast from here, the distance though has its compensations as the scenery in the Inside Passage can only be described as stunning and with a companion to share the experience, why not?

I couldn't help myself now the opportunity presented itself to ask. "Why the name, 'Butch Cassidy'?

"It wasn't my choice, it came with the boat, that is what it was called when I bought it and considered it too expensive to change the registration. I must admit to being a little weary of the many people alluding to those two romantic outlaws. But, that is life; we often get stuck with something we can do without."

Observing the companionship between these two good people gave me a twinge of regret that I was travelling alone, but then, as the man said we quite often get stuck with situations we can do without. Tomorrow would be the run home and about time too if I was entertaining regrets at this solitude.

Most of the conversation was devoted to boat building. Patrick and Heather had both been involved in the construction of a sailboat and as a consequence showed a keen interest in how my boat was put together. It was at this juncture that I cursed myself, having built this boat and written a, 'How to," book on the subject. I had been remiss in not anticipating possible interested parties.

After chatting for only a short time after they took their leave. Probably they could hear the grumbling of my insides crying out to be fed. My stomach was most probably thinking that my throat had been cut.

By bedtime the wind had still not eased, if it was still blowing in the morning it was just as well I heading south. At least the wind would be behind me going down the Johnstone strait.

Day Seventeen

For some inexplicable reason I was wide awake well before daylight with no inclination to return into the arms of Morpheus. So, out of bed was the order of the day, to find that it was only 0430, a good hour before daylight. Oh! Well may as well start the day. While the kettle was boiling the water for the morning tea I popped my head out the hatch to get an idea as to what the day might promise. The sky was obscured by cloud and the wind was as brisk as ever which brought grimness to my thoughts and a sense that it was to going to be a miserable day. Well the weather would be behind me on the run down to Chatham Point, so that was a small mercy to be thankful for as I wouldn't be shivering into a head wind.

Over the morning tea ceremony I resolved that as soon as it was light enough to see any kelp rafts or lurking logs hanging about I would take off. It was about this time that an unusual discomfort had developed in my stomach which had me wondering what I had eaten, or drunk to bring this on. The Bridie consumed the night before had tasted alright with no hint of the meat being off, but then who knows what germ might have been introduced when handled by a preparer. Anyway I wasn't long contemplating the possibilities before a dash for the pot became imperative. Strange though that there was no other symptoms like a fever that would indicate food poisoning, in fact apart from the discomfort and the need to dash I felt perfectly fine. Which clinched the decision to get a move on and get home; if I was going to be incapacitated it would not be in the wilderness.

I was pleased to note that my appetite was not affected and the breakfast of bran flakes stayed down.

This sort of happening does not make for a pleasurable trip and takes the gloss off the gingerbread so to speak, but I took comfort in the fact that this indisposition was happening at the closing days of the trip and not the beginning.

Daylight was creeping into the bay and by five-thirty it was bright enough to sight any hazards that might be in the way. The engine starting procedure is always a noisy affair as full throttle is required with the gears disengaged. The reason for this is that if the full throttle is not applied the alarms are activated, a feature of this engine type unfortunately but one which we must live with. Don't ask me why this is so, it just is.

However, with a silent thought for non disturbance for my neighbours sleeping soundly, hopefully, the engine fired with a mighty roar then the revolutions reduced to a minimum noise level immediately. During the warm up period no irate bodies emerged with curses on their lips. So all was well.

Within half an hour of the first attack another dash for the pot was called for. Oh! Boy what an outlook for the coming day's sport, it certainly promised to be an interesting day.

By the time I had cleared Port Neville it was full daylight, but what a cold miserable day it was for August. Bundled up and huddled behind the wheel didn't make for any less of the misery either. Well out into the strait and heading for Race Passage the sea had built up astern causing the boat to lift and gyrate. Fortunately the need for the potty was behind me as matters seem to have settled in that department, it wouldn't do at all to leave the wheel in conditions such as these.

Approaching the traffic separation zone off West Thurlough the seas fell away and in these more sheltered waters the effect of the wind lessened also. It was at this juncture that I observed a large cruise ship heading north which with our combined speeds soon put us to passing. Looking up at this huge wall of steel the pilot stood at the bridge wing waving down at me in a most friendly manner, but then he would as this is the custom, probably relieved that I hadn't been run down or swamped in the process of such a close encounter. With equal feeling of relief and friendliness I returned the gesture. As the 'Norwegian Sky' passed by I put the helm over to take his wake on the port bow. As the boat lifted and fell into the trough of his wake I couldn't but help think about the experience with the wake of the power boat on leaving Prideaux Haven. With a ship the size of this cruise ship one would expect a larger wake and consequently a rougher transit but this was not the case in fact much less turbulence was created. This had my imagination fired up on a fantasy involving boat designs. Which went something along these lines, if a prospective customer approached a boat builder for a power boat, could it be that different designs were offered depending on the wave criteria and how big a wake could be produced to cause the maximum distress to other boat users? No conclusions were reached on this one, but this is the sort of fantasy that one travelling alone indulges in I suppose, at least I haven't got to the stage of, 'beg your pardon', not just yet anyway.

As the morning progressed the weather improved with no sign of the expected fog, the wind died away completely and the air became warmer allowing for the shedding of a few layers of clothing. As always with this type of change in the weather one's spirits improve and this was the case in this particular instance, and it was at this time that I observed someone waving from a passing sailboat. As this person was too far away to make out with the naked eye I located the binoculars and then could see who it was. Well bless my little cotton socks it was a fellow boater with his wife from the same home marina as myself, yet one more member of the Pender Island community, it was getting to be just like old home week. This was the second person of my acquaintance met with on this perambulation, (if I could borrow the meaning of the word,) around the island. Thank goodness I was on my own and not entertaining a lady other than my wife on this trip. Just a passing thought you understand and not even a remote possibility of such an occurrence. Now that would have had the tongues wagging in such a small close knit community.

This chance meeting required a communication without a doubt, a short circling movement and a reduction in the speed brought us close enough for a chat. Wayne and Leigh McNab who spend a lot of time cruising together were now heading north to realise a dream that they had been hatching for the past twenty years and planned to take six weeks in so doing.

Expressing wonderment at this chance meeting we parted company. They were hoping to meet up with Jim Rendal, the other Pender boater I'd met at Big Bay. and with me in dire need of the pot again we parted company.

Shortly after this interlude and my toilet completed I rounded Chatham Point and headed down Discovery Passage. The sun came out to warm the day some more so off came another layer of clothing. What a nice change from yesterday and early this morning, apart from passing a deadhead the second sighted on this trip which had me wondering on the adage that things invariably happen in threes. One more deadhead and one more chance meeting with a Penderite?

The remaining part of the trip down Discovery Passage to Seymour Narrows was uneventful, no more meetings with people I neither knew nor deadheads either, just the coastline passing by with a barely perceptible increasing speed.

Once again the passage through the Narrows was made with the full flood and moving with a body of water I was beginning to feel like an old hand at this game it was so familiar.

At the narrowest part of the Narrows a boat of about eighty feet of the workboat design was attempting to come through against the flood and making heavy going of it, he didn't seem to be making much headway just stemming the tide. At least he wasn't going backwards from what I could make out so I suppose he would get through eventually. As I shot past the thought of his problems became of no account to me and I was soon in the turbulence of the Discovery Bay tide rips.

Whether or not I fancied myself as an old hand at this game of transiting turbulent waters this particular area didn't seem to be much of a concern on this occasion, there were no whirlpools to contend with to give an adrenaline rush. A piece of cake really giving a slight feeling of disappointment, well as they say if you have done a job once you are an expert. In all fairness there was the time difference between the last one and this transit. The moon phase was losing its gravitational pull and the neap tides were approaching, ergo, slower movement of the water through the narrows.

So it was then that I arrived at Discovery Bay Marina at eleven thirty just six hours after leaving Port Neville thus making an average speed over the ground of just eight knots, a most satisfying rate of progress.

On approaching the fuel dock a pleasant young man took my lines and assisted in my requirements for fuel and water, albeit the boaters are required to stick the nozzle in and perform the function of filling the tanks themselves. This is I suppose is in case of an overflow then the fuel dock attendant could not be blamed. Having said that he couldn't have been more helpful in other ways for when I suggested a smaller nozzle would be more appropriate off he went and soon returned with a nozzle of a more suitable size, and when asking for fresh water to wash down he most kindly offered soap and a brush.

"Thank you, no," I said almost pleading with him to desist from his insistent attention. "I only want to wash the salt off."

"There is the hose, sir; you just turn the hose on with this valve," pointing to a ball valve, "Just help yourself and if there is anything else you require please let me know." And off he went to attend to another boat that was approaching no doubt to give equally attentive service.

One can't be but pleased at the attitude of these young people who take on these obviously low paid summer jobs. Both the Ozzie lad at Big Bay and this young man here couldn't have been more courteous and helpful.

At this time of day a stopover at this delightful haven was, alas, not to be considered as it was much too early as this old horse was beginning to smell the stable and the urge to get on was dominating my thoughts, so by twelve of the clock I was passing through the breakwater and heading south.

The Georgia Strait compared to Johnstone Strait was like comparing chalk to cheese. Here, heading as yet to an undecided destination the air was still and balmy and the sun hot, compared to the Johnstone Strait during the disagreeable morning which was rough and very cold, not the weather one could expect at this season of the year, though all part of life's rich pageant, and when the sun shines these discomforts are soon forgotten.

So it was then that chugging along at an economical revolution I was still making good time. With plotting progress with the GPS by three in the afternoon and still on reduced revs the speed was a touch over eight knots and French Creek not very far away. This port was foremost in my deliberations for an overnight stopover but, on second thoughts the idea was abandoned as on a previous occasion I was most fortunate in getting a berth at all and that in a slot for a sixty foot boats only. The place was so crowded boats were rafted up four and five abreast. All this contrary to the published dock guide which states that during the fishing season there are lots of berths for the transient boater.

The estimated time to reach French Creek would be seven in the evening and had there been no possibility of getting a berth, what then? It would be a long run to any other alternative haven and much too late in the day to be a sensible decision. It was on this premise that Lasquieti was decided upon.

With this decision made I made a sandwich and a cup of tea and enjoyed this repast seated in the cockpit in the sunshine. Ah! Ain't life wonderfully sublime when one cannot see into the future?

On checking the Tide Tables for Dodd Narrows which I planned to transit on the morrow at slack water so the decision to stop over at Lasquieti made sense as the run down the Strait would then place me there comfortably at a reasonable time to make the transit.

It is always a conundrum when planning to stay at a place of repose in the boating world anyway. Where on earth does one stay in a strange place? There are many bays on Lasquieti that would be suitable and on this particular occasion there would be no agonising as to what would be the choice. It had been a long tiring day and I was getting very weary. So what better choice then the nearest? As it turned out, not a fortuitous choice, False Bay.

False Bay was a new experience for me so after carefully consulting the chart for possible dangers I entered close to the south shore giving Jeffrey Rock a wide berth, and. bearing in mind problems that might arise from the noted Qualicum winds anchored in twenty feet of water close to the north part of the bay tucked behind Higgens Island for shelter should it start to blow.

It had been a long day, thirteen hours from Port Neville after a very early start, not to mention the upset tummy, which now thankfully seemed to have settled down after the third potty run and ceased to be a consideration since then. I poured myself a generous Grouse and began to unwind. So it was then that come eight o'clock I stirred my stumps and started dinner. I had fond memories of the earlier delight of eggs and bacon of a few days ago which would not involve any great effort to produce and as this was to be my last supper on this journey, why not relive this culinary pleasure?

Now this is where fate revealed itself to my everlasting amazement, this was to be my last meal of this Odyssey and would you believe here lying before me was my last carrot? Now if that wasn't an extraordinary coincidence I don't know what is. Coincidences on this trip had become the norm rather than not, so accept. So it was then that in this happy frame of mind I prepared the last evening meal of bacon, eggs, potato, peas and carrot, with only one glass of wine as I had other plans for the evening.

The remains of the day, therefore, where I devoted to the last of the scotch which provided only two trips around the buoy, before turning in tired but happy for a well earned night's sleep, content with my achievements of the past couple of weeks thankfully without any moments of alarm and immediately zonked.

DAY EIGHTEEN

As usual at this time of year, and as I've stated before, many times, I come awake when daylight arrives. This day was a little different though for at one o'clock in the morning I came awake with a shock. Standing next to my bunk was a Coastguard officer, booted and spurred so to speak in heavy weather survival gear.

"Whaa?" mumbled I.

"Sir, you dragged anchor."

This announcement brought me upright and out of bed in a trice, and making my way to the cockpit in the gloom of early morning where several like dressed gentlemen waited my arrival, and one in the inflatable tied up alongside. I was stopped on my way to the cockpit by whom I took to be the man in charge and requested to fire the engine then get some clothes on. An excellent idea as the night air was quite chilly standing around in my underwear amongst men in survival suits had a touch of the ridiculous.

The near disaster of probably ending up on the rocks I was informed was prevented by a gentleman on another boat whom I had bumped into in my journey across the bay. He claimed that he had tried without success to waken me so had called the Coastguard at French Creek. In silently thanking my unknown saviour I couldn't help but wonder and asked myself the questions, just how hard and by what method had he tried to wake me, although I allowed that I must have been dead to the world after the long trip down from Port Neville, and also if I had bump into him surely he could have put a line on my boat to stop the drift until he had woken me? These questions I asked myself should not be considered an ungracious criticism rather to clarify my curiosity. And I do thank him for calling the coastguard for assistance.

Apparently, the wind had increased causing the anchor to drag. Even so, with forty feet of chain and a goodly amount of line assessed at being twenty feet, i.e. three times the depth of water should have been enough to hold the boat. No doubt the anchorage didn't provide a good holding ground. The amount of chain and line would have been self evident to the officer who helped me bring the anchor on board had he been interested, so there could be no criticism that insufficient line was out. Three times the depth plus a bit more to give a spring is the accepted norm.

However they soon had me moored securely alongside the Public Dock at the seaplane berth, which with an amused thought I reflected that had I moored there instead of anchoring I would have soon been told to move. Still in these wee small hours it was most unlikely that there would be a seaplane needing the berth.

On being interviewed by the officer in charge certain questions were asked apart from the above, which had me somewhat puzzled by the nature of them and wondering as to what they had to do with dragging anchor.

"Was I on medication?"

"No."

"Name, address, telephone number?"

This information supplied and in an attempt to find out what they needed this for, and out of curiosity mind, I asked if I was to be charged for their time. I wasn't and there was no explanation forthcoming as to why they wanted to know if I was taking medication either. Thinking it prudent to drop the matter I kept silent, not that I would have objected to being charged for their time as they had acted in a prompt and professional manner throughout the whole exercise in preventing my boat going onto the rocks or drifting out into the channel trailing sixty feet of anchor rode.

After they had left I thought for a moment, only a moment mind you, wondering how to spend the rest of the night. Should I take off home or go back to bed? As it wasn't yet two o'clock I decided to take the bed option even though I was much disillusioned with this False Bay, at least the boat was securely moored now and not likely to be going anywhere. Much to my surprise, as my brain was working overtime sleep overtook me in no time at all.

On waking a little before daylight my stomach was warning me to be prepared for a change in the daily routine. As it turned out I was able to make the morning tea before making the dash. Obviously I had picked up something, a bug maybe, on these travels but, I could only wonder where as there had been no diversion from my eating habits in the past two days, all food had been cooked by yours truly from food bought mostly from home. Maybe the stress from motoring all the way from Port Neville and the incident of anchor dragging mostly brought it on. No matter I would be home today, and if it is a problem then medication could soon sort this problem out, Imodium please.

As daylight was creeping into the bay I left Lasquieti vowing that this would be the first and last time I would seek shelter here, False Bay is well named.

The morning was still without a breath of wind, and except for the disturbance caused by my progress the sea was like glass. A nice day was in the offing.

My estimated time of arrival at Dodd narrows was a little out, but no matter as half an hour either side of slack water didn't make much difference as there is a lull between tides of about half an hour anyway and as the tide was to turn to the ebb that would be to my advantage.

This time I was the only boat making the transit, a definite plus. On a previous occasion there were so many boats pushing and shoving to get through at slack water from both directions that there was much cause for alarm. Quite unnecessary were the antics of some of these boaters. Power boaters I might add who seem to have little or no regard for any other boat in the vicinity making rapid and un-indicated alterations of course to cut across the bows of others, with the accompanying mini tsunamis from their wakes that if they had any sense or knowledge of the rule of the road they would have kept to the starboard side of the channel until well clear and proceeded with a moderate speed.

But then no license is required to operate a boat, unlike a car which is mandatory. Strange that, in my experience there are more idiots in charge of boats that you can shake a stick at, even those flying the Power Boat Squadron flag. More times than I care to mention I've had to take evasion action to avoid a probable collision when I had the right of way.

The un-initiated in the ways of the sea may wonder why it is necessary a transit of a passage like Dodd Narrows should be made at slack water or nearly so. Well, if I may state the obvious when a flow of water meets a narrowing of an immovable object such as the coastline the water has to move faster to get through this restricted opening. This increased velocity can and does in most cases create dangerous whirlpools and eddies which it is wise for a small craft to stay away from until a calmer moment when the tide eases off and ready to go in the opposite direction, i.e. slack water.

There are many openings between the islands of British Columbia and everyone should be approached with respect after careful consultation with the Tide Tables.

So it was then that after the transit progress was made through familiar waters that I had sailed many times, sailed being the figurative word as almost invariably there was not enough wind to actually sail and motoring was the necessary means of propulsion on these occasions. In effect this was a tried and trusted stamping ground if one may use the phrase in a maritime setting.

The day was clear and the water was wide so the Autopilot had the responsibility of guiding us, my floating chariot and me, as we progressed down Trincomali Channel as we had done so many times before. While sitting in my favourite seat just inside the cabin entrance, which gave an un-restricted visibility through the wrap around windows enjoying a cup of coffee and a muffin, and all the while keeping a sharp lookout for those lurking logs and at the same time enjoying the scenery.

The autopilot, in these sheltered waters could be trusted to steer the boat and not flip the breaker and as I had put a slack lashing on the wheel as a back-up, belt and braces one might say, I felt at peace with the world and took this much earned relaxation with confidence. In this relaxed mood I decided to take a different route homeward.

This new direction took me to the west of the Secretary Islands and east of Kuyper and Thetis. It was quiet out here with very little traffic to bother with. How different this was from having to cling to the wheel for hours on end on the Pacific side of Vancouver Island. It is on these wonderful days in BC that I can find peace within myself. My mind kicks into a happy mode unadulterated with my usual opinionated thoughts on solving the world's problems. Even the loonies with their personal agendas and the so called experts with their theories on global warming trouble me not. Ah! Happy days. How wonderful it is to live in this glorious country.

Off Norfolk Island I sighted an unusual object. I say unusual because one doesn't normally see a white pole riding upright in the water. I estimate that upper part of this pole to be three feet out of the water and closing this object I could make out the lettering or what remained of it, the wave action had probably eroded parts of the name. The top letter, as the word was written top to bottom looked like a '3' then 'I', 'I', 'I'. The meaning of this dawned on me then because I knew the story behind this the full name came to me immediately. This was a marker for Biddle Rock.

Some years ago a friend of mine related a story of how he had hit an uncharted rock in this area which had sunk his boat. The Coast Guard had arrived on the scene in double quick time on receiving his 'Mayday' call, bless those intrepid gentlemen, to find Ken Biddle clutching a teapot the only item he could save, being an Englishman this incident spoke volumes. Well to cut a long story short Ken Biddle had this rock officially named after him. Shortly after this tale was related to me, me being of little faith, but of an inquisitive mind, I searched the charts of this area to try and locate a rock named Biddle with no success. Over the years I had more or less put the matter out of my mind but, here it was, Biddle Rock, the marker a little worn but large as life. Unfortunately, Ken no longer lives on Pender and has passed from my acquaintance and unable to tell him of this co-incidence.

So it was then with plenty to think about the journey south progressed with each mile getting us closer to home. Surprising myself on passing Wallace Island with no more than a glance, this island at one time during my earlier days of sailing these waters was a preferred destination where I had enjoyed many hours socialising with friends and hiking the trails. Over the years as I became more adventurous seeking wider horizons this lovely island was by-passed for places further afield. The fact is that Conover Cove had become so popular and crowded it would be difficult to find a place to park the boat added to the decline of interest, being a Marine Park the powers that be have realised that the place is now a source of income charging for the privilege of being here overnight.

On approaching Captain's Passage these reveries came to an end and time to man the wheel for the run across Swanson Channel to the home marina and journeys end. Not without a final rude intrusion from power boat wakes. On this occasion from four in line astern all of the same design. No doubt a club outing oblivious to the curses and fist waving from the boater in torment from the confused seas their passage created. For this I could now mouth my usual expletive in the plural.

Just as I was entering Swanson Channel a brisk breeze sprang up, an ideal situation for sailing. Now isn't that Sod's Law? After motoring all the way around Vancouver Island it is only on the last lap of three miles does a situation arise to put this sail boat through its paces? Tough, with only three more miles to go I had no intention of changing the mode of transportation so it was a case of motoring on.

So it was then that I arrived home with a great feeling of achievement and a sense of well being over the challenge. I hadn't found myself, as what was suggested I might do on this trip. But then I wasn't lost, and had no idea where I should have looked anyway as one is supposed to do under these circumstances.

After mooring in my appointed slip I walked along the dock towards the telephone booth to phone home for a ride and let them know I had arrived safe and sound when a voice accosted me.

"Been away have you, Ron?"

Looking around and upwards I sighted a fellow marina resident clinging half way up the mast of his boat.

"Yeah, just been around Vancouver Island."

"How long did it take you?

"This is the eighteenth day. What are you up to? No pun intended."

"Fixing this Radar reflector."

"Doesn't look like much." I observed, noting the frailty of the object. "Does it work?"

"It's the latest design and more efficient than a lump of tin hanging off the rigging."

"Ah!"

And so it was that this great adventure came to a close with so casual a comment.

REFLECTIONS

On completing the narrative and re-reading what is contained in the body of the Kirk so to speak I was struck by a number of impressions from this trip. The first being the warmth and friendliness of the fellow boaters I met with on this same odyssey albeit in opposite directions. The small act of taking a mooring line could lead to a generously warm attitude completely out of proportion to this simple gesture. These kindnesses that I met with both pleased and perplexed me, I say this because I have often been told that because I seldom smile I give the impression of being aloof. Well that is as maybe. I know in myself that unless an introduction has been made I feel it rude to impose myself on other people and generally speaking that introduction should have come from a third party. It is because of this hang-up that I have I therefore quite often keep to myself.

Never-the-less I believe I do respond favourably to others even to the point of talking too much at times. This could be blamed on two things, the length of time I spend on my own and secondly the effect of a drink or two. Should any of the nice people that showed kindness to this sinner be reading this narrative then with my whole heart I apologise for any presumptions I might have made on your company.

Why boaters should warm to strangers I can only imagine. Could it be I wonder an underlying pride in the ownership of their particular vessels that prompts this outgoing warmth, for myself I am always pleased to show people around my boat. (That is if they have been introduced.) This point of protocol may seem to be a bit stuffy but that is how I was brought up. Wait until you are asked. Don't push yourself on others. Don't interrupt when others are talking. Good Heavens! I can still here my mother voicing these admonishments to me as a child, particularly when it came to an offering of cakes, I would mentally cringe when the cake I particularly fancied was on the far side of the cake stand as I was always told to take the one nearest to me as it was rude to reach. What cruelties parents unknowingly impose on their offspring.

Having made that observation I'll allow that there are exceptions to the rule as in all things, no less the boating community. What comes to mind are boaters that are renters or give that impression from the way they handle a boat. These people do not seem to have a confidence in what they are doing as though unfamiliar with their charge which shows in the apparent lack of confidence. Or conversely those that obviously haven't any idea but behave as though they are expert sailors. Then there are those that have big power boats where they and their guests sit around on the top deck sipping their drinks looking down on us lesser beings, or tearing around at high speeds creating noise and disturbing the ocean into bow waves that give moments of alarm to small boats.

What really does bother me, and I view this subject with alarm, are those irresponsible people who rent a boat and have no idea what they are up to in matters nautical.

A few years ago when with a group of friends rafted up in Montague Harbour on the last day of our cruise, three boats rafted together sitting comfortably at anchor enjoying the late evening watching the sun go down with the obligatory companionable drink. Another boat was observed with a large group of teenagers on board ranging widely about the anchorage. In due course as this boat came alongside our group it was patently obvious that they had too much anchor line out probably with the range of swing across the anchorage they had paid out to the bitter end. However, this young kid started to berate one of my friends, a man with of vast experience in the subject of boating, accusing him of dragging his anchor. The fact that the tide was contrary to what could have made this possible, or for that matter of insufficient strength, seemed to have passed unnoticed to this callow youth who was told in no uncertain terms and much to his obvious chagrin just what the situation was and duly advised to shorten his anchor line.

Earlier, during the course of the afternoon this particular boat was heard to be having a detailed conversation with what transpired to be a companion vessel and this on Channel 16, the channel reserved for calling and the handling of distress messages only. As it transpired there was an actual distress being handled at the time by the Coastguard. And would these kids get off this frequency? Not on your Nellie. All this lack of following the laid down procedures begs the question. Why is it that a person who wishes to drive a car must first prove competency before getting a licence yet inexplicably get into a boat without proving responsibility to be a possible threat to others? There are courses run by Power Boat Squadrons but these are not mandatory. The examination is based on the multi-choice system which seems to me to defeat the whole purpose of an examination, just take an educated guess at what the answer would be. Even passing the course and holding the required certificate does not prove competency either.

The most profound emotion that I came home with was the respect for the resolve, dedication and fortitude of the early explorers on this coast. Whom, to borrow that modern expression: 'To boldly go where no other has gone before.' These dedicated seamen not knowing what dangers could be met with, neither nautical nor native, made thorough and comprehensive surveys of what, in this instance, is the west coast of North America in general and British Columbia in particular. Starting with Francis Drake in 1579, whose contempt for the Spanish claims to the whole Pacific as their own private lake named the coast and hinterland from just north of San Francisco Bay to Alaska, New Albion and claimed it for Queen Elizabeth the First. Not that anything could become of this claim as the area was too remote from England to colonise and would have to wait another two hundred years for James Cook to regenerate an interest, and only that for the benefits of the fur trade.

The old Greek pilot Juan de Fuca with his claim to have sailed from the Pacific to the Atlantic in these waters in 1592, rightfully disclaimed by Spain, is never-the-less remembered by the Strait between Vancouver Island and Washington State by bearing his name.

James Cook of course whose expedition to finally prove or disprove the existence of a passage over the top of North America after stopping at Nootka Sound for repairs continued on until stopped by ice charting the coast up to and including the Aleutians and coast of the Bering Sea. This presence along with Spanish fears of encroachment by the Russians into the north Pacific prompted them to send their navigators, Malaspina, (Italian), Hecate, Valdez, Galiano, Perez, to establish title to this area by charting and surveying the coast during the years 1774 to 1792, thus giving credibility to their claim.

The credit for the most comprehensive surveys and charting of the British Columbia coast during this period of exploration goes without doubt to George Vancouver's expedition and the dedicated officers under his guidance and command in the years 1792 to 1795.

Having myself journeyed in these same waters they had charted, although much less comprehensively equipped with the latest navigation aids than I had, filled me with admiration for their achievements. Not for them the sophisticated satellite navigation systems and up to date charts. Everything they had was basic and a continuous challenge. The whole coastline had the sameness about it, trees, trees and more trees and rocks to lie in wait to ground the unwary. No pubs to visit and break the monotony of being cooped up in their ships, relying on the local habitants to provide fresh provisions. It is no wonder that Vancouver named the Sound on the mainland side of Georgia Strait, Desolation Sound, there where very few indigenous people and an even greater scarcity of provisions.

They did get ashore of course now and again for relaxation and exercise not always to their advantage though if one bears in mind the incident at Flea Village, mentioned in a previous chapter. The other problem they had to contend with, that we now know the danger of which is fully understood and warnings posted is, Red Tide. This is caused by pollutants in the water that affect bi-valves. The eating of which on Johnstone's boat survey of the Strait named for him resulted in most of the boat crew being poisoned, which only by purging with hot water had any results in divesting them of this, unfortunately, with one man dying.

On the plus side they had little or no problems with the indigenous people.

The trials and tribulations that these early explorers must have endured and the admiration for their achievements that they invoked in me is, I believe, the most memorable of this circum-navigation.

INTERVAL

During the next three years after the circumnavigation of Vancouver Island many smaller adventures were undertaken, but none of any great interest to relate. These were shorter trips more suited to taking our dart team to neighbouring island for matches, and maybe now and again to Sidney for shopping or trips of this nature, nothing of great moment.

So it was then that this proved to be the last time I would travel far and wide in these waters on my own for any extended period. What with all the time I had spent on the boat by myself and the time spent away from my spouse each having developed our own interests it came as no surprise that a separation of a permanent nature came about, and we went our separate ways.

As a result of this break-up the germ of an idea that had been presented to me while building the boat took seed and blossomed. 'Get away and circumnavigate the world.' To this I devoted my time in getting ready and preparing for this grand adventure.

A HOLE IN THE OCEAN

In the folk law of the boating community a boat is said to be a hole in the ocean into which one forever throws money

Now, land and life, finale, and farewell!
Now Voyager departs! (Much, much for there is yet in store;)
Often enough hast thou adventur'd o'er the seas,
Cautiously cruising, studying the charts,
Duly again in port, and hawser's tie, returning:
But now obey, thy cherished secret wish,
Embrace thy friends-leave all in order;
To port, and hawser's tie, no more returning,
Depart upon the endless cruise, old sailor!

"Now Finale to the Shore," from Walt Whitman's Leaves of Grass, 1871/1891.

Part Two

Chapter One
Preparation

... chance favours only the prepared mind
Louis Pasteur

"I don't want you to go."

The intensity of the statement made me look at her with surprise. It had never occurred to me that anyone cared enough to worry about my taking this trip. But then for the last several months I had been totally absorbed in the planning and the purchasing of the extra equipment needed for a single handed round the world voyage to consider much else.

With as much re-assurance that I could muster I reached out and grasped her arm, and smiled. "I'll be alright, don't worry."

If anything the concern deepened. "It's dangerous, and I don't want you to go."

"Life is dangerous, and there have been many that have done this single handed thing before." I looked at her, willing an understanding. Then with a touch of asperity, I said, "You forget I've spent my whole working life at sea."

Her look didn't change any. And it made me feel uncomfortable. To give me time to think I looked away and scanned the Marina, resting my gaze on my boat at the far end of the dock. 'Ron's Endeavour', a forty foot sloop of van de Statd design. This boat was built with a foam core hull, a strong construction and was a fine sea boat. And I had no qualms about taking off in such a vessel.

The boat was so named by my wife. Endeavour was Captain Cook's ship on his first voyage of discovery to the Pacific, and as I have an abiding interest in all things Cook, what better name?

This diversion gave me time to reflect on a previous conversation with a neighbour who was also concerned about me going of into the wild blue ocean. This lady believed that sea creatures had human qualities. In this particular instance a memory of hurt and revenge being the topic. She was convinced of this to the point of being concerned that I could maybe be attacked by a whale or some other sea creature that had suffered injury by some other person. A Moby Dick situation one would assume no doubt. When a person has such convictions, and although one doesn't necessarily agree, one can only respect the concern. And I don't mind saying this premise stuck in my mind.

'Good heavens,' I thought. 'If there is this much concern from both these friends, it is just as well there isn't someone with a deeper and more personal relationship in my life.'

Turning again and thinking a note of humour might ease the situation, "Come on now, lighten up," I said, breezily. "You know how it is when you are young? You feel that you can do anything and will live forever."

At least the look of concern went, only to be replaced by exasperation, then a pitying shake of the head. "For goodness sake, Ron, you are seventy-one." At this she couldn't help but laugh. A short derisive laugh maybe, but at least it eased the situation.

"I still don't like the idea of you going."

I nodded trying, to understand her concern. "You know my situation. There is nothing here for me now." If I stayed I would have to put up with people gossiping about my wife and I having split up. Already there was a cock-eyed rumour going around about our finances, as if that was any concern to anyone but us. That's the Island for you. A small community thrives on gossip. They do say that if you haven't heard a rumour by 10 o'clock in the morning, then start one.

There was a time during the past few months when I questioned the wisdom of what I was planning. But that was purely financial. Having purchased high priced items necessary for an off shore venture, I baulked at having to spend even more. By then the money had been spent and the equipment would have been of no use had I not gone deep sea. After all, a life-raft may be of some use, should the expedition be abandoned but, certainly not necessary in close waters when equipped with an inflatable dinghy. A Hydrovane self steering system? A sea-anchor with six hundred feet of one inch nylon line? Certainly these would not be necessary in the enclosed waters of British Columbia either. And a Satellite telephone would have been a luxury on this coast. However, I consoled myself by the conviction that the expenditure was one off and before the voyage was over my financial state would be less parlous. Ah! Yes. 'The best laid schemes, o' mice and men gang aft agley', to quote Robbie Burns. But then one cannot foretell the future.

Insurance for the boat was not forth-coming as no company would insure unless there were at least four people on board. Which begs the question: How can one sail single-handed with four people on board? Once the word was out that I was setting out around the world via all the exotic places there were many people wanting to come along but all were politely turned down. In my present frame of mind I didn't want to be bothered with people. In one case a female acquaintance became quite insistent on coming along and was only dissuaded by a mutual friend who made it quite clear that it wasn't all cocktails in the cockpit. When told of this, I couldn't help remarking that sometimes one had to go below for cocktails if the weather was bad. Fortunately the issue was dropped without me having to become rude. Medical insurance was not forth-coming either. Yes, this was possible, but the premiums would have been prohibitive. And let's face it. Would a doctor come out to the middle of the Pacific should I need medical assistance? In cases like these one must weigh the risks and make a decision. A recent kidney infection got me thinking on medical lines but, as they say lightning doesn't strike in the same place twice. One concession I did make was to get a prescription for pain killers, just in case I was hurt badly.

It was my intention to set off the middle of April, after the Spring Equinox and the expected gales which are prevalent at this time of year. This plan fell through almost immediately as I was laid up with the aforementioned kidney infection. As this was accompanied with a fever of 103, this delay was most fortuitous. Then there came the business with the lawyers dealing with the legal separation. This became a most trying and frustrating time, which delayed departure until early May.

So here we were, we two, one convinced I was nuts, the other believing it was probably true but going on this adventure anyway.

"You'll see me off on Saturday, won't you?"

"Yes, of course." Not too happily, I surmised.

****

Planning a blue water cruise is no small task. There are so many things to think of, and so many pieces of equipment to check. When there is only one brain dealing with these problems then it is no surprise that something will get left out and especially when there is an urgent desire to get the show on the road, so to speak.

Purchasing and fitting the big, expensive items took priority in the early stages, particularly the Hydrovane steering system as this required hauling the boat. Fitting the brackets to carry this equipment could be done in the water, but is not advisable, for the obvious reasons that something may be dropped in the water and possibly lost. After hauling the boat, cleaning and painting the bottom with anti-fouling paint can be carried out to deter marine growth becoming attached to the hull and creating a drag. A topside coat of paint also gives a well maintained look to the boat. Checking the cooling water and service intakes for blockage and, if necessary, clearing; checking the propeller; securing nuts for tightness, and the rudder for slackness in the seals; are small but important jobs that can only be done at this time.

There are quite a few self steering systems on the market, and no doubt they all have their good points. I chose Hydrovane particularly for the fact that there are no lines leading into and cluttering the cockpit. In fact it steers the boat quite independently of the boat's integral steering capabilities. When the boat is put on the required course and the vane positioned to the wind for steering, it is only required for the boats rudder to be set to counter the pressure on the boat's bow. If the boat tends to go off course the wind on the vane alters, causing it to compensate the self steering rudder, so bringing the boat back on course. It is almost like having the three extra people on board that the insurance company required. The message being: If a long sea passage is planned then don't leave home without one. In life not everything is perfect, and in this, even this wonderful device needs to be watched, as I later found out. That, however, didn't detract from the Hydrovane's efficiency.

The rigging of the Satellite phone antennae, fixing the life-raft and arranging the sea-anchor parachute and rode was just a matter of course and proceeded without any problems. It must be said though that a bulky life-raft and a sea-anchor with six hundred feet of rode hanging off the cockpit rails caused a bit of a clutter, albeit arranged on the port side only. But then, safety at sea is paramount and some clutter would be willingly tolerated during this adventure.

In the event of a storm, a set of fibreglass shutters were fabricated and bolted to the forward facing windows. The design of the boat called for windows on three sides of the cabin and made allowance for the fact that should a storm develop the boat would be heading into the wind and therefore only the forward facing windows would bear the brunt of the weather. Although I had been assured that the glass was guaranteed to withstand a solid object being hurled against it with a wind of hurricane force, I felt compelled to take out this extra insurance. The shutters could easily be removed for maintenance if required, or to enjoy sunnier climes.

It was during this preparation time that I had to engage a lawyer to represent my case regarding a separation agreement with my wife. It was the start of April, and as I was nearly ready to leave this became a source of irritation. However, this delay as it turned out, was a blessing in disguise, a double whammy even. Quite by surprise I was taken with the aforementioned kidney infection and laid low with a fever. Even taking a pee was a slow, uncomfortable process. During this enforced stay a violent storm passed through our area. My boat was determined to leave the dock without me by parting its mooring lines. Fortunately, a group of fellow boat owners came to the rescue as I was laid low and put out extra lines, securing the boat safely to the dock.

The local marina is usually sheltered, with the prevailing winds being from the SW and giving shelter on all sides but one. On this occasion the wind from the NW exposed the marina entrance to the elements, and as my boat was on the last finger it took the brunt of the wind and the seas that surged around the breakwater.

April rolled by with the interminable delays with the lawyers doing their thing. The good side was, with the help of antibiotics my infection had cleared up. Waiting is always frustrating when on the threshold of something eagerly anticipated and, in this case, there was the added concern of getting to Panama and through the Canal in time to cross the Caribbean and the Atlantic before the hurricane season. 'If you can wait, and not be tired by waiting', to quote Kipling. That is a comfort of sorts I suppose and as there was no alternative then one must put up with a little frustration. All things come to an end sometime and by the beginning of May I had the clearance to leave. All that remained to do was the storing of provisions. This was the first occasion when the gremlins struck.

On this Saturday morning, the planned day of departure, my friend was helping bring on board the frozen provisions, and much to my relief no mention of her not wanting me to go came up in the conversation. She had probably accepted the inevitable. Most of these items were meats accumulated over the past few months won at the Legion meat draw, and also the frozen vegetables purchased for the trip. It was now that the deep freezer refused to operate. On checking the compressor I found that the fuse had blown. This prompted a dash to the service centre for replacement fuses. As it turned out this was not the problem. The freezer still didn't work. As it was a weekend there was no chance of getting a fridge technician to check it out. Besides, all the people who were coming down to see me off at the allotted time would start to show within the hour. To send them away was not a consideration, and I wasn't prepared to have another delay. On discussing the problem we decided to get blocks of ice and hope the products would last for a few days and delay the inevitable spoiling. Some small items would go into the fridge freezer section and keep frozen that way. After a trip to the grocery store for tinned meat, I felt life wouldn't be too hard. A food freezer was a luxury anyway and I resolved to carry on without it.

So it was then that the trip would start without a freezer.

At ten o'clock quite a crowd of friends and well-wishers had gathered on the dock. I'm not considered to be an emotional sort, but I was quite flattered by this gathering and some people that I would never have thought would be present turned up, and it was quite touching. After hugs with the ladies and handshakes with the men I went on board with the many gifts from these good people. The muffins, the wine, and the single malt scotch more than made up for the loss of frozen meat, as these were given out of friendship.

The lines were cast off and putting the engine on slow ahead I eased the boat around the end of the dock. With many waves of farewell I was off on the odyssey of my life.

CHAPTER TWO
British Columbia to Panama

Now voyager, sail thou forth, to seek and find
Walt Whitman, The untold want

The first part of this momentous adventure was from my home base to Oak Bay Marina, on Vancouver Island, a matter of only four, maybe five hours motoring. There I took on fuel and water, and spent the last but one night in the bunk before Panama.

Maybe I shouldn't refer to a home base, as on the expiry of the yearly contract I had given up the right to the berth my boat had occupied. This relinquishment had caused some discussion as I could have kept the rights to the berth by continuing the payments, and been assured of a place when I returned. The Marina was part of the housing sub-division and as such was private to those who owned property and lived there full time. The fees were nominal; other boat owners would use my slip while I was away, and I would be assured of a berth on my return. I gave this some consideration, but rejected it on the grounds of the length of time I anticipated being away, and the possibility that I might not return. This thought could be called a premonition, although a possibility would be a better description. Besides, due to the terms of the separation agreement I didn't own any property anyway, which made the whole exercise academic.

When some distance away into Swanson Channel I turned and took one last look at the Island that had been my home for the last eighteen years, it must be said that there was no deep emotion attached to this. Just a look, as one does on these occasions. I'd had a good life there, but it was time for the next part of my life, and to find out what that would hold. The weather was fine, with hardly any wind and the waters calm, glassy almost. The clear skies and warming sun cheered me on my way. So it was goodbye Pender for a while.

Life was good; contentment was creeping in, as it always did when I was at sea. I had travelled these waters many times over the past few years and they were familiar enough to have no special interest apart from which route to take amongst the many islands that dotted this part of the world. As it was to be some time before I sailed these waters again, and as the tides were favourable, I decided on transiting John Channel and pass close by the town of Sidney, and then James Channel to transit Merry Channel into Oak Bay and the marina there. This route would be close enough to the shore to have one last look at this wonderful part of the B.C. coast and to store in the memory bouquet. Could I be inadvertently storing nostalgia I wondered? Time to put on the autopilot and make a cup of tea.

By early afternoon I was passing through Merry Channel, and today the usual turbulence from the tide rips wasn't too bad. The steering, had to be constantly corrected as the up-welling eddies pushed the bow one way then the other. It is a short passage into the Bay so we were soon through and heading towards the marina. The Bay is dotted with several small islands, most of which are not much bigger than rocks which must be avoided, or one could, embarrassingly, come to grief. Although I had been through here on several occasions I still felt the need, and the mental security, of steering with my eyes on the chart and directing my course accordingly. Occasionally an open boat propelled by a roaring outboard motor would hurtle by at high speed, leaving me rocking in its wake. No doubt they knew where they were going. Oh! For such familiar optimism.

Before long I was tied up to the fuel dock and attended to by a pleasant fellow of middle age. This I found interesting. Usually the dock-jocks are much younger. I don't suppose it matters one way or the other in this modern day of political correctness. There wouldn't be any discrimination here in a marina than anywhere else I suppose. But then it is noticeable when faced with the unfamiliar. He was very pleasant, helpful and chatty.

"Nice boat," he said, with a look of wistful envy. "Where are you going?"

"Panama, first. Then hopefully around the world."

"I'm going to do that one day." Then as an afterthought. "I guess I'll have to get a boat though."

This statement gave me cause for reflection.

"You could always crew for someone," I said, trying to be helpful.

"Yeah, that's true. Maybe I should take sailing lessons, though."

I looked at him for a moment as he gazed into the distance. He was thinking no doubt of sailing away to tropical climes.

"Yes, that might help." I offered.

The conversation threatened to become ridiculous at this point, and as the fuelling was completed I busied myself with handing the hose back to him and securing the filling cap.

The fuel tank arrangement consisted of a 50 gallon main, and a 25 gallon secondary. Over the past year or so, long before this planned voyage, the secondary tank had been used for the warm air cabin heating system and the diesel fuel content had been gradually diluted with kerosene. Kerosene is a much better fuel for the heater as the summer diesel available in BC is likely to gum up the works. However, with kerosene being mixed in with diesel this tank now contained fuel that was not recommended for the engine, and as I would be operating in warmer climes this tank and its contents as a consequence became extra to requirements. All the effort to convert to the heating system did seem like a good idea at the time.

"I need a berth for the night," I remarked to the dock jock.

"Sure. I'll just check with the office." With this he pulled out his walkie-talkie and made the arrangements.

The berth that I was assigned was a bit of a squeeze with forty feet of boat to manoeuvre around a tight turn, and the wind picking up didn't help any. After a couple of tries at getting in bow first and not doing much good a stern first finagling did the trick with helping hands taking the mooring lines.

Securely moored it was time to take on water. There were two tanks on board, one on each side of the fuel tank compartment, interconnected, and both holding a hundred gallons each. I had been assured by experienced deep water sailors that water was never a problem, but then, I had the capacity. So why not use it?

So, by early evening the boat was fuelled and watered. Being well aware of my cooking skills I considered taking a walk and one last meal ashore. However, on reflection it would be sensible to cook at least one piece of meat before it went off, and there were frozen vegetables that would soon become inedible. There was still time to go and pay the Marina dues before the office closed though, and so stretch the legs before making a decision about the evening meal.

*****

Being a morning person it was no problem to wake up as soon as it started to get light, have the usual cups of tea, breakfast and potty time and be ready to leave. Having stayed in this Marina on previous occasions I took the precaution of not accepting a key for the gate as this was on deposit and the office didn't open until seven o'clock. To hang about so the key could be returned was not a considered option.

The wind had died over night and the morning air was still with not a soul moving about. When I started the engine I was concerned whether nearby boaters would be startled from their bunks this peaceful Sunday morning. To avoid the engine alarms doing their irritating thing it is necessary to first put the disengaged throttle on full power before switching on. The initial roar is a unique feature of the Volvo Penta. It likes a boost of revolutions when first starting to reset the alarms. Immediately on firing I returned the throttle to neutral and the engine was set for operation. No irate bodies appeared demanding to know what the racket was all about, so, it was just a case of slipping the moorings and moving out of the berth and onto the next stage of the adventure.

The air was cool as I moved out into the channel and I put on a warm jacket. The sun was coming up though, so it promised to be a warm day.

It was just a short run out of Oak Bay and to the Trial Islands. The tides were once again favourable. To take the shorter route between these islands and the near shore would save the best part of an hour on the passage to Port Renfrew some sixty miles away.

As the early morning had promised, it was turning out to be a lovely day. A little cool out on the water but out of the breeze the sun was warming and pleasant. Apart from the occasional recreational fishermen there was not much to take note of and I was absorbed by the scenic shores of lower Vancouver Island. Coffee time came around at ten o'clock, and having restrained my desires up until now, I could sample one of those wonderful muffins Bertie and Pammy had given me. And what a delight they were. I was hard pressed to restrict myself to only one. It would be a long trip and only right that the pleasures should be prolonged as long as possible. High fibre they were too, so it made sense to spread the load as one might say. No pun intended.

The morning passed quickly. Then lunch came with a cold meat and salad. Afternoon progressed with nothing to mar the pleasure of being out on the boat enjoying the solitude. The constant noise of the engine was a distraction of sorts, but then the batteries needed a good run up while there was still a chance of topping up with fuel.

By mid-afternoon I was entering the indentation of the coastline that was Port San Juan. It was so named by the Spanish when they explored this coast in the mid 1700's. These days this part of the coast is generally referred to as Port Renfrew, named after the small town that lies some 3 mile towards the head of this indentation.

The marina, such as it was, lay behind the protection of the Government jetty. While rounding the end of the jetty to locate a berth, I was puzzled to find that there was just one float, and that secured in a temporary manner to the side of the jetty. In fact the marina didn't exist. The last time I came here, and the first, it was on my circumnavigation of Vancouver Island and it was in thick fog. Then I made no attempt to approach the marina but rather chose to anchor off for the night. When the fog had lifted a little it was possible to make out the masts of numerous boats. So it was that I deduced that a marina of sorts actually existed.

Shortly after mooring to the float and viewing the situation with some dismay, I realised that, as it was low water, the jetty top was some considerable height above, and I had no means of getting ashore. While I pondered this problem a man appeared and looked down.

"Afternoon!" I called. "There doesn't seem to be a ladder here so I can get ashore."

At this obvious statement he shook his head. "We had a storm come through here a couple of weeks ago and took out the floats. They will be replacing them later this year when they've completed the work on the jetty."

I looked around at the jetty. It seemed to be complete to me but then I couldn't see it from the top. I did notice though, and then I wasn't surprised that the floats had been taken out by a storm. Probably it was the same storm that came through while I was laid up with the kidney infection. Although the marina was on the landward side of the jetty, supposedly to give protection from the elements, the view through the pilings was unrestricted as far as the eye could see, as far as the Pacific Ocean. The jetty pilings would have given no protection at all and the wind and waves would probably have roared right through and carried away the floats. The simple answer to this would be a breakwater on the seaward side of this jetty. Maybe this would be included in the new plans.

While pondering the problem of marina protection I was distracted by a rattling noise. I turned around towards this disturbance and a ladder appeared over the edge of the jetty and was lowered down onto the float. The gentleman who greeted me earlier popped his head over the edge.

"I brought this along. Don't take it away with you," he said, grinning.

"I won't," I said with a derisory laugh. The thought of carrying away an article of this size was being farcical to the extreme. "Thank you."

With a grin and a friendly wave he disappeared leaving me to put out extra mooring lines and shut down the engine. As a reserve I carry a five gallon container of diesel and this I added to the main tank. This was in the scheme of things as I could refill the container here at Port Renfrew. Or so I thought. Fish boats came in here so it followed there would be a refuelling facility. But apparently not. Oh well, the lack of five gallons of extra diesel wasn't the end of the world as I didn't anticipate motoring. The engine would be used only to charge the batteries should the solar panel not keep them topped up.

As a security measure I tied the bottom of the ladder to the float leaving it free to move up and down against the jetty with the movement of the tide.

So it was then that I was settled down for the last night in Canada before taking off into the broad Pacific Ocean. Surprising though it may seem, the enormity of this didn't particularly provoke any emotional response. Not that I didn't wonder why. I supposed that if this is what I'd planned to do, therefore would get done, having no need to vacillate makes for a much simpler life.

After dinner I climbed ashore to take a walk and make a phone call. I could see then, when reaching the jetty deck, what had been meant by other work being carried out first before tackling the marina. The jetty deck had been concreted with a thick slab which must have taken some planning and effort, not to mention vast amounts of concrete. There was probably no money left in the budget to attend to floats.

While on shore I soon found that most places were closed, not that there was much in the way of facilities anyway. Port Renfrew is a small community, a pub, and an hotel and not much else. But there was a call box so it was possible to phone to base and give a progress report. No doubt my need to make contact was more to do with easing the transition from those that I've known to the prospect of spending some weeks without the social contact of other human beings. It had been my decision to take on this adventure, and my resolve to see it through, so the separation was totally acceptable. The revelation that my dog just lay on the front step apparently waiting for me to come home was hard to take, and gave me some remorse. Consoling myself that she was well looked after and would no doubt have plenty of people to take her for walks, all I could do was harden my heart.

Boarding the boat was made a little easier by the fact that the tide had come in sufficiently to make the descent shorter. It was with some apprehension that the weather report for the morrow gave 40 knot winds from the southwest. This was troubling; to set out with such winds right on the nose was discouraging to say the least. To stay here on this float after the marina had been wiped out gave cause for even more apprehension. The latter though, would be the lesser of the two evils. Deciding to wait and see, which the best therapy often is, I settled down to make the first of many daily entries into the journal. This was a duty that would become an evening ritual, and would be something in my old age to read and relive. Maybe, even something to write about on my return.

*****

My first task upon waking this Monday morning was not to prepare tea as usual, but rather to switch on the VHF for the weather. It was with some relief that the high winds reported the previous evening had passed over central Vancouver Island to give a gentler weather pattern.

With an easier mind I turned my attention to making tea. There is only one thing better than a cup of tea in the morning and that is two cups. I never have been able to adopt the North American habit of drinking copious cups of coffee first thing in the morning and throughout the day. It strikes me as being more of a drug than a pleasure. Having one cup of coffee for elevenses with a muffin is, however, civilised. Although I must admit to elevenses being at ten o'clock which can be construed as a habit of sorts I suppose?

The morning formality of tea and a breakfast of cereals, dried fruit, nuts and banana took a little over half an hour. This conglomerate of good things to eat would keep me healthy and, I hoped regular. As there was little chance of exercise to ward off constipation, what better way was there than eating a high fibre breakfast? This I could do while the supplies lasted, which from the amount that I laid in, would be for quite some time.

The morning was bright and clear, a perfect day for a sail. The tide had risen high enough to just push the ladder onto the jetty deck. There was no one about this early in the morning so it was fortunate that the tide had come in and I needed no assistance.

Letting go of the mooring lines and backing off the pontoon I gave myself clearance to turn into the channel and head for the open sea. Up went the mainsail as soon as it was prudent to do so. Having to clamber out of the cockpit to perform this task I found it better to do so in still waters rather than be bouncing about in a swell. At the same time the fenders and mooring lines were collected and taken back into the cockpit for stowage. It would be quite some time before these items would be used again. There is a saying that any task performed at sea should be with one hand for the boat and one hand for oneself. A steady platform to work on is a bonus too. With-in half an hour the buoy at the entrance to Port San Juan was abeam and I set a course to cross the Juan de Fuca Strait for Cape Flattery and away into the Pacific Ocean. The intention was to first make for the outer edge of the Continental Shelf before heading south, some 200 hundred miles off shore. This is to avoid considerable discomfort from standing seas should the weather deteriorate bringing high winds. It is when the sea bed becomes shallower that waves drag on the bottom causing them to become steep and dangerous to small vessels. I don't suppose that big ships care too much for them either. However as long as the weather remained clement there would be no reason for concern.

Now that the die was cast, there was no turning back; I had a chance to look around at my new environment. The coastline of Vancouver Island was becoming blurred and the features which were earlier pronounced had become indistinct, while Cape Flattery as yet seemed so far away. I must admit at this point I had a vague feeling of sadness at leaving all this behind.

A large container ship on my port side was heading out to sea, its size making me feel insignificant and vulnerable. There was no danger from him though as ocean going ships stay within the traffic separation zone and he would be long gone before I needed to cross. This thought prompted me to take another look around for any other vessel that wanted to share this part of the world.

Away from the shelter of Port Renfrew the boat, starting to feel the swell lifting the bow, rolled easily as the waves passed underneath. The breeze was proving to be quite cool so abandoning the course to the autopilot I went below to put on a survival suit. These I consider to be misnamed in the present circumstances: rather a 'warm and cosy' suit would be more appropriate, as having donned this item of clothing I was immediately insulated from the chill.

It was now mid-morning and time for elevenses. After taking another look around the horizon to check on any shipping and finding that I was alone in the world I busied myself with the kettle and preparing a filter of coffee. The distance to Cape Flattery was fifteen miles which gave me plenty of time to enjoy the coffee and the muffin before stopping the engine and giving over the voyage to sail. At this early stage I felt I needed time to become acclimatised and comfortable with my surroundings. There was no need to rush. There was a long time ahead before arriving in Panama. The wind was out of the northwest at five knots, not a great velocity to propel the boat forward at speed, and as it would be advisable to round Flattery before dark, I kept the motor running.

Cape Flattery was so named by Captain James Cook in 1778 while on his third and last epic voyage to the Pacific, claiming that he was 'flattered' into thinking there would be a safe harbour beyond this point of land. Alas! He was not to find out as he was soon driven off shore by a gale and would not make landfall again until Nootka Sound halfway up the west coast of Vancouver Island.

Cape Flattery is the north-west extremity of what is now Washington State, between the continental mainland and the coastline of Vancouver Island lays a stretch of waterway called the Strait of Juan de Fuca.

As previously mentioned Juan de Fuca, an old Greek pilot in the employ of Spain discovered the Strait in 1592. Alleged, because these claims to his discoveries were treated with scepticism by his employers. And, in the light of subsequent proof to the contrary, his claims really were far fetched.

According to the story, Juan de Fuca was sent by the Viceroy of Mexico in search of the Strait of Anian, the fabled passage which would enable a more direct and quicker route to the Orient from Europe. The Northwest Passage if you will.

And I quote: In 1592, beyond California, between latitudes 47 degrees and 48 degrees, I found a broad inlet, into which I entered, sailing for more than twenty days, passing by islands and landing at divers places, seeing people clad in beasts' skins. A fruitful place it was, rich in gold, silver, pearl and other things. In due course he arrived at the Atlantic Ocean, and sailing back through his passage to Acapulco.

He received neither reward nor gratitude from his masters. This in the light of things is not surprising, as we now know, in this modern day that this is blatant fantasy. But even at the time in history the Spanish knew that such a passage to the Atlantic could not be true, because the English had given all their voyages over to the search for the Northwest Passage from the Atlantic side of the continent, and as the Hudson Bay was so well charted, and the only ice free possibility, there could be no easy passage from the Atlantic to the Pacific.

Juan de Fuca was dismissed, his services no longer required.

How different history would have been if Cook had entered the Strait of Juan de Fuca and charted the coastline to disprove once and for all the claims of this eccentric pilot. It remained for Captain Barkley, a fur trader, in his ship the 'Imperial Eagle' in July 1787 to honour Juan de Fuca. Captain Barkley immediately recognised the strait as the one discovered by de Fuca and so named it after him.

Shortly after noon Cape Flattery was safely rounded, the engine was now shut down, the foresail run out, and I was on my way. With several hundred miles of ocean to traverse I must admit to feeling somewhat cut off from the world. Oddly though, now the earlier feeling of sadness had passed, a sense of elation that I had undertaken this venture became dominant. To sail around the world in a small boat was something that I had denied ever wanting to do, my argument being that I had stared at enough seawater during my years in a seagoing career to ever want to do so again. But now to be on my own was infinitely more desirable than to be amongst people. It's a funny old world.

During the afternoon the wind increased to fifteen knots and right on the starboard beam. This was a most favourable point of sail for making a course for the deep water off the Continental Shelf. If the weather held, then tomorrow evening we would be cruising on a southerly course in the deeper waters of the Pacific.

After a sandwich and a cup of tea (Ah! that so delightful nectar.) for lunch the afternoon progressed easily until dinner time. When I opened the freezer the euphoria built up during the day suddenly dissipated at the sight before my eyes. It hadn't taken long for the ice blocks to melt, partially granted, but sufficient, for what should have been individually wrapped meat and packets of frozen vegetables in an unmoving block were items swilling back and forth with each roll of the boat. With dismay I selected a piece of pork, surmising that this selection of meat would last the least length of time before spoiling. I also rescued a soggy bag of peas I might as well make the most of the vegetables as well while the going was good as I didn't hold out much hope for the contents of the freezer to last for many more days. So it was then that I ate dinner with a slight feeling of dejection, only to be lifted a little by a glass of wine.

Twilight is a time of day when it is the most difficult to see ships. It is not dark enough to see their navigation lights and losing the brightness of the day it is difficult to make out their shape. It was a placid evening with the clouds clearing to let out the stars, and the pleasure of keeping watch for shipping in the cockpit made the chagrin of the freezer problem soon evaporate. The enormity of the clear night sky and the millions of stars soon had my whole being at peace. No longer did I have the feeling of being cut off. I now had the profound sensation of being somewhere special. This pleasure was complemented by gazing at the myriad stars, and locating the constellations that still remained in my memory from my sea-going days. Orion in particular brought back fond memories, as I sat in the cockpit locating each star that made up the outline of the mighty hunter and his dog Sirius. I must admit to a smile of pleasure at the many memories that came to mind.

In mythology Orion pursued the Pleiades and for his trouble was eventually slain by Artemis, and was then placed in the sky as a constellation. Not such a bad ending I suppose; at least he is so obvious that he cannot be ignored. Turning to look astern I located the Plough bright and clearly pointing to the North Star, the only fixed star in the heavens. This star over the centuries had been a sure beacon to navigators in the northern hemisphere in providing a means of determining their latitude.

The day had progressed favourably. Sufficient distance had been gained off-shore to be clear of any coastwise shipping, should there be any. There was no sign of steaming lights to landward, or anywhere else for that matter. As the evening was nearing an end, the sea air gave the sleepy suggestion that it was time for me to lie down and get some rest.

While preparing for this voyage there was one important adjustment made to the radar. To do this a technician fitted an alarm to the radar that would sound when a target came within the pre-set guard range. This worked marvellously when along side in the marina but, when switched on out on the briny the alarm sounded loud enough to wake the dead, and continuously with no target in sight. So this was item two to malfunction. For the rest of this voyage I would be hoping that this alarm system fitted on other vessels would be working to give warning of my presence. To rely on a sailboat's navigation lights to be seen from a large vessel was tempting fate. Although very bright, they were low to the water and tended to be difficult to see, especially with a boat rising and falling in a sea, and even assuming that the large vessels in question would be keeping a good lookout for small craft.

It was considered impractical to undress and climb into the forward bunk due to the struggle that would ensue should I have to get out in a hurry. The layout of the berth was designed to take the full width of this section of the boat, and as one would lie feet forward, to throw off the bedding and swing one's legs round to clamber out and get dressed takes time, and at my stage of stiffening advanced years, it was considered prudent not to take advantage of this comfort but to lay out the cockpit cushions on the main cabin deck and fully booted and spurred, so to speak and take my rest thus.

One more thing I did before lying down for the night was a trip to the bathroom. There had been considerable movement with the boat generated by the waves during the day. Most of the time with an easy pitching and rolling, and the infrequent jerk when the boat hit a wave at an awkward angle, this is known in the trade as hitting a milestone. Sod's Law and true to form this is what happened when I entered the bathroom and was thrown off balance, falling heavily against the door. The door was of louvered construction secured against the weather by a wind hook at the bottom section. With my not inconsiderable weight coming into contact with an immovable object with some force, the obvious happened, the door broke. Several slats came out of their sockets and rattled onto the deck but apart from that the door remained intact and usable. As I was the only one on board and had no need for the privacy of a closed door the situation was left as it was. I made a mental note to make repairs when circumstance became more favourable.

Returning to my place of rest I set my mental clock to wake up at frequent intervals during the night and soon fell into the arms of Morpheus.

Setting the mental clock, as it turned out, was quite uncalled for because the position I was lying in on the hard cushion, combined with my body weight caused the elastic in my underpants to dig into my upper leg creating enough discomfort to bring me awake after only a short time of maybe an hour at most. The only way to solve this problem, as I was wearing the survival suit, was to turn over when one side became a bother and ease the soreness, turning over again when the lower side became a bother, and so on through the night. In between the turning over, I got up to check that all was clear and free from danger. Not a bad alarm system, come to think of it, and I didn't seem to suffer from any sleep deprivation, dropping off to sleep again without any appreciable time lapse.

*****

When daylight started to lighten the horizon my new day commenced. First, I took a look around the watery wilderness for any sign of shipping. Satisfied that there was no danger, the kettle was put on and tea made. Two cups of tea then breakfast. This sequence of events became the norm for starting the days during the rest of the trip. And a more perfect way to start a day I cannot imagine. The reader must forgive me for the frequent reference to this morning ritual but it was a very important part of the trip and also of my mental wellbeing.

After checking my position by satellite I realised that with the weather being favourable it was unnecessary to continue on a course south of west to cross the 100 fathom line. A change of course would make it more convenient to cross the line further south and thus save some distance. An alteration of course to due south was thus made, and so brought me on a track parallel with the Washington coast and, a healthy distance off shore away from the coastal traffic routes.

A high pressure system, called the North Pacific High, covers a vast area of the north Pacific with the winds flowing out in a clockwise motion from around the centre. There are several permanent high pressure systems situated over the oceans of the world, which provide well known tracks for sailing vessels. So it was then that steady progress could be made on the eastern side of this high with winds from a constant direction, giving the most favourable point of sail. Now I could relax and enjoy the solitude, feeling the caressing wind and the movement of the boat, both adding to the pleasure of just being here.

The accident with the bathroom door weighed heavily on my mind this morning. It wouldn't take too much to totally destroy it, should the same thing happen again. As mentioned I didn't require privacy, but when transiting the Panama Canal the extra people on board would. I was expecting to make the transit on arrival so there would be no time to make repairs should the door be totally demolished. Ah, yes! If only our expectations came to fruition. Wouldn't it be a wonderful world?

The best solution I could come up for the time being was to use the bathroom as little as possible, and as there is no time like the present, I moved to the stern lockers and kneeling there with one hand for myself and one for the job, took a pee over the stern.

Soon it was ten o'clock and time for elevenses, then soon after in no time at all it seemed a sandwich and a cup of tea for the mid-day meal. After lunch a much welcome snooze, for half an hour, to replenish the batteries that had been run down with constantly getting up and checking for shipping during the night. Pottering about until dinner at six I created a daily routine that became pleasurably time consuming and comfortable interspersed with reading for relaxation, and so the days passed.

The loss of freezer capacity was a nuisance but had to be accepted and the choice of another pork item was considered to be safe. It was thawed out and floppy but didn't smell. Each time that I approached the choice of meat I became a little more despondent at the sight of all this waste of produce. Before much longer I would have to bite the bullet and dump all of this lovely grub. There was no point in taking chances with eating possibly tainted meat and becoming ill.

The peas had thawed also, but were still firm enough for a meal. With carrots and potatoes a meal fit for a king was prepared. With a glass of red wine to wash it down what more could one ask for in the art of culinary delights? At least there wasn't any chance of the wine being in short supply soon. All of the wine was home brew, sixty litres in plastic waiter bags. Bottles were considered to be too fragile to carry on a boat. In the sea going environment with a boat bouncing about in the waves carrying bottled wine was asking for trouble, not to mention all the space that they would take up.

While I ate the evening meal, the wind increased to 25 knots, causing the boat to heel more than desired. Rather than scrabble about in the dark taking in a reef in the mainsail the boom was let out to spill some wind. A fisherman's reef as it is called. The boat behaved most favourably under these conditions. Spray was starting to come on board with the increase of wind, the tops of the seas being whipped away to splatter the full length of the boat. The SatNav put our position on the same latitude as the mouth of the Columbia River. So it was satisfying to know that good progress was being made under these conditions and the spray became just something to put up with, a minor irritation when out on deck.

While sitting in the cabin waiting for a suitable time to lie down for sleep I was awakened from my reverie by the sound of water, not a pouring sound but rather water falling. Curious, I got up to investigate, only to find that water was coming into the galley by way of the cabin heater chimney. Odd, I thought, the chimney cowl has a canvas cover to stop this sort of thing. Going out into cockpit and looking forward made it obvious what the problem was: both the canvas and the cowl had disappeared.

This problem had to be addressed now; it was not a favourable option to have water coming into the boat via a chimney or anywhere else for that matter. Giving a mental expletive of pique at the inconvenience I went below, donned the safety harness, and collected the necessary tools and a small piece of plywood suitably coated with sealant for the task. Making ones way forward on a bouncy boat requires two hands and great care. However, by first shoving the cordless drill, and plywood piece ahead of me along the cabin top, and waiting for lulls in the spray and the heavier plunging movements of the boat, I arrived at the scene of action. The task didn't take long, for I needed only to drill the holes and screw down the plywood piece. I was soon back down below, wondering what would be the next problem to arise.

I wasn't kept waiting too long to find out. At half past three in the morning I sensed something was amiss, and by glancing at the compass readout above the chart table it was obvious there was a problem. The boat was seriously off course. I could only wonder why this would happen as the Hydrovane steering had so far proved to be most reliable. The only reason that came to mind, and this was conjecture only, was if the wind had increased it would cause an increase of pressure on the opposite bow, causing the boat to come round to the wind and set another course. Whatever the reason the boat was heading towards Hawaii, and no matter how much I'd enjoyed Hawaii when visiting there, it was not my intention or wish to visit this trip.

It was quite possible that being awake at such an early hour had made me a little dopey and in attempting to get the boat back on course I kept getting the steering set-up wrong. And off we would head towards Hawaii again. For a while I left the steering to the autopilot while I thought the Hydrovane set-up procedure through more attentively. It wasn't difficult really to come to a conclusion. I'd been failing to apply counter rudder on the main steering. I guess it was too early in the day for conscious thought. However, it seemed that my theory of wind pressure on the bow could be right. It was quite cool out in the wind and it was a relief to go below again to lie down and, maybe doze as I was now too mentally alert with the recent excitement to sleep, until the next call out.

Daylight came, and the sun rose on a bright clear day. The usual routine of tea and breakfast, then potty time, all passed by and I could relax. After such a hectic night I felt the need to have an after breakfast snooze. Just half an hour's repose worked wonders. So in the light of this experience a regimen of relaxing whenever the occasion allowed came into being. It also became a matter of conjecture as to whether I spent more time horizontal or vertical in the pursuit of this theory.

The noon position gave the distance over the previous twenty-four hours of 110 miles including whatever time was taken travelling in the wrong direction. An achievement not to be sneezed at: in fact quite a good run when one considers a daily estimate of 100 miles as a yardstick. Even the dolphins had trouble keeping up.

This daily progress wasn't achieved again for the rest of the week; the wind became erratic in intensity, although fortunately the direction remained favourable. On only one day was the 100 mile criteria reached. The least distance covered in one twenty-four hour period was just 48 miles. No matter. Progress was being made and I wasn't in a round the world race. Saturday noon put the position 160 miles due west of Crescent City, Oregon.

Saturday evening I sent a progress report by e-mail with the Satellite phone link to the pre-arranged contacts. They then would forward the message to all interested parties. This may seem a convoluted way of letting people know what I was up to, but it was decided during the planning stage that with the cost of satellite communication, and my indecisiveness with modern technology, it would be better to let just two people handle the distribution.

During the following week the weather became much warmer and I could finally get out of my Andy Pandy survival suit. The freedom of movement and the joy of feeling the sun and breeze unrestricted by this heavy article of clothing was a pleasure indeed. Lying down on the cushions with a lack of restraint by bulky apparel also allowed me an adjustment of my underpants elastic. A positive plus and much appreciated. All was not well with this sleeping arrangement though because when I needed to get up to check on the current situation, I found that it was difficult with my stiff old bones to stand upright easily. I achieved this only with much grunting, oohing and aahing, after rolling onto my side and struggling to my knees and with considerable effort hoisting myself upright, a most awkward exercise definitely not conducive to speed and ease should the occasion demand. Obviously some other arrangement had to be considered, a place of repose somewhere that called for putting my legs down to stand, rather than having to roll over onto my knees before attempting to come upright. The forward bunk was out of the question for reason previously mentioned. The after berth was being used for storage, so that wasn't an option. This left the settee. I viewed this possibility with some dismay. It was curved, only the width of a chair seat, and wrapped around a table. The design called for this table to be lowered to make up another bed, should that be called for. This then could resolve the present problem, only to create more problems. Not only did I take my meals at this table, it was also used for writing up the journal and many other uses. However, I seemed to be faced with Hobson's choice. At least this option of kipping on the settee should be given a trial run.

The next morning I was asking myself why I didn't sleep on the settee from day one. It was a most restful spot. The only problem that arose was when needing to change sides. The settee was too narrow for me to roll over, so it was a case of getting up and changing end for end. The plus side of this action was that I could check on the situation outside while on my feet.

The days progressed pleasantly; the weather was fair with the sea slight. Once a routine had been established the days just flew by. Boredom, as one might think, would be a problem under these circumstances, but boredom never happened. I must qualify that statement, however. Boredom did crop up now and again but this had nothing to do with the circumstances of being alone on a boat in the middle of the ocean. Rather, strangely to say, from doing the crosswords. These had been given to me by a very good friend with the admonishment to do them if I became bored. As it turned out the crosswords created a reverse reaction. The first crosswords were reasonably easy, although the lay-out of the blocks were not in the accepted format of being equal on each side, and top and bottom of the square. But, no matter, these puzzles would exercise the brain. Or so I thought. After completing the first one and moving on to a second and third I realised that some of the clues were being repeated, and so it became a test of memory. This was true with each puzzle right through the book. It must be said though that I now know that a Dace is a fresh water fish. An interesting development evolved over the ensuing weeks because of having a go at these crosswords. Whenever I felt a need to be bored, irritated, cross or whatever, I would pick up the crossword book and start a puzzle. I could then become frustrated and toss the stupid thing to one side with a curse. This seemed to work wonders with my perverse psyche, a therapy of sorts.

Before I knew it, it was Saturday again and time to make a report, but when it was entered into the lap-top and ready to be transmitted by satellite it would not go. Several attempts proved to be futile. The only recourse now was to phone the help line, and, after half an hour of being walked through a re-installation of the program the message finally went, leaving me wondering what else would happen to make my days fruitfully frustrating.

Sunday was, strange though it may seem, considered to be my day off. Unless called away to make refreshments or meals, checking on the probability of shipping, etc, I kept the phone handy. This had a two fold purpose: the ring tone was very low, not helped by my standard of hearing: and, this was the day set aside for friends to call should they so wish. The day then was taken up with reading, of which there was a varied selection, or listening to CDs, of which again there was a varied selection, or just sitting and thinking. Surprisingly the day didn't drag and boredom never happened under these circumstances contentment must have had a hand in this I suspect. The problem with sending the report bothered me though, and I spent some time thinking on the subject.

As I must admit when it comes to technologies I am a dummy, and not a little suspicious of what goes on in the little box of tricks called a computer. So it was about this time I got to wondering if my last report had got through as there had been no confirmation of this, and I must admit with the way this trip was panning out with all the hiccups a touch of paranoia could be creeping in. There was only one way to find out and that was to phone base. Well! What do you know? The satellite phone didn't work.

What to do now? Obviously, if I couldn't have communication with the base then they would not know if I was still above the waves.

The position of the boat at noon was south of the latitude of San Diego and a hundred miles from the coast of Mexico. Should I go back to San Diego to have the phone fixed? To carry on to Panama was out of the question. The distance was too great to be without communication and keep the folks back home in the dark worrying about my safety. After pondering the situation and with much perusing of the chart, I decided that my one remaining option was to make for Cabo San Lucas at the tip of Baja California, an estimated five days away, still a cause for concern for those who would be waiting for the weekly news, but the best option.

It was during this period that a bit of luck came my way. A vessel steaming south was overtaking at a distance of five miles on my starboard side, and after several attempts answered my call on the VHF radio. The officer of the watch called the captain who graciously agreed to pass a message via e-mail to base. A kindness that certainly took a load off my mind.

Had I known the true outcome at the time I wouldn't have been so complacent. As it turned out the message was not received and the non-recipient hadn't been unduly concerned about my lack of contact anyway. I was not a little miffed after all the worry about lack of contact. I could not accept that the message would not have been sent. More likely the recipient didn't recognise the sender's address and didn't open it. Doesn't it make you want to curse the spam and virus merchants for all the trouble they cause?

But that was in the future.

Having made this change of plan and accepted that a diversion from the original idea of making directly to Panama was now the order of the day, I settled down to the prospect of a few days' break in the Cabo. I had spent a vacation there a few years previously and apart from being pestered by the Timeshare people, quite enjoyed the place. At least I knew where to go and how to approach the harbour. The next few days passed in a relaxed and trouble free manner. The weather remained clement, the seas slight and the sails full. If I had been of a poetic nature no doubt I could have waxed eloquent on the joys of cruising in relaxing surroundings. 'Just give me a tall ship, and a star to steer her by,' that sort of thing. Although being of a practical turn of mind I could hardly have set out on this venture with such limited equipment which had suited John Masefield.

In due course I sighted the coast in the region of Cabo San Lucas just after daybreak and set a course to close the land. During the night a tear had appeared in the leach of the genoa. Probably it had got caught on the spreader, but as it was only a small tear, it didn't concern me all that much. With the repair kit on board it would be attended to while alongside. However, the wind was starting to blow quite strongly and as the land was getting close I took the sails down and started the engine. This was most timely as the wind increased alarmingly and by mid morning was up to forty knots from the north. The wind direction running as it was along the coast started to bring up a rough sea with quite a swell running, throwing spray across the deck as each wave slammed against the side. These conditions had me manning the steering, because with the rolling and pitching I did not consider it prudent to engage the autopilot. With the push of a wave against the bow threatening to throw the boat off course I had to anticipate and put the helm over to meet the pressure. The wheel was constantly in use as the boat bucked and gyrated to the action of the sea.

In this situation one could use the flyer's maxim transferred to a nautical environment: flying by the seat of one's pants. Wonderful as an autopilot is, it cannot anticipate a wave action, and to have the boat broach to a wave would be most undesirable.

Within the hour the land provided a lee and it was then easy motoring along the easterly trend of the coast, around that magnificent rock that has a hole in it, Los Arcos (the arch) and then on a reverse course to the harbour of Cabo San Lucas and the fuel dock and marina. I was twenty-five days out from Pender Island.

CHAPTER THREE
Cabo San Lucas

The Spanish Conquistador Hernan Cortez, in 1535, was the first European to come to this part of the world after subduing the Aztecs, to seek a fortune in gold and silver that was supposed to abound here. He was disappointed in this assumption, but left his name to the sea on the east side of the peninsula of Lower California a sea that stretches all the way back to where the Colorado River exits to the sea, a distance of 700 miles. Lying as it does at the southernmost point of the Baja, Cabo San Lucas remained very much a backwater until after the Second World War, when American celebrities from the movie industry discovered that they could access this part of the world by plane or with their long distance pleasure boats and take advantage of the abundance of marine life which provided a sport fisherman's paradise. From then on, and after the road was built, there was no looking back. As a tourist attraction the Cabo just took off, and is now a vacation spot for those who seek the sun and the beautiful beaches, and the world class sports fishing.

None of these pleasures were for me though; mine was just a stay of convenience, an interruption of the original plan of proceeding directly to Panama. As it turned out this break in the original arrangement proved to be pleasantly relaxing. The climate at this time of the year was dry and warm. The tourist season was coming to an end so there would be a marked downturn of people bent on enjoying themselves. This of course was no concern to me as I was here for more mundane matters. Namely, to contact the Satellite phone people and seek direction as to where to send the offending object, refuel, fix the tear in the genoa, and boost the charge on the batteries. I also wanted a meal that comprised meat that didn't come out of a tin. The original fresh meat had long gone to the fish that is if it was still fresh enough for them. It certainly wasn't for me. There had been another little mishap during the previous few days that also needed attention: the plug for charging the phone and the electric shaver had gone into destruct mode and was completely useless. So that would have to be replaced. A car cigar lighter is such a useful item but, so delicate that the moist atmosphere takes its toll on the connections and soon corrodes them. The way things had been going this diversion to Cabo San Lucas was a blessing in disguise.

The approach to the fuel dock couldn't have been simpler as it was directly inside the entrance and at the end of the marina floats. Willing hands soon had the boat tied up and refuelled. I took the short walk along the floats to the office for the assignment of a berth, payment for the moorage, and there I was, all secure and ready to do the necessary paperwork for the inward clearance. First, though, I considered a call to the satellite phone people, but was stymied from the word go. In the Marina Office I had noticed a telephone in the lobby, and it was with this that I proceeded to make the call, only to find out that one needed a call card, that irritating invention that seems to have frustration attached to it. In the same building as the Marina Office was a store that catered in a small way to the boating trade and luckily they also sold phone cards. The call I had to make was long distance, and an 800 number. The call went through alright but before you could say Jack Robinson the call was cut off through lack of funds on the card. Obviously, the 800 number didn't mean anything. The store owner proved to be quite helpful, and also spoke excellent English. He sold me another card. This, although a little more time was used before I was cut off again, still didn't get me to the person that could deal with the information required. The store owner, whom I shall call Alex, as that was his name, came to the rescue once again and suggested I ask the Marina manager if I could use his phone. After all, it was a collect call. For some reason that I didn't quite grasp this alternative was not forthcoming. Something to do with telephone system being an internal set-up and would not accept long distance calls. At this point it became more important to have the inward clearance into Mexico and, I took the Marina manager's direction to the Port Captain's office, which he pointed out, was just over there, a five minute walk. When over there, there was no indication of the place I wanted. Not being shy about asking directions even in a foreign country, I approached the guard at the gate of the Naval Base, and in my best Spanish, asked, "Que es el Porto Capitan's offico?" At this question surprising though it may seem he looked blank. Maybe it was my Yorkshire accent? While I was figuring out how to rephrase the question, another armed guard sauntered over who, when I repeated my question, also looked blank. He must however, have caught the key words and things brightened up.

"Ah! Capitan del Porto?" he asked, looking pleased with himself.

"Si." Now we were getting somewhere, I thought.

Up went his arm and pointed in the direction of the town. This didn't gel with what I had been told at the marina and arguing wasn't a consideration. So, after a pleasant "Mucho Gracias, to the guard I took myself off in the direction indicated, none too happy though at the way things seemed to be developing.

It was a hot afternoon and walking was becoming uncomfortably warm, with my skin taking on a definite glow. To return to the boat would not solve anything though as was the thought that crossed my mind. So I continued in the general direction of town. Soon I came to what proved to be a small market selling tourist merchandise, the sort of thing that holiday makers buy as a memento, put in a cupboard on arriving home and promptly forgot. Big wide Mexican sombreros magnificently studded, and curly brimmed, that sort of thing. Wearing such apparel in northern countries would possibly bring unwelcome attention and would definitely be out of place on the street of a northern city, one could hang it on the living room wall though as a conversation piece if one was that way inclined. There were a few men hanging about who looked like locals, and it was to them I directed my next question.

"Do you speak English?" I asked, not wanting to confuse these good people with my Spanish.

"Yas, I spic a leetle," a tall man answered.

"I'm looking for the Port Captains Office," I said, much relieved at finally getting somewhere.

"Come," he said, "I take you," and he walked away towards a car. Just like that, no preliminaries.

Slightly surprised at the way things were developing I hesitated, but only for a second. This was a chance not to be passed up. Quickly catching up with him and on the passenger side of the car, I noticed there was no handle on the door; it was to be opened from the inside by the driver. With a feeling of slight dismay at this introduction and the general decrepit state of the vehicle I climbed in, wondering if I was taking the right course of action.

Churlish I may have been to harbour these thought at the outset because it wasn't long before I was becoming very impressed with this Good Samaritan. It was quite a distance to the Port Captain's building, and the thought of walking there and not knowing the way gave rise to daunting thoughts. During the journey he asked me not to tell anyone that he was taking me, because if the taxi drivers found out he would be in big trouble. After all this kindness, how could I?

Not only had he driven me to my destination but insisted on coming in as an interpreter. This was most fortuitous as the clerk didn't speak English and it transpired that we would first have to go to immigration, and then return with the necessary papers before he could give me clearance. So off we went on, to me, another mystery tour. The process of legally entering Mexico was far from completed because waiting in line while bureaucracy took its interminable time, I was presented with a form and told to go across the road to the Bank and pay up, then come back to complete the paperwork. So off we went, at least down to the street where my companion suggested that he must go about his business. Not in a million years could I fault his decision; he had been very attentive to my problems which had taken so much of his time and, I would be able to handle the rest of the procedure alone. To show how much I appreciated his help I suggested that he be given something for his trouble.

"No, no, nada, nothing," he protested.

And so started an argument that I later realised was the polite way of settling a debt.

"Come now," I said, "you have taken so much trouble on my behalf, you deserve something." And I took out my wallet.

"OK, a couple of dollars."

"A couple? How much? You tell me."

At this he held up his hands and shrugged. "It's up to you."

I was becoming a little exasperated at this game and said, "I have no idea what the right amount would be." Then, "Ten dollars? Would that be OK?"

Another shrug and a hand gesture of acceptance, "Sure."

And so ten dollars changed hands with a hand shake and we parted company. I was most grateful for his help but, wondered if ten dollars had been enough. No doubt he would have been too polite to question this amount. It was pointless pondering the subject so I took myself off to the Bank.

It seemed as though everyone and his uncle and aunt were lining up waiting for service and as it was well into the afternoon, I was becoming anxious whether this business of clearing inwards, and negotiating the outward clearance, would be completed this day. As it turned out it wasn't to be. After the immigration side of this procedure was satisfactorily completed and the necessary papers presented to take to the Port Captain, this wasn't the end of it. Next in this chain of bureaucracy it was required of me to go to yet another department before the clearance could be given. This as it turned out was close by the marina and the office I should have gone to in the first place. Well we live and learn, don't we? It was hot and I was weary so I engaged a taxi. As it turned out, although the office was open, the man in charge had gone home and I was requested to return in the morning. I said to myself, enough for this day, dismissed the taxi and returned to the boat. By the time I would have returned to the Port Captain's office they would most likely have been closed anyway.

While on the boat I noticed an almost continuous procession of buses passing around the Marina office. They would travel along the road from town, disappear behind the marina building then re-appear from the other side and return towards the town, stopping only long enough to pick up passengers should there be any. What made me curious was that there were so many buses, nothing like a regular schedule, when a person would wait for ages then two buses would turn up. Here it was more like a regular cavalcade approaching from town, circling the building and speeding away again. To satisfy my curiosity, and after the solitude of the boat and my own company I was now getting to like people, so I wandered up to Alex's shop and made enquiries. True to form Alex was most helpful and explained that these buses were independently owned and operated, and apparently anyone could go and buy an old bus and run a service in and out of town. The beauty of this arrangement was there was no long wait and the fare was only six pesos. Deciding to try out this mode of transport I went back to the boat and took a shower, got dressed up, and presented myself at the bus stop. A vehicle of uncertain pedigree, painted yellow with the words, 'School Bus' showing through an attempt at being camouflaged soon pulled to a stop. The word, old, in old bus was an understatement. Ancient would be nearer the mark. But, for six pesos who was complaining? A bone shaking ride on a seat of torn vinyl with a coil spring threatening to pierce ones bum was the consequence. But then, the alternative of a taxi for ten dollars wasn't even to be considered.

During my quest around the town for inward clearance I had seen an Internet café and it was to this that I made my way. Not only was there internet, there was, joy upon joy, a telephone, a telephone that worked by dialling without the insertion of a card. Just make the call and pay at the desk, at least a nominal fee for the collect call as the café owner had to make a living I was advised. Matters seemed to be taking a turn for the better now. Within no time at all the satellite phone people had been contacted, the problem discussed, and I was given an address where to send the offending article would be forwarded to my e-mail. The next call confirmed that no message had been received from the vessel contacted during the previous week. At this I was a little bit miffed, after all, brotherhood of the sea and all that jazz. But as previously mentioned this attempt at contact could have been considered spam.

Much enlightened by getting matters moving, and fortified with a happy heart I sought out a suitable restaurant. There are many eating places to choose from in downtown Cabo so I chose the first one I came to and I was soon tucking into a delightful meal of baked red snapper on a bed of rice, with just a suggestion of assorted vegetables. The fish was served whole, complete with the staring eyes, or I should say, eye, as the fish was lying on its side. As I was famished the stare was completely ignored and the flesh soon scraped down to the bones. After three weeks at sea to tuck into a meal that was protein rich and hadn't been prised from a can was a delight indeed. All washed down with two bottles of Tecata beer. Lovely.

It had been a long hot and tiring day so taking a short walk in the direction of home base to settle the meal, I then caught the first available independently operated bus. Much to my relief this bus, albeit hurtling along the road at an alarming rate, was much less of a bone shaker than the one on the outward journey. Even the seat was in one piece.

And so it was that I retired for an early night and in the comfort of the forward berth. Much pleased with the latter events of the day, and thoughts on tomorrow, I fell into a sound sleep.

*****

Without the necessity of having to frequently awaken during the night to check on shipping, weather, and make sure the boat was travelling in the direction it was supposed to, I enjoyed a sound, full night's sleep awakening only when it started to get light. After a normal start to the day with tea, breakfast, and the usual routine I was out on deck appreciating the prospect of yet another warm sunny day, and washing the torn sail with fresh water prior to the repair.

While waiting for the sun to dry the genoa I filled the time by packing up the satellite phone ready for posting. Nothing would be open at this time of day, neither the post office, nor, any Government offices which still had to be dealt with, so matters took on a leisurely pace. Apart from repairing the sail once it was dry, there were the water tanks to fill and the batteries to charge from shore power.

With modern materials a preliminary sail repair is quite an easy task. There is still the repair that can only be tackled with a palm and needle but, in the case of a small tear more often than not this can be dealt with by what is known as Sail makers Duct Tape. This is a fabric that comes in varying widths with a peel off covering that reveals an adhesive backing. All that is required is to cut to length, round off the corners to prevent the tape lifting, remove the peel off backing and stick the tape over the tear, and Bob's your uncle, repair completed. This is a stopgap method, and only recommended as a repair until the services of a sail maker can be engaged. In the present circumstance with such a minor tear this patch would have to suffice as my time here in the Cabo was limited and any delay was for the purpose of getting the phone away for repair. So it was then, with the minor chores out of the way, and the morning progressing, I took myself off to the first place of call to pay another fee, collect the piece of paper for the Port Captain's office and catch the bus into town. Now that I knew the correct procedure and destinations the frustrations of yesterday were not repeated. Matters took on a flow of their own, and when I walked into the office the clerk noticed me and left the person that he had been attending to and came over and took the offered paper. The office was quite crowded and would otherwise, had I not received immediate attention, have promised a long delay. This attention, much to the looks of annoyance from the other people waiting for attention pleased me no end. My irritations had been suffered on the previous day so there was little sympathy for their discomfort. In a matter of a few minutes, not counting yesterday, my Inward and Outward Clearances had been attended to and I was free to leave Mexico for Panama. But first, check the e-mails for the address for the phone and to get that off, buy a cigar lighter to replace the duff one, and dowel and glue to fix the broken bathroom door. When these chores had been satisfactorily completed it was back to the boat and away. Or at least that was the intention.

However, fate was taking a hand again.

After posting off the phone and returning to the boat with a happy heart in preparation for departure I noticed, while checking the engine oil, that there was a considerable flow of water alongside the engine bed coming from the back of the boat. There had been a slight ingress of water prior to this but nothing the bilge pump couldn't handle. This leak had emanated from the seal where the rudder post came through the hull. This was a weak area of the steering system as the tiller bearing was only about nine inches above the bottom seal. Above that there was two feet of rudder post. This arrangement had been fine in relatively still waters but out in the ocean with the rolling of the boat the spade rudder had worked like a loose tooth on the seal causing it to leak. What to do? The boat ideally should be hauled and the leak fixed from underneath. As an alternative if Alex had a quick drying adhesive in his shop that might solve the problem.

After much discussion on the subject and dismissing the products offered as being unusable, Alec had a bright idea. He phoned his friend the boatyard owner and had a word with him to see if he could fit me in for a haul out. What transpired during the conversation and what arrangements had been made, I couldn't say, as I don't speak Spanish. When Alex got off the phone he looked thoughtful, then, as though a brilliant idea had formulated, advised that I go and talk to his friend the boatyard man. What else could I do but concede to this suggestion? He had gone to this trouble on my behalf and the problem had me worried. So it was then that I returned to town to have a word and see if it would be convenient for the boat to be taken out of the water.

This turned out to be a wasted effort as the yard man was quite emphatic about not putting me ahead of his other customers. This left me wondering why Alex had sent me on this wild goose chase. It would appear, and I came across this helpfulness time and again in the Latin American world, that in their eagerness to be helpful they would suggest anything to try and solve a problem. As they say, you live and learn. And these situations are not to be taken with offence. Just make one's own decisions on any given suggestion. Or better still don't even ask in the first place.

When I returned to the boat the afternoon had progressed to the point were it would be pointless leaving until an attempt had at least been made to stop the leak. So it was then that an arrangement was made to stay yet another night.

A liberal application of fibreglass cloth and thick epoxy putty with enough hardener to set it off rapidly was then applied around the area of the leak, after drying this appeared to solve the problem. This then had to suffice. So, with an incongruous thought that water is best kept outside of a boat I left for another meal in town. The good thing about all this, and I do try to look on the bright side, is that I could look forward to missing yet another one of my home cooked meal, which was a blessing.

CHAPTER FOUR
Cabo San Lucas to Panama

...to suffer
The slings and arrows of outrageous fortune
Hamlet Act 111

Another good night's sleep put me in the mood to get my act together and get on my way, but first another trip into town to purchase a few extra provisions and a final check for any messages that had come in, and one or two to send off. Friends had expressed the wish to transit the Panama Canal with the boat and act as line handlers. This arrangement would be most welcome and to see friends again would break up an otherwise long spell away. Also the line handling would cut the cost of the transit a little. As there was to be no communication from the boat between the Cabo and Panama, all I could do was send an estimated time of arrival (ETA) from here.

Before noon goodbyes had been said, not to Alex though as he wasn't around. His wife did wish me a safe journey and hoped that I would return, which was nice to hear. I hadn't thought much on that subject but, meeting such friendly people maybe in the years to come that could be a possibility? So it was that, before noon the lines were cast off, I motored out of the harbour and cleared Los Arcos headland. In no time at all the sails were up, the engine switched off and I headed in a south-easterly course towards the bulge of Mexico in the vicinity of Manzanillo, with the intention of keeping well off the coast and coastwise shipping. With the peace and the quiet of moving through the water at a brisk pace a feeling of freedom from civilisation took over again. There is a great deal of truth in the saying that one can only find peace away from the land, and I could almost feel the blanket of tranquillity closing over me. With the warm wind on my skin and the slapping of the waves against the hull to thrill the senses, life was good. Heeling slightly on a port tack with the wind on the beam I gave over the steering to the Hydrovane.

A fair wind and a trouble free passage would bring me to Panama in a matter of three weeks. How optimistic can one be? But then the future can only be experienced, not foreseen. With these pleasant thoughts I prepared and consumed lunch, then took a refreshing snooze. Having a lie down in the afternoon for ten, maybe fifteen minutes, surprising though such a short siesta may seem certainly worked wonders, a pleasure to be indulged in at every opportunity.

The land by the Cabo was soon becoming a blurred mass and by late afternoon as I sat in the cockpit looking back there was no distinguishable shape at all. Once again there was only the boat, the sea and me.

Over the next ten days sailing parallel to, but out of sight of the coast of Mexico, life was sublime. A fair wind on the port beam gave a perfect point of sail; progress was being made at a reasonable average of just less than one hundred miles a day. The weather was warm enough for me to take a shower out in the cockpit. The plastic Solar Shower had been filled with fresh water previously and left out in the sun all day on the coach top to warm. They are a great invention these showers; a plastic bag with a shut off valve at the end of a spout, then hung off the end of the boom gives a most adequate means for a body wash, and most importantly with a slow delivery from the spout, is a water saver. In this situation though there was one point that needed attention. With the boat rolling easily in the swell the bag would swing about in a most erratic and alarming manner, requiring one's attention to avoid being slapped by the bag while soaping down, particularly so when one's face is covered in soap with the eyes closed. With a little practice this oscillating action can be anticipated and with a deft movement one can duck.

My birthday rolled around on this stretch of the voyage, and as one does on these occasions there is a need to do something special, or if not special, then different to the everyday run-of-the-mill routines. Glumly I perused the provision cupboard, and there wasn't much that could be done for a change in the food line. The excitement of corned beef, or spam for that matter, had long been exhausted. Pondering this problem for some time I decided that maybe a serving of fried rice with a fried egg on top, if nothing to write home about, was at least different. So this sumptuous repast was put into being. This I took with a glass of red wine to wash it down. It made for a feast that could not be scoffed at. The thoughts, as they do on festive occasions, go back to other times when I celebrated with people around, and today on my seventy-first was no different. Last year was a milestone of sorts when friends helped in the celebrations. But, today? Undaunted and there being no-one else, I gave a hearty rendition of, 'Happy Birthday to Me', and felt greatly elated at the experience.

Evening was coming on and the light fading, so taking a cup of coffee out to the cockpit I sat and reminisced while keeping a sharp lookout for any traffic that might be in the area until darkness blanketed this part of the Pacific. No shipping had been sighted, not this evening nor any previous evening since leaving the Cabo so, after only a little thought on the subject I opened Peter Binner's bon voyage gift of the bottle of Glen Morangie. Strict instructions had been issued about when this should be opened, and not until Panama. Also this act was contravening my own rule of partaking only in a glass of wine with the evening meal, no beer, no hard liquor. Well it was my birthday so why not, and rules were made to be broken, so it was a case of, 'Cheers, Ron,' a lift of the glass and a sip of the single malt with a hearty happy birthday. Needless to say this self-imposed forbidden fruit was a nectar indeed and most enjoyable, more so because of it being forbidden.

To paraphrase Newton's Second law of Motion, for every action there is an equal and opposite reaction. The following morning the residual euphoria from the previous evening was replaced by glumness on the sight of the genoa. During the night and unnoticed in the dark during the checks, a tear had appeared along the leach seam. This was only a few inches in length and apparently not getting any worse. The old adage, 'a stitch in time saves nine,' came to mind but this was the middle of the ocean with a brisk breeze blowing. The tear was close to the leach seam which presented difficulty in sewing. Should the tear become worse then it would only go as far as the next cross seam, so I decided to leave the problem until there was a lull in the wind. As progress was being made out of the favourable effects of the Pacific High, I made a reasonable assumption that there would be the anticipated lull before picking up the trade winds off the lower part of Mexico.

As I progressed to the south the coast tended towards the southeast, then easterly. In the next two days the wind changed to the trades which required a change of course to follow the trend of the coast. This put the wind forward of the port beam and the mainsail adjusted accordingly; the boom was hauled amidships to flatten the mainsail and the genoa trimmed to sail as close to the wind as reasonable, with the wind at sixty degrees on the port bow. There had not been the anticipated lull in the wind to allow the repair, and as the tear on the genoa leach had remained static I was pleased to let the matter rest.

The noon position having been taken and plotted, I anticipated a good day's run and went below for lunch and the afternoon snooze. The rest of the day and through the night was a relaxing time, just a steady progress towards my destination. The usual chores had been carried out, which involved reading the latest book while seated in the cockpit: 'The Conquest of Mexico,' was rather appropriate I thought as we were still paralleling the coast of this country. After preparing and eating dinner I had a relaxing interlude in the dark listening to a music disc. There was quite a selection of CDs on board with a wide variety of music ranging from classical to jazz. Shirley Bassey was there, too, and Kiri te Kanawa at the other end of the singing scale. It became a much anticipated relaxation, these music evenings, and something of which I never tired. That is how the evening progressed until the time came to check if any dangers threatened on the broad ocean.

On the warm balmy evenings when the stars came out I would stand on the top step of the companionway and lean with my arms on the hatch opening just gazing into the night with my thoughts dwelling on the good things, and good people that have been part of my life, the gentle warm wind almost a sensual caress on my exposed skin, directing my thoughts to matters not to be mentioned. Life could never hold such contentment as those moments. All too soon it would be time to go to bed or, should I say, time to go to settee to rest.

*****

During the night the frequent checks produced no worries and even the steering behaved. However, something strange was going on that was difficult to pin down. While taking my rest between visits to the great outdoors, with my head on the pillow, I was hearing voices. These were in the form of a conversation between a man and a woman the actual words undistinguishable but the inflection unmistakable. When I lifted my head they stopped and started again when my head was set to the pillow. Not given to fantasy I didn't put this down to visitations from outer space or other such imaginings. Having said that, these thoughts must have come to mind I suppose. Rather I surmised that it had to do with the movement of the boat, and the bilge water swilling from side to side, or at least that is what I told myself, and I would fall asleep trying to interpret what was being said, nosey that I am eavesdropping on other people's conversations. Be that as it may, there were far more important matters to consider than the possibility of supernatural beings.

To conserve the batteries it had been my habit to limit the use of electric power by switching off any unnecessary circuits, particularly during the night.

So it was then that when checking the position the following noon I found that the boat was in almost the same position as the previous noon. This was a most odd turn of events which caused me great deal of consternation. The wind had eased to around ten knots since the last fix but we were still moving. Rechecking the GPS didn't give any indication of errors from that department which was also checked against the hand held GPS. Puzzlement indeed and what to do? At least the problem wasn't electrical, so discharged batteries could be discounted from the equation. The boat was not going the way that it should, in fact, not making any progress towards the appointed destination at all. The reason for this anomaly was only revealed much later in the voyage. At this time, however I could not come up with an answer except to carry on for another day and see if the situation improved.

The following noon indicated a little progress in the right direction but still very unsatisfactory. Obviously this point of sail was not suitable for getting us to Panama, or anywhere else for that matter, as the trend of the coast would increasingly bear towards the east and bring the wind ahead even more.

It didn't take me long to come to an alternative decision. In fact, under the circumstances the only way to go was to put the wind on the beam again and the best point of sail, head south until I met the Southeast trades from the southern hemisphere which, when they cross the equator, blow from a southwest direction. This would entail a much greater distance to travel because with the coast tending away to the southeast and the boat travelling towards the south, the distance between us and Panama was getting wider. The way I saw it there was no alternative, unless I was prepared to doodle about here hopelessly trying to close the coast. The other positive thought was that I could cross the Inter Tropical Convergence Zone sooner and faster. The ITCZ is the area between the two trade winds and much influenced by squalls and heavy rainfall. So I then set the course to the south and with my spirits lifted the boat heeled on a port tack picking up speed.

Not all was a bed of roses though. A problem had developed with the cigar lighter purchased in the Cabo; this it turned out was defunct. This was an important piece of equipment as it was this that the inverter plugged into to charge the lap-top. As the laptop was redundant due to the satellite phone being ashore it was no problem in this respect. However, the electric shaver also plugged in to this receptacle to be charged, and with this being redundant my beard would inevitably develop. Facial hair is not considered desirable in my case and I was not keen on developing a full set of hair on my face, not for vanity, but rather for the feel of it. When looking in the mirror I would have the uncanny feeling of looking at another being staring through a hedge, not a desirable state of affairs but, alas, one it seemed that would have to be borne under the circumstances.

The next day the wind died sufficiently for me to get the genoa down to make repairs to the tears that had appeared over the last few days. The sailors duct tape that had been applied in the Cabo had not held so the morning was spent stitching a patch over this particular area, and folding and stitching a patch over the leach. It was quite a nice interlude sitting out in the sunshine doing the needlework and taking on a tan. As it turned out this interlude didn't last, as the wind started to pick up before the jobs were completed, and so the sail went up again with the resolve on my part to return to playing the seamstress during the next lull. I was thankful that during the period between the first tear and when it had been possible to make a repair there had not been anything alarming like a violent ripping of the sail, just tears that caused some concern but which held.

The gloriously sunny weather lasted for some days more, a time of relaxation which I enjoyed principally because it was not necessary to wear much in the way of clothing. Even the wind was warm, so I wore just a pair of underpants, and why even this limited clothing one might ask? After all there was no-one to be bothered by my nakedness should I be so. But one should preserve some sort of decorum I suppose if only just for forms sake. This state of affairs sure saved on the laundry.

All good things must come to an end though, and before many days had passed the sky clouded over and darkened ominously. Rain appeared towards the eastern horizon and the wind rose to twenty-five knots. This was a sure indication that ITCZ was nigh and would soon have to be dealt with. As evening was coming on and in anticipation of squalls arriving during the night and, being reluctant to fight with the sails in the dark, I doubled reefed the mainsail and reduced the genoa to a third of its area.

In the planning stage for this voyage, amongst the many preparations that I made for this, that, and the other, a plastic sheet with a spout stuck in the middle had been fabricated. This rig was to be arranged to collect rain water and direct it via the spout into the water tanks. In preparation for catching the approaching rain this plastic sheet I secured in position with the spout inserted into the filler pipe to the water tanks. The filler cap was on the side deck between the rails and the cabin top. Alas, this proved to be impracticable as the wind got under the plastic sheet, ejecting the spout from the filler pipe. So to Plan B: the sheet was moved into the cockpit, spread out with fastenings secured to the rails on either side of the boat. The spout was now in a bucket. This too wasn't entirely satisfactory as the spout wouldn't stay in the bucket with the wind flapping the sheet about. As a variation on Plan B, I filled plastic bottle with water and placed it in the sheet to hold it in place. This proved admirable for the purpose. The spout stayed in the bucket and when a sufficient amount of rain water was harvested poured into the water tank.

And so the rains came with the squalls, intermittently as squalls do, and flashes of lightning were followed by the crash of thunder. This heavenly display made for a diversion of sorts: with each flash I counted the seconds before the thunder gave the distance from the lightning. The closest lightning flash was twenty miles away which perversely gave me a feeling of disappointment as a flash of lightning immediately followed by a deafening crash of thunder usually gives me a mental jump and an adrenalin surge. My, but what one will do for kicks?

The bucket that collected the rain water which when sufficiently full was transferred to the water tanks gave me alternative entertainment during an otherwise quiet evening. Unfortunately there was an uncalled for side effect to this manna from heaven. The working of the boat in the waves had opened cracks between dissimilar materials, i.e. the wooden window frame and the fibreglass coaming causing leaks. With the wind driving the rain through what must have been just small apertures, this ingress of water ran down behind the settee back to accumulate on the seat, soaking the cushions. As the leaks were small they took quite some time to create puddles. I placed the cushions on their edge, and mopped the puddles, and waited for the rain to cease, which it did, as is the case with squally weather. Then it blew again bringing more rain, with the gust at times reaching forty knots. How pleased I was with having the foresight to reef down the sails before these gusts made life difficult. What with the window leaks and my tramping water in from outside after checking for shipping and such during the lulls, the cabin became quite damp. Apart from these nuisances the boat was making good progress, and I comforted myself with the thought that it wouldn't last forever. As the days passed though, the noise of the wind and the lashing of the rain on the windows, and the leaks, and the mopping up, became quite tiresome. Ennui crept in too, and under such depressing circumstance this wasn't unusual. One evening after the meal I was sitting listening to the Mozart's 21st Piano concerto, the 'Elvira Madigan,' the rain had eased off a little, and it occurred to me to get up and check around for any shipping. I debated whether to go out on deck or not; if anything was there I probably wouldn't see in the rain anyway. I decided stay where I was. Why go and get wet when it was much better to stay inside where it was damp. From this another train of thought developed: was it possible for a human to be affected by rising damp? Couldn't say that I'd heard of such a case. When I was an apprentice on cargo ships in the tropics it was not unknown to get athletes foot from sweating, but then that is a far cry from rising damp. I had to give an inward smile though at the thought of maybe getting athlete's foot of the butt. Such thoughts I considered to be the result of apathy and a tired mind and I wondering how much longer it would be before getting back into finer weather.

A few days later there was an occurrence that shook out any feelings of ennui and had me in a state of energetic alacrity. It happened during the afternoon: the rain had eased with only the odd shower during the morning and early afternoon, and the sun was shining spasmodically through the clouds, promising a passing of the squalls. I was relaxing in the cabin reading about Cortez doing his Conquistador thing in Mexico when my senses were directed to an increase of wind. The wind had been reasonably steady at twenty-five knots but with a glance at the wind indicator I saw the needle was showing gusting to thirty-five. At this wind speed the tops of the waves were being blown into a spray and the boat speed had increased also. The waves were about twelve feet which was no cause for alarm as they were running faster than the boat, which is how it should be. The problem that could develop, however, would be if the boat started to run faster than the waves. In such a situation when the boat went into the trough it could possibly broach to and be swamped. This would be a most unpleasant situation to be in. The main sail was double reefed and the genoa reduced, but obviously this wasn't enough to slow the boat. The option that faced me was to impede progress sufficiently to keep the waves passing under the hull and moving faster. The recommended practice was to trail a drogue behind, thus arresting the forward motion. This I didn't have. Similarly, trailing a heavy line, the sea anchor rode would do but that would have to be manhandled back on board when more clement weather returned. The next option was to heave-to, an option under the present circumstances regarded to be the most favourable and the quickest. Another glance at the wind indicator showed the wind had increased to forty-five knots. In these situations as speed is of the essence but not so speedy as to take an unnecessary risk. Taking the time to don the safety harness I was soon on the coach top dropping the main sail and lightly lashing it to the boom. Back in the cockpit the wheel was put hard over to bring the boat's head into the wind. Nothing happened with this manoeuvre, the boat just kept on going ahead. In the matter of only a few minutes I was in the cabin firing the engine, then back to the cockpit to engage the gears to bring the boat around. Well, imagine my surprise. The boat had turned itself around during my absence and was riding the waves with the sea on the port bow where it should be. After all the frantic energy expended, not to mention the adrenaline surge, I was gob smacked that the boat had first refused my efforts, then gone and done what was required without any guidance from me. Does this boat have a will all of its own? Considering the other occasions when it had tried to make for Hawaii, I couldn't help but consider that possibility. Having said all that I must admit to a profound exhilaration while on the coach top securing the main sail. The boat had skidded and sheared in the following seas, the full force of the spray whipped off the wave tops to sting my skin, the scudding clouds and the warm sunshine all contributing to my elation.

After this expenditure of energy and mental gymnastics the wind dropped back to twenty-five knots. A state of affairs I was not about to act on immediately, first a cup of tea and waited to see which way the cat would jump. After half an hour the wind had settled and I resumed direction and progress towards the south.

During the unpleasant interlude of the ITCZ yet another event happened to mar the pleasures of boating. As is my wont the engine was run for an hour every third day to top up the batteries; the solar panel didn't seem to have any effect in this line of work. On the last attempt to fire the engine nothing happened except for a grating noise. At this I deduced that the cranking battery was flat. On checking this battery and the four house batteries with the hydrometer all showed a full charge, and yet the electric panel volt meter indicated less than nine volts. This was indeed a puzzle compounded by the fact that when it comes to understanding the mysteries of electricity my knowledge is basic indeed. This was of great concern; apart from not being able to charge the batteries there was the problem of not motoring into the anchorage at Panama. But that was sometime in the future and now I had to try and find a possible fault between the batteries and the panel. If this could be solved then maybe the engine would fire. But, niggling at the back of my mind was that the fault might lie in the batteries being duff. After doing all that my limited experience would allow I had to admit that from now on until expert help was available it would be a case of conserving what electrical energy remained.

And so the days passed. In time the ITCZ was crossed and the squalls and gusting winds and the rain were behind. The cushions from the settee were dragged out into the sunshine to dry, and the forward hatch opened up to allow a flow of air to pass through the cabin, hopefully to dry it out. The wind had eased considerably and the reefs were taken out of the sails. The genoa had suffered a little more and the mainsail had also torn. The ties on the reef points had ripped down the sail to be stopped only by the battens. The three tears were only six inches in length so nothing serious there and they couldn't go any further. On the luff of the mainsail are slides that fit into a track on the mast to keep the sail tight against the mast. Several of these slides had broken and it was with not a little dismay that the luff now had bellied out in places, allowing the wind to pass through with a resultant loss of efficiency. The redeeming feature of this problem, if one could call it that, was that the broken slides could be replaced by redistributing the good ones to more strategic positions. To do this the sail only had to be lowered without taking it right off the mast to do the change over, as is the case with the foresail when making repairs.

The return of the sunshine and fair winds compensated immensely for the previous unpleasant weather conditions and, with a lifting of the spirit I anticipated reaching the south-west trade winds. All thoughts of the past boisterous weather were gone. It was at this time that I was joined by several boobies, the feathered kind. For the most part they settled down in a raft to ride the waves when night came on, but some squabbled and fought each other for a perch on the forward rails of the pulpit. One particularly cheeky character found a perch on the aft rails and stayed there for days keeping in tune with the rolling of the boat. How this was possible eluded me for the rail was smooth and the bird had webbed feet, but he did, and made this balancing act look easy. These birds are about eighteen inches in length with brown feathers. The area around the eyes is purple, and the eyes stare unafraid. The beak gives the impression of the nose on Pinocchio after telling a few lies. A most interesting bird which never moved from its position on the rail even when I passed close enough to poke him. Not that I did for he was far too cute to frighten off, and company of a sort, the first thing to look for when I came on deck.

In the fullness of time I reached the trade winds and put the boat on a course for Panama. I had previously directed the course to the south so the distance to Panama had been greatly increased. Good sailing weather was anticipated but, with a distance of sixteen hundred miles to go would take some time, adding considerably to the length of the voyage. And what of the friends who would be expecting my arrival on the announced twenty-one days? There was no way to contact them to abandon the idea of joining the boat for the transit, which became one more worry. And I hated to think what they would be thinking: stuck in Panama on an enforced holiday not knowing what had happened, whether I was dead or alive. All I could hope for was that, having no contact, they would not even start out.

There was one bonus to put on the list and that was we were now south of ten degrees north latitude which meant there would be no tropical storms to worry about. These monsters, thankfully, do not operate in the band of ten north and ten south latitudes.

The trade winds, for the most part, remained constant with the occasional lulls that allowed the foresail to be taken down and repairs attempted. The genoa had suffered during the squally weather and was now in a most parlous state with the leach torn away from the rest of the sail. The sail had also torn part of the way along the bottom edge of two of the seams. Despite this, the sail still held together and was pulling the boat along efficiently, considering the injuries it had suffered. The sail-makers duct tape had long since come away and disappeared, suggesting the stuff had no meaningful repair qualities. Household duct tape had been tried on the last attempt at repair and that too had come away and was flapping around in the wind like a demented crow. The patch that had been sewn on was holding out magnificently but the sail was showing signs of coming apart around it. In the time allowed between the winds picking up again I attempted to repair the seams which were coming apart. And, also, to stop any further progression of the tears I stitched across the seam. This particular lull lasted about two hours before the winds picked up again. Well satisfied with the effort and keeping a watchful eye on the sails behaviour I progressed eastwards, with the boat rolling easily in the swell.

Just after dark I sighted the bright lights of a fishing boat on the starboard quarter. At this time the wind had eased again and my boat was not making much forward motion above keeping steerage way. I deduced from his speed and direction that he was laying the long nets that have been the subject of so much controversy during the past few years. These nets are made with indestructible monofilament which catches anything and everything. The fishermen claim that they are fishing for squid only but, can they claim this to be true. Any other species of marine life is also in danger of getting caught up in these nets and unable to free themselves, die. There have been reports of nets, which are miles in length, breaking free and becoming so loaded with dead marine life that they sink, and when the catch has rotted away they rise to the surface again to carry on with their evil work. And so the process is repeated, and as the monofilament is indestructible it can go on ad infinitum, a truly terrible example of man's greed and indifference to the creatures of the ocean.

While I pondered these problems the fish boat gradually reduced the distance between us and was getting quite close. Something happened to my thought processes at this juncture, which I'm hard pressed to explain for I went below to put on a pair of shorts. No doubt I thought that if he was to bump into my boat

I'd better be presentable. A crazy idea, even in the subconscious, but I had been on my own for some time so it should be allowed that a lapse in sanity could happen under these circumstances. However, he moved off across my stern and stopped some distance away, while my leisurely pace to the east increased the distance between us and I could take off my shorts again.

During the course of the following week all power from the batteries died. This was a nuisance for quite a few reasons. There was to be no readout from the instruments; no GPS, wind speed, and no gyro compass. Without power the bilge pump wouldn't work and to empty the bilges which were making quite a lot of water at this time I had to resort to the hand pump. No problems there, at least for the next few days until that also quit operating. On investigating and taking out the suction hose I discovered a hole allowing air to be sucked in with the result that the bilge water was not being lifted. The application of that most wonderful duct tape soon had the fault repaired and the bilges kept low, at least for a few more days when the pump acted up again with no evidence of a hose leak. It was then a matter of baling the bilge with a saucepan, transferring the water into a bucket, and then emptying this into the kitchen sink, and thus out the drain back to its original environment. Wherever the leak came from it got progressively worse as we headed to our distant destination, and before long the bilge was being baled three times a day. The water didn't at any time come over the floor boards but it was close. The leak from the rudder seal had been inspected closely since leaving the Cabo but there wasn't enough leakage to justify the amount of water entering the boat. So where did it come from? There was nothing to do but keep baling until I arrived in Panama and the services of a haul out would hopefully reveal all.

It so happened that in planning this trip I'd had the foresight to buy a hand held GPS. If this had not been so I wouldn't have known where I was on this planet at this time. Just head east by magnetic compass until land was sighted, I suppose. Ah! The joys of boating are not experienced by many. One must admire the early explorers who just wandered about the oceans looking for new discoveries not knowing what they would find. Not to mention the shipboard diseases. At least I wouldn't get scurvy.

There wasn't much that went wrong after this. But then there wasn't much else that could go wrong, but, that was a dangerous assumption, for the solar shower disappearing one night. This had been sitting on the coach top between the hatch coaming and the grab rail. Quite difficult one would imagine for a bag of water to escape from these restraints. But it did. No doubt a free surface effect had been set up inside the bag with the boat rolling in the swell and working itself over the grab rail and, plop, over the side it went. At least that is what I surmised. A loss but not critical, as there was always a bucket to get an overall body wash from. To be quite honest I should have anticipated this happening because on a previous occasion I placed a four litre bag of wine on the kitchen counter only to have it plunge to the deck and burst open when the boat rolled. A different situation and conditions, maybe, but one should observe and learn I suppose.

The loss that was felt more critically though was the flashlights. These had been bought as a set of four. Bright yellow they were and of varying sizes, from big chunky to pencil size. One by one they gave up the ghost, for what reason I never did fathom. Occasionally, by giving them a good shaking, a glimmer would appear then give up again. The batteries were up to snuff so that wasn't the problem which was just as well. During the pre-voyage shopping spare batteries I had purchased in quantity. Alas, these had suffered from the all pervading damp and became quite useless. This loss of flashlights was particularly annoying as this was the only means there was of checking the compass course on a dark night. All these little anomalies paled into insignificance though when the self lighting picot for the stove failed, no doubt due to the dampness. That in itself was not critical as there was always the BBQ lighter, at least until that fell apart. Even then, as I had by now developed resilience and a resigned acceptance to all these petty happenings, all was not lost. Ha! Ha! I said to myself there is one more means of lighting the stove. And, I must say here that this wasn't going to beat me, no way was I going to do without a cup of tea. There was an alternative should the stove be out of action as there was an electric kettle and the generator. But more of that later. Having planned well ahead for lighting the stove, a box of matches had been put on board in a watertight plastic container. Carefully opening the box and taking out a match and placing the box on the counter, as lighting the stove is a two handed affair, one hand to press and hold in the knob for a few seconds the other to light the gas, I successfully lit the match. Just as the flame was approaching the gas, the boat took a violent roll, putting me off balance and causing me to drop the match, and would you believe because of this wave action the box of matches was thrown into the sink. At this I must admit to a small gesture of despair by throwing my hands up and crying out, 'Why me Lord?'

There was no answer from above. But, I had a few derogatory thoughts on the subject. Why ask anyway? The Lord moves in mysterious ways, and in my case, with violent movement of the waves.

However, all was still not lost. Maybe the propane stove was out of commission until something brilliant came to mind about the problem of lighting the gas. In the meantime there was still the portable generator and not only an electric kettle but, and this is were forethought brought its rewards, an electric frying pan, purchased at the great expense of two dollars at the local thrift store. These then were put to use to prepare that nights dinner. The clouds of black, smelly smoke that emitted from the fry pan thermostat were a little alarming, probably the damp again, and although the thermostat didn't work, I cooked a reasonable dinner of stew.

These items were put to good use for the next couple of days, the frying pan to cook dinner, fried rice with peas and carrots being the meal of choice for this were the most suitable for this type of cooking utensil. And, although the thermostat did not work it had stopped smoking. The kettle boiled the water for the ubiquitous tea, a beverage that one cannot live without, not this one anyway. Using the generator for these tasks was all very well in an emergency such as this but, the propane stove should be handling the cooking and, should the fuel supply for the generator run out I would be in a right pickle. Apart from any other consideration the stove provided more scope with four burners and a capacious oven. After mulling over the problem for a day or two the bright idea then struck me about how to light the propane. Why didn't I think of that before? Dragging out one of the batteries from below and baring the ends of two lengths of electrical wire of suitable length, I attached one length to the positive side of the battery and the other length of wire to the negative side. Striking one wire against the other produced a spark of sufficient intensity to light the gas. Eureka! The manoeuvre though called for a little contortion as two hands were needed to strike a spark and a knee to hold in the stove knob. With a little practice balancing on one leg against the roll I found this manoeuvre to be eminently successful. We were back in the cooking business. A mental pat on the back for this act of inventiveness was duly applied.

The sin of pride it seems carries a penalty, for having proudly cooked and eaten the first meal on the regenerated stove I went out on deck for a bucket of sea water for washing the dirty pots, when the boat took a heavy roll. The mainsail boom swung over causing the sheets to catch me unawares. Off balance I was thrown violently to slam my back in way of the lumber region against the coaming. Obviously the wind was not strong enough to create sufficient pressure on the sail to resist the force of that particular wave. The pain this caused in my lower back was such that I didn't dare move. I just sat still wondering if anything was broken or any organs damaged. Well, I couldn't stay in this position forever, so easing myself off the coaming and gritting my teeth against the pain I managed to get below onto a more comfortable seat. Although it hurt like the blazes I came to the conclusion that nothing was broken. Why not was a puzzle, from the force with which my back met the coaming would suggest that something would have to give, but thankfully that this wasn't the case. The result of all the milk I drank as a child building strong bones I would guess, unless of course what they say about Yorkshire men being, 'strong in the back, and thick in the head.' Whatever, this incident had me taking pain killers, something that I had almost never done. Funny though, how a situation like this can bring to mind an amusing anecdote. On this occasion it was when I was at the chemists having a prescription filled for pain killers, foresight again. There was a bit of banter going on between the chemist and me, with me claiming not to take pills but rather put up with pain because of a high pain threshold. There is no bragging element to this statement; it is just that taking pills of any sort goes against my principle of not wanting to become reliant on them. This conversation was being avidly followed by the girl assistant and the Chemist became impatient with my attitude and told me with some asperity that the pills would be needed if I got toothache.

"I don't get toothache," I stated.

"Everybody gets toothache," said the chemist with a hint of exasperation.

As she had her back to me, and the conversation was threatening to get out of hand, I just clacked my dentures at the assistant. We both had great difficulty keeping straight faces at this.

Sometimes the devil gets into me.

Now these painkillers came in handy and I silently conceded the argument to the chemist.

Over the next few days the weather remained constant and the boat required only a little sail handling. When this chore did have to be dealt with, it required gritted teeth and very careful movements. Time heals all things, as they say, and in due course apart from the occasional muscle pull which brought on an involuntary, 'Aaagh', life progressed. After a few days I gave up the painkillers as it occurred to me that when I took them the pain would become subdued, then when the affect of the pills wore off the pain seemed to be worse. There was nothing for it but, when the occasion arose, to take careful movements and grin and bear the discomfort.

When the land came into view towards evening some days later, my pleasure can well be appreciated. It had been a very long time since I had sighted land. The boobies though had long past departed; I had become used to having them around as they had been company of sorts. A cheery, 'Good Morning,' when I came to the cockpit at daylight to the bird on the cockpit rail never met with any response, only a blank stare from the beady eyes. Well, they had gone now and I silently wished them well. Possibly they would meet up with another boat and provide company there.

The speed of the boat being as it was we soon came abeam of Punta Mariato, the headland at the southwest corner of the Peninsula de Aguero, and only one hundred and fifty miles from our destination. The end of the journey would soon be in my grasp.

Oh, dear! Will I never learn not to look forward in naïve anticipation?

*****

Several ships were sighted closer to the shore, more than likely having transited the Canal and heading out into the Pacific. These observations prompted my decision to continue my present course and keep the distance off the coast and the shipping until abeam of Cabo Mala on the southeast corner of the Peninsula de Aguero, when a course change to the north into the Gulf of Panama could be safely carried out and be clear of the traffic from the Canal.

Through the morning and into the afternoon I made progress at a reasonable speed eating up the miles to Cabo Mala, then to make sure that the big boys wouldn't get in the way, directed the course a little to west of north. This alteration would also bring the coast in a better position for viewing. After all the time spent on the trip down from the Cabo San Lucas just having the ocean to look at, a change of scenery would most certainly be a welcome alternative to the passing waves. Not only was there the dense jungle to admire, there was the added bonus of examining all the rubbish floating by. The amount of flotsam drifting in the Gulf of Panama was something to behold. Had there been a fast flowing river in the vicinity that brought down trees and other rubbish from the interior, then this would have been understood. But, this rubbish was man-made, mainly: plastic bottles, plastic bags, plastic milk containers and cartons of varying sizes, and much to my amusement, a condom heading west. At least that was the way it was pointing. It would seem that not everyone in this Catholic country followed the dictates of the Pope regarding birth control. He obviously doesn't advocate recycling either.

By mid afternoon the wind died to nothing, not a breath. It was as though the boat was sitting in a sheet of glass. Well, with no engine there was nothing else to do but wait it out until a breeze picked up again. The vagaries of the wind in the Gulf of Panama are well documented so I was prepared for a wait, or not, and trusted to whatever. If lucky the wind would pick up again with an evening sea breeze.

That evening, just after sunset, there was a slight breeze, and we were moving, at not more than a drift, but at least there was movement and in the right direction. This gave the boat steerage so it was possible to direct the boat, which was a blessing indeed as it took a direction between a headland and a small islet, then passed close to an outcrop of rocks, which now had a low swell breaking over them. As the sea was generally calm I took this wave action to be a result of ships' wakes. Needless to say, with our movement no more than a drift I watched these rocks with no little apprehension until we had safely drifted by. Even though it was very dark by this time there was enough light from the shore buildings to make out the white of the breaking surf.

At this time of day it appeared that the locals chose to do their fishing, not commercial, but rather a couple of guys in a small boat with bright lanterns, no doubt to attract the fish. What surprised me while sitting on the aft lockers with my feet on the wheel steering the boat was that there was no recognition of my being there even though at times they came close enough to be almost touching. I'm sure if I had said, 'Boo', they would have jumped, so engrossed were they in their activities. Although I had no power for navigation lights, it was a bright tropical night, the clouds having gone to allow the stars to come out, and therefore I was not exactly invisible. It was getting on for midnight before I reached open water and all the other boats had left. Even the little breeze had died away and we were stopped again, so I felt secure enough to lie down and get some rest. Through the remainder of the night it was a case of coming awake at more frequent intervals than out in the ocean, for after all there was no possibility of sound sleep under these conditions.

Daylight comes fast and early in these latitudes so I was soon able to assess the situation. Although there was no breeze to speak of there was a slight movement of the boat parallel to the shore over which I had no control. At this point the drift was close to another group of rocks below a lighthouse. This had me making tentative plans about what to do if the boat struck. There would be no force to drive the boat onto the rocks, there being neither wind nor swell. So I hoped the boat might just bump and be pushed off again with the boathook. There was nothing to do but sit and wait for events to develop. If this situation called for abandonment it wasn't more than a short clamber up the rocks to the lighthouse, and maybe get help from there. My mind also mulled over what could be rescued under these circumstances, and I wondered what the reaction would be from the lighthouse keeper when a soaking wet sailor appeared at his door toting his goods and chattels. As it turned out none of this planning needed to be put into effect as the drift took the boat clear, very close but clear nonetheless, causing a relaxation of tension and my sigh of relief from these anxious moments. This part of the voyage was fast becoming an experience garnished with much anxiety. Having cleared this particular potential hazard I continued to drift in the direction along the coast which presented a view of yet more rocky outcrops. Another nasty situation seemed to be developing. Within the half hour though, a movement of air sufficient to lift the sails out of their torpor came off the land. Casting away all thoughts of keeping out of any potential ship running me down, I directed the boat away from the shore, thinking that at least ships can manoeuvre, rocks can't. The gods must have been looking out for me, for when I was at a safe distance off the shore the wind, or should I say air movement, died away again. And there the boat lay, drifting towards the ocean again. The next twenty-four hours set my progress back some ten miles. Then progress towards Panama for a while, then drifting back, then progress one way then the other across the Gulf. This went on for ten days just being at the mercy of nature, but thankfully I was in no danger from either rocks or ships. On the eleventh day that lovely southwest trade wind picked up again, blowing right into the Gulf. And off we went again as fast as the tatty sails would take us towards Panama. That evening put my position twelve miles from and in sight of the signal station on Flamenco Island at the entrance to the Canal. Then the wind died again leaving us drifting. Daylight comes quickly in these latitudes and so does darkness. And so it seemed did the local fish boats. These, and there were many of them apparently trolling, progressed up and down in procession on each side of me throughout the night. Working on the principle that they could see me on their radars, and were slow moving, should they bump me, it would bring me awake. I lay down to doze a little after midnight.

Well before sunrise the fish boats had departed, gone to wherever fish boats go after a night out. Now it was time to head towards the anchorage below the signal station. Having given some thought about how to make contact with the port to announce my arrival, I had brought the anchor battery from its place forward and connected it to the house circuits. This gave power to use the VHF radio, and thus contact with shore. Much to my pleasure this worked admirably and contact was made, loud and clear. Odd though, as on being directed to the anchorage, I was instructed to then go ashore and phone.

"Who should I phone?" said I. A reasonable question I thought.

"You will find out when you get ashore," came the answer.

This puzzled me, but then, when in Panama do as the Panamanians do. No doubt all will be revealed in the fullness of time. And true to form there was plenty of time.

There was only a light breeze, but the boat was moving in the right direction towards the anchorage below the signal station and to the east of the Canal approach channel. There were a great number of ships at anchor, but no ship movements that could be observed, so the slow speed of the boat would not be an impediment to them. With chronic lack of progress over the last days I couldn't help but think that my beard was growing faster than the progress of this odyssey.

The wind, breeze, air movement, whatever, died again and so drifting once again became the norm. Then a little puff, just to tease, then calm again. But, wonder of wonders progress, slow though it was gave a closing towards the destination.

After starting out at four this morning from the night's position until I came into the anchorage took twelve hours, a distance of three miles. But then fate hadn't finished with me just yet. At the very moment that I was ready to go forward to drop the anchor a reasonably strong breeze sprung up, pushing the bow onto a heading away from the direction required to make the anchorage. From previous experience the bow would not come across the wind to take another course, and to put the wind on the opposite bow required a jibe manoeuvre, or in other words bring the wind across the stern. By the time this had been completed the boat had been blown out of the anchorage and into the approach channel to the Canal. The wind dropped and there I was sitting becalmed waiting for another breeze. Feeling a little pissed off by how events had carried me out of the anchorage just when success was in my grasp, my attention was attracted by the sound of a ship's whistle giving five short rapid blasts indicating that danger loomed and I should vacate my position to somewhere safe. This ship had the right of way of course; after all it was the Panama Canal and he wanted to get to the locks. But then what could I do? Well I suppose I did what anyone else would do under the circumstances. I raised my arms aloft, hands outstretched in a gesture of helplessness. At this, much to my anxiety the ship increased speed and headed in my direction. Crikey! After all this time during the past weeks keeping clear of all shipping I was now to be run down only a matter of minutes from my goal. Life at this moment seemed to be vindictive. All that I could do was watch the relentless approach of this monster and gulp to keep my heart from vacating its normal position to choke my now dried out mouth.

The distance between us was closing rapidly, the ship bearing down in what I considered a most dangerous manner. Then a slight alteration of course took him to the other side of the channel and across my bow. As this wall of steel passed close enough to spit on, had I any saliva and the will to do so. I could see the rails were lined with crew expressing complete indifference to my predicament. The strangest thought came to me at this. A line from Albert and the Lion came to mind when I looked into the eyes of these people as if reading their thoughts: 'There weren't no shipwreck nor drowning, in fact nothing to laugh at all.' A strange thought but maybe I had been too long at this game? What really miffed me was that no one came from the bridge to see if they had missed or not. As I lay rocking in the wake of this ship I thought how callous of them. At least if someone had come out to check I would have waved in acknowledgement of his courtesy.

The vagaries of the wind being as they were in the Gulf of Panama they came up again and from the right direction to blow the boat slowly back into the anchorage and out of the way of any ship that might be using the channel. It was with a slump of the shoulders in a gesture of profound relaxation and relief that I had finally arrived and the anchor was down in a safe berth, albeit with tatty sails, mainsail tied to the mast with rope replacing the non-existent slides, no engine, batteries flat and this, that, and the other out of commission. The initial estimate of twenty-one days had stretched to fifty-one which must be a record of sorts. The last one hundred and fifty miles took an incredible ten days

But, I was 'appy. I'd arrived.

CHAPTER FIVE
Panama

.....if you can wait and not be tired by waiting

Kipling. 'If'

So this was where Balboa waded into the sea and proclaimed the whole South Sea for Ferdinand, King of Spain. Vasco Nunez de Balboa (1475 to 1519), a Spanish colonist, conquistador and explorer, was the first European to see the eastern shore of the Pacific Ocean. It is also claimed to have been he who named this vast ocean, Pacifico, due to the calmness of the waters, although some say it was the Portuguese explorer Magellan who gave this name. My money would be on Balboa based on the assumption that the Gulf of Panama, which he was looking at, would be much more 'pacifico' than the waters off the Strait of Magellan, i.e. the Southern Ocean. Nevertheless, this proclamation opened up the whole western coast of South America to exploration and the conquest of Peru which provided vast wealth in gold and silver to the Spanish Treasury.

Although born into an impoverished noble Spanish family with little or no influence Balboa managed to aspire to Governor of Panama under Pedro Arias de Avila, an elderly nobleman, Avila was an extremely jealous man who resented the growing popularity and influence of Balboa with the Indians and local Spanish population. In 1518 Governor de Avila falsely accused Balboa of treason, speedily had him tried and sentenced him to death. On 21st January 1519, with four friends, Balboa was beheaded. Unlike de Avila, who has passed into obscurity, Balboa has been remembered. The Panamanian currency, shows his portrait although nowadays only on the small coins, the American dollar being the currency of choice, and the city at the southern end of the Canal also bears his name.

*****

It was pleasant lying at anchor observing the activity on shore. The anchorage where I lay was just off the causeway that stretched from Balboa to Flamenco Island; although this was no longer an island as it was joined by the causeway to the mainland. During the building of the Panama Canal this island was a popular excursion and picnicking spot for the wives and families of the American engineers and executives working on the construction of the Canal. John Stevens, an American railroad engineer in charge of the construction, used the spoil from the diggings to create this causeway. Over the years various shops, restaurants, nightclubs and marinas have cropped up at various points along the roadway. This was a Saturday evening and it was interesting to see a procession of vehicles coming along the road, reaching the end, turning and heading back towards town. This I surmised must be an outing of sorts where the local populace drove out in the cool of the evening to take the sea air. It would seem that the tradition of going out to Flamenco Island was still alive but these days by road rather than by boat. One mode of transport that was plying the causeway was a vehicle that at first sighting gave me the impression of an awning with several people under it moving with no apparent means of propulsion. It became a lot clearer once I trained the binoculars in that direction. It reminded me of a horse drawn carriage from movies of the Old West: Paint Your Wagon comes to mind where one of these carriages was bringing in the ladies of pleasure to No Name City. The carriage in question was similar to these I observed this evening but lacking horse propulsion. The canopy was, open on all sides, and people were seated with their knees pumping. This phenomenon I observed more closely the following week while I was on the causeway and the knee pumping of four adults became clear. This was the means of propulsion: four bicycle pedal arrangement geared and linked to the back axle. The contraptions were a rental item to give pleasure to whoever wished to put in the effort to ride the causeway and view the surrounding waterside scenery, a neat idea, but hot work in this climate.

There were not many boats in the anchorage; one sailboat close by appeared to be the size of a rich man's play thing. I was later to learn that it was a hundred and ten feet in length and quite an impressive boat it was too. Judging by the activity on board it carried a crew; at least these people were observed to be active and not sitting around having sundowners or whatever it is rich folks do while on their gin palaces.

The evening was still, with not a breath of wind, but what's new, and it was most pleasant standing on the top step of the companionway leaning on the coaming just watching the activities of the people around and about. Restful one might say listening to the muted sounds of the traffic on the road and the bursts of laughter from the people. Not having seen people for so long it was a kind of companionship, but with the added pleasure of not having to make contact. A long time spent in one's own company makes one a bit of a recluse I guess.

It had been a long day and the anxieties, excitements and now the relaxation had made me weary and ready to turn in, happy in the knowledge that I could sleep the night through without the need to regularly check on any imminent dangers. Tomorrow would be soon enough to go ashore and make the phone call. At about this time loud music started up in the near distance which seemed to come from a group of buildings at the turn around below Flamenco Signal Station. So be it. There was no way this was going to interfere with my rest. With the hatch closed and the doors pulled to, the music faded to an undulating murmur, and in my weariness it was no bother at all.

*****

True to expectations I had fallen asleep in record time on the settee, a habit I guess. The forward berth was available and ready for use with no need to get out in a hurry, but then old habits die hard. Had I taken the berth then there wouldn't have been the shock that met me on waking. It was still dark when I awoke but with bright lights shining through the windows. This gave me an initial fright as mentally I was still out on the ocean and these lights struck my mind as an approaching fish boat. Not for long though as I soon realised the lights were from floodlights on the shore. The adrenaline rush though had me rattled for a moment or two. The few hours of continuous sleep had been most refreshing and although it was too early to be active the remainder of the night was spent musing over cups of tea about what actions should be adopted to clear inwards. The first of these chores, after checking in over the telephone, would be to get a new battery to fire the engine, as I was still convinced that insufficient oomph! from the batteries was the cause of the problem.

It wasn't long before daylight came and the daily routine started. After breakfast I hauled out the dinghy and inflated it in preparation for going ashore. It was while I was doing this that a man in a kayak passed by. Without a break in his paddling he gave a cheery, "Good morning," and the advice to move to a safer anchorage away from the rocks. Should the wind get up from the north I was in a dangerous place. From my past experience with the wind, or lack of same, this advice seemed to be a bit over the top. However, I conceded to his better knowledge of the area and resolved if a wind came up I would so move. I told him this and the reasons why. With a wave he paddled on his merry way disappearing around the adjacent headland, leaving me to finish inflating the dinghy and put it over the side, ready to take me to the first dry land my feet had been on for some weeks.

Where to go to telephone to announce my arrival was still a mystery. When I contacted the signal station again this didn't resolve anything and I was told that I would find out once on shore. Indifferent to say the least, I deduced the attitude to be, but, nothing ventured, nothing gained as they say. And so I rowed ashore to a landing on a shallow stone strewn beach and, with much difficulty, having to nurse my still painful back, dragged the dinghy up the beach out of the reach of the rising tide. Well aware of my luck of the recent weeks, I took the extra precaution of tying the painter to a convenient bush. Belt and braces one might say. It would be most frustrating to return to see the only means of getting back to the boat disappearing over the horizon. Satisfied that all would be well I clambered up the low bank slipping and sliding on the loose surface to gain the top with the assistance of clumps of grass and undergrowth, then walked towards where habitation might be found.

On reflection, the row ashore and the effort of dragging the dinghy up the beach, had prompted the thought that my back pain had lasted more than was welcome. Surely in the time that had passed since the accident there should have been an improvement? The thought was dismissed just as quickly as it came; there wasn't any evidence of a broken rib or damage to the internal organs that I knew of. Therefore it must be bruising which, I hoped, would go away in time. The nuisance value was that I was unable to perform a task without a sudden relieving movement, and a, 'Bloody hell', to bring the task to an abrupt stop. This was particularly so when I hauled on a rope or worked a winch, which was a principal activity on a boat. I couldn't let these inconveniences be any deterrent to continuing the voyage though, so just grin and bear and get on with life.

There were buildings close by the landing, cleanly attractive in their newness, a short distance and across the road from where the traffic had been observed on the previous evening, These low two story buildings were spread out over a wide expanse separated by open gardens and parking spaces, empty of vehicles at this early hour, all looking as though recently built and pleasingly attractive to an eye used to staring at an empty ocean. The restaurants and shops housed in these buildings gave the impression that this was a resort of sorts. There were a few people about, service staff no doubt, cleaning up after the previous nights reveries, and it was to these that I made my way. After accosting a person or two who seemed that they might help I finally found someone who spoke English, and he very kindly walked with me across a parking lot to a building and pointing through the glass fronted entrance gave directions up a flight of stairs to the Port Captain's office situated on the first floor. At this level a balcony formed three sides of the building above the entrance hall. Looking across to the far side and behind a glass fronted office I noticed two men in conversation. One was seated behind a desk, the other in a chair at one end. It was to this place that I made my way, hoping to gain some information about becoming a legal visitor.

Luck was on my side; the notice on the door stated that this was the office of the Port Captain, and even though it was Sunday the Port Captain was in residence. However, over the period that I was to stay in Panama I came to realise that the gentleman that occupied this office was not actually the Port Captain. Such a luminary was to be found in the main offices in Balboa. But of course I was not to know this at the time. Justino, as I came to know him, was more of an assistant who attended to the business of clearing vessels inwards that visited the Flamenco Marina and Resort. This place, situated at the end of the causeway was where five weeks would be taken out of my voyage, not that I realised this at the time. I was still planning on just hauling the boat getting the sails repaired, having the batteries checked or replaced as necessary, and transiting to the Atlantic side.

In time as my acquaintance with Justino developed I came to realise what a nice helpful man he was. He showed a mixture of shyness and kindness, deferential almost, which from my past experience with officialdom was an odd combination. These qualities were evident because the help he gave was far beyond the parameters one would expect of his job description.

As I entered his office and approached his desk he stood up and smiling, held out his hand. The handshake was firm and friendly which was comforting as all too often, when a handshake is soft and limp this is sure sign that the giver is indifferent to the receiver, and so speaks volumes regarding his approachability. The second man who had been seated at the end of the desk stood to be introduced as the Port Health Inspector, and speaking in Spanish to Justino, nodded and smiled to me. He then took his leave, slinging the strap of a canvas satchel over his shoulder.

Taking the proffered chair. I said, "My boat is anchored," indicating with a wave of a hand in the general direction of where it was. "I arrived yesterday evening from Cabo San Lucas." Then I placed the clearance from the Cabo on his desk.

"Si!" he acknowledged and nodded.

"I wish to clear Inwards," I said, a little nonplussed at what seemed to be his indifference. But then, as I was to learn, in Panama one takes a languid approach to life's tasks. He only appeared to be indifferent. It was an adopted macho attitude which one often meets in dealing with the male population of Panama.

"Also," I said, leaning forward in the hope that this move would demonstrate my seriousness, "I need to haul the boat. You know, take it out of the water."

"Si!" He nodded again.

I waited.

"Come," he said. "We go your boat, then immigration." After gathering the papers he handed them back to me.

Ah! A sign of progress, I thought, but I was curious about the procedure.

So it was then that we left the building and headed across the parking lot. Not to his car or in the direction of the boat, as one would think, but after skirting another building the marina boatyard was before us. It was a most impressive sight which filled me with pleasure for the boat could be hauled out here and I would not have to go to the trouble of trying to sail along the shipping channel to Balboa. As we approached the marina office building a gentleman driving a golf cart came up and stopped, got out, then moved to go into the office. Justino hailed this gentleman in Spanish, and he came over.

"Buenos dios."

"Buenos dios," said Justino, then spoke again at length as though explaining something important. In my ignorance of Spanish I could only speculate what it was about.

The new arrival, a man of medium height with thinning light brown hair and moustache, turned and addressed me in perfect English, accented with an American inflection.

"You want to haul your boat?"

"Why, yes, if that is possible," I said politely and greatly pleased at such a prompt response to my problems and with no struggling to make someone understand. Then noticing the name tag inscription, 'John Cole, Director,' I deduced he actually was an American.

"It won't be until tomorrow. I don't have a crew today with it being Sunday."

"That's fine," I said. "But I don't have any power, the engine quit on me."

"No problem, I'll send a tow." After a short pause, he announced, "It will be a dollar fifty a foot, a day. Ten dollars for water and electricity."

I nodded acceptance. 'Forty feet means, sixty dollars a day, plus ten.' I'm no slouch when it comes to sums. Especially when I have to pay.

"Do you have a sail maker in the yard?" I asked, as he was climbing back into the golf cart.

"No, but I can call one in if you want."

"Sure, thank you."

Then as an afterthought, he added, "We're quite a new facility and don't have our own trades here. In time maybe, but not at the moment." Then reflecting as though he had forgotten what he had come for he got out of the golf cart and walked to the office.

"The tow will be for you at eight tomorrow," he called over his shoulder.

"Lovely. I'll be ready." I was much relieved at the way the boat's problems were being addressed with such ease.

He walked away with what appeared to be a sense of urgency towards the office. During my time here Mr. Cole was the only person I met who showed any sense of urgency, but then he wasn't Panamanian.

Justino and I then proceeded to the beach.

Launching the dinghy again became a painful exercise. Justino in his willingness to help would enthusiastically pull on one side, while I was holding on to the other trying to favour my back and having acute pain with each movement. Eventually, after many instructions to him to take it easy and not pull against me, we managed to get the dinghy into the water and rowed out to the boat.

"Coffee?" I asked when he was seated, waving the kettle to emphasise the question.

"Si."

I wondered if our conversation would progress beyond this one word. Up to now communication had been conducted by gestures and English from me and not much more than the one word, "Si" from him. Not to worry though, we were making progress with the clearing inwards.

While waiting for the kettle to boil, Justino busied himself with the paperwork. Then curious, sipping the coffee, I wondered why he was so quiet and spare with his words. After all he was reading the forms that were written in English without too much trouble.

"You said we would go to the Immigration," I stated.

"Si."

"Would it be possible for me to send an e-mail? You know, internet."

"Si."

Flush with success at this communication lark I added, "I also require a battery," I might as well make the most of his largesse.

"Si, no problem," he answered, smiling.

Well, he may not speak English, but he certainly understands the language, I thought with relief. Therefore it wasn't going to be too difficult to get my requests across the language barrier.

Inward clearance now issued, coffee drunk and passport tucked safely into a shirt pocket, we made our way back to shore, dragging the dinghy back over the stones of the beach to a secure mooring once again to the shrubbery, but it was not without much gritting of teeth, and admonishments against Justino's painful enthusiasm. The word sorry or its Spanish equivalent doesn't seem to be used much. Justino just gave a surprised look and an acknowledgement of, "Ah! Si." Until the next time.

The journey to Balboa in Justino's tired old car was a revelation. The way it would cough and splutter had me wondering whether we would make it to immigration but it did. The route took the full length of the causeway, some two miles, before we came into the city of Balboa, a community built by the

American engineers to house their Canal workers. Fine, clean houses they were too with large overhanging roofs to shed the tropical downpours. There is little American presence now that the Panamanians are taking over responsibility for the Canal and these residences looked unused, I found this a little odd as the buildings and grounds seemed well maintained and I wondered why they weren't occupied.

The visit to Immigration didn't take long. A stamp in my Passport and we were on our way. By this time I had given all direction over to Justino. I just contented myself to being driven around Balboa and out to a place called Albrook which proved to be a new and vast complex of railway station, bus terminal, food stores, shopping mall and joy upon joy, an internet location. Bless you, Justino, you are a kind man. Under the circumstances I didn't think it to fair to keep my Guardian Angel hanging about so it was sufficient for me to just send a quick message to let the folks back home know that I had arrived and was safe. A more detailed announcement could be sent when more private time was available. The shortness of this visit at least prompted a response from Justino that proved that he could speak English.

"You were only two minutes," he announced, surprised.

A little taken aback, but pleased that communication was possible between us I contented myself with just explaining that the recipients would know that I was safe.

Outside the noise of the traffic was deafening. The road through the complex between the terminal and the buildings on the other side was roofed over causing the traffic roar to be amplified. Background noise from the roaring busses added to this maelstrom of noise. Everywhere there were people, crowds moving every which way. With the volume of traffic and the crowds of people all wanting the right of way it was easy to understand why the police controlled the pedestrian crossing. There was no doubt without some control mayhem would have ensued. I've never seen such a surging mass of humanity, or so it seemed after my recent solo existence.

I had explained to Justino that a battery was required so that the engine could be fired. So it was into the superstore that we directed ourselves. This place was a veritable Aladdin's cave. There seemed to be everything that one would wish for contained under one roof. But, it was lunch time and I was hungry. So minding the adage not to go shopping when hungry we repaired to the Deli before embarking on a shopping spree.

"What would you like, Justino?" I asked viewing the menu board.

This question only seemed to cause embarrassment as Justino just waved his hands around in refusal. "Ah! No, no," he said.

"But you must eat something," I said, surprised at his response.

"OK! Maybe the fruit salad," he answered, rather reluctantly I thought, and I hoped this wasn't going to be a contest between us on the subject of food.

It didn't seem much to me but, if that is what he wanted then so be it. I let him order for both of us. After all he had the language. What I had asked for turned out to be a sandwich far larger than I'd anticipated, so half was offered to Justino. At first he refused, but after my insistence that it was more than I could manage, he accepted. Was I being introduced to Latin American politeness? Justino had no qualms about sharing this feast once the courtesies had been observed while I, reflecting on his meagre fruit salad, felt better for the sharing.

Apart from purchasing a battery the advantage of being in such a store, prompted me to stock up on grocery items. One purchase that filled me with joy was my favourite scotch, Famous Grouse. Not only did they stock such a treasure, a free scotch glass was part of the promotion. No doubt I was going to have a good selection of scotch glasses by the time I left Panama.

Returning to the marina Justino insisted on helping get the groceries on board which I found to be a very kind gesture and felt for all the trouble he had gone to on my behalf he should have some remuneration.

But first there was the battery to connect up and the engine to run. If this could be accomplished then there would be no need for a tow to the boatyard. Much to my chagrin nothing happened. Nada, (Spanish creeping in now; must be the climate). Dead as a dodo. Now what? Checking the battery connections didn't change the situation. Obviously, something beyond my limited knowledge of things mechanical was the problem. As there was Justino to ferry ashore I might just as well seek out John Cole and order a mechanic. If I wished to transit the Canal in the near future then expediting the repairs was of the essence.

This was explained to Justino.

"Si!" nodding his head in agreement. "Bueno."

"Can I give you something for your trouble, Justino?" as I took out my wallet mindful of his assistance in matters grocery.

"No, no, no problemo," he said, waving his hands again in refusal.

It seemed to me that this performance had a familiar ring to it. Although it has to be admitted that Justino was a different kettle of fish to the gentleman in the Cabo, this initial refusal to accept remuneration for being helpful can only be construed as Latin good manners.

"Come now, I must give you something for all that you have done," I said as I opened my wallet.

After a moments hesitation, with again the hand gesture, and obvious embarrassment he suggested, “Ten dollars, okay?”

That was a small sum to pay for his attention to my welfare bearing in mind had he not taken me to the Immigration and shopping I would have been at a loss what to do or where to go, but, if that is what he wanted who am I to complain?

“Please, don’t tell the taxi drivers,” he asked with concern.

His request was understandable when one comes to think about it.

“Si,” I said with a grin. Cheeky, I suppose, but the urge to reply in his language was irresistible.

*****

John Cole I tracked down in the eatery cum bar on the corner across from his office eating a pizza. As the weather had turned hot and humid and the Bar was air-conditioned it made sense to sit with him for a while and have a beer. The beer was very cold but also very thin without much strength to it, a disappointment after being so long without. A buzz to satisfy the senses would have been welcome. John promised to arrange for a mechanic for the next day and as he was ready to go home we parted and went our separate ways.

This busy day was not over yet though for when I left the Bar the Port Health Inspector was waiting and wanted to go on board the boat for an inspection. So once again into the breech, so to speak. This dinghy launching and rowing people out to the boat was proving to be something of a behaviour pattern, and let’s not forget the back pains from the effort.

Senor Health Inspector was a different personality from Justino. Where Justino was deferential in his dealings, Senor Health was only interested in completing the formalities with no distraction, not even a cup of coffee. The paperwork was completed in no time at all, and then came the questions and instruction.

“Have you any animals on board?” he asked in English.

“Only myself,” I answered smiling, introducing a moment of levity, and unable to resist a tease at his seriousness.

He only looked blank at this facetious comment. Couldn’t blame him for that.

“No,” I said.

“There is only you on board?”

“Si.” Seemed as though the Spanish was getting to me. “Yes,”

“There have been cases of dengue fever in Panama.”

This statement took me a little aback as I was under the impression that when the Canal was being built all these fevers had been eradicated by the spraying and draining of the mosquito's breeding areas. Still, I suppose there was nothing to stop them returning. While pondering this, with half an ear I was listening to Senor Health extol the virtues of frequent spraying of the cabin, and to inform him should I see any mosquitoes.

Gathering up his papers he pushed them into his canvas satchel and stood ready to leave, waiting for me to play the part of the ferry man.

Finally, after taking him ashore, I could relax a little or so I thought. As I was sitting on the settee with a cup of tea contemplating the events of the day and thinking of the morrow and what that would bring, a breeze came up strong enough to dispel a little of the afternoon heat. What better time than this to move to another anchorage as advised by the kayaker.

Oh, dear! No sooner had the anchor been brought on board and the foresail unfurled than the breeze died away. So what's new? While contemplating whether to drop the anchor again or wait for another puff, the decision was taken out of my hands. From the aforementioned gin palace an inflatable dinghy had put out and headed my way.

"Need a tow?" the occupant asked.

"Would I? That would be kind of you," I replied with relief.

A tow line was quickly rigged and the dinghy started to take up the slack. Unknown to me, as my concentration was on the dinghy, the bight in the towline had hooked onto the anchor locker gooseneck vent. The dinghy took off, the towline slack came up with a rush, and the gooseneck vent parted company with its deck fixture, up and over the side, tracing a graceful parabolic arc up into the evening air then to go plop, never to be seen again. There was only time for me to shake my head in exasperation at this latest calamity and say to myself, "Not again," before having to pay attention to the rapid progress to the new anchorage. Boy! Could that dinghy pull?

Well, this day came to end as most days do; anchored though in a safer position, albeit at a greater distance from the landing place should I wish to row ashore again, I enjoyed a pleasant relaxing dinner complete with wine, music from the CDs. After the evening had taken on its dark shroud, I had a nightcap of The Famous Grouse, much appreciated after the enforced abstinence of the previous weeks. This was the life.

*****

The tow arrived shortly after eight the following morning as promised. As I was an early riser I had finished the morning routine, and had checked the bilge which had not risen appreciably, which I put down to the fact that the boat was not moving, and therefore no water had been forced into the boat from the rudder seal. My, how one can be deluded by false assumptions by hanging on to an original thought with mindless conviction, which would be all too evident at a later date.

The boat that was to do the towing came alongside and the crew soon had a line on board. There was little I could do except stand around as everything that could be done was done by the boarding gang. They handled the job admirably with little or no verbal instruction among them. Much to my relief they even pulled up the anchor; with the state of my back this action pleased me no end. The boat that was doing the tow was a powerful launch, as long as my boat and rather big for the job at hand I thought. As I came to know the yard and its operations better I learned that this launch was intended for nobler tasks than towing disabled yachts. Its size, power and range enabled it to deliver supplies to vessels off-shore.

Before the hour was up the boat had been towed around Flamenco Island, between the breakwaters enclosing the marina proper, and positioned under the hoist. The positioning of the lifting straps was an interesting exercise. On previous haul-outs in Canada the owner of the boat instructs the people responsible for hauling the boat where to position the straps to avoid fouling underwater obstructions, such as propeller shafts and transducers. In this yard a diver went under the hull to position the straps. One other interesting feature that I noticed while the boat was being transported from the lifting dock to the hard stand was a large sign fixed on the side of the Travelift announcing that no personnel were to be on board vessels being moved. Bit late for that I thought as no one had instructed me on that fact, and with the boat centred over the dock one would need wings or considerably more agility than I possessed to get off. Well, if the yard ignored this rule why should I care?

It became even more evident that the Flamenco Resort and Marina was still in the development stage at least the repair yard part of it. Refinements come last I would suspect as once in position on the hard and the Travelift departed, there was no ladder to get off the boat. Fortunately, there were still yard personnel hanging around who at my indication of my marooned situation dragged a painter's tubular scaffolding over and positioned it at the stern. A ladder would have been nice but, beggars can't be choosers. The scaffolding was awkward to negotiate with only a single plank on the top section and diagonal tubing for a foot hold on the way down.

On inspection the underside of the boat was a revelation, which left little doubt as to why progress through the water had been so slow and erratic. Just below the waterline for full area of the hull was entirely covered with gooseneck barnacles, heaving and writhing in protest at being removed from their environment, which prompted a mental thought of disgust at the qualities of this particular paint, so much for the anti-fouling product that had been applied only six months previously.

Among the people hanging about admiring this maritime phenomenon were two young lads who, their spokesman said, would remove the barnacles for fifty dollars. Of course one should always negotiate even if already decided on an offer.

"Fifty dollars?" I asked, not keeping the disbelief from my voice.

He wasn't to be deterred though, "Si. Him," pointing at his buddy, "And me, twenty-five dollars each. We clean everything."

It was at this point that I realised what had been niggling at the back of my mind since being lifted out of the water. There was no power washing facilities which is normal in any yard that takes boats out of the water. There being no better way to clean off barnacles, seaweed or any other maritime gunk and the like to which this deficiency was viewed with dismay. However, on reflection it did give employment to the local casual labour force to perform this task by hand.

I looked at this writhing mass and the work that would be required to remove this growth; also the awkward positions that would be needed to be perform this task decided the matter. My back gave a little twinge in confirmation.

"Alright, fifty dollars."

"Another fifty dollars and we paint for you. He very good painter," he said, indicating his mate, whom I gathered was the silent partner.

"First clean, then we will see. Okay?"

I saw the lads started on the removal of the barnacles when John Cole turned up with the mechanics and the sail maker. There might be a paucity of facilities, but there was no faulting John's organisation in this yard. As neither of these gentlemen could speak English, John very kindly did the translations about what was required. They then came onboard and were shown to their respective areas of expertise.

I struck a deal with the sail maker on the price to first repair the genoa for which he wrote out a rough contract with the request for six hundred dollars up front, for materials I was given to understand. When the genoa was finished we would negotiate for the mainsail repair. This system of cash hand-outs either before or after a job of work was completed became all too clear during my stay here. It was the favoured mode of payment if any work was to be carried out. No cheques, no credit cards, only cash, and then no bill higher than a twenty due to fear of counterfeiting. This, over time, became an imposition and inconvenience, but something one had to go along with.

I didn't have that sort of money on the boat and told him so. This didn't faze him as he had a taxi waiting and we could go to the Bank. Unknown to me at this stage was the fact that my PIN number on the Credit card had crashed. So after numerous futile attempts at the ATM I finally managed to get the daily limit of five hundred dollars. With this he had to be satisfied until I could get the balance on return of the repaired sail, when he would be paid. With this mutual agreement he was dropped off at his place of business and I returned to the yard to be presented with the bill for the taxi which included the sail maker's original journey out to the yard.

"Cheeky bugger," I thought.

John had seen my arrival and came over to tell me the worst.

"The mechanic says that the engine is seized."

"What," I said in disbelief, "how can that be? It has always been most reliable." It occurred to me that I was in denial; the engine had to be operational. This belief in such a piece of machinery was ridiculous I know but, these past few weeks since it had failed to fire I had believed, in my ignorance, the problem was with the batteries.

"Well they have tried to turn it over and it won't move. They are waiting to show you."

"Bloody hell!" I thought with a twinge of gloom. "What next?" Then just as quickly so as not to tempt fate, "Don't ask," was the mental response.

Back on board a demonstration of the problem was enacted for my benefit. A long handled box spanner had been fitted to the fore part of the engine and an attempt to turn the shaft proved that it was indeed immovable

"Can't they fit a pipe over that to get better leverage," I asked hopefully.

This request was passed on by John and the reply returned. "They say that no matter the engine is seized," he said.

"So what do they suggest," I asked, feeling the gloom deepening.

After discussion in Spanish I was advised that the engine would have to come out and taken to their Workshop.

Well, what could I do but agree. They were the experts and accredited by the yard management, so they wouldn't be conning me I thought with unreasonable suspicion. At least there was some satisfaction in that revelation. This day was not going too well so far. As these gloomy thoughts were going through my head I realised that John was speaking to me.

"They will bring a truck tomorrow. I'll arrange for the crane."

One of the mechanics was speaking again. Chubby and indolent was he, and subsequently I came to understand that he was the one with the expertise who never laid his hand on any tool except to pass it to the younger guy who did all the work.

"When they get it to their workshop and open it up you will be required to go and inspect it," John translated.

"Why on earth should they want me to do that? Just fix the thing," I said feeling things were getting to be a little too much.

"You'll find that no-one will do anything without authorisation. They need to cover themselves," he said.

Digesting this information didn't take long as I was becoming well aware of the need to go with the flow.

"Alright. Let's get the ball rolling," I agreed.

*****

"Will you be transiting the Canal?" a voice behind me asked. I had been watching the lads scraping the barnacles and listening politely to the chatter of the one who had proposed the job. It seemed to me that he chatted up the punters while the quiet one did the work. Still if that was their arrangement who was I to interfere. I was having enough put on my plate now to bother with other people's work ethic.

"Sorry," I said, turning to a slightly built man of middle age and noting his grey hair and beard.

"Will you be transiting the Canal?" He asked again.

"That is my intention."

"Could you use a couple of line handlers? My wife and I are making our way to Cartegena."

I was a little off balance at this time with not knowing when the engine might be ready, and as yet I hadn't registered with the Canal authority to do the transit. I had far too much on my mind to make yet another decision, especially catering to some strangers needs.

After explaining to him that I had no idea when I would be ready to go but, if and when I was ready and they were still interested then we could get together and talk some more. After all, one normally has to pay for line handlers, and as four are required to perform this task in the locks, it would make sense to make use of two free ones.

"How can I contact you?"

At this he took out a pen and wrote his name and the hotel he was staying at in a small notebook, tore out the page, and handed it to me.

"Okay, Gerry," I said after glancing at the paper. "My name's Ron."

"I gathered that from the name of your boat," he replied knowingly, grinning his pleasure at being so observant.

I smiled in agreement. "Dead giveaway isn't it?"

He then fell into telling a rather interesting story. His wife and he had travelled from New York by car and decided to see the world while they were still capable. The car would be sold and they were waiting in Panama for the next part of their adventure, if possible a passage to Cartegena. During the course of my travels I was to meet with quite a few people who had cast caution to the winds and got out of the rat race to go wherever life took them. Well, there was no way I could fault that, only applaud. After all wasn't I in the same business with the only difference being the method.

Before long he went to meet his wife, whom he said was around somewhere, no doubt meaning the general vicinity of the Flamenco Resort and Marina.

I wasn't left alone for long for yet another person approached and introduced himself as Luis, a taxi driver who was frequently in the yard and should I require a taxi to go into Balboa or Panama to let him know. Being the new boy on the block and not knowing the routine vis-à-vis transport this solved a problem for me as I needed to get to an Internet facility that evening and contact the folks at home to inform them of the situation here. An arrangement was made and he would pick me up at 6 o'clock outside the office.

The barnacle scrapers had finished their job to satisfaction, cleaned up the debris, and were paid. After many assurances that should I require the boat painted they were first class painters and would do a first class job, they took their leave. At last the source of water ingress could be examined and a plan of action determined. The bottom rudder post seal had, with the working of the rudder, broken off parts of the epoxy securing the seal to the hull, which in my estimation when repaired would only be a stop gap solution. What was needed to resolve the problem of the rudder post working on the seal was a bracket arrangement at the top of the post to resist the rudder movement. It now became a case of which project had priority: the engine, sails, or possibly new batteries. New sails should also be factored into this wish list, somewhere down the road. These items were at the top of the list. In my limited financial state careful consideration to this was a must. A wind generator was also a must if the batteries were to be kept fully charged without recourse to the engine, but not this week. The "must have" list seemed to be growing. With efficient batteries the bilges could be kept low as the bilge pump would be operative. This fact carried the day. A repair to the hull in way of the seal would have to suffice. I had so many worries it is not surprising that I hadn't thought that the reason why so much water could have entered the boat might be something other than the rudder seal. The outside of the boat had been inspected with no evidence of ingress apart from the rudder seal, so I had convinced myself that this was the source of the problem.

*****

The workers finished at four thirty leaving the yard deserted but for the security guard and the occasional boat owners still working on their boats. Just to my right there was a seventy foot yacht undergoing painting below the waterline. During the day three young men of a northern origin who, due to their Caucasian features I guessed must be crew, periodically climbed on and off the boat going about their business. Although I was taking an interest in what went on in the yard I was loath to approach people, content to just keep a watch on what went on. Must be from spending so much time on my own. The boat was called Dynasty, which, if one used a certain inflection on the last syllable could sound ominous.

Ahead of Dynasty was a large cabin cruiser with the crew still working, removing the anti-fouling paint with a noisy power tool, sounding something like a power planer but not as big. Judging from the way it was being held upside down under the hull I couldn't help but feel for the operator. His arms must have become numb from holding the machine for so long in such a position. Curiosity as to just what was going on had me thinking I should go and investigate sometime. At the moment though I had enough on my plate to worry about what other people were up to. Once matters settled down and I could see which way the cat was going to jump would be soon enough to be nosey.

To my left was another cruiser of Panamanian registry. The interesting thing about this boat was the people engaged for maintenance. Only once during my stay in the yard did I see them activated into any sign of labour, and that was when a well dressed gentleman, presumably the owner, appeared to inspect progress. For the rest of the time they just lounged about under the boat. They must have been planning on a long stay judging by the arm chairs which were positioned under the boat in the shade for their comfort. Nice work if you can get it.

All this surrounding activity I viewed with a beer to relax with. Now it was time for me to make a move. First take a shower and get cleaned up before venturing into town. The facilities for taking a shower in the yard were conspicuous by their absence. Toilets? Yes. They were something to be thankful for, and a relief, if one would accept the pun. I did not have to manage on the boat. But no showers; these would be built in due course I was informed. This I had a hard time understanding. Surely when the toilets were built it would not have been too much of a problem to include shower facilities. While they were at it they could have also included laundry facilities which were promised for sometime down the road. It would seem my wish list had extended to the Flamenco Resort and Marina facilities.

This is how matters stood at the end of the first day high and dry in Panama. It had been a hot day and to get cleaned up was a priority. Obviously, to be successful in this enterprise caused a direction away from the norm. There was plenty of water in the tanks, but the freshwater pump had decided to go into destruct mode, probably in sympathy with all the other mini disasters of the past few weeks. Under these circumstances the need to get a shower became an obsession. Away from people, out on the ocean alone the lack of hygiene is of little importance but now, faced with mixing with other humans, there was no chance that I was about to be smelly. There was no alternative but to take a bucket bath. The easiest way to get water now was not from the tanks but to go ashore to the standpipe and carry a bucket of water back to the boat, stand in the shower stall and perform the ablutions that way. Having enough water so as not to run out while still soapy took some planning, and to climb out of the boat and trot across the yard covered in soap suds was not something I would relish, not to mention scaring any of the locals that might be about. It is amazing really what planning can go into a simple task like getting clean. A new fresh water pump was a definite must, one which I made a mental note to attend to on the morrow. There was a Marine store in the general area of the Yard so we would see what was offered there.

Otherwise all went according to plan with the bathing and I was shortly ready at the appointed place awaiting the taxi driver, Luis. This was to be my first lesson in Panamanian reliability. Whatever arrangements are made for whatever time, don't believe it. Either add an hour onto the time or ignore the arrangement entirely seems to be the norm. In this particular instance after waiting for half an hour it was fortunate that Gerry, the erstwhile transit line handler, came by with his wife and car, in this otherwise deserted place.

"Want a ride, Ron?" he called out the window.

"Thanks, but I've arranged for a taxi."

Gerry gave an ever widening grin at this remark. "Been waiting long?"

"Half an hour or so," I replied.

"You will be better off coming with us; otherwise you will be here all night."

Somewhat puzzled, but not wanting to pass up the chance of a ride, I walked over to the car and got in.

"Hello," I said to the lady in the passenger seat.

Gerry made the introductions.

"I don't like the idea of leaving," I stated, expressing my concern at abandoning the arrangement with the taxi driver.

Gerry and his wife both gave a short laugh.

"When you have been here a while you will realise that arrangements mean nothing," said Gerry. "He is probably doing his thing, don't worry about it. Where do you want to go?"

"Well mainly an Internet location, then get a meal." I ran my fingers through my hair. "And a haircut if possible. I'll soon be tripping over this lot," I said.

"No problem, all three are right by our hotel."

On this assurance we fell silent and took an interest in the passing scene. Coming off the causeway Gerry directed the car towards Balboa with the explanation that at this time of day the traffic was much lighter than the direct route into Panama. He took us through the streets of the old American canal family residences, which was impressive in the orderly cleanliness, and the quiet peaceful atmosphere.

Gerry's attention must have been distracted by the scenery for he hit a speed bump without slowing. Sitting in the back seat the force of this contact with the immovable object caused me to rise up slightly; the pain this caused to my injured back brought forth a loud and involuntary cry of anguish, startling all of us. Between gritted teeth, in an attempt to ease the discomfort, I explained the problem. To his credit, Gerry slowed at each new sleeping policeman and eased over with exaggerated care.

Soon after leaving Balboa we passed through the older part of Panama with its rundown buildings, intense traffic and streets crowded with locals going about their business, such a seedy change from the Balboa sector, Gerry pulled up outside a barber shop advertising two dollar haircuts.

Gerry was pointing across the road giving instructions. "There's our hotel. The Hotel Lisboa."

"Mmhuh!" I answered, still favouring my back and not wanting to risk speech.

"Round the corner there are a few places to eat. Quite reasonably priced too. And right here is the barbershop."

"That's very good of you," I said showing my appreciation for not having to seek out these places for myself. "Your help is much appreciated."

Even though I had the door open ready to make my exit, I was considering the flooded gutter and the best way to keep my feet dry. Gerry hadn't finished talking about them being line handlers. His wife's comment that we were three feet from the curb and the gutter was flooded brought him back to the real world.

"Sorry," he said. "Just a minute. I'll pull up."

This solved the problem of keeping my feet dry allowing me to exit the car and assure them that when the time for transit came I'd be in touch. And so we made our farewells.

Shortly after I was sitting having my ears lowered, always a relaxing time listening to the clip of the scissors and watching the hair roll down the sheet to fall onto the floor. The hairdresser was a young lad, early twenties I would think, and keen, as though he had been allowed to perform on his first customer. Who knows? Maybe I was. For when the hair had been cut he insisted on having a go at my beard, much against my protestations. It was my intention to shave it off at the first opportunity, besides it was time to eat, and with my blood sugar problems, a task that should be attended to without delay. But, he was already getting on with the job. I couldn't fault the guy's enthusiasm and to resist at this stage was to leave with a partly trimmed beard, which would have been ridiculous. I had to admit that he made a good job of it, taking the hair from the cheeks but leaving it full along the ridge of the jaw.

From here a routine developed that would be followed whenever I came to town to eat and deal with e-mailing. Across the road outside the Hotel Lisboa I would alight from the taxi, walk around the corner to eat dinner, and then go back to the Internet next door to the Hotel. These duties having been attended to, I just stood at the curb and hailed a taxi to go out to Albrook and the Super 99 supermarket to buy the groceries for the next leg of the voyage. Altogether, this system was convenient to the extreme as it saved organising a suitable vehicle to transport the amount of food required in one go. Also, I could eat the evening meal cooked by someone infinitely more capable than I, and check any messages in the inbox. On this occasion I made contact with the satellite phone people to arrange for the phone to be returned. However, they assured me that they could find nothing wrong and that the unit was in good order. This made me feel rather sceptical as it didn't perform prior to Cabo San Lucas.

I now learned that none of my friends had attempted to turn up in Panama. I was disappointed that they would not be coming, but relieved that they had the sense not to venture out when there had been no contact from me for so long.

*****

The following morning dawned bright and clear, promising another warm day. I took my usual morning tea into the cockpit to sit and watch the yard come alive. The workers wandered in with no sense of urgency, just drifting towards the place of the day's employment. It was with some amusement that I watched the guys that were presumably supposed to be working on the boat to my left gather to lounge around in the shade under the boat, and remain in a state of repose until, to the best of my knowledge, the end of the day. In counterpoint to these layabouts the work on the large power boat over on my starboard bow had resumed as soon as the personnel and equipment had been assembled. It was a strange feeling to sit observing other people's activities and not be observed myself, at least no one deigned to look my way or acknowledge my presence.

Sitting in the cockpit sipping tea I realised that my back wasn't hurting anymore. Strange, I thought, as I eased my back to find out if this was true. Much to my delight it was. Could it be that Gerry's speed bump therapy had done this? Regardless, it certainly was a pleasure to be able to walk, and to work without the need to favour this part of the anatomy. Thank you, Gerry.

Although I had work to do on the boat I was loath to start. Today the engine was to be taken out and I didn't wish to be part way through a job and have to attend to the requirements of the mechanics or for that matter, be absent buying a freshwater pump. Apart from the obvious repair to the rudder seal which required mixing epoxy and applying fibreglass to the injured area, there were also areas of the top side paintwork to attend to where the original paint had come off in sheets, exposing the filler coat, and giving the topsides paintwork a look of being inflicted with the mange. The hull below the waterline needed a coat of antifouling paint, but this required an investment that would have to be deferred until my finances were known and could be allocated in order of priority. At this time the cost of repairs to the engine was as yet unknown. No doubt all would be revealed by day's end.

Still there was no way I could sit around all day so armed with a scraper I started the task of removing what loose paint remained on the topside, ready for a patch painting. There didn't seem to be much point in giving an overall coat of paint when the original would likely shed away again with wave action. Although the paint I had used was a well-known brand, of an internationally approved quality, or so they claimed, and the same manufacturer as the anti-fouling. I resolved to not to be taken in by their claims again.

After lunch John Cole came over.

"See you've had your beard trimmed. It suits you," he offered, looking critically at the barber's handiwork.

That being a matter of opinion to which I didn't subscribe I made no comment.

"No sign of the truck for the engine?" I asked. The concerned tone of my voice must have sounded more like a statement. The mobile crane had arrived sometime previously and was parked close by and I hoped I wasn't going to be charged waiting time.

"I'll find out what's happening," he said. He pulled out his cell phone to make the call in rapid and unintelligible language. The call ended, he closed the phone and with an air of someone who is familiar with the train of events imparted the information.

"The truck was taken out on another job this morning, and hasn't returned."

John cocked his head to one side in an attitude of one anticipating a response of an unexpected nature. He must have noticed my lips tighten in exasperation.

"So we wait all day and they can't let us know what the situation is," I said, not trying to hide the annoyance in my voice. "So what now?"

John shrugged not so much as an apology, but rather to express that this is Panama. This is the way it is.

"They will come tomorrow, ten o'clock."

'Yeah! Right.' I thought.

The uncertainty of the way events seem to be happening didn't exactly fill me with happiness. Visions of being a captive in Panama's apparent hairy fairy life style were looming large. My impatience at wanting to get through the Canal and across the Caribbean before the Hurricane season got underway was heavy on my mind and needed to be addressed.

In the meantime other people had wandered over requiring John's attention and leaving me with my thoughts, half listening to the chatter. The conversation ended and without another word to me John got into his golf buggy and drove off. This I realised was a factor of life in John's day. If ever a man had nervous energy it was him. This seemed so opposite to the people who worked for him. A good man, and one whose good will and energy I came to rely on in the coming weeks.

Not wanting to hang about I left to see what was on offer with fresh water pumps.

*****

They didn't come for the engine the next day either, making some other excuse, so it was another inactive day. Not entirely wasted though as an interesting conversation came up with the owner of the large power boat. Having wandered over to see what kind of tool was being used on the antifouling area it transpired that it was similar to a power planer, which accounted for the high pitched whine. This tool shaved off a predetermined thickness of paint, cleaning to the aluminium plating only. What I found to be particularly interesting was the person operating this tool. He was of Central American origin but put to shame the lack of enthusiasm regarding work in the local populace; in the two days that I had been there he had worked continuously with only the occasional break for refreshment.

When I remarked on this fact to the owner, an American, he expressed disgust for the local work force, using for an example the guys lying about under the other boat. He had brought his man down with him from Costa Rica, where he lived, as crew and general dogsbody and praised him for the effort he was putting in to maintain the boat.

During our conversation I remarked on the unusual keel the boat had; this was boxed shaped, maybe eighteen inches in height and the same in width, running the full length of the boat, some thirty feet. When I was told that it was full of mercury that really threw me. It must have cost a fortune to fill that cavity. The owner explained that the boat had been built for the Coastguard as a rescue vessel with self righting capabilities and, as it was built with taxpayer's money, expense was no object. A little cynical even if true. The weight that the mercury provided was to create a self righting effect should the boat turn over in a heavy sea. The boat had been bought by its present owner at Government auction. Should he ever decide to scrap this vessel his outlay most certainly would be more than returned by the contents of the keel, I have no idea of the price of mercury but it is generally known to be very expensive.

So the day passed with little activity on my part. The projects on the hull were considered, only to be shelved until I could get a good run at them without being interrupted, the engine guys being uppermost in my thinking. These people were not the only ones I was waiting for. The electrician was conspicuous by his absence which I had occasion to remind John. It was a matter of urgency to have the electrical system checked. The trip down from the Cabo had created many doubts, not to mention frustration brought on by my ignorance of things electrical, as to why power was not available. A continuity check on all the circuits was high on the list, something that required equipment that I didn't possess. For my part I hadn't been exactly remiss in this enterprise, and the yard electrician had run a power line to the boat which made it possible to put the batteries on charge. After twenty-four hours there had been no appreciable result. When the refrigerator was switched on the volt meter needle fluctuated most alarmingly indicating that it was grabbing at low and insufficient voltage. To my limited knowledge this suggested that there was something definitely wrong. Either the batteries were duff or there was a circuit grounding, draining the batteries.

Well the day hadn't been totally wasted as I bought and installed a very efficient fresh water pump that was unlike the original in construction. Whereas the original relied on an accumulator tank to supply air pressure, the new one operated when a tap was opened and marvels of marvels had no part of its construction that would rust or rot out, being all neoprene.

By four thirty when the yard activity started to peter out, all hope of a truck coming to take the engine was abandoned. John Cole very kindly offered to go by the mechanic's place of work to check on what the hold up might be. And for this I had to be satisfied. So left to my own devices again I got myself cleaned up and went into Panama for a meal, to check for any messages at the internet café, then to Albrook to grocery shop. On returning to the boatyard I decided to have a beer at the corner watering hole. Stopping for a beer before returning to the boat to sleep developed into a nightly routine and I became well known by the staff to the point of being addressed as Mister Ron. "Ah! Good evening, Mister Ron," became the cry. "You want pasteurised beer?" This greeting was a result of me passing a beer before my eyes on an earlier visit and stating that it was, “Past your eyes.” It was a pleasure to see the delight this simple little jest gave these young people.

*****

During late morning the following day, much to my delight, the truck arrived for the engine. The vehicle that did the transporting gave me doubts as to what sort of engineering outfit I had got tied into. The size of this vehicle would have been more suited to transporting cattle. The logo on the door didn’t suggest anything to do with engineering trades either. But, who was I to comment on this? My little engine would be quite happy for the ride, and I certainly was not going to complain. At last things were starting to happen.

The mechanics of removing the engine and, indeed everything that was do with bringing this injured machine back to good health started an all too familiar process. Of the two bodies that came to attend the operation, one was the chubby fellow previously mentioned who sat around giving orders, and the young lad who provided the sweat and the labour. No doubt this was the accepted system. Probably Chubby was the qualified mechanic and the lad his apprentice. More respect for Chubby would have been generated on my part had he become more involved than occasionally passing a spanner.

Some days the climate in Panama can be exceedingly hot depending on whether there is cloud cover or clear skies, a breeze or still air, or a combination of these factors. Today, fortunately for the lad, it was cool, for working in such a tight space as the engine compartment disconnecting the engine can be quite a trial. All went well though and the mobile crane was soon lifting the engine out of the boat into the cattle truck. By noon I was left engineless, to ponder my next move. First lunch then tackle the rudder seal.

With the engine ashore with its problems being dealt with I felt a certain calm in my daily routine. All the other problems would be taken care of in their proper place when the occasion arose. It had been established during the last contact with home base just how much my wealth amounted to. Nothing to go daft about in this revelation but at least it gave a certain solvency to my life and I could deal with bringing the boat back up to operational perfection. Or close to it. This fact was a comfort as I could now keep a close watch on spending in order of priority. There was one irritation in the scheme of things: my debit card seemed to have thrown wobblers by refusing to produce cash from ATMs. This was a nuisance but not critical as I could get cash back from the supermarket when paying for groceries, enough for pocket money to pay for small purchases in day to day living.

My mind at ease, the days passed pleasantly and took on a certain leisurely pace. The sail maker returned with the foresail suitably repaired, although the material he had used didn’t look much like sail cloth. To my fertile mind this material conjured up visions of old army blankets. Beggars can't be choosers though and I had been made aware of the scarcity of people in the trade of sail repairing. Since the departure of the American Canal personnel sailboats were to all intents and purposes non-existent. The sail maker was a big man in both build and voice, forceful in speech and demanding in tone. This didn't faze me though as he didn't speak English, only loud rapid Spanish which, I couldn't understand, so I just closed my ears. This bombast and other similar attitudes met with on other occasions, mainly with taxi drivers, I took to be the local interpretation of machismo. The way certain taxi drivers would lean out of the vehicle windows to gesture and verbally accost the local females, who I might add, took not the slightest interest, was to me most embarrassing. If this behaviour was a sign of manliness I wondered what they would be like if they ever grew up.

Later on towards the end of the week I was summoned to view the engine which had been opened up for my inspection. What that would achieve was lost on me; the cylinders were full of water which had caused the engine to malfunction, but looking at this didn't help solve the problem. Just an explanation would have sufficed if that was the only reason for bringing me all the way out to their yard to which they had sent a taxi to bring me to see the offending object. A driver who spoke English whose help in negotiating a price to fix the engine was most welcome. All spares were to be extra, which I thought to be fair, and so I gave my consent to proceed. Had I known then what was to transpire an alternative arrangement would have been made. But then hind-sight is ever infallible.

During this sojourn at Flamenco Resort and Marina I had made the acquaintance of an American marine engineer whose services I would have much preferred. His name was Joe Brassiere, or at least that is how his last name sounded and judging by the ribald comments from others of his acquaintance this could well have been. Joe was highly respected for his professionalism and work ethic, all much desired, but in my ignorance of yard practices not to be for my benefit. The mechanics allotted to my problem were on contract to the Marina and therefore John Cole was honour bound to recommend their services. Because Joe operated independently, his services could be engaged by arrangement with the management on request from the customer only. None of this was known to me at the time which was a great pity for at the very least a communication would have been established, and without the run-around I would receive from the people appointed to my project.

In the fullness of time the 'electrician' presented himself. Ah! now things are beginning to happen,' I thought. Alas, the language problem cropped up again. Not for want of fluency though; this gentleman was quite voluble in his needs which he wrote down for me to take to the Marina store to purchase for him. My explanation of the problem and what was expected was another kettle of fish with which I was soon to be acquainted.

Needless to say he hadn't budged by the time I had returned, but give him his due he was soon on the job. A nagging doubt as to his qualification to fix the electrical problem soon had me regretting employing the guy as well as the mechanics.

The house batteries were located under the settee and required a bit of manoeuvring to get at, although for one person to work there was quite acceptable. Two bodies getting in each other's way was not desirable in the cramped space, the lack of ventilation which caused the air to quickly become hot and humid didn't help matters either, so I stayed in the cabin and waited. Before too much time had elapsed he emerged pleased with himself and sweating profusely, which was not surprising as it could get quite warm in such an airless location. Through his voluble Spanish I was given to understand that the work had been completed. I was sceptical that he had not done any more than clean the battery leads. This point was not raised at this moment because of something else that had taken my interest so I just let him rabbit on sweating profusely, while I watched a bead of perspiration hanging off the end of his nose like a dewdrop ready to fall off a leaf, and willing it to drop. In due course nature had its way and the dewdrop dropped to be replaced by yet another gathering in readiness to follow its predecessor, and strangely with no effort from its owner to do any sweat mopping. Fascinating though this show was, it was not getting on with the job. Besides, I'd not understood a word he had said.

"Battery. OK?" I asked, interrupting. Knowing full well that it wasn't

"Si. Batterier Bueno." This was accompanied by more voluble Spanish. By this time I got the impression he was trying to convince himself.

Time to interrupt him again.

"No, Bueno," I said, switching the volt meter to show the needle bouncing up and down the scale like a thing demented.

"Ahh!" he said, knowingly, "No Bueno,"

"Bloody right mate. No Bueno," By this time I was becoming annoyed with this person. Obviously he hadn't a clue about electrics, boat electrics anyway. All I wanted now was to get rid of him.

"How much do I owe you?" I asked, pulling out my wallet. I felt that he wasn't worth anything but was not prepared to create a scene.

The twenty dollars he asked for was small payment to get rid of him.

After he had left I pondered the situation for a while then came to the conclusion that new batteries might solve the problem, but I was very reluctant to do this not knowing if the existing batteries were salvageable.

As luck would have it, John Cole was about to come on board to check on the progress. My irritation with the departing, 'electrician' was still needling me coupled with my frustration at being no further on with the electrical problems. In no uncertain terms I told John what I thought of the guy and that I would go and buy another battery.

"Don't do that just yet, Ron, let's find out if these batteries are dead," he remarked wisely.

That threw me for a moment, "How can we do that?"

"I'll phone the House of Batteries and tell them to come down. They have the equipment for testing batteries."

John was on the phone for a few moments only when he turned to me and asked, "What sort of batteries do you have?"

When I told him he explained that they would bring batteries in case the original ones were finished. I was relieved at the possibility of my troubles in this regard being solved, and John received my profuse thanks.

Before the afternoon was over the old batteries had been declared defunct and new batteries installed. The added bonus to this wonderful experience was that the fridge would operate and the beer could be cooled. I was now a much happier camper. As an added assurance the charger was connected to make sure the batteries remained topped up to the maximum charge. A loss of power when the means to avoid this were readily available would be stupid at least, not to say criminal. The more I thought about batteries the more I desired a wind generator. Had I not listened to false witness before embarking on this adventure more than likely the problems resulting from lack of electricity might never have arisen? But that was hindsight again. Sadly, this item would have to wait for sometime and place in the future, the ever spectre of low funds was rearing its ugly head. The next most pressing item on the agenda now that the power was restored was to connect the water pump and to purchase and install a cigar lighter. The one to provide the means to shower, and the other to charge the shaver to get rid of the hair on my face, the inverter for the lap-top and the Satellite phone when this was returned. Life was taking on a much rosier outlook; finally a fully operational boat was in the offing.

*****

The following day the repair to the rudder seal was made and suitably boosted in a belt and braces mode; covering the whole seal and backing onto the hull with fibreglass cloth and epoxy putty. Satisfaction guaranteed, at least until a brace for the rudder post could be fabricated. Comfortable with the results, I approached John about returning the boat to the water. It seemed to me that waiting on the hard at seventy dollars a day was somewhat ridiculous, when I could anchor off to wait for the engine. A much better solution was proposed that would facilitate getting on shore with less effort than having to row the dinghy from outside the breakwater; tie up to a mooring buoy inside. There would be a charge, however. But what is new? And ten dollars a day seemed reasonable compared to the seventy on the hard.

Nothing happens immediately in Panama, so it was another three days before the tide was right. By this I mean that the high tide had to coincide with the working day, time and tide waiting for these men involved in the operation presumably.

These waiting days were not wasted however; during this period I took the opportunity to register for transit something which I still planned to do. No sooner had this been done than information filtered down that the Canal was closed to small craft due to one chamber at Miriflores Lock being closed for maintenance. This put a completely different outlook on my plans. The hurricane season wasn't going to wait for me to get clear so it would be the height of folly to try and trust to luck to dodge these terrible winds. Also there were other considerations to patch into this equation. Should I make a timely transit and an Atlantic crossing then that would put me into the English ports getting on towards late in the year and, the Autumnal Equinox and the gales that accompany this season of the year thus creating a knock on effect to delay my plans for the circumnavigation even further. By that time I would have done the rounds of friends and family, winter would be on the threshold, making a passage south undesirable. Besides, the engine hadn't been returned and who knows when that would be, and having covered the cost, would there be enough funds to pay for a transit? Change of plan: I would sail west and make the circumnavigation the other way via the Marquesas, and Tahiti, with the added consideration that the funds would be greatly increased in the additional time to make the crossing. Not to mention by sailing in the ten degree latitude band there should be constant winds and no storms. What a clever plan: I gave myself a mental pat on the back for such a clever proposal, ignoring the fact that circumstances had thrust this on me. Well why not; it was really only in recognition of circumstances starting to go my way.

The information of the closure was confirmed by John. While we were discussing the delays of the return of the engine and what information John had received on this subject when we were approached by a couple who had come into the yard seeking passage as line handlers to the Atlantic side of the Canal. John informed them of the closure and left to phone about the engine. It was then that I mentioned there was more scope for getting a berth at the Balboa Yacht Club as this was where the boats congregated awaiting transit, should the Canal be opened again at a time suitable to them, that is.

"Will you be going through?" the woman asked.

"No, I'll be going the other way, Marquesas, then on to Australia."

"Ooh! I have a son in Brisbane. Could I come with you?" asked the woman eagerly.

"Sorry, I travel alone," I said without a second's hesitation, ignoring her enthusiasm but not without a twinge of regret at the crushed look she gave me.

"Pity," she said, walking away.

My reaction had been spontaneous. Instinctive I suppose, because after all I didn't know her. For all I knew she could have been a psychopath or something. Had to admit she was a comely looking woman. Besides if the man she was with was included in the request the boat would have been too crowded for comfort.

On John's return he had good news. He had spoken to the girl in the mechanics office who had told him they had gone to customs to clear the spare parts.

This information was indeed good news; as the engine would soon be returned and the saga could be resumed. Right?

Later that evening while sitting having a 'pasteurised' beer I noticed two of the crew from the Dynasty sitting outside, during the time in the Yard the only conversation that had passed between us was the time of day; or good morning. Rather limited but one has to respect others' privacy. On this occasion they were not working. What better time to make their acquaintance? Once the formalities were over a friendly rapport was established. Of the two, Geoff soon went his way leaving me with Damien and, later by Damien's girlfriend. It developed into a most pleasant evening. Damien had a wealth of experience for someone his age, which I put at mid to late twenties. Footloose and fancy free was Damien, seeing the world by crewing on other people's boats. Also he had taught English for a year at a school in Korea, lack of qualifications didn't seem to be an important factor for either party. The world is certainly a young person's oyster. Because of this chance encounter, there were many enjoyable evenings I spent in the company of Damien and his girl friend, Vivien. Vivien Lee would you believe? Her mother was Panamanian, her father Chinese.

There was another fortuitous happening that came out of this decision to make the acquaintance of the Dynasty crew. The following day, Geoff, with the skipper, came on board my boat for a look around. Stan, the skipper, stared at the cabin deck with what I took to be a look of dismay, and well he might. The cabin deck had suffered grievously from the marine environment. I will admit here that the material I used, house wood flooring, was not the best choice but at the time it seemed acceptable. However, the top veneer had peeled away due to the damp and was looking quite tatty and forlorn.

"Would you like some teak decking?" asked Stan. "Our decks have been replaced and there is some planking left over. You can have it if you like."

What came to mind was he was probably offering the old decking which would need some cleaning up. Why I would think that is difficult to say except why would anyone part with the good stuff?

"What would you want for it?" I asked, delaying the decision.

"No! You can have it. It's extra to what we needed. The fibreglasser wanted it but sod him, I'm not doing him any favours." His voice carried the tone of one that was displeased with the person in question. "A bottle of scotch, if you like" he added.

Needless to say, the teak decking was on board my boat and the Famous Grouse changed hands with almost indecent haste, long before Stan had a change of mind. Beautiful wood it was too, not a knot or shakes in the lot, and more than enough to completely replace the whole of the interior decking. Today was indeed my lucky day. As it so happened there was a bottle of Famous Grouse on board which changed hands before the transfer of decking was completed even, an added incentive to deter any change of mind on the part of this benefactor.

As I was still waiting to have the boat returned to the water, what better time than this to make a start? The project would have to be done in sections to facilitate walking about while the glue dried, so I tackled the main cabin deck first, ripping out the old planking with gusto.

Stan's good will had not yet expired. While engaged in this project he and Geoff came by and asked, as they were going into Panama would I like to go along and get some supplies, caulking for the new decking, that sort of thing? This day it seemed as though I was really on a roll.

As it turned out there was no caulking left as Stan had cleared them out for his project but for just one tube. No matter, I purchased a back saw and Set Square, thinking the caulking could wait for a later date.

Elated at being able to replace the old decking I soon had a completed section of deck to admire, and what a pleasure it was too, regardless of the lack of caulking. Progression towards an efficient and fully appointed boat was being realised.

While working on this arrangement the sail maker returned with the mainsail, full of himself and bragging by gestures and voluble Spanish on what a good job he had made of it, until I pointed out that he had sewn across one of the batten pockets and therefore the batten could not be returned to its rightful place. Also, he had repaired the tears in the way of the reef points but made no provision for passing a line through the sail for reefing. The bragging ended but not the voluble Spanish which he directed to his young assistant. Grievously hurt I would have guessed, at this lack of professionalism, his assistant looked long suffering, no doubt having gone through similar situations before. So it was back to the sail loft to make adjustments. When he did return there was still the problem of mast slides; these apparently were unobtainable in Panama. The sail maker had made an effort to redress this problem and had tracked down a few slides that were too large. These required reducing to fit the mast slide, which was easily done by sandpapering the nylon edges. With this method a sort of Heath Robinson arrangement was cobbled together. That solved the problem of some of the slides but there was still the connection of the slide to the sail. This was resolved temporarily by using small shackles. After settling the bill with the sail maker I ordered suitable slides from the United States which, due to an efficient service arrived within a couple of days.

That evening Damien and I took the short walk along the causeway to a restaurant to meet Vivien for a meal. The restaurant being close to the waters edge was open to the cooling sea breeze which made for a most enjoyable evening. Vivien being fluent in both English and Spanish took a lot of effort out of ordering. In fact being the owner of her own business she was quite happy making decisions which Damien and I were quite content to go along with as it left us to have our banter. At the close of this most delightful evening with these two young people, the first social evening spent in company since leaving British Columbia, it was suggested that a friend of Vivien's should be roped in for a nightclubbing foursome to which I begged off, excusing myself on the grounds that tomorrow early the boat was going back into the water. At least that was the excuse I made. Damien and Vivien liked to party into the small hours night clubbing, which to me in my advanced years was very low on the agenda of things to do, in fact not a consideration at all. A pleasant constitutional stroll back to the Marina set me up nicely for a nightcap of 'past your eyes beer' at the local watering hole, then back to the boat and bed.

*****

There was some delay in the launching for when the Travelift was positioned over the ramp the heavens opened up with a tropical downpour scattering the attendant crew to seek shelter. This deluge lasted for some twenty minutes before the operation was resumed with the crew chattering excitingly over the experience. As a result of the rain the air was much cooler and cleaner, a pleasant change from the previously muggy weather.

To my horror and distress when the boat was returned to the water and safely tied to the buoy the bilges were fast taking water. The leak from the rudder seals was obviously not the only means of ingress. To cap this frustration the bilge pump wouldn't work either. Well as they say in the boating world, 'if it isn't one thing to go wrong, it's five others.' This state of affairs could not be tolerated and the source of the leak would have to be investigated. I soon realised that the best way to detect a leak was to use a reverse process, i.e. take the boat out of the water again with the water still in the bilges and observe where the water came out and not by guessing where it came in.

As mentioned earlier, nothing happens in Panama just when you want it to, so it was a few more days before a second haul-out would be carried out. As luck would have it I came across Joe in the yard during this waiting for the second haul out, and I related the problem with the electrics, and the bilge pump in particular. Although mechanical problems were his forte, he was pleased to have a look and see what was what. Now that is what I call a professional. The result of this investigation revealed that the float switch was kaput, and the three way control switch iffy. So, a new float switch was purchased and fitted, the switch cleaned up, the wiring checked out. All this effort by Joe on my behalf left me very pleased with the way progress was made in the matter of electrics. It also restored my faith in human nature, re Panama. There was one other matter that had to be resolved which would have to wait until suitable equipment was available. Were the batteries discharging to ground?

Shortly after rowing Joe ashore I was informed that there was a parcel for me in the office. You can imagine my delight that the Satellite phone was now returned and communication with the outside world was again possible. Back on board and the phone connected to the aerial I made a call to base back in British Columbia which went through, loud and clear without a hitch. My star of confidence was rising. The indicator on the phone showed a low battery reading, which was no problem, just plug it into the socket and all would be well. Except that the phone wouldn't take a charge. Several attempts with the different charging leads gave no satisfaction and it was with the star of confidence fast sinking towards the horizon of gloom that I realised that there was still a fault with the system. With dejection and frustration fighting each other for dominance I realised that the offending article would have to go back again. Time was now pressing as I fully expected to get away from here within a few days. So the phone was boxed up, Luis' taxi engaged and out I went to the Fed-Ex office. The phone people were contacted that same evening to be told in no uncertain terms that their product was non-functioning, and would they please do something about fixing it.

*****

It was during this waiting period on the buoy that I was called to the office to be confronted by a tall sophisticated looking gentleman whom it turned out was the accountant for the engine people. A dour gentleman he was too, emanating disapproval. At what, one could only guess. He didn't, or more likely wouldn't, speak English. I say this because it has been my experience that the better class of educated people in the Latin American countries do speak English, and very well too. So it was left to John to do the translating. It transpired that before any spare parts would be ordered I would have to sign a letter of approval, which the Senor presented, silent and aloof in a most imperious manner. No excuse was offered as to why we had been told, many days previously, that they had been to the Customs to pick up these very same parts. Not to mention that I had already given verbal approval. Apparently, no-one is trusted to pay up even after giving their word, which I found irritating, not to mention this latest delay while the spares were ordered and waiting for them to come from England. As I was totally in the hands of these aggravating and suspicious minded people there was no alternative but to grin and bear the situation. Needless to say, I was not in any way endeared to them for their cavalier attitude. I signed his form, and he departed, glum as ever. In fact I decided that he should be dubbed Senor Glum for future reference.

So the days passed lying on the buoy, with me pottering about and working on the cabin deck until they came to haul me out again.

When this happened I made sure I was in such a position on shore to observe where the leak came from. There was no doubt about where, as the water just streamed out from the fore part of the keel where it joined the hull. It would appear that sometime during the passage down from Canada the keel had worked in the seaway, loosening the connecting bolt allowing ingress of water through the bolt hole and into the inside of my little world. To tighten these bolts at this time was impossible; the construction of the boat precluded this. The only alterative would be to seal the leak from the outside. No doubt the leak could start again sometime in the future, but until a return home and a comprehensive haul-out this method would have to do.

I shuddered at the thought what such a haul out would entail as this would mean cutting out bulkheads and decking, in fact ripping out most of the interior to get at the six by nine inch white oak keel bearers. These then would need to be cut to free up the bolts; all eleven of them. Drop the keel, then reseal to the hull. A daunting thought to say the least.

As the source of this leak had been missed on the first haul-out I could only surmise that when the weight of the boat had rested on the keel the gap, as small as it must be, had closed up.

The provisional repair to this leak didn't take long and while the boat was out of the water a fresh coat of anti-fouling was applied. The finances were healthy enough to put this project into fulfilment. The original coating was serviceable but with the amount of fouling it had attracted, I didn't trust it to the expected six week passage to the Marquesas and beyond.

The time required to make this repair and apply the antifouling to a satisfactory conclusion didn't take more than a day which in this, the original manana country, didn't mean diddly squat. Regardless of frequent requests to be put back in the water I was still there a week later. This, however, turned to be an advantage as the engine came back towards the end of this period all nicely painted. With the boat out of the water putting the engine back was much more convenient to my mind for the use of the crane, although John had assured me that to return the engine while in the water would not be a problem,. The delay in putting the boat back in the water, and then the engine turning up when it did had me deeply suspicious that matters were being controlled behind the scenes. My needs seemed secondary to the controllers' desires. Ah! Well, go with the flow, life is much less frustrating that way. Besides, I was becoming as laid back as the locals by this time.

One would think that with the engine back in the boat, it would just be a matter of connecting up all the parts, put the boat back in the water, test the engine and away we go. No way, not here in Panama anyway. The mechanics, Chubby and his lad, were quite content to connect the engine onto the bed and connect the propeller shaft before taking off again.

Just so the reader has no doubts about the actual situation, the lad did the hands-on part of the operation with a little help from me in guiding the engine through the hatch into position on the holding down bolts, Chubby being content to give voluble verbal directions accompanied by much waving of hands towards the crane operator. This approach to work ethics would seem to be the norm here but, Chubby made no effort to help the lad and I developed an even lower regard for him.

The haul out had happened on a Friday, with a promise of being returned to the buoy on the coming Monday. It was on the following Friday before being water-borne again. With the extra cost of sitting on the hard on my mind I took up the matter with John with no satisfaction. What had been going on behind the scenes over the delay I was not privy to, and was given no satisfaction. John, kindly waived the cost of the tow over to the buoy, a small gesture to compensate for the wait on the hard for which I had to be thankful.

Lying on the buoy proved to be a relaxing time, each morning I would take my tea out the cockpit to enjoy the early morning. Without fail, Derek would pass by at speed in his dinghy on his way to work in the boatyard. Derek, an American, had arrived in Panama from Hawaii fifteen years previously and never left. His boat, a catamaran had been converted into permanent living quarters and was moored close to the shore on the far side of the marina. He had married a Panamanian girl and was thus allowed to work in the country. They had a child together who, at the time I was there, was about six years of age. Imagine my surprise, when one afternoon relaxing in the cockpit, this child of such a young age came hurtling past in the dinghy in full and sole control. She obviously knew what she was doing as she very professionally put the dinghy alongside, embarked her father and came hurtling back to return to their boat.

They do say that women mature quickly in the tropics.

There was a job that I had been putting off for some time. Emptying the holding tank so the macerator pump could be inspected, Joe had assured me that there was power there, which suggested something mechanical was the cause. Derek had told me there would be no problem with dumping the contents of the holding tank over the side as no-body cared anyway. So, putting aside my reluctance I began siphoning the contents into a bucket then throwing the slop over the side. I soon lost count of how many buckets there were, maybe twelve at a guess, before finally emptying the tank. Not a pleasant task, what with the smell. The siphon hose had a bulb to draw the delivery, so I considered myself lucky I didn't have to suck the hose to get the job going. The cause of the problem was that the cutter, which broke up the solids, had jammed with hair, which when one considers this, is not a very clever feature of this type of pump. However, the pump was working again which had been the object of the enterprise.

During the following week the engine was connected and a speed trial into the Bay carried out to my satisfaction, with one complaint: the engine alarm wouldn't shut off. Being Panama this problem would have to wait for another day before being attended to. At least matters were progressing towards a departure date which, with all things being equal, couldn't be far off. Alas, this was not as close as one would have hoped; another delay of a different stripe was in the offing.

On checking the e-mail that evening I was informed that the satellite phone people had found the fault and had returned it to the manufacturer under warranty, and it would be returned within ten days. This was good news of a sort, but no cause for jumping with joy and therefore I adopted a wait and see attitude and hoped that the phone really would work when returned.

Senor Glum appeared again on the next day with Chubby and his lad. With John interpreting I was given to understand that a trip to the Bank was now required for funds to settle the bill. Cash only, no Credit Cards. To this request I objected as there was still the matter of the engine alarm. To my delight it was agreed that this would be seen to the very same day, so while the lad worked on the engine with Chubby supervising, and me in attendance, Senor Glum was left to cool his heels on shore. It was mid afternoon, and hot, before the job was completed, which didn't improve his outlook on life judging by his look of disapproval:

Off we went to the bank or should I say banks as the one in Balboa which I usually dealt with was closed, necessitating a tour of Panama to find another branch. If this traipsing around hadn't been so tiresome sitting in the same vehicle as these people, it could have been entertaining. The bank would only allow a withdrawal of five hundred dollars in one day to which Senor Glum, if this was possible, became even more annoyed, but which delighted me no end. Through all this seeking of funds I was kept out of the conversation, due to my lack of Spanish. I gathered though that my travelling companions, by the tone of their conversation, were not at all delighted. Finally we ended up at the mechanic's place of work to report to the owner. These people had given me the run-around during the past few weeks so the shoe was now on the other foot. It gave me a great deal of pleasure to inform them that as I could only draw a daily amount of five hundred dollars they would have to wait until there were enough funds accumulated to settle the bill, and would they kindly return me to the Marina. No sooner had I got to my feet to leave the office than I was asked for my Credit Card. 'Ah! I thought, they do take plastic.' Not so, they only wanted to check my credit. The cheek of it? Now if they had the facility to check a person's credit they obviously could take credit cards. So, what were they up to? Tax dodges maybe? The half hour ride back to the Marina with Senor Glum was carried out in total silence, in an atmosphere that was fraught with resentment. Cutting the air with a knife came to mind. What could be the guy's problem? He wouldn't even respond to my thank you when I got out of the car.

The accumulation of funds was performed on a daily basis as there was the maximum amount that I could draw at any one time. The bank opened at eight o'clock, which was an ideal time for me as I could be there before they became busy. The procedure was to present my credit card and passport to the girl at the front desk, which would check my credit rating and then give me a slip with the amount to present to the cashier. Who would then count out the required dollars.

On the second day the girl asked me if I was married. A strange question I thought, and wondered what that had to do with drawing cash. It did occur to me later that the question was a form of invitation. If the answer was no, then one is free to ask the person for a date. Being a little slow on the uptake I didn't follow through with this. She was a very attractive woman, in her early thirties, I would guess, but my recent past and disappointing experiences with the opposite sex precluded any interest in taking up on another relationship. On the following days the subject was not raised again. Just a good morning greeting of friendly recognition.

During the time it took to accumulate the amount to settle the bill, strangely enough, Chubby and his lad attended to the engine. Just what they were doing was beyond me as the engine had been run to satisfaction. The alarm wasn't silenced satisfactorily but they didn't appear to be tending to that, rather the lad was disconnecting parts of the engine and re-assembling. It crossed my mind that they were probably making sure I didn't take off without paying. This presumed suspicion of their motives towards me seemed to have become mutual.

In the fullness of time the funds to settle the bill was accumulated, but another problem arose. Having spoken to Justino at the Marina requesting outward clearance I was informed that this would have to take place in Balboa and we set out in Justino's car to the office that we attended on arrival, calling at the Bank on the way for the last of the engine fee. For whatever reason the Immigration Officer was quite angry when he inspected my passport, and kept saying, "Diablo, Diablo." This I understood was Spanish for devil. He didn't seem to be using the word as an expletive but rather, with throw away gestures of the right hand, was trying to tell me something. For whatever reason Justino had made himself scarce and was unavailable to explain what this irate gentleman was on about. Could it be he was telling me to go to, the devil? Surely not, for this was official business. The official appeared to realise that we were getting nowhere and the problem was solved by taking me outside to speak to a taxi driver that happened to be there. The driver, having listened to the immigration chappie, turned to me and speaking very good English advised that he would take me to Diablo, which housed another section of the Immigration Offices. There I must pay a fee and come back here to complete the formalities. So that is what all the Diablo business was about. Diablo was another area of Balboa.

This taxi driver obviously wasn't going to miss out on making a little money out of this trip which took a mere five minutes there and five back, with a wait long enough to part with a considerable amount of the day's banking. Having been long enough in Panama to know taxi prices what this guy charged was double the going rate. Obviously I protested, but his mate adopted an intimidating manner suggesting that the request was reasonable. For my part I didn't fancy being duffed up for a mere five dollars so with as much grace as possible under the circumstances, coughed up.

Then once again I presented myself to Immigration Part One, had my passport stamped and was directed across the yard to another building housing the Port Authority. The desire to gain officialdom's largesse to be allowed to leave Panama required a lengthy form filling session. The door to this office had been left open which allowed me to see Justino in the hallway sidling out through another door. Although he didn't acknowledge me his look was apologetic, enough for me to keep silent, feeling that a word from me would not be welcome.

The form filling itself was not a lengthy affair, if the typist had attended to the matter without interruption it would have been over within just a matter of probably ten minutes. But this was Panama where social graces and good manners are paramount. Amongst a certain level of society that is, and if the occasion suits. The preliminaries to the form filling were conducted by me putting down under the secretary's guidance details of the boat. And I should say at this point she didn't speak any English either, no more than the Immigration chap. So the directions for information were conducted by understanding boat measurements and details in word sounds and descriptive gestures. This information was then taken to the typewriter to be made into an official format. At this juncture another person then entered the office and sat down, starting what was to be a long conversation with the typist who, one presumed, had the aforementioned social graces. One must be polite and pay attention to the speaker. The form filling stopped with only an occasional peck at the keys when the conversation had a lull. I deduced from the papers he was holding and his air of familiarity with the office that he was an agent for some other boat, and well known to the typist. By the intense tone of the conversation I also deduced that the subject was one of some importance, as either one or the other of the participants would strengthen their verbal delivery, not in the sense that there was a conflict of opinion but rather an important point on which they both agreed. Nothing they said had any interest to me as I hadn't a clue what they were discussing anyway. All my emotions were directed at getting my form completed and leaving. Certainly I could have been rude and reminded the form filler that I was still there and would she kindly complete my bloody form. But, that didn't seem to be the best approach and I decided to wait it out. When the discourse finally ended and the form completed, to my surprise and chagrin, it wasn't a clearance that had been filled out but an invoice regarding the dues connected with my nearly five weeks stay in Panama. Now if that wasn't adding insult to injury I don't know what would be, particularly as the bill came to a tidy sum, just about cleaning me out of the daily bank allowance. With yet another visit to the bank looming on the morrow I paid the bill with the compensating thought that the girl in the bank was quite pretty and friendly. My, but what the mind conjures up to soothe when faced with a financial injury.

The next move in this saga of attempting to leave Panama was to be directed to the next office to present the proof of payment and receive the permission to leave. At least I could be thankful it wasn't the Cabo and have to tramp all over town to complete these formalities.

*****

Thankfully, Senor Glum was not awaiting my return holding out his sweaty palm for his due. At this, perversely, I entertained a twinge of regret. It would have given me some satisfaction to send him on his way to return the next day. After all, having put up with the run-around from his company for the five weeks and being held against my will, being petty in retaliation for a sense of satisfaction would have been some compensation.

Justino showed up though, regretful at abandoning my cause. It transpired that his boss had sent him to an arriving ship to transact its clearance inwards. He did, however, offer to take me shopping for groceries prior to my imminent departure, for which I was grateful. To have a helping hand and ready transport was preferable to struggling on my own and engaging taxis.

All was not peace in the old homestead though, for later that day when a relaxing beer would have been welcome the kitchen tap riser split, spewing water at great pressure across the galley. It seemed that the new water pump was not lacking in efficiency. So a trip to the hardware store for a new riser took precedence over a relaxing beer.

By the time the new riser was fitted it was evening and time to meet with Damien for a beer, and an amusing banter session. Good company was Damien and a welcome relaxing change from the day's trials. Vivien joined us later when, I'm sad to say we, were both a little affected by the intake of beer. For my part I had trouble getting into the car, which was commented on by the office girls the next morning that ignored my protestations that it was due to stiffness brought on by old age and not necessarily from any effects of imbibing. The effects of the beer can't have been too bad though because after Vivian dropped me off in town I managed to down a meal and return to the boat without incident. Rather I would suggest that my perceived happy mood commented on by the girls was due to elation at the imminent departure after such a long period of inaction and not from the intake of alcohol: besides, I have difficulty getting into cars anyway even when I'm not influenced by outside forces.

*****

Nothing is ever perfect in this life, and I make this comment thinking of what happened the following morning after being to the bank for the balance of funds; I was enjoying a cup of coffee in the cockpit watching the day develop, when I was abruptly brought out of my reverie by the sound of water under pressure. With the previous day's occurrence still fresh in mind I dashed below to find that the tap riser under the bathroom sink had split, no doubt in sympathy with the galley sink. So it was off to the hardware store again for parts and spent an unpleasant interlude as a sweaty contortionist crammed into the sink unit doing plumbing repairs again. On the bright side of this event if one cares to consider that life is not all doom and gloom, the water pump is proving its efficiency.

No sooner had this problem been solved than Chubby and his sidekick turned up to tinker with the engine. The boat was on a mooring and it was up to me to ferry these characters from the dock, and believe me it was quite a pull. Chubby being on the heavy side can only be described as unwelcome ballast. For the next two hours it was my dubious pleasure to hang around watching the poor lad, with sweat pouring from him, doing whatever with the engine, which to my mind was in good shape anyway. Chubby spent the whole session just sitting watching, offering the odd comment. And, the cheek of it asking me for a beer; needless to say this request was sharply refused. It truly was a very hot afternoon and I could have downed a beer myself, and my sympathies were with the lad who looked as though he could use a beer if only to replace the lost fluids. I would have willing shared a beer with him, but he couldn't be given one without the other, and there was no way the idle Chubby would be offered. This refusal of refreshment served a purpose though, as they shortly reassembled what they had been pottering with and requested a ferrying to the dock.

Senor Glum had been sighted earlier in the day hovering around the office area and as I was anxious to depart this place I gathered up the wherewithal to settle his bill and ferried his off-spring ashore. True to form Chubby had left his gate pass on the boat, again, so it was up to me to row back and get it. Truly I would be glad to see the back of this slothful person.

Arriving at the office the transaction to settle the bill was carried out under the amused, interested eye of Christina, one of the office girls who was on duty that day. Not that her interest was of an official nature rather that she happened to be attracted by the amount of money that was changing hands. The banks were not issuing notes of a higher denomination than twenties due to a counterfeiting scare so the pile was quite impressive. The amusement came when having handed over this considerable number of dollar bills I asked Senor Glum for change of fifty cents for the remaining forty-three cents. One would think that for a mere seven cents it was not worth the bother, but then after all the delays sanctioned by this engineering firm an urge to be devilish possessed me. Imagine my glee when he didn't have the change so he had to ask Christina. I'm quite sure that if Christina and I had exchanged glances mirth would have taken over. As it were only we two that saw the humour in the situation.

John Cole had come into the outer office at this moment and must have wondered what was going on. With a stack of bills on the counter to have three people sorting out a few cents must have looked odd to say the least.

"John;" I said, "Would you tell him that although the engine is satisfactory, the alarm sounds continuously."

After an exchange in Spanish, John said that they would come back tomorrow to fix it.

By this time I'd had all I cared to take of their hedging and interminable delays and there was no way that I was going for that one. The alarm wasn't that much of a bother and I only mentioned this to let Senor Glum know that their attention to detail was nothing to be proud of.

"No way," said I. "I'm leaving first thing tomorrow."

Ignoring the Senor who was busy stuffing the settlement into his pockets I directed my next statement to John.

"I'll go over to the fuel dock now, John, then come and settle up with you. I'd like an early start in the morning."

"OK. Your bill will be ready."

However, even yet matters were not going to run smoothly. Returning to the office after fuelling to settle the marina dues I found that my debit card would not be accepted. It appeared that I was temporarily broke, at least for this particular bill, until my pension was paid into my account in three days. A further hold-up of three days in Panama was not the option that I was prepared to choose. The other alternative was to pay with my back-up credit card, one that was kept in reserve, which when funds were removed could not be replaced without considerable problems. In this situation there was nothing for it but to bite the bullet and dip into this reserve.

"What time will you be leaving, Ron?" asked John.

"As soon after first light as possible. Well, after my morning ritual anyway, can't set out without the morning tea."

John nodded, accepting the importance of this statement. "I'll be in the yard at seven, make sure you come and say goodbye before you leave."

I must admit to being touched by this, but then, our relationship during my stay had been one of goodwill, and to leave without saying goodbye would have been churlish to say the least. It had been my intention to say cheerio this evening, but then at the outset of a six week trip what does a couple of hours difference make?

*****

At the promise of finally getting away from Panama I felt elation, but also a twinge of regret. Having been there for five weeks the place and people must have got to me. Their laid back attitude to life I found to be opposite to my get a move on approach. But then, by the time I came to leave their relaxed way of life seemed to be the way to go. Too late to change though; as one gets older one tends to get a fixed attitude and set in one's ways, and in the morning all this would be in the past. So move on and be happy.

The last evening was spent pleasurably in the company of Damien and Vivien over dinner at the restaurant partway down the causeway, and then much against my wishes I conceded to their pressure to visit a nightclub. The reason for giving in to this alien pursuit was due to the fact that the nightclub in question was within the Flamenco Resort and only a few minutes walk from the boat. Needless to say the racket was deafening, drowning out all possibility of conversation. It wasn't long before I slipped away for a farewell 'Pasteurised' beer at the regular watering hole, then went back to the boat for a good night's sleep.

Chapter Six
Panama to Marquesas

'.....a procurer of contentedness; and that it begat habits of peace and patience in those that professed and practiced it'

Izaak Walton 1593-1683

Having made the goodbyes to John and his staff, I rowed back to the boat, deflated and stowed the dinghy, and got away from the mooring at 0730 motoring out of the marina and around Flamenco Island into the Gulf of Panama to find a breeze awaiting me. This was not long in coming as by eight o'clock it was soon blowing briskly at fifteen knots out of the south-west. A sure sign that the trade winds were here to greet me, the sails were soon hoisted with the boat then making an exhilarating progress. That feeling of peace and contentment gradually took hold of me again as we headed out from the constraints of shore-side living with its crowds and noise. I was beginning to believe that I didn't care much for the company of people, nice and pleasant that they can be, or for that matter their environment. The further away from Panama I went the greater the feeling of happiness became. The solitude of sailing truly was the life to have.

True to form though, as this was the Gulf of Panama, the wind died away around noon. From the past experience the vagaries of the wind in this part of the world could not be relied on for making any appreciable progress, but this did not worry me unduly as I now had an operative engine. Normally, when the wind fails one just sits and waits for it to come up again. After all to use fuel unnecessarily is folly. Of course there is always an exception to any rule, and in this particular case it was a wise move to fire up the engine and get clear of the busy shipping lanes and out into the Pacific proper.

The gremlins hadn't given up just yet though. The engine fired and was put into gear. As there was no wind the Hydrovane steering was inoperative which didn't present a real problem as there was the Autopilot. The idea was to engage this method of steering while I made lunch. So far, so good, at least until it came to setting a course by the gyro compass, when something about the compass struck me as odd. The compass indicated the direction we were travelling was to the north which was a hundred and eighty degrees out of whack. Something amiss here, but what? Well may I ask. And that is all I could do as I don't know anything about electronics either. All was not lost though as the autopilot was keeping the course it was set for, probably as fooled as I was by the compass. There was no way I would go back to Panama to try and find someone who could fix it; from now on the courses would be set by magnetic compass.

An anecdote came to mind at this time, one that Joe had told about a boat owner engaging a local to fix a problem with his electronics. He ended up with his in destruct mode, thanks to the technician he had engaged, requiring a new unit shipped down from the United States. Not for me, thank you; the magnetic compass would be fine until such time that a representative of this particular system could be engaged.

Lunch passed pleasantly while I was in the cockpit with the boat chugging along famously. This venue for lunch was so I could keep a watchful eye on the gyro compass to see if maybe it would sort itself out, but alas no satisfactory results in that direction.

The wind came up again within the hour, so it was off with the engine and back to sailing. This lasted until the following noon when we were comfortably in the steady south west trade winds. In twenty-four hours the boat covered the same distance as it did in ten days when I was trying to get to Panama. There is certainly something to be said for having a clean bottom and an operating engine. Truly life had taken a turn for the better. All that was needed now was to get across the equator into the south-east trades, of which this wind we were experiencing now was a part, and then it would be just a case of boogying along to Heva-Oa in the Marquesas with the wind on the port quarter, a most admirable point of sail.

*****

For the next few days with the wind constant on the starboard beam I made a course towards the bulge of Ecuador. This was not the original intention but for some inexplicable reason this boat would not travel in the direction asked of it when the wind was forward of the beam by more than two points. This situation had also evolved when I was trying to make a better course coming down from Cabo San Lucas. Obviously the sailing qualities of this design left something to be desired. Enough said of this phenomenon, remarkable though it may seem, but one must work with what one has. Once again distance would be added to the overall trip, something to write about I suppose, if nothing else.

Some sixty miles short of the equator and too close to Ecuador for my liking I brought the boat around on the other tack with the hope of passing south of the Galapagos Islands. This tack was held for the next few days when I realised that, due to the crab like qualities inherent in my boat, we would pass to the north of this archipelago. Hawaii was in that direction but as mentioned before, much as I like Hawaii this trip was to be elsewhere. So it was a case of changing tack again and turning back the way I had come and try to make more distance to the south before changing course to cross the Equator.

During this interlude of backing and filling I sighted a ship heading on a reciprocal course. As it came closer it altered course slightly to pass nearer, no doubt to get a better look at this thing which was me in the middle of nowhere. By the size of this vessel I guessed that it was a small trader plying between Ecuador and the Galapagos. As it passed close by I gave a merry wave, which, when I considered this in retrospect struck me as the sort of wave that President Nixon gave when boarding the helicopter on leaving the office of President of the United States. If the reader can recall this wave was distinctive, given by the lifting of the arm with open palm giving a circular motion, then turning to proffer the back of the hand. It struck me at the time that this turning of the hand seemed to be a gesture of contempt. Must remember to wave with a more distinctive courtesy. Obviously the people on the ship didn't take this as an offensive gesture for they gave two very nice toots on the ship's whistle and I gave a merry wave in return.

The next afternoon I sighted a boat approaching at speed from right ahead. My first thought was, 'bloody, hell! Pirates'. This thought was short-lived, however, as fine on the starboard bow a Dan buoy was clearly seen, no doubt marking the nets vis-à-vis the boat, and as we were one hundred and fifty miles from the nearest land it was extremely unlikely that pirates would operate this far from a land base. As the boat came nearer I saw it was an open boat about twenty feet in length propelled by a large outboard engine, and containing three men in oilskins all of whom were gesticulating towards the buoy. By this time I had altered course to give the buoy a wide berth and by hand signals I alleviated their concern. They appeared to be well pleased as they closed close on my port side keeping station; they then changed the arm motions to a dumb show which I took to be asking for cigarettes. As I don't smoke all I could do was to show by apologetic hand signals that I didn't have any. This was taken in good humour and off they went at a great rate of knots. As I watched them leave it occurred to me that they might have been asking for something to eat, but they had left now. Not that there was much to offer that didn't require cooking, a tin of sardines maybe, but that would have been inappropriate under the circumstances; after all they were fishermen. This meeting did raise the question: as to what on earth they were doing so far from land, fishing obviously but, in such a small boat? One can only assume that there was a mother ship in the vicinity. Later that evening when dark had settled in I sighted lights far to the south, which judging by their intensity would certainly be those of a fisherman's working lights. By this time there was considerable distance between me and the small boat and relating association of the two was now academic.

For several days since leaving Panama one of the tasks that I had to perform as soon as convenient after the morning ritual, was to climb out of the cockpit and throw the dead flying fish back over the side that had landed on board during the night and expired there. After all they couldn't be left to rot in the sun. The fish were quite a reasonable size, maybe four or five inches in length which on reflection could, with a number of them make an acceptable meal. Sod's Law now took over; only one flying fish on subsequent days came on board. Plenty of shoals were sighted skimming the waves having been disturbed by the boat but they were all heading away. The one I did have to eat was very tasty if very scant in bulk. No matter. Maybe in the future they would grace me in abundance sufficient to make a meal. As the opportunity never arose again I could only surmise that the word was out in the flying fish population that there was a boating guy eager to have them in the frying pan, so beware.

On this return tack towards Ecuador I did make sufficient southing to get across the equator into the South-east Trades then directed the course to the west passing south of the Galapagos. The band of latitude between the equator and ten degrees south on which Heva-Oa lay was now my bailiwick. The wind at twenty knots was now on the port quarter giving the boat a very satisfactory speed towards this destination. There was quite a high swell running, no doubt created by the constant direction of the wind, which apart from giving the boat a rolling and dipping motion was no problem at all, the boat lifting easily to allow the waves to pass under. At no time during the months of sailing did the boat take a wave on board, heavy spray at times of inclement high wind weather conditions, but nothing green and solid. In that respect this was a good sea boat.

The days and nights passed pleasantly with the wind constant in direction varying slightly in intensity that only made for a more interesting passage. No ships or other traffic was sighted, making the solitude even more acute. In fact there was nothing to disturb this happy experience. The skies varied between cloudy some days and clear on others, the clear nights being particularly delightful with the stars appearing to be enormous. Orion was right over head with the disconcerting view of Sirius pointing in the opposite direction from what it does in the northern hemisphere. This took some getting used to. Viewing it from the south of the equator rather than the north latitude one can see what happens. As Orion's belt travels along the celestial equator, i.e. directly above the geographical equator, the whole constellation appears in reverse order in south latitudes. However, the clear nights were not as frequent as one would wish so there wasn't too much time to worry about the configuration of the constellation of Orion. Most nights being overcast precluded star gazing, and at these times I sought contentment by standing in the hatch feeling the wind and the easy roll of the boat in the swell. After all the hiccups prior to my arrival in Panama this problem free passage was indeed a balm to the spirit to be enjoyed to the fullest.

Ah! Yes. Complacency has no place on a boat, like anywhere else it only leads to a feeling of false security. Something like three weeks out from the start of this idyllic cruise, with 2440 miles to go from noon to the Marquesas, while I was enjoying an evening concert with Shirley Bassey belting out a selection of songs, the fresh water pump started up with a high pitched whine. Something wrong there I said to myself and switched off the circuit at the panel. Suspecting that the pump was being starved of water and assuming that with the boat heeled over on the port tack I thought the port tank would be the most likely culprit. Sure enough it was bone dry; and checking the starboard tank that wasn't much better being about a third full, or should I say, two thirds empty. This was a pretty pickle. The tanks were filled in Panama and it was unreasonable to have used such a large amount in so short a time. A leak in the water line, or the tank, was the most obvious reason, but could not be investigated at this time of night. I resolved to take up the problem of water loss in the morning and both tanks were isolated. There was some comfort in this predicament of water loss, and here we were looking on the bright side: the starboard tank could be accessed from the main cabin, whereas with the port tank one had to clamber over the engine and under the settee. Judging by the amount of water left for general use, serious restrictions would have to be adopted. With an estimated eighteen days to go that would mean diluting cooking water with sea water. After all one normally puts salt into the cooking of potatoes, not that there were any on board as the supermarket in Balboa didn't seem to cater in bulk for this item. There was plenty of rice however so here was a possibility to cook with sea water. Then it occurred to me there was an untapped source of noodles, both chicken and beef in large quantities, having been bought in bulk from the original storing. There would be no showers unless it rained. Not much hope there as it hadn't rained for a week and then not enough to make any difference. Tea was the one item that wouldn't be curtailed at the moment; after all, one had to get one's priorities right, and a little indulgence in the right direction could mean keeping one's sanity.

Searching for a possible leak would mean putting a pressure test on the line, a situation that would only reduce the amount of water in the remaining tank. Hobson's choice, which is no choice at all, so the test would have to wait until the tanks had been filled. The pump would remain shut down and the water accessed through the inspection port. Who knows, it might rain.

There was little to record during the following weeks but agreeable weather, clear skies for the most part, wind constant in velocity and direction, in fact perfect sailing weather. Record the noon position, calculate the day's run and write up the journal. Now and again the weather bow would bang into a wave to slop water on the foredeck. Taking water on board forward had created an annoying situation, annoying in as much as somehow puddles of water had formed in the forward berth under the cushions. How this water had entered the boat to settle as it did remained a mystery, at first I suspected that ingress was through the chain locker and along the wire trace to seep behind the lining fabric. I sealed off this suspected area but the puddles still formed. It is well known that where water comes in is no indication of where it will come out, or conversely where it comes out is no indication of where it comes in, so there was nothing to do at this stage but wait until I made a thorough inspection on the outside. As the forward berth was not in use the cushions were placed on edge and away from the accumulated water and the hatch that accessed the space under the berth was removed to allow the water to be drained into the bilges.

With this poser on the back burner I turned my attention to the teak deck. Progress had been made where the main cabin deck had been completely laid and one tube of caulking applied. The overall effect was stunning to the point where I was eager to purchase more caulking to finish the remaining section. However, as this was somewhere in the future, it was now considered practical to apply a sealing coat of varnish, and then tackle the raised section of deck in the dining area, the engine box top and the step into the cockpit. After a few days, this project I completed, *sans* caulking, a most pleasing appearance that dispelled all the bad happenings of the voyage from my mind.

The guys from the Dynasty in Panama had explained how best to approach the matter of inserting the caulking and these instructions were followed to the letter as it made the most sense for a clean application and avoided messing up the teak surface. Masking tape was placed on the teak, leaving the space between the strips open to receive the caulking by the caulking gun which could then be pressed into the joints and any excess pushed into the next seam. When a skin had formed the masking tape could be removed, leaving a perfectly clean deck ready for sanding and varnishing once the sealant had hardened.

Contact with base by e-mail had failed early on in this leg of the passage from Panama in that it was only possible to write a message while connected on line, which with the cost per minute of air time was not an option I considered. It just didn't make sense to communicate this way; rather it was more economical to telephone what was happening and have the message distributed by e-mail from base. At least there was contact so all the recipients would know I was safe and sound. Still some days away from Heva-Oa I decided to phone a friend in England to invite her to join the boat in Tahiti. I know this was going against my resolve to sail single handed, but then about this time I was enjoying this experience so much that a sense of wanting to share had taken hold, and what better person than Judy who was at this time between jobs and feeling very much down. As sailing was a new experience for her, not having been on boat before, it could be argued that it was still, for my part in effect, a single handed experience. Well there was some logic in this premise. To my delight the offer was accepted and she made plans to her advantage. She would go as far as New Zealand only a short two week run from Tahiti. Ah! Yes, here we go again. Will I never learn not to anticipate the future?

Joy upon joy, the rain came. This unexpected occasion had me scrabbling to set up the water catchments plastic sheet and bucket. The rain came down in torrents, unfortunately though for only a few minutes before passing away to the north. No matter, beggars cannot be choosers and at least there was three inches of water in the bucket. Sadly this amount had a brownish tint and contained specks of black dirt, a tantalising situation, not clean enough for consumption and not enough for a body bath. What to do? The answer soon materialised and I stripped off, fetched the soap and towel and washed the parts of my body with water in order of priority: face, under arms and the nether regions. Not having bathed for quite some time this limited cleaning of selected body parts created a most unusual sensation. The washed areas felt fresh and clean in counterpoint to the grotty unwashed parts. No matter, something in the manner of hygiene had been accomplished and I felt a new man. Well, a partly new man anyway.

To add to the delight of this experience, for the first time on this leg a school of dolphins came to play around the boat. It is always a pleasure to watch these wonderful creatures streaming through the clear water with no visible effort, to leap and cavort around the boat, racing ahead and under the boat yet never in any danger of being hit. On this occasion, there must have a dozen or more, but sadly they only seemed to stay long enough for the watcher to anticipate a performance of some duration before, sadly then heading off to other locations. As compensation though, they left me with a profound feeling of pleasure and a further lifting of spirits.

Prior to starting out on this adventure a neighbour, a young lady of maybe thirty years, had given me advice that I found amusing at the time, and which now came to mind. As previously mentioned apparently she was worried that I might be attacked by a whale or some other large sea creature. It was difficult to suppress my amusement at this piece of information and for my lack of faith I was promptly chastised. She was concerned that a creature may have been hurt by someone else and believing it was me, would attack my boat. Although I didn't put much credibility to her fears the memory of it remained. So it was then that during the latter part of the run to the Marquesas I was kneeling on the stern lockers, in the failing light of day, taking a leak when from under the boat what I took to be a sheet of plywood appeared. Odd, I thought, a sheet of plywood way out here? Then it flapped proving it to be not a sheet of plywood but a rather large ray. The neighbour's advice came like a shock to my mind causing me to step quickly back to gain the safety of the cockpit, somewhat shamefaced I might, and realising that a ray was not likely to leap out of the sea and attack. Ah! The powers of suggestion can be quite a force on the mind.

For some days, what I had taken to be a length of seaweed, kelp by the nature of it, seemed to have caught up on the stem and was streaming along the starboard side. Numerous attempts I had made with the boathook from the cockpit to capture this offending article and release it, all to no avail as it kept slipping off the hook. One day the wind and swell having calmed a little, and the boat being steadier, I clambered forward to have a better look at where the kelp had been caught up. Well, to my surprise it wasn't kelp at all but the tubular insert of the rub rail. As there was no way to re-insert it out here in the middle of no-where, I just coiled it up and secured it to the rail with a mental resolve to deal with it in due course at the next haul out whenever that might be. I shook my head in wonder at what else would go amiss. Later I contemplated the rub rail insert coming free and wondered if this could be related to the water coming in to the forward berth. I was clutching at straws maybe, but it was something else to check on when time and place allowed.

On the last evening of this passage I was relaxing in the cabin after the evening meal thinking how nice it would be to have a glass of wine or something similar to celebrate the near conclusion of the six week run from Panama. A drink of anything alcoholic would do as all supplies had for some days been exhausted. I was jolted out of this reverie by a loud thud above my head. This bump in the night needed investigating of course, so I stirred my stumps and went on deck to find that the mainsail was lying in a heap on the coach roof. With a sigh of acceptance that things do happen on this boat I clambered onto the coach roof to find that the topping lift halyard had frayed through. This shouldn't happen I thought in wonderment; there are sheaves to prevent this happening. Well there was nothing I could do about this matter at this time, being disinclined to scrabble around in the dark connecting the spare halyard. A gathering up of the offending heap on to the boom and a light lashing around the sail would have to suffice. Sorting this out would have to wait until morning as we seemed to be making reasonable progress under the genoa. The Hydrovane seemed quite happy with the situation also, so I went below determined to fix the problem in the morning.

So it was that after six weeks of easy sailing I saw Heva-Oa in the Marquesas rise above the horizon soon after first light. Throughout the morning this island loomed larger until more detail began to emerge. As I closed with the island I took the mainsail off the boom and stowed it, furled the genoa, and then, fired the engine to cruise along the coast to find a safe haven. Unlike most islands in the south Pacific there was not the expected coral reef protecting the shore, just sheer cliffs rising several hundred feet out of the ocean at the base of which the swells broke relentlessly. These cliffs were interspersed with deep, lush valleys leaving one wondering if there was any easy means of travelling from one valley to the next. It just didn't seem possible there were any roads that could reasonably be constructed through the dense jungle and around these steep sided mountains, and there were definitely no signs of habitation.

CHAPTER SEVEN
Heva-Oa Marquesas

After an hour motoring along the coast, the entrance to the harbour at the western end of the island came into view. Now a sense of dread possessed me at the likelihood of numerous boats being in the harbour. After all wasn't Heva-Oa the first stop on the way to the South Pacific. Not that boats crowding the harbour was a problem, it was the thought of the people on board wanting to socialise that bothered me. Time spent on my own was becoming an obsession. Not to worry though for on rounding the breakwater there was only one sailboat at anchor. With a feeling of relief that my fears were unfounded I came to anchor. My relief was brief, however, as a head appeared at the hatch of a boat shouting and gesticulating towards the shore. I must admit to a twinge of irritation, for it seemed that I was to be bothered by people after all. All I could do was to gesticulate in return, indicating that his signalling meant nothing. At this he jumped into his inflatable and came over, which indicated a matter of urgency to his signals.

"Parlez vous, français?" he asked, as his boat came to rest by my bow.

"No, English."

He proceeded to inform me in perfect English that I was anchored in a restricted area, and pointed out two markers on the shore which indicated the no-go zone. It appeared that the spot in which I was anchored was plumb in the middle of the approach to the quay for the trading steamers. Nothing for it then but to move. It now came to light that the gremlins were still at work, for the electric windlass decided to go on strike requiring the anchor to be hauled in by Armstrong's patent.

During the shifting of anchorage the gentleman in the inflatable stayed close by to advise me of a good position, and because of his help my irritation was replaced by a feeling of goodwill and we soon fell into conversation. How fortuitous this was to my needs is beyond explanation, for a stranger who didn't speak French would have no idea of how to clear inwards or the best and only way to get to the police station to perform this function. There was no public transport so the only way to get into Atuona was by thumbing a ride, or shank's pony and the road which was long and tortuous was something to be avoided by the less energetic. Matters with this agent of goodwill were becoming more and more to my benefit and understanding my need for an alcoholic beverage he took me over to the store, to buy supplies. Bad luck though for the store didn't sell alcohol, so a drink less evening was looming. Pity as a little of what does one good would have helped me unwind.

This Good Samaritan it transpired was retired from the French Army, still a young man on a pension that allowed him to spend his future on his boat just cruising around the islands of the Marquesas and visit with his many friends and contacts accumulated over the years he had spent here. Something like a latter day Paul Gauguin. As he had a female companion on board, and in a part of the world where there was no fear of storms, his life must have been idyllic, just pottering around from island to island as the inclination took him. The French painter Paul Gauguin found these islands compelling, so why not modern man? The twelve islands that make up the Marquesas cover an area of 1000 square kilometres so there would be plenty of scope for an island hopper to fill one's days. Unfortunately, though there is a down side as supplies are very expensive, having to be brought over from Tahiti. Heva-Oa was also without any services for the boater either. The sail repairs would have to wait until Tahiti where I was informed by my new found enlightener there was everything the heart could desire.

In due course all the information that would be required to have a trouble free stay in Heva-Oa had been passed on and my French friend took his leave to leave me planning the adventures of tomorrow. This would incur inflating the dinghy to get ashore then hope for a ride into town to get inward clearance. These thoughts were distracted by a knocking on the hull, which on investigation proved to be the Frenchman again. On this occasion he was an angel of mercy as holding his inflatable steady alongside with one hand he waved a bottle of wine with the other.

"For your evening meal," he announced, handing the bottle over.

"Well, thank you kindly," said I, "you are a lifesaver. What do I owe you?" I asked, reaching for my wallet.

"Nothing, enjoy. Maybe one day you can return the favour." And with a Gallic wave he was zooming back to his boat.

The slight discomfort at having been the recipient of this fortuitous gift was short lived and I was soon tucking in to the evening meal and raising a glass of this wonderful libation towards the boat of this kind man. Is there anything more worthwhile than a glass of fine wine to excite the pallet?

*****

After a good night's rest in the forward berth I was ready for the new day. After breakfast the dinghy was inflated and launched in readiness to go ashore. Viewing the harbour wall through the binoculars for a possible landing place didn't reveal anything that filled my heart with joy. There was but one set of steps to effect a landing on which the water surged with an incoming swell. To avoid getting my feet wet would need some nimble footwork.

While contemplating the best method of getting ashore my erstwhile friend from the previous evening had up-anchored and was motoring past, no doubt to yet one of the other islands. With a merry wave and a hearty 'Bon Voyage', he was gone.

The scramble up the steps wasn't all that difficult as it turned out. Being sockless it was just a matter of carrying my sandals to dry ground. In fact, there was nothing difficult to cause any concern. It was just a short walk to the road where a passing car gave me a lift into the town of Atuona. Having located the Gendarmerie only proved that nothing ever goes smoothly, as they were closed for the weekend, this being Saturday. This must be a crime free island for the police to close up shop for the weekend. Well, there was nothing for it but to return on Monday. First though I wanted to wander around the shops and see what they had to offer. Bread was high on my wish list and as I am partial to those long French loaves, what better place than a French island to satisfy this whim? Oops! Not to be. Bread baking was only carried out for Monday delivery to the shops. What I did find odd was the number of shops all selling general merchandise and three of these were on the same street. There wasn't anything to keep me in town, which was just a collection of shops. Post Office, a bank all spread out as though to give the impression of size I supposed. So it was back to thumbing a ride to the other side of the harbour and the boat. Before clambering into the dinghy though I wandered up to the store visited the previous evening. Might as well do some grocery shopping here where it isn't too far to carry the goods. What they had to offer in the way of food appeared to be only canned goods. If this was the situation on Heva-Oa life must be very dreary meal wise and no, no bread until Monday.

Water and fuel though, were available but, not without difficulty, or so I first thought. The procedure was to take up the anchor and approach the store, then turn to present the stern of the boat to the steps that led down from the store into the harbour, drop anchor and back up to within two feet of the steps. The store owner would then take the mooring line securing the boat in position. Surprisingly, this manoeuvre didn't present any difficulty even for little me on my own. I made a few adjustments to the anchor line which required a few trips to the foredeck, but apart from that everything went smoothly. Within the hour the boat was back in the anchorage where a pressure test was put on the water line. This proved nothing except to present a mystery as to where the fresh water had disappeared. Well if there was no evidence of a leak in the line there was nothing to fix; however, a close watch would have to be made on the water level in the tanks on the passage to Tahiti.

Having rigged a spare halyard for the main sail and the afternoon having progressed to what would have been time for sundowners and as there was nothing to drink anyway; I contented myself with watching what would appear to be the local sport. This involved an individual paddling an outrigger canoe at a furious pace. The design was more like a kayak of some fifteen feet in length with an outrigger, and like most things these days, of a fibreglass construction. Although there were several people involved, all paddling with impressive energy, there didn't seem to be any competition amongst them. Could it be they were in training for some event? What did interest me however was when the exercise was over the boats went around the end of the quay wall at the inner end of the harbour. Could there be a better landing place there? Something to be investigated on Monday when it was time to re-visit the Gendarmerie for the inward clearance and, now I had decided not to tarry here I would also acquire the outward clearance for Tahiti.

Early Sunday morning I observed a great deal of activity at the landing place, with people dressed in white tropical uniforms setting up an awning and tables. The reason soon came to light as a Cruise ship had anchored in the outer bay and was disembarking passengers into the ship's boats which soon came chugging around the breakwater to disgorge them at the landing there to board busses. More than likely to tour the delights of the island, this traffic went on all morning and into the afternoon bringing people ashore and taking them back to the ship. Well a sight such as this can only hold one's attention for so long and I had wonders to perform, so it was then that I attended to replacing broken slides on the mast. To my surprise a voice addressed me by name and enquired what part of Victoria I was from. Of course this grabbed my attention, and on turning I noticed that one of the liberty boats was lying just off my stern with a body leaning half way out of the hatch.

"What part of Victoria are you from?" he asked again, volunteering that he was from the James Bay area.

It was obvious that he had read the boat's name and port of registry on the stern. No prizes for reading 'Ron's Endeavour. Victoria.'

"Pender Island, actually. The boat's registered in Victoria."

A short conversation followed with this fellow of goodwill, along the lines of what he was doing on this floating hotel, and what I was up to. Then it was back to ferrying passengers to base. I was assured they never left anyone behind. Quite a feat I thought, all these bodies wandering around and not losing one.

During the night a swell had built up running around the breakwater which produced a discomforting rocking motion making it difficult to get any sleep. This confirmed my decision and the plan of action for the next day: clear inwards and outwards at the same time, then get away for Tahiti. The run to this port would put me well ahead of the arrival of my friend Judy, but at least I could be doing something constructive in the way of bringing the boat up to operational efficiency.

So, the following morning these plans were put into action. The observed landing place proved to be ideal, a low sloping shingle beach sheltered from the swell by the projecting end of the seawall. It was only a matter of clambering out of the dinghy dry footed and pulling it clear of the incoming tide and off to town.

By mid-morning, after the brief visit to the gendarmerie and availing myself of the bread delivery, I was chugging out of the harbour into the Bordelais Channel between Heva-Oa and Tahuata.

*****

This archipelago was first discovered by the Spanish sailor Alvaro de Mendana in 1595, landing at Tahuata. He named the islands after the wife of the Viceroy of Peru, Marquesas de Mendoza, soon to be shortened to the name that it now bears. Sadly, the Islanders first meeting with an European was bloody as the Spaniards massacred 200 locals causing a violent hostility to future visitors to the island. Even as late as 1842 a Polynesian chief set up a fierce resistance to the French, who tried to take control of Tahuata, France having annexed the Marquesas in that year.

Captain James Cook rediscovered the islands in April 1774, fixing more accurately their latitude and longitude. As with most other islands in the Pacific Ocean, the Western sailors brought diseases that devastated the local populations. French missionaries and colonial administrators nearly destroyed the ancient culture of these Polynesians by forcing European religion and mores into their way of life. According to Cook and his officers these people of the Marquesas were not merely the most beautiful people in the South Seas, but the finest race ever beheld, all tall and well proportioned, with good features.

The Marquesas comprise 12 islands spread over an area of 997 square kilometres with each of the islands being very similar in structure. They are high and volcanic in origin, dominated by peaks of lava, five of which are higher than 1000 metres. Apart from Tahuata there are no coral reefs to protect the islands from the pounding of the Pacific Ocean swells, and flat coastal areas of land are extremely rare.

Chapter Eight
Heva-Oa to Tahiti

With winged heels, as English Mercuries,
For now sits expectation in the air
Henry V. act 2

Once clear of the Bordelais Channel the sails went up, and what a sad sight they presented. The Genoa had suffered the most injury on the passage from Panama with the repairs made there having come apart. The leach or what was left of it was wrapped around the starboard spreader with a flapping remnant entangled with the shroud. An attempt to untangle this unsightly symbol of heavy sailing with the boat hook had come to naught with the spreader being tantalisingly just too high, or conversely my arms being too short, to be able to unwind this fluttering rag. A further encumbrance was having to hold on with one hand and stand on tiptoe taking swipes with an unwieldy boathook on a heaving deck. What was needed was for someone to be hauled up the mast to cut it free. However, as it was physically impossible to haul myself up the mast the offending article would have to remain in situ until Tahiti when the sail maker/rigger's services could be engaged. Renewing the broken slides on the mainsail I had attended to in Heva-Oa which solved the problem of losing the wind through the luff. Some satisfaction had been gained there; it was now only a matter of repairing the Panamanian repairs around the area of the reef points. Thankfully, the battens had prevented the sail from ripping down to the foot so, if not perfect, at least all was functioning satisfactorily with the main, for now anyway. This business of having to make do with sails that had seen better days had me thinking about new sails of sturdier construction. But when? As the South-East Trade winds still prevailed and the passage to Tahiti being just a week's sailing the decision could be put off until then.

There were four halyards on the mast, two leading forward and two leading aft. One of the forward halyards was used for hoisting the genoa, with the other as a spare. Of the two from aft one had parted, allowing the mainsail to come down with a thump the night before arriving at Heva-Oa, which left the spare. This halyard had shown admirable service by hauling the Radar reflector up the backstay. The situation now was that this halyard had been rigged to hoist the mainsail and the reflector switched to the forward spare halyard. To prevent a repeat of a breakage and lose the services of this now mainsail halyard on the trip to Tahiti was going to require regular checks for any sign of fraying. Lowering the sail, twice a day, to check for any sign of fraying was a bit of a nuisance but it would be foolish to ignore such a critical exercise. As it turned out this halyard remained in perfect condition, which in turn had me wondering what could have caused the initial halyard to fray. Some things it seems are destined to remain forever unanswered.

Leaving Heva-Oa earlier than expected I would arrive in Papeete with days to spare before my good friend Judy arrived. This early arrival would be needed to sort out the lay of the land so to speak. Being a stranger to this part of the world it would make sense to first get established, and then find out the best way to get to the Airport. The flight was due to arrive at one-thirty Saturday morning which added a problem of getting to the airport at such an ungodly hour. No doubt all would be revealed in the fullness of time and it was pointless worrying at this early stage. For the time being there was nothing to do but enjoy the cruise and ponder the problem in the abstract form.

The course I set was in a south-westerly direction to pass to the north of King George Island in the Taumotu Archipelago and the numerous reefs in the area, thence south to Tahiti. The first part of this plan went well and I made good progress as far as the course alteration to the south. This change of direction put the wind forward of the beam, and although the sails were flattened to sail to windward the boat still made considerable drift widening the distance to close Tahiti. Realising that before long yet another change of course would be necessary to reach Papeete, thus putting the wind right ahead, I decided to take down the sails, fire up the engine, then motor the rest of the way. While lowering the mainsail I noticed that the lower batten had disappeared, which was yet another puzzlement to ponder, as this batten prevented the reef points ripping the sail to the foot when reefed. This problem would have to be addressed before any future reefing could be carried out.

Originally, before leaving Panama my intention was to make for Fiji from the Marquesas so the appropriate charts were purchased. However, the best laid plans often change and during the previous weeks it had been decided to call in at Tahiti instead, this island being on a more direct line with New Zealand. Time was the guiding factor in this decision as I deemed it sensible to be out of the area before the onset of the storm season. After all making a decision to avoid the Atlantic Hurricanes only to find myself in a Pacific storm would not be a very clever situation to be in. The problem was there was no large scale chart on board as Heva-Oa, true to form, was destitute of a seaman's requirements. The only chart on board was of the general area showing Tahiti but not Papeete. All was not lost, however, as there was on board the Admiralty publication, Ocean Passages of the World, which gave the geographical position of Papeete. With this information it was possible to set a course by GPS from where I was to where I wanted to be.

The morning was bright and sunny, the wind brisk from right ahead bringing the occasional spray over the bow. Otherwise the cruise along the north coast of Moorea was most pleasantly relaxing. Within the hour Moorea had been left behind and I crossed the channel to Papeete. Next problem to address was to find out how to get into the harbour with the lack of chart information. Viewing the situation through the binoculars I saw a long whitish wall which seemed to be the outer limit of the port but, no break that would indicate the entrance. There was nothing for it but to observe and watch for any other vessels leaving the port, or failing that, proceed as close as possible to see if anything lent itself to an obvious answer. As I closed the distance towards the breakwater to about two miles, a large vessel which turned out to be the Moorea ferry came steaming out of port. Although, due to the angle, a break in the seawall couldn't be located the general area could. Step one solved. Now to proceed until the opening could be located. During this period of trying to locate the entrance to Papeete harbour a person on a Skidoo was observed bouncing about in the waves, no doubt having a great deal of fun. As fate would have it when the entrance opened into view this Skidoo decided to put an end to his games and made for the opening in the seawall. In a situation such as mine could one wish for a better pilot?

The island of Tahiti is nearly totally enclosed by coral reefs on the west side and the approaches to Papeete were no exception. However, there are passages well marked by beacons, and as the ferry had come through the reef there was no reason to think that my little boat could not do the same, not to mention the Skidoo operator. All that the situation required now was to navigate the darker blue water through the reef into the port of Papeete, which soon found me inside the breakwater wondering where to go. There was no indication of a marina; from what could be observed this port seemed to handle big ships only. While chugging slowly past various structures for the benefit of big vessels, I noticed a familiar sight of a Travelift situated on the inside of the seawall, so it was to that place I directed my course. My arrival produced a great deal of consternation with many people gesticulating in a Gallic manner, presumably indicating that my presence was not welcome. Eventually someone who spoke English arrived to whom I expressed a desire to book a haul-out, not that that was my intention at this moment but a possibility to be decided on at a later date, but then what else could I do to appease these gentlemen, and I might as well do just that while I was here. So Friday at ten-thirty was agreed on, and I got directions where to moor in the meantime.

Once more I was chugging around the port of Papeete, this time though with a better knowledge and confidence of where to go. To my delight when rounding the stern of an ocean going freighter, before me were a few sailboats of varying sizes moored stern to the quay wall. That was not the only delight for the moorage was right in town, something like the pictures one sees of places like Monte Carlo. Before long, the anchor was down and with the assistance of a lady and her two teenaged children from a boat with the unusual name of 'Fruity Fruit', I was securely moored stern to the quay and lying with a pontoon on the port side.

CHAPTER NINE
Tahiti

Look stranger at this island now, the leaping light for your delight discovers.

Auden.

The first Europeans to visit Tahiti were Captain Samuel Wallace and the crew of His Majesties Frigate, Dolphin on the 21st June 1767. They had been commissioned to search the Southern Ocean between Cape Horn and New Zealand to establish the possibility of a temperate land in these latitudes. After battling storms for four months to pass through the straight of Magellan they came upon Tahiti, the first land of any note that would provide the necessities for replenishment of provisions. Their arrival in Matavai Bay on the north coast was vigorously challenged by the natives, who were only subdued by the firing of the guns, a display of the white man's superiority. Henceforth trade was established, with nails being the unit of currency, for both the securing of provisions and the favours of the local women. Wallace named this island King George's Island after the young British monarch. Once friendly relations were established with the Tahitians and the easy favours of the women extended to the ship's company this island soon earned the recognition of Paradise. The Dolphin was just five weeks at Tahiti when having replenished water and provisions she left to return to England.

The second European leader to arrive at Tahiti was the French commander Bougainville in1768, remaining for just over a week.

This discovery of Tahiti led to an expedition under the command of Lieutenant James Cook in 1769 to observe the transit of Venus across the face of the sun. This, with other observations of a similar nature around the world hoped to determine the distance between the earth and the sun. Cook had a fort built on the low lying land on the north side of Matavai Bay to protect the valuable instruments from the thieving which was prevalent among the natives at this time. This point of land is still known today as Point Venus.

William Bligh of HMS Bounty was also here to collect breadfruit plants which it was believed would provide food for the West Indies slaves. It is a well known fact of history what the results of that visit became.

After the sailors, came the Missionaries to oversee the decline of this sailor's paradise. In 1816, however, two Roman Catholic Priests were expelled to the great annoyance of the French Government who demanded an apology and a most favoured nation treaty extracted from the Tahitians. In 1843 the island became a French Protectorate, the British more than once refusing such an offer. 1880 saw Tahiti become a French Colony.

As a result of western influence the island soon became less than the Paradise that it was seen to be when first discovered. Paul Gauguin on his arrival soon realised that Tahiti was not the place he had expected and took himself off to the Marquesas, hoping for a better life.

*****

By the time the boat was secured it was noon and time for lunch and a snooze. After these most important obligations I took myself ashore to report inwards to the Immigration. The location of these offices must have been designed with boaters in mind as they were only a matter of a few minutes walk along the quay wall and all departments were located together in the same low one story building. Indeed a better organisation could not be imagined for the benefit of the boating community, and bearing in mind the difficulties faced in the Cabo a blessing to be thankful for. Another piece of good fortune was the fact that the officials all spoke excellent English which eased the process of clearance. However, before the formalities could be entered into I was required to go to the bank and make a security deposit against overstaying my welcome then return with the proper documentation to formalise my approval. The amount of the security deposit, paid by credit card, was quite considerable, but as it would be returned on departure the pain was therefore, if not convenient, at least bearable.

These formalities concluded I was free to explore the immediate locale. Having noticed a Tavern across the road from the berth I proceeded there for a beer and to watch the world go by while pondering a plan of action. My euphoria at being on land again with the prospect of having all my troubles with the boat put to rights was rudely shattered when it came to paying for the beer. To say it was expensive would be an understatement, the price was exorbitant. But then I came to realise in the following days that everything was. This apparently came about when France was carrying out nuclear tests in the Polynesian Islands. Highly paid French personnel competed with the locals for the basics of life to the disadvantage of the locals; riots followed which resulted in the wages of the populace coming into line with the French. Although resolving the problem locally not the best deal for tourists however.

The inner man being satisfied, if not my pocket I took time to take a wander and find out the lay of the land. In the immediate vicinity of the boat moorings parallel to the sea wall a wide pavement presented benches and planters, and discretely hidden by a low containing wall, garbage containers for use of the boating community, all very neatly kept and functional. Next to this was a wide road of two lanes, each way separated by a median. I later learned that this road encompassed the whole island. The traffic was heavy indeed but, thankfully disciplined, as all vehicles came to a stop when a pedestrian chose to use the designated crossing. On the far side of the road where shops, hotels, banks and the like, in fact quite the commercial section of Papeete. Supplying the needs of the boat began to look promising; however, these needs would have to wait until the morrow as it was too late in the day to conduct a search to track down the help that was required. My stomach was telling of a far greater need, and I decided that someone else's cooking was more desirable than mine, so a restaurant became the object of my search. Down one of the side streets and not too far from the boat a restaurant presented itself. The hour was still early for most diners so I had the place to myself with personalised service. The meal of a main course of the local fish, followed by a cheese plate with French bread and several glasses of excellent red wine was an absolute delight. So much so, that from my position in sight of the kitchen door, I could observe the waiter showing the cook the returned plates which held not a morsel of food, which they seemed to be viewed with a great deal of surprise. Must admit though that the bread served admirably for wiping up the juices and the small specks of the meal, and they weren't to know just how starved I was for such a well cooked meal. It had been a long day and as is the case in a strange place with its traffic noise and unfamiliar crowds, a tiring one mentally as much as physically. After a short constitutional stroll along the quay wall it was back to the boat to read for a while and an early night, happy and content with the thought that all would be right with the proposed boat projects during the coming days.

*****

The following morning as soon as reasonably possible in regard to the opening of business I took myself off on a search of the service agent for the gyro compass. The waiter of the previous evening had given me directions to a shop selling charts only a short distance away as the best place to start. This morning though I was better prepared and had taken the precaution of writing down the address of the agent from the service manual. The gentleman who attended me, much to my surprise, looked at the name and address on my piece of paper and with much confidence denounced my information and wrote out directions to an establishment called Nauti-Sport. This left me a little perplexed as to how he knew the right people to approach, but who was I to argue. As I searched for this place of business I soon came to understand that in Papeete it was a case of wheels within wheels so to speak. Each business operated with other businesses in the boating industry, hand in glove for their mutual benefit no doubt. It certainly was beneficial for the customer also not having to drag around town trying to find the services required.

It was a long hot trek, but soon I presented myself at Nauti-Sport to make my request for the particular service agent only to be told that this gentleman didn't do repairs only installations. The service agent had no ties with Nauti-Sport but, as mentioned everyone seemed to be aware of everyone else's movements I must point out at this stage that each person that I spoke to on this quest spoke excellent English, which posed the question, would a Frenchman meet with the same novel gratification in an English speaking country? However, that is by the by, although I was relieved at not having to make myself understood by signs. The help that was forthcoming I much appreciated as another person was recommended and contacted on the office telephone; the result of this was an arrangement for him to come to the boat the same afternoon. Feeling I was on a roll I also asked if a sail maker could be recommended. This prompted yet another telephone conversation and another arrangement for tomorrow, Friday morning, before moving over to the boatyard. As previously stated, ask one person and, like a domino effect all other needs are met. To a visiting boater, a stranger, could there be a better arrangement? The morning was not yet over and here we were with all requirements duly arranged. Conscious of all the agreeable help that had been forthcoming the least I could do was to purchase a few small but necessary items of a chandlery nature for the further prosecution of the voyage.

Heading back to the boat at a leisurely pace gave me the chance to look around a few unexplored areas of the back streets of Papeete. A laundrette and also a car rental establishment were noted for future reference. Had I been thinking right and not just letting the mind dwell on future needs, or for that matter letting my mind wander with the sights and sounds, I would have enquired about renting a car. After all I had to be at the airport in the wee hours of Saturday and some mode of transport would be needed. Well there was always tomorrow. For the moment I was basking in the euphoria of having arranged so many tasks so easily to bring the boat back to an operational standard and didn't worry too much over the needs of two days hence.

The back streets of Papeete seemed to be of no consistent nature as one would expect from the orderly manner of what I'm pleased to call the Corniche encompassing the waterfront, rather they wandered off at different angles and directions all built up with shops and like establishments. Soon I realised that if I didn't get my bearings and make my way back to the Corniche I would probably end up in the outlying countryside. The morning was becoming quite warm, this coupled with the low blood sugar telling me it would soon be time to eat, brought urgency to the situation. Abandoning the meandering I took the first right hand turn regardless of where it might bring me. All I was certain of was that the harbour lay in that direction, which proved to be correct although not much further towards the boat from where I originally turned off. No matter, at least I wasn't wandering any longer. A relaxing lunch and a beer at the open air restaurant across from the berth soon had my good feelings restored. This happy attitude had me accepting the high prices. It seemed there were no mental protestations, only a resolve that in these circumstances one beer was better being cheaper than two or more, and most certainly sufficient.

The family from the Fruity Fruit were heading in to the restaurant as I was leaving which gave occasion for a few pleasantries and an exchange of local information. The lady of the group dominated the conversation while the man, whom I took to be her husband, said not a word. Subdued came to mind, which could well be the case as the lady's opinions were most positive and brooked no argument. The two teenagers also remained silent, not looking too happy. It must have been an odd situation for them to be cooped up on a boat with their parents and not have any friends to do teenager things with. All that could be said about such a situation is that it would be an experience the memory of which would last a life time. To sail around the South Pacific was not an experience that everyone would have in their lifetime. I was given to understand that they would shortly be leaving for the Marquesas to wait out the storm season. I too would have to get my skates on also and make tracks for New Zealand before too long.

After I had a short snooze and pottered around on the boat the gentleman came to fix the gyro. However, nothing was done and after asking what the problem was he just looked at the offending object and announced that he would return on the morrow with a replacement gyro compass and make more tests. That was the last I saw him.

Nothing much seemed to go seamlessly on this boat and after breakfast on the Friday morning I attempted to start the engine prior to proceeding to the boatyard. This proved to be futile, nothing, nix, nada, the thing had died. This presented a bit of a quandary as without a telephone number I couldn't contact the yard, and for that matter I had no idea how to get there except by water. Quite a pickle it seemed. While pondering the problem for a period of time, who should turn up but the sail-maker, deus ex machina one might say. On being acquainted with the engine problem he pulled out his mobile and made a call, conversing in French. He then advised me that the mechanic could not come to attend to the problem until Monday which helped matters not at all. Although I appreciated his input it still didn't get me over to the boatyard, so yet another call was made resulting in the information that the yard was sending a boat over to tow me there. All this strengthened my belief that all the people involved in matters boat worked hand in glove with each other, quite a bonus for one seeking help with no knowledge of Papeete. All these machinations had the effect of taking the matter out of my hands making me feel rather extra to requirement, but certainly appreciative. As the haul out wasn't all that critical and the appointment only made to calm the irate boatyard workers on my intrusion on their bailiwick on arrival when it was directions to an appropriate berth that was really wanted. The haul out could have waited until a more appropriate occasion in the future, and therefore I was quite prepared to wait where I was for the mechanic. As matters turned out the whole business proved to be an advantage for the gremlins hadn't finished with me just yet. The yard manager promptly arrived with his boat and an assistant, in a mood I took to be concern for the falling tide and whether there would be enough water at the boatyard over this delay. After several attempts to haul in the anchor it proved to be impossibly fouled on some underwater obstruction resulting the manager's behest to cut the rope rode at the chain, and be ignobly towed away, leaving a valuable anchor and forty feet of chain lying on the bottom of Papeete harbour. Had an appointment for the boatyard not been made, then on departure from Papeete I must have allowed for maybe the total loss of the anchor and chain, the worst scenario, or be left with trying to engage the diver which the yard would provide? That's how it goes sometimes, chance taking a helpful hand.

The lift out and positioning on the hard was soon accomplished. We had enough water to remain afloat regardless of the delay, which was fortuitous; otherwise a rescheduling for the following week would have been necessary as the yard closed at two-thirty on a Friday until seven-thirty on Monday morning. On the hard the boat had been placed by the fence bordering the road which proved to be a bit of a nuisance as this area on the far side of the road was used as a late night party spot for the younger generation. Fortunately, when disturbed, I could stand in the cockpit and bellow my displeasure, accompanied with arm gestures for the revellers to turn down the volume on the ghetto blasters and move further down the road. Another feature of this position on the hard was the close proximity of a stand pipe located immediately under the stern, handy for water both for the workers to clean up after their days labour and as a supply for the boat tanks. In the absence of a drain, puddles had formed around the boat, which proved that the convenience of an available water supply could be a less favourable benefit in the days ahead.

The first task after being settled and for getting down off the boat was to present myself at the office to do the paperwork. I must say that the manager of the yard was more than helpful over and above matters relating to a haul out. The first item on the agenda was the filling of the propane tanks to which he instructed his assistant to take me to the depot, which was only five minutes away but too far to walk carrying two ten pound canisters. It was a most welcome and generous gesture and much appreciated. Alas! As they only filled tanks during the mornings it was too late in the day to cater to my needs. But all was not lost for with yet another kindness from these Tahitians of French extraction I was instructed by the operator whom presented a marker pen to write the name of the boat on the tanks and was assured they would be ready to be picked up on the Monday morning. I was really warming to these considerate people.

What work that I needed to do on the boat could be completed by the following Monday so it was arranged to go back in the water at noon on Tuesday. The anti-fouling that was applied in Panama was still in excellent condition with no evidence of breakdown or marine growth becoming attached to it. This was indeed a bonus that gave me the resolve to use Glidden's paints in future maintenance work. While I was arranging the propane a diver had been organised for the Tuesday afternoon to retrieve the anchor and chain so everything was coming together again. The one problem that remained was how to get out to the airport at such an early hour. In consultation with the manager various options were bruited about. Renting a car? On phoning around both of us considered a rental to be too expensive? Hiring a taxi? Could this be relied upon to turn up in the middle of the night? Close by the town berth there was a taxi rank to which I had made enquiries and I was assured that there were taxis there throughout the night. This revelation was comforting, but to get to the rank would require a walk of about two miles as the boatyard was located on the outer seawall of Papeete harbour. Out in the sticks one might say. This business of getting out to the airport in the wee hours of the morning had developed into somewhat of a quandary.

Both the manager and I fell into a silence no doubt pondering the options, certainly on my part with no small concern. I was more or less resolved to walk into town well before the witching hour, get a taxi out to the airport and hang around until flight time, not an option particularly filling my soul with joy.

"You can take my car," The manager announced bringing me out of my reverie in a most abrupt manner, as though I didn't believe what I'd heard.

"Sorry?" I asked, in disbelief as to whether he was being serious.

"You can take my car," he repeated, showing amusement at my confusion.

"But what will you do? How will you get home?"

"I have my motorbike. Come, I'll show you."

We went down into the yard and across to a vehicle parked close to the boat. It wasn't a car as such but rather a small van, but who's complaining. It transpired that the van was for the yard usage, fetching supplies and errands of that nature. Having explained the workings he handed over the gate keys with the admonishment to make sure the yard was not left open and then took his leave. So this problem had been solved with a profound relief and greatly appreciative at this kindness.

Promptly at two-thirty the yard suddenly emptied, leaving me with silence and two or three cats that rolled around in the dust, no doubt aware that they would not be disturbed until Monday morning. Left to my own devices I took the opportunity to wander around the yard for the sake of familiarisation before tackling the boat jobs. Not only was this establishment not just for the haul-out and maintenance of small craft, it was also a boat building enterprise. Inside a large construction shed an aluminium fish boat was in the final stages of completion with yet another being fitted out in the yard. During this walkabout I came across a scrap bin of cast out aluminium bits which brought to mind my need for a strut to stabilise the rudder post. After mulling the idea around about the best way to construct this bracket, I realised that with funds running low and already spoken for regarding the sails it would serve my purpose best to wait until New Zealand where prices, I hoped, would be more reasonable.

With the working of the rudder post the bottom seal was showing signs of cracking in way of the hull again. Although it wasn't about to break away, for the sake of good order until the aforementioned bracket could be fabricated a strengthening with fibreglass cloth and epoxy would have to suffice, if for no other reason than to reduce the ingress of water into the boat in this area. This project was put to one side as there was another job that also required an epoxy application and it made sense to perform these tasks at the same time.

For some time now I had convinced myself that the only place water could be getting into the forward berth was via the rub rail, at least all other avenues had been explored and rejected. In fact, it could remain a mystery forever given the right circumstances. It was to this task that I attended, by pulling out the insert that earlier had been assumed to be a length of kelp caught up on the anchor, and throwing it onto the scrap heap. Likewise, the actual rub-rail would also end up in the same place, extra to requirement, another example of something being a good idea at the time, but subsequently becoming useless. While removing the retaining screws my mind was working on a more suitable replacement rub-rail of teak to be installed when my odyssey was finally completed, another project to add to a growing list of things to do when I finally returned to my home port. By the time the rub-rail was consigned to the scrapheap it was too late to start mixing up an epoxy putty rather it made sense to get cleaned up, make something for dinner then have a lie down and snooze until midnight, the designated time to take off for the airport.

*****

Over the years, out of interest rather than necessity, I had trained my metabolism to wake me up at any given time, thus doing away with the need of an alarm clock. On occasions of great need to be awake at a certain time this acquired gift often goes into overdrive which has me waking up several times before the appointed time. I check on the clock then drop off again. Fear of oversleeping is probably the reason for this. Well, what can I say? No-one is perfect and a purpose is served. This particular night proved to be of this nature, which gave me the opportunity to have a cup of tea before setting out.

The road out of the industrial section and the docks of Papeete where the boatyard is located joins up with the main highway that encircles the whole island, and from here it is a short run of ten minutes to the airport. At this time of night there was no traffic and the whole of Papeete was as quiet as the grave. This appeared to be peculiar to French Colonial life in the tropics. Having noticed this phenomenon on several other occasions in my younger days on returning to my ship after a night out, it came as no surprise to have the town to myself. With the roads empty I could concentrate on driving this strange vehicle and watch for the turn off for the Airport without being concerned with how other traffic would behave.

The airport terminal seemed strangely deserted too, with only one or two young people kipping on the floor. Wandering around looking for other signs of life I found a lady who by her uniform belonged to either the airport staff or an airline. I asked her when the Air New Zealand flight from the UK was due. Being very helpful she used her mobile and phoned for advice. Much to my dismay the flight had been delayed in Los Angeles and would not arrive until two o'clock in the afternoon. Well, there you go, nothing unusual in airline delays, so I thanked her for the information and set out to the boat to turn in again.

I was a little uncomfortable about driving out to the Airport again as the manager of the yard had given me the understanding, but not stressed, that the use of the van was for a middle of the night run only and not for general use. To my credit I did agonise over this unfortunate turn of events, whether to take the van on this necessary second run, or to walk the two miles into town and get a taxi. Did another trip to the Airport constitute general usage? With the yard empty of personnel this Saturday with no one to ask to solve this dilemma I suppressed the uncomfortable guilty feelings and took the van, commonsense prevailing over the niggling minor guilt being my logic.

Arriving in good time at the airport I went to the Cafeteria for refreshment. However, the only means of getting refreshment was from coin operated dispenser, not what one would expect where a coin is popped in the slot and voila, one's choice is produced, Oh, no! After depositing the required coins nothing happened. Puzzling over this hiccup for a while I then went over to the counter to complain and was directed to the instructions on the side of the machine. Now, I ask why put instructions around the side of a machine. Well there was no way I was going to get my choice of refreshment. Although the instructions were in English as well as French the machine would only work with a token purchased from the main counter, presumably after purchasing something to eat. All this nonsense became academic because by putting proper coins into the infernal thing it had become inoperative, with the coins jamming up the works no doubt. Time to make myself scarce.

Tahiti Airport is uncomplicated, comprising one low building on the level of the road outside with no stairs for the visitor to negotiate. At one end there is the cafeteria and washrooms, a few shops and lounges, and arrival and departure gates along the length of the concourse, all open to the pleasantly cooling air on the road side of the building. A mezzanine floor over the lower facilities contains what one would presume are offices relating to the operation of the Airport.

Quite a few people had started to gather around the arrival gate which suggested the flight had arrived. The 'meeters and greeters' in their bright and colourful dresses and holding the traditional garlands of flowers began to gather which strengthened the suggestion that the flight was discharging its passengers. Time to take up a watching position at the gate. Soon the passengers started to drift through in dribs and drabs at first, some avoiding making eye contact with the waiting people, no doubt not expecting to be met. Others were anxiously scanning the crowd and breaking into wreaths of smiles when contact with those known was made. After a little while a loose group came into view and, there in the middle a head above the others was Judy looking remarkably refreshed after such a long delayed flight. What always gave me pleasure when meeting with Judy was the way she walked, tall and self assured with a slight movement of the shoulders, something akin to a nautical roll. Indeed she was a pleasure to behold, a posture developed no doubt by her love of hiking, horse riding, cycling and other outdoor activities.

After I remarked how fresh she looked after such a disrupted flight, she told me that due to the pilot getting earache the flight was suspended at Los Angeles to await a new crew, all the passengers being put up in hotels for the night. Then in conversation we considered how much an earache could cost an airline.

There being little traffic on the road this Saturday afternoon we were shortly back at the boatyard. It must have been somewhat of a letdown for Judy to have to climb up a ladder to get into the boat; after all this doesn't suggest a cruising mode, a boat high and dry is not the same as a boat in the water. By the time Judy had been given a tour of the boat, shown where everything lived and her gear stowed it was time for pre-dinner drinks. A duty-free bottle of Famous Grouse was produced like magic from the depths of the dear lady's bag to celebrate this occasion. What a delightful thought and, so considerate to cater to my preferences. There was much to discuss with reference to the objections from a family member for her to come out to Tahiti for this adventure, quite unfounded in everyone else's opinion and although noted, the objections she ignored. Time passed quickly as it does in good company and in no time at all dinner had to be started, so out with the electric frying pan to cook some rice and diced tinned veggies. Not an auspicious fare to welcome the new crew but, needs must when the devil drives. Not having located a Supermarket to shop for provisions we would have to make do with what was on board. Tomorrow we could walk into town to that restaurant which provided such wonderful fare on my first night in Papeete. Judy never commented on my cooking but in subsequent days she took over these duties which I suppose could be considered as comment enough. As long as the cook was kept supplied with wine during the preparation of our evening meal my input was considered satisfactory.

As my duties didn't require me to keep a lookout for shipping or attend to the sailing of the boat I was able to do justice to the FG and relax in great company with an easy and wide ranging conversation.

*****

The morning tea was my bailiwick and as I'm an early riser I was able to give my guest her tea in bed with the suggestion that she should relax and take her time before facing the first day in Tahiti. Judy was not a person who required constant attention so I could leave her to her own devices while I got on with the epoxy jobs on the rudder shaft seal and the area of the removed rub rail. These projects took most of the day and as the epoxy hardened in a reasonable time it could be sanded down in readiness for painting. The topside paint was showing signs of mange again with large areas coming away and exposing the filler coat. Much as this needed attention I was prepared to delay this until New Zealand where, I was hoping, materials would be less expensive. Not that I was averse to subscribing to the Tahitian economy but I would have upcoming expenses, new fore sail, wind generator and the like. Another haul out to fit a large through-hull valve for the holding tank was required so it made sense to carry out the painting of the hull topsides at such time.

The yard being deserted made it possible to carry out what maintenance was needed without any distractions at least that is what should have been. During the lunch break Judy drew my attention to her exposed skin which to my horror, as well as hers, was covered in mosquito bites. Once over the initial shock and discussion about how this could happen, I realised that the creatures must have been breeding on the stagnant water under and around the boat. But why had Judy and not I been subjected to this attack? One possibility could have been I was tanned and Judy wasn't, but out of deference to Judy's situation I accepted her comment regarding my ancient meat being less preferable than the younger fresh quality. Nothing could be done about it until the shops opened on the morrow and a balm could be purchased. In the meantime I sloshed some petrol on the stagnant puddles in the hope of killing the mosquito eggs and suggested that all that she could do was keep covered up and hopefully deter another night attack from these bloodsuckers. A fine introduction to a sailing holiday, but at least it was understood and comforting to know that this species of mosquito didn't carry disease.

The walk into town for the evening meal was pleasant as the temperature cools, and the slight humidity clears at this time of day. For me the meal was a bit of a disappointment. The staff were less friendly than the first time I was there, and Judy disapproved of the cost. Sure it was expensive but this was Tahiti and that is what one must get used to if one wishes to eat out. From my point of view I was prepared to put up with the cost, at least until I'd got over my own cooking to which I'd suffered prior to arriving at Papeete, and could purchase provisions at the yet to be found supermarket. With this walk into town at least the shops where mosquito repellent could be purchased were located, so it was not altogether a futile adventure.

*****

Monday: First thing after the yard personnel had arrived was to buttonhole Henry the foreman for a ride to the propane depot. The securing of propane at such a fortuitous time in the scheme of things was most timely as the electric frying pan had finally given up the ghost. On its last outing the previous lunchtime it had expired without even giving out the usual puff of smoke from the thermostat. With a kind thought for the service it had given I committed it to the garbage heap. This act prompted me to think that during this voyage I seemed to be staggering from one minor calamity to another. At least we were still mobile and hopefully all the necessary work to put the boat fully operational again would be finalised at New Zealand which seemed to be the most likely place. I was pinning this premise on the fact New Zealand has a viable sailing community. Cost too was a factor that was uppermost in my mind.

As the engine mechanic was expected that morning and my presence would be required, Judy took off for town by herself in search of a salve for the mosquito bites. Having been bitten myself in past years, although not to such a degree, I could sympathise with her situation. Even one bite is an aggravating experience never mind having both legs covered with the damn things. Her stoic manner in putting up with the torment had my whole-hearted admiration.

The mechanic arrived in due course, another Frenchman who spoke perfect English. His efficiency didn't end there as within a matter of a few minutes he had sussed out the problem, something in my ignorance of all things mechanical I would never have traced in a hundred years should god forbid I would live that long. Watching him work I thought whether it wouldn't be sensible to take a course in engine mechanics. When and how this opportunity would come about was also a subject for debate, and I realised that a long apprenticeship might be involved before proficiency would be gained. The idea was reluctantly shelved. Between the engine and the control panel is a harness of sixteen wires, some sixteen feet in length, supplying the power and information for the engine to be started. Apparently there was a broken wire somewhere in the bundle. To trace which wire was the offending one would have only been academic as it couldn't be repaired anyway. So, fortunately there was a replacement harness in the mechanic's shop, and off he went. Before noon he was back and had the engine in service again. Now this strengthened the premise that all trades, or businesses, were working hand in glove as he instructed me to settle his bill with the sail-maker.

After lunch and for the rest of the afternoon I worked on sanding and painting the area of the removed rub-rail. Arrangements also were made with the office to put the boat back in the water the following morning with the happy thought that in the next few days it would only be a matter of the sail-maker finishing his tasks, and then we could take off for Rarotonga. There I go again, anticipating the un-anticipatable.

*****

The first casualty in the expected line-up of events for a smooth running progress towards departure was the fact that the boatyard would not take credit cards, cash only. This arrangement had Judy and me hoofing it into town to the bank. This unexpected turn of events, due to the launching time set for eleven-thirty left little time to do anything but hurry there and back. Hurrying in the Tahitian climate soon had both of us working up, in Judy's case, a glow and in mine a free flowing perspiration, but at least we made it back to the yard in sufficient time to pay the bill and make the tide.

The engine fired on the first attempt with a satisfying roar and with a merry wave to Henry of Propane fame, we were heading back to the original berth at the town quay to await the diver and the repaired sails. Happy in the knowledge that there were no mosquitoes there to create a bother, and once moored on the pontoon, we crossed the road for lunch and a celebratory beer.

During the following days the anchor and chain were rescued from the bottom of Papeete harbour. With the anchor having caught on the pontoon mooring chains the diver found it quite easy to lift the flukes off the obstruction and it was soon back on board, the rope rode spliced onto the chain and all stowed in the chain locker. The mainsail was repaired to a much better condition than the Panamanian effort, and securing the luff to the slides the sail maker had used was particularly satisfying with bindings sewn to the slide and the sail. This method, as long as the slide didn't break, was preferable to the old method which tended to rip the sail. So far matters seemed to be on the up and up, at least on these first few days. This illusion was soon shattered though as the genoa, in the sail maker's estimation, had become so worn that it was pointless trying to repair it. This put me on the horns of a financial dilemma as a new sail was beyond my current means. The sail-maker, however, thought he could locate a used foresail of better quality, and with a little adjustment have it fit the furling system. This was agreed to as a satisfactory alternative but we were not out of the woods yet. The sail-maker, having climbed the mast to reeve a new halyard, had noticed that several strands of the fore-stay were broken. I had a slight feeling of despair, with thoughts of staggering from one critical situation to another seeming to be never ending. There was nothing for it but to replace the forestay as it would be the height of folly to leave it partially broken and at some time in the future have it part completely with the subsequent bringing down of the mast, an option not to be considered. On recommendation from the sail-maker I agreed to a heavier wire which the furling system was capable of handling.

With all these projects in hand it left plenty of time for Judy and I to wander around town exploring the back streets, getting a little lost and finding our way back to the main road and the harbour. I don't think we ever really sorted out which direction to take without confusion of some sort, but that is Papeete. I was convinced that it would take quite some time to be absolutely sure of which direction to take for any given location. Frequenting the internet cafes, to keep in touch with the outside world became a daily routine. Once the Super-market which was within walking distance of the boat had been located shopping for groceries for the next leg of the voyage also became a regular feature for the remainder of our stay. An item that gave an immense feeling of pleasure in exciting the taste buds was the local pineapple, a like of which I had never experienced before; so sweet and juicy, one fairly drooled in anticipation while one was being cut open and prepared for eating.

On Saturday, as no work was in hand, we hired a car, which to my surprise was nowhere near as expensive as previously quoted when in the boatyard, and drove around the Island. This didn't raise any problems regarding navigation as there is only one road and one travels either right handed or left handed on this circumnavigation. Just follow the road to return to the starting point. This premise holds good for Tahiti-Nui which is the largest section of the island. Tahiti-Iti is the smaller section stuck like an appendix on the south-east side of Tahiti-Nui by a narrow strip of land. Here the road branches in the direction of the settlement of Teahupoo on the south side and its world famous surfing beaches, although no surf was up when we arrived. On the north side the road leads to Tautira. Both these roads are dead ends and one must turn around and go back to Tahiti-Nui to continue the circumnavigation. No need for route planning on Tahiti. There were one or two sights to visit which were taken advantage of, the Paul Gauguin museum to which Judy wished to visit, and particularly, for me, Venus Point on the north of the Island. It was easy to see why Captain Cook chose this place for the observation of the transit of Venus across the face of the Sun in 1769. Venus Point is low lying and encompasses to the north the natural harbour of Matavai Bay within the reef system, and must be about the only flat area of land suitable to build a fort and also have access to his ship and of course have Venus and the Sun on the right side of the island. Being a keen follower of all things Cook, and this was a highlight of his career, I started taking photos of the obelisk that presumably, although the descriptive plaque had fallen off, marked the spot of Cook's observations, and snaps of the surrounding Bay. Much to my chagrin, the gremlins were still at work as the film transporter lever had jammed, preventing any further records of this delightful and historic place. To really put an end to this photo-op Judy's camera had also failed. I think this was the most disappointing event of the whole trip so far. This was a place I had often read about and anticipated visiting for so many years, and to be denied a factual record was, well, what could one say? The memory of this historic site had been stored away in my brain and I had managed to get four shots of the place, so there was some satisfaction in that.

All in all it was a most enjoyable day out, even though it took only half a day. There is a road across the island through the mountainous interior but, being accessible to four wheel drive vehicles only, rental cars being excluded on the agreement, this section of discovery was denied us. Pity really as the scenery and views must have been spectacular from the high mountains of the interior, if the travel brochures are to be believed.

The remainder of the following week was spent waiting for the sail-maker to complete his tasks with side trips to his loft to check progress with the replacement sail which, although not full size was at least serviceable for our needs until a sail could be made in New Zealand. The replacement forestay and furling system also was proceeding satisfactorily, so all that remained was to obtain the clearance and retrieve the posted bond from the bank. Nothing seems to proceed in a satisfactory manner and having the bond returned proved to be no exception, for although the security had been paid by debit card I was offered local currency as repayment, with no option. Now, one can only wonder at the uselessness of a great wad of Pacific francs when departure was imminent? For whatever reason repayment by debit card reversal was not possible so it was a case of buying New Zealand dollars. There was some remuneration gained in the exchange rate, and it would give me a ready supply of currency for Auckland and Rarotonga without having to seek out a bank.

On the Friday we went last minute grocery shopping, the water tanks were topped up from the shore supply, and the rigging of the replacement genoa, which had somewhat less sail area than the original but was acceptable for the run to New Zealand via Rarotonga, was also fitted. By early afternoon and, after a last lunch at the cantina across the road, all was ready to make our way to the refuelling depot further down the coast. As previously mentioned this side of the island was protected by coral reefs so, on leaving Papeete, we wended our way inside the reef following the numerous beacons. The airport runway extends into the lagoon and we required permission from the Control Tower to proceed past and around to the far end of the runway where we had to report the completion of the passage. No doubt this precaution was to ensure that any aircraft taking off doesn't take off a sailboat's mast.

There was an interesting cluster of thatched roof cabins between the airport and the fuelling station. These cabins were perched over the lagoon on stilts and connected each to the other and to the shore by walk ways and numbering twelve in all. These apparently were part of the hotel, providing interesting accommodation for guests. Quite an impressive display they made, although on reflection it would be interesting to find out how waste water and the like were disposed of; not into the lagoon one would hope.

Fuelling was completed in good order and we were soon heading through the gap in the reef to the open sea. This presented a disconcertingly strange spectacle as while we were passing through the narrow opening in the reef there was a young lad standing on the reef with the water only half way up his shins. A strange apparition it was while passing only a few feet from him. However we were soon clear and making a course for the south of Moorea, so up went the sails and off with the engine to ride easily on a low swell.

CHAPTER TEN
Tahiti to Rarotonga

.....in whose company I delight myself
Pilgrim's Progress

It is always good to get away from civilisation out into the peaceful ocean, although it must be said I enjoyed Tahiti and the people we came in contact with, so helpful and pleasingly proficient in the English language. It is not surprising the early sailors came to consider this beautiful island with its delightful climate and the accommodating females to be Paradise.

Shortly after sunset while we were passing the reefs off Moorea the wind died, no doubt due to us being under the lee of the land. In the stillness of darkness the surf could be heard breaking on the reef which, although not presenting any immediate danger gave me cause to fire up the engine again until the wind picked up once more until we left the lee of the land. Judy, although under the effects of a bout of mal de mer, had produced the evening meal. Considering how the effects of seasickness had laid me low, during that period of my life when I had succumbed to the debilitating effects of this malady I could only have admiration for Judy's fortitude on remaining on her feet, not to mention cooking a meal. Seasickness, if my memory served me right, can be a most incapacitating experience so my admiration also had a hint of envy.

Prior to lying down to rest I went on deck to check the situation vis-à-vis the surrounding world, and as circumstances would have it, was just in time to see the replacement sail rip vertically from top to bottom and bizarrely across the seams also. As the wind was only twenty-five knots and not even strong enough for me to need to reef down the mainsail, the destruction of this new replacement caused considerable chagrin. There was nothing for it but to roll up the useless article, furl it completely and get along best we could with the mainsail. I pondered this new setback for a while then decided to phone the sail maker and advise him what had happened with the view to him taking the matter up with the person he had bought it from, and maybe securing some compensation. On making contact and exchanging pleasantries I had only just advised him of the situation when the phone went dead. Odd, I thought, and tried to make contact again only to eventually get an unanswered ringing. Rather impolite of him not to hear me out I thought, then I got to wondering if he had knowingly sold me a sail that was suspect. Well, as I would never know the answer to that one, all that could be done was to proceed on our way the best we could under the circumstances. To return to Papeete and demand retribution I briefly considered but soon rejected that as futile. No doubt if he saw me coming and he was guilty as charged he would make himself scarce. This late in the game with so many problems behind me I was becoming quite philosophical to what fate was handing out. Having one more problem didn't worry me too much. Soldier on was the order of the day. Maybe Rarotonga would produce some reconciliation in the way of having this sail repaired.

Having fallen back into the old routine of getting up to make frequent checks on the surrounding ocean during the night I was ready for a cup of tea come daylight. I debated with myself whether to let Judy have a lie in, what with her being seasick the previous evening, but then resolved to take her a cup of tea instead. Might as well get her on her feet, as this was the best way to overcome the debilitating effects of the old Mal de Mary's. No sooner had I entered the forward berth and woke her up than we hit a milestone which caused a heavy spray to come over the bow and down the partially open hatch drenching the pair of us and overflowing the cup of tea. The humour of such a rude awakening tickled my sense of the ridiculous which produced a hearty, 'bloody hell' accompanied with a snort of mirth. Although Judy took it all in good humour she was suspicious of the cause of such a rude awakening and I was hard pressed denying that I had not planned it that way. From that time on Judy occupied the other end of the settee for her night time rest, probably reasoning that I wouldn't pull another stunt like that if I was in the firing line. What cruel thoughts some people harbour.

The following days were pleasantly balmy and in the warm sunshine with a cooling wind tanning sessions were enjoyed. During the evenings, once the meal was over, we passed the time listening to a selection of music, with Kiri Te Kanawa's 'Heart to Heart' being a firm favourite. Not all was decadence though as Judy expressed an interest in learning to sail. This request raised something of a dilemma as she had never been on a boat before and wasn't going to be long enough on the boat for any schooling in this subject to be of much use. However, such an interest could not in all honesty be denied and as pulling up sails was unnecessary as they were already up; the sailor's bible was produced with the intention for her of at least learning the sail parts and other nautical nomenclature. The difficulty of learning this new language and the totally alien practice of the tying of knots presented some interesting moments but her interest and perseverance brought some rewards. On the subject of crewing I had given some thought, should we keep watches being uppermost in this thinking.

In all honesty this would have been the ideal way of ship keeping but then it would not have been very responsible of me to leave Judy on deck alone with no experience, and no doubt I would be checking on her more than I do with the normal run of things. As I had been following the routine of checking matters as a single-handed sailor and as Judy's tenure was going to be brief, there was no point in disturbing the rest of two people.

On the subject of rest, Judy reported hearing voices during one night of this passage. Odd that, as previously mentioned I, too, thought that I'd heard voices. As there was definitely no one else on board it can only be assumed that this weird occurrence was due to water swilling around in the bilges, or maybe the wind catching an obstruction at a certain angle and the sound being carried through the boat's structure. At least those assumptions gave us some comfort. As there had only been these two occasions it was better not to dwell too long on what else may have caused this phenomenon, unless of course one believes in bogeymen.

The passage to Rarotonga was an easy sail of ten days even with just the main, the trade wind still in the south-east, and the days passed pleasantly with no necessity to reef this one remaining sail. The movement of the boat in the seas however, caused some interesting moments attempting to get from the galley to the table with plates of food or cups of tea. This required waiting for the boat to steady and then give an easy roll to port and then the one carrying the objects in question could launch oneself up the two steps from the galley and cross to the table where one would be relieved of the burden. This became quite an exercise of skill with the object of making the journey without spilling food or slopping the contents of the mugs. Because there were two people on board the load was double and did not give one the luxury of having one hand free for steadying one's progress.

On the evening before the day of arrival at Rarotonga the trade wind died and a westerly picked up. No doubt some low pressure disturbance had caused this change of direction in an otherwise reliable wind system. The wind was not very strong and as the boat didn't perform well into the wind I decided to put the wind on the port beam and doodle along on a course to the north until daylight, hoping that the trade wind would pick up again. Come the dawn not much in the way of progress had resulted from this manoeuvre. The wind was still out of the west and being only forty miles from our destination I decided to motor the rest of the way. An excellent opportunity for Judy to get some serious steering practice and I was much impressed how quickly she picked this up. Just one explanation: when changing direction one should move the lubber line across the compass card and not the other way round, a common mistake with first trippers. She soon had the steering off like an old hand.

Rarotonga soon lifted over the horizon, just an indistinct blur at first but taking on a more detailed form the closer we came. By mid afternoon we entered the one harbour suitable for sea going vessels, the other being too shallow even for our boat. By the time we had moored up stern to the quay it was too late to report to the harbour authorities so we would have to wait until the next day. Meanwhile, as it was exceedingly difficult to get ashore over the stern without manipulating the anchor rode at the bow and the mooring lines from the stern, I busied myself inflating the dinghy and launching that for ferrying to a rather rickety set of steps for getting on land again. About twenty feet along the wall there was a boat moored which we had noticed in Papeete. It was particularly noticeable by having different company logos painted on the hull and, in large letters NSA, which caused a certain amount of conjecture as to what it meant. About this we were soon to become acquainted.

CHAPTER ELEVEN
Rarotonga

The long arm of coincidence
Chambers 1860-1921

Raro, meaning down, Tonga, meaning south. Thus called by Iro, the famous Tahitian navigator when asked where he was going, at least that is a popular version of where the name originated. But then, so did the Samoan navigator, Karika, use the same terminology, calling it Rarotonga because to him Raro meant to leeward and Tonga also to the south. Both gentlemen being Polynesian, one can assume they spoke the same language and therefore we can allow both meanings.

Rarotonga is the administrative capital of a group of fifteen islands named the Cook Islands which cover an area of the Pacific the size of India and centre on the town of Avarua on the north coast. Although James Cook sighted the islands and landed on many of the southern group, it is not recorded that he even sighted Rarotonga nor was he responsible for naming them after himself. The name Cook Islands was given to the group by the Russians in honour of Cook, the name first appearing on a Russian naval chart early in the nineteenth century.

The island of Rarotonga is the furthest south of the Cook Islands and is roughly round in shape and surrounded by protecting coral reefs. The centre of the island is extremely mountainous and rises to a height of 2140 feet which was originally formed by volcanic action. Now extinct the volcanoes are covered with tropical jungle. The principal road runs around the island close to the sea with the occasional side roads running to settlements and farms which produce, in the inland swamps, taro, the main crop of the island. To the west of Avarua and just a little way along from the harbour is a modern international airport that also serves the other islands in the group.

The weather is generally equitable with temperatures averaging highs of 28C with lots of sunshine. The wet season is from January to early May, and the Cyclone season from December to April.

*****

Due to the approaching cyclone season I was anxious to have the sail repaired and to get on our way, but then as Robert Burns said, ‘the best laid schemes o’ mice and men, aft times gang a'gley,' and my situation was no different. On reporting in to the Marine Office for clearance and requesting information of a sail maker I was informed that to the best of the Port Captain's knowledge he didn't know of one. This information gave cause for concern as there was a tear in the sail fifteen feet long and to sew a patch of that length, even if I had that much material, would have taken some considerable time. As it turned out two different good Samaritans appeared, (Deus ex Machina again), to redress this problem. During the first day while I mulled over this problem a gentleman appeared on the quay, and seeing my boat's registry was Victoria and he being from that city we fell into conversation. With the sail being uppermost in my mind I broached the subject of how to have it repaired and he advised that he had a friend who had a sailboat and would ask him and report back. Well, I thought things were looking up and if there are sailboats it follows there must be services.

Also, while moored to the quay we got into conversation with the young man on the boat with NSA emblazoned on the side and he very generously offered to lend me one of his spare sails. As we were both heading to New Zealand, it could be returned there. Although reluctant to take him up on this offer as I was concerned that for whatever reason I couldn't return the sail, this didn't seem to bother him so; it was left in abeyance until the situation with the injured sail was reconciled.

This young man and I use this terminology from a distance of my great age, had a stroke at the age of thirty-five and, on recovery decided to collect sponsors and make a voyage of awareness for the National Stroke Foundation. What a noble gesture I thought, eyeing all the Company logos painted on the side of his boat. Maybe I should have gone that route? It certainly would have reduced the expenses, but no use being regretful in this matter, for I'm far too independently minded to have thought about it anyway. His boat was about thirty feet in length with a Heath Robinson repair job to the self steering arrangement, which I was given to understand had suffered grievously on passage. This apparently had caused little concern as he had a girl even younger than himself as crew and between them could take turns at steering. At least this arrangement had been useful for the time being as she was shortly to leave and go home to her boyfriend. I have to wonder how the younger generation view their lives; it seems they have an enviable independent spirit that was denied my generation. Roam the world? We were lucky if we could borrow a bike, never mind own one, to cycle to the next town a distance of eighteen miles and have the entrance fee of two shillings for the swimming pool, now that was considered to be a real outing in those days of my youth just after the Second World War.

The young man, Les Bissell by name didn't seem too perturbed about losing his little helper as with the self confidence of the young he had expectations of recruiting some other wanderer for the onward journey.

Tony McCulloch, the gentleman from Victoria, returned a little later with the news that there wasn't a sail maker on the island but at the Airport the upholsterer might help as he repaired airplane seating and the like, ergo, heavy sewing machine. Well this was good news so Judy and I took a walk to meet with this man who could help us out of our predicament. As it turned out he was just about to leave on a job on one of the other islands and, should we wish to bring the offending article to his shop he would have a look at it on his return in two days time. Things seemed to be definitely picking up with hope, the flavour of the month, boosting my confidence of yet once again being fully operational.

During the interim yet another sailboat arrived and with a bit of a squeeze moored on the other side of Les's boat. The interesting aspect of this boat was that it was the same design as mine, something that I had never seen before. The drawings for the design called for either aluminium or steel, and this new arrival had taken the steel option and had numerous rust runs tracking down the sides I was pleased to have requested from the designers drawings for a foam core hull laminated with fibreglass inner and outer skins. It was not a pretty sight having a boat streaked with brown unsightly runs. Not a pristine yacht with white paintwork glistening in the sunlight as one would expect of a boat. A great pity, as the design is very attractive.

Sunday, having taken Tony up on his invitation, Judy and I were given a tour of the island and introduced to the local history. Legend has it that the great Polynesian voyages started from Rarotonga, crossing the vast Pacific in their double hulled canoes to populate places as far away as New Zealand and the Hawaiian Islands. Indeed, we were shown a replica of one of these canoes and close up they looked truly large, large enough to carry several families and their provisions for immense distances. Having two hulls with a connecting platform between, one can imagine them capable of impressive speeds. A forerunner of the modern day Catamaran with the exception of the rig, the Polynesian canoe was rigged with two masts and mutton chop sails which, being wider at the top, gave lift as well as forward drive.

The main part of the town of Avarua stretches along the main road to the east of the harbour and comprises modern shops, restaurants, an open air market and all the modern amenities of business. The Law Courts and Police Headquarters were built with Chinese funds, thus developing close ties with China. A cyclone proof highway and an enclosed sports stadium have also been built with Chinese largesse. Hotels and holiday accommodation are for the most part right on the water's edge and, it was one of these holiday homes that Tony and his partner Nancy, our hosts for the afternoon, rented for their stay on Rarotonga. It was a most delightful low bank location right on the edge of the Lagoon, protected from the ocean waves by the reef some hundreds of yards away, cooled by the prevailing southeast trade winds, and shaded amongst the Palm trees. The

Lagoon is safe for swimming if one stays well away from the Channels that cut through to the ocean; it is at these points that swift currents often run strong, strong enough to carry the unwary swimmer to a watery grave. However, the Lagoon is large and safe and Judy, Tony and I made good use of it well away from these channels. However, the effort of keeping afloat made me realise how the lack of exercise on a boat can put one out of condition. No longer the water dog (and I use the term informally), of my youth, I begged off on the second dip and the suggestion of going snorkelling. Judy, however, delighted in searching the seabed under Tony's guidance for the myriad marine life. I was content to sit and watch and socialise with Nancy and her other guests.

All too soon, as is always the case when enjoying oneself, the time came to return to the boat and dwell on what a wonderful time we had.

*****

During the coming week there were interesting developments, and the sail was repaired and returned. This repair it turned out was a helpful attempt to get us mobile again as the upholsterer at the airport could only run a straight seam whereas sails require zigzag stitching for strength on the seams. But what could one do? The man didn't have a sail maker's sewing machine. Although he understood the need for sail repairs on the island, his company just wasn't going to invest in such an item. Well, beggars can't be choosers and one could only hope that the repair would hold. It was not a happy state of affairs so I took Les up on his offer of one of his spare sails. Its return didn't present a problem as we, Judy and I, were now going to Whangerai rather than Auckland which was much nearer to Les's destination of Opua. The reason for the change of plan came about purely by chance, as it often does in this life. While having my haircut by a New Zealand lady it came out in the conversation that we would be leaving for Auckland in a day or two. The lady hairdresser pooh-poohed the idea as being not very clever as the place was inconvenient for transient boaters. The moorage was vast and most problematic for taking on stores and access to the amenities that I would require and it was most difficult to find a place to park, anyway. Rather, she said, Whangerai marina was right in the centre of town and the supermarket a short walk away and just across the road. She knew the place well having lived there before moving to Rarotonga. The sail maker, the marine stores and everything a boater would require was within easy walking distance. Who was I to ignore such advice? Besides on consulting the chart I found Whangerai was much further north than Auckland, and Opua would be on my way when passing to the north of the North Island on the way to Melbourne. Once again matters were falling into their convenient places.

One other incident that was purely coincidental happened while Judy and I were sitting in the cockpit relaxing with a coffee. A couple had ridden up on a motor bike and stopped to look at the boats in the harbour. Noticing the Port of

Registry on the transom I was asked if we were from Victoria. They received the stock answer, "No, Pender Island. Victoria is the Port of Registry." "Oh!" The man said, "We are from Pender." Now Pender isn't all that big, maybe two thousand souls but there was no way I recognised them. This surprised me a little as having lived there for twenty years one generally runs into nearly everyone who lives there. Ah! Well, we live and learn. The point of this anecdote, however, lies in the fact that within a matter of days there was an e-mail demanding to know who that woman was who was with me. As I am foot loose and fancy free it never occurred to me to report my every action to the outside world. Funny though, even being so far away from base one is never safe from prying eyes.

It was getting late in the year and the cyclone season was in the offing which made me anxious to get away. I know I keep harping on that subject but, it was a real concern. Being caught in a storm anywhere, never mind at sea, would be sheer folly, not to mention having the added responsibility of an extra person.

The south east trades had returned which gave favourable conditions for the run to Whangerai. Water and fuel had been taken on, food also, for the anticipated relatively short run, so there was no point in hanging around any longer. The harbour dues were quite hefty I thought for the lack of amenities available, particularly the water supply which could not be accessed at the edge of the quay due to someone having cut off the hose connection. Les and I had to join both our hoses together to be able to connect to the tap at the hotdog stand on the far side of the quay. The complaint was passed on to the Port Captain who gave the impression that it had been reported and maybe something might be done about it one day. Not very reassuring but not everything in this life is perfect and this didn't detract from the overall pleasure of this beautiful island and the good people we had met. The means of refuelling were a bit unusual also as this required a walk up the road to the fuel depot where one ordered the required quantity of diesel, this was then delivered by tanker truck at a pre-arranged time. With Les and I both ordering at the same time it took a careful calculation from us both not to over order, or more importantly under order.

So it was then that we made our goodbyes, with promises to keep in touch with Les by e-mail on our respective voyages to New Zealand. Up with the anchor then, and with Judy steering we passed through the harbour entrance into the ocean again.

CHAPTER TWELVE

Rarotonga to Whangerai

Expect nothing. Live frugally on surprise
Alice Walker

At the risk of repeating myself, as always is the case, it was good to get away from civilisation, to be out on the solitude of the ocean again. It had been touch and go whether I would have been on my own for this leg of the trip as Judy had been seriously considering jumping ship to fly to New Zealand. I couldn't fault her for this as she had always wanted to visit the country and do a bit of touring. She had friends there too, whom she hadn't seen for a very long time so it was quite in the cards for an early visit. Needless to say my thoughts on this need not be described, only to say that I didn't wish for such a good companion to leave. As it turned out she did decide to stay on the understanding that it was only a sixteen day run to Whangerai. Oh, Dear! Here we go again.

Judy hadn't slept too well during the past few nights so took to the forward berth in the afternoon for a snooze and to admire the upholsterer's handy work on the foresail through the hatch and on the thorough job he had made on the repair. I kept my counsel on this matter not wanting to tempt fate over the lack of zigzag stitching, but appreciative of the effort he had put into this with the limited facilities he had.

For the first week the trades held with wind velocities of no more than twenty-five knots and we made comfortable progress towards our destination. Alas! The repair on the foresail didn't hold though and ripped again to a two part piece of rag flapping uselessly in the breeze. So down it came to be replaced by Les' contribution, which being of a laminated construction with the laminates separating, presented something less than a joy to behold. However, one doesn't look a gift horse in the mouth and no matter what the condition of the sail as long as it held together and was serviceable as far as Whangerai the object of the lesson would have been achieved.

Then the wind came around to the west again. Les had been sending us daily weather reports so it was obvious that the change in the wind direction was the result of a low pressure system to the southeast of our position, some distance away, which meant that we would not be bothered by it apart from the disruption of the trades. Well there was nothing we could do about the situation but wait for the trades to pick up again and sail at a tangent to the wind, heading north for half a day then change tack to head south again, as the boat would not make any headway in any point of sail but with the wind on the beam. I suppose one should be thankful that it was only leeway that was affected and not lost distance by being pushed back. Had this been the case it would have meant heaving to; at least as we were moving we did have the psychological effect of going somewhere.

After three days of this the wind shifted again back to the trades so we made progress once more at a satisfactory pace. The latest news from Les announced that high winds had hit Rarotonga which was good news for us if not for Raro. It seems the wind was strong enough for him to warrant streaming another anchor and running extra mooring lines to the quay. It had been his intention to leave a day or two after we had departed, but with one thing and another he was delayed. That's how it goes in the sailing world, very little goes according to plan. We were pleased to hear, however, that his crew had decided to stay on until New Zealand, saving him the unlikely possibility of finding a replacement.

In the fullness of time we reached 170 West Longitude the psychological position where the trades are expected to die away. As luck or whatever motivates these things the wind held for a few more days with our anticipation of moving into the Eastern Hemisphere. Whoops! The wind came around to right ahead again just half a degree short of the International Date Line and increased to 30knts. The swell too became heavier causing the boat to labour uncomfortably, with the result that getting food and or mugs of tea to the table became very much a matter of gymnastics. The warm sunny days departed to be replaced by grey, overcast dreary skies. Time to reef the mainsail before the darkness made the exercise risky. As the wind might increase it was deemed sensible to double reef the main and take in some of Les's sail which was already beginning to tear upwards from the foot. Dreams of a new Genoa were now almost constantly on my mind. Les's sail would also have to be repaired before being returned, which is par for the course it seems as no matter what I borrow it ends up having to be mended. Not, I might add, that things get rough usage by my hands, but rather that they are somewhat suspect to start with.

We were now twenty-three days out of Rarotonga and still three hundred miles to go with no progress being made in that direction. Another matter of concern was that the food was getting low and the water for some reason tasted salty maybe salt water in the bilges was somehow being picked up. This was one of life's mysteries as having put pressure on the line previously I found that no hole or split in the waterline. There wasn't anything for it but to shut off the tanks and resort to drawing water by dipping via the access ports again. At least the fact that the system was drawing salt water into the line would reduce the area to investigate as there wasn't much of the fresh water line that passed through the bilges.

It was about this time that the bilge float switch gave up the ghost, the second one this trip. So much for the salesman's comment that this particular type of switch would last ten years, but he was a salesman and these people will say anything to make the customer happy and clinch a sale, which goes with the territory I suppose, so it was a case of emptying the bilges with the switch in manual mode; this worked for a day or two until one of the connections broke off. No problem as we still had power to the switch so it was a case of touching the bare wire to the broken connection to activate the pump. Strange though, regardless of the inconvenience of having to operate the pump in this way, I felt blessed and thankful that we still had power and didn't have to resort to Armstrong's Patent and bale the bilges with a saucepan. This voyage seems to have developed a tolerance to inconveniences in my daily life that I had never been aware of having the patience for previously.

The latest report from Les had him catching up with us; even though he had left Rarotonga a week after us he had managed to keep favourable winds and was now only a matter of two days behind. Not for long though as he would soon be experiencing the weather that we were putting up with, unless his boat sailed better into the wind than did ours.

After a week of the head winds they once again turned in our favour and we crossed the International Date Line thus gaining an extra day on the calendar. For two days we made good and hopeful progress towards Whangarei, and then what do you know the wind came around out of the west again. Back to the same old, same old, up and down parallel with the New Zealand coast and only ninety miles to go. So much for the promise to Judy of only taking sixteen days for the passage. The loss of time was eating into her plans to see something of New Zealand and still be home for Christmas. But what could I say? Although I felt bad about it all there was nothing I could do, or say. We were at the mercy of the vagaries of the winds. She was very good about the whole business though and never complained.

On the dawning of the 18th December the wind having died away during the night came up again out of the north-west with a most favourable velocity thus creating a handsome speed towards our haven. The ETA off Bream Head would be at noon and put us under the lee of the land. It was my intention then to take down the mainsail and motor in after lunch. This meal was timely as the food supply had become exhausted. An Old Mother Hubbard cupboard situation and just as well we didn't have a dog. During the interim the VHF had been switched on in preparation to report our arrival when the weather report came on for Bream Head, 'winds southwest imminent 60 knots'. This alarming news had the engine fired up, Judy at the wheel, and me on deck taking in the sail like a man possessed. None too soon as before the sail was properly stowed the wind came howling down the Bay right on the nose again, the sea was whipped up in no time at all to a steep low swell with breaking tops and spray driving the full length of the boat. As luck would have it I'd had the foresight before relieving Judy at the wheel to don oilskin leggings and jacket and with the canvas wheel cover for extra protection managed to endure the cold and stinging spray while battering into this maelstrom, hoping against hope that the engine would keep going. It would have been too much to bear for the engine to conk out and drive us out to sea again. While all this was going on dodging the spray, steering with one hand and a leg and trying to keep the wheel cover in a protective position, the legging part of the heavy weather gear started to slide down around my ankles. At least it was heading that way before I arrested them in mid slide and made vain attempts to pull them up again. Some consideration was given to becoming a contortionist at some time in my life. My prayers regarding the engine were answered though and within the hour we were into the river and getting some shelter if not from the wind certainly from the breaking seas. This is where Judy came to be appreciated again, for had I been on my own, tired and cold as I was from the battering, I would not have been relieved at the wheel to dry off and warm up in the survival suit. Although the waterproofs were bought in Panama the leggings had not been used before, only the jacket. So it was with some dismay that on inspecting the reason for the leggings to behave in such a strange manner I found that both buttons on the bib had come off with a sizable piece of cloth, allowing the whole lot to make a downward progress. As the saying goes, buy cheap, pay dear.

Whangarei is some twenty miles up the Hatea River and deep water as far as the port for seagoing ships which was a little under half way there. It was to there we were directed to the Customs and Immigration Station for clearance. The wind was still strong as we came alongside the Customs barge and off the berth but, with a little clever manoeuvring and with willing hands to take the lines, we were soon safely moored. Twenty-eight days from Rarotonga.

Boarding with the Immigration Officer also came the Food Inspector clutching a large garbage bag to remove all imported food stuffs. This gave cause for some amusement as we were completely out of fresh food apart from a piece of ginger which Judy had bought to make a curry but never used. This item with all good will and humour was ceremoniously dropped into the garbage bag. The formalities I found to be rather tedious as all equipment had to be entered onto the proper form complete with product numbers, and expiry dates where applicable, which had me running back and forward to each item calling out the required data, all this with the added distractions of answering questions from the Port Health.

The formalities over with, permission was granted by the Port Captain's office to stay on this berth until morning when we would proceed to the marina. Judy had expressed the wish to stay over night at a hotel where we could have hot showers and a decent meal and a dry bed, a request I acceded to with alacrity. Nothing could be more desirable after the trials and tribulations of getting into port than a hot shower, and a meal that was not dominated by rice. It was then that we were introduced to New Zealand hospitality for, 'Bruce the Immigration' offered to drive us into town, some distance away, to a hotel, saving us the difficulty of securing transport from this lonely place out in the sticks. So kind of him and much appreciated. The hot shower at the hotel was everything one desired and a sense of pleasure of not now being grotty and uncomfortable. The meal however was not much to our liking and a big disappointment after the anticipation, but then being hungry none was wasted. And, it was a pleasure to sleep in a comfortable bed with clean sheets and not on a curved settee with a blanket for warmth.

CHAPTER THIRTEEN
Whangarei

Life has no greater pleasure than the joy of anticipation

Meron

Whangarei is Maori for bountiful land, for which I can only accept their word as I have no contest with this accolade.

The immediate vicinity of Town Basin where the Marina was situated was all the lady hairdresser in Rarotonga had claimed it to be, with the close proximity of shops, restaurants and marine hardware stores for the delight of the visiting boater. We were fortunate to secure a berth here because with the strong winds that had been experienced during the past several days no boats had ventured out. However, the Marina manager had us rafted up in the river to a boat from Montreal. This port is truly an international gathering place with boats from just about every seafaring country moored in this crowded Marina.

Once secured in our berth we launched the dinghy and rowed over to the Office to make ourselves known and make the request for a sail maker, this being the first priority. The two boatyards which we had passed coming up river were also contacted for a haul out date which, due to the fact that Christmas was almost on us and no one worked over the holidays, was left in abeyance, it making no sense to pay for being on the hard with no services. Other matters concerning bringing the boat back to efficiency would be attended to in due course as and when convenient. For the present it was a case of finding an internet café and a visit to the supermarket. The exposed film from Tahiti was also left to be developed and the address of a camera repairer acquired.

Over the next couple of days things started to happen. Judy, being disappointed in her efforts to secure a touring holiday as due to it being the Christmas holiday season everything in that line was booked solid, therefore she decided to return home to England for Christmas. It would appear that at this time of year the population of New Zealand decide to travel and every possibility for Judy to do just that had resulted in all accommodations and bus tours being fully booked. A shame really, as she had set her heart on seeing at least something of the country. While in town making arrangements at the travel agents she also went to pick up my film, which could not be developed as it had been spoiled by salt water, a great disappointment but no surprise. After all most things had suffered from the elements. The sail maker came down to the boat and took away the sails that needed repairing and advised us that due to a heavy workload a new sail could not be made until the end of January. This news was something of a let down as I was anxious to proceed with the itinerary and set out for Melbourne where my sister lived. All other needs would have to be shelved too, as all other businesses whose services were required would also be closed for the holidays. So what to do? I didn't like the idea of hanging around the marina until the population returned to work in the New Year, so, I decided to fly to Melbourne and spend Christmas and see in the New Year with my sister's family. As a precaution a float switch for the bilge pump, this time of a different manufacture than the unreliable kind that had let me down so often, and a panel control were purchased and installed. These items were considered essential if my peace of mind was to be guaranteed while away. I had no wish to return to a flooded boat or for that matter one lying at the bottom of the harbour. It seems that I had developed a sense of paranoia over the past months with regard to the ingress of water into my home.

So Judy and I parted and went our separate ways, sad in many respects as she had been excellent company. I could only be thankful for the time she was on the boat and accept that it had been longer than originally planned, having taken so long over the original estimated passage time to get here. The parting wasn't without anxiety though for while waiting at the appointed place for the taxi the arranged time came and went, resulting in a frantic phone call to the taxi office. Shortly it appeared, having been waiting at a different location. Then we said our goodbyes with Judy waving from the taxi, and me standing on the pavement with a sense of loss wondering what to do with myself. Well, what does one do in these circumstances? With only a slight hesitation, instinctively I went over to the supermarket, in a sense for comfort food and, practicing the premise of purchasing provisions when the opportunity arose. With a supermarket so close it made sense to ease the loads by carrying small amounts more frequently than to struggle with a large load nearer to departure time.

*****

On investigating alternatives regarding travel to Melbourne I decided to take the bus to Auckland and fly from there. Apart from any consideration of cost, the travelling by road gave a rare chance to see the countryside in this part of New Zealand, also to appreciate how fortunate it was to have had my hair cut in Rarotonga. The road into Auckland gave a good view across Waitemata Harbour to the crowded Marinas which, from my view point gave no indication of having any easy or obvious facilities for boat repairs, or for that matter easy access to storing for the next leg of the voyage. It was just a mass of boats moored fore and aft between mooring piles. How comforting it was to think, thanks to the lady hairdresser, that not all aspects of this saga were hapless happenings. Fate had certainly been kind on this occasion.

The inter-city bus terminal was conveniently located for the shuttle bus out to the airport, so after just a short wait and a tour around the city we arrived in plenty of time for the flight.

My nephew Stephen met me at the Airport as it was more convenient for him to come directly from work than anyone to take the long drive from the suburbs to the airport. The time spent with my sister and her family was a delight. Although I had been with them for a visit the previous year it was still a pleasure to see how close a family they all were. In fact I cannot remember ever seeing a family so lovingly close to each other.

With Christmas over I got to wondering if the boat was making any water, or maybe the bilge pump was misbehaving again. This morbid train of thought brought me to the point that I should return to Whangerai to put my mind at rest. And so I made arrangements to change the flight and take an earlier departure than otherwise planned. These arrangements caused something of a disappointment for my brother-in-law and nephew as a night out with the boys had been planned. Still what could one do? It would have been no fun to have a drink or two with visions of my boat lying at the bottom of the Hatea River.

As it turned out my fears were not totally unwarranted because although the bilges were dry, the house batteries had gone flat. Once again my thoughts turned to the need for a wind generator, which, as a promise to myself would be put in hand as soon as Whangarei businesses became operational again in the coming week. In the meantime the batteries were charged with the engine. This early return had another bonus as on New Years Day who should appear on the scene but the owner of the sail maker's business. This was somewhat of a surprise as he wasn't expected until later in January, but much to my pleasure another customer had cancelled his order allowing mine to be put forward. However, I was advised not to get too many hopes up as he was only on board to take measurements. The finished article was still some days in the future. Incidentally the sail-loft was in Opua, north of Whangarei which is where Les was moored, thus making matters easier for the borrowed sail to be returned to the rightful owner directly from the repair shop, saving either Les a journey here, or for me to go to Opua. Seems as though the decision to come to Whangarei was bearing a veritable harvest of good fortune.

Having said that, there was an incident that if not of good fortune certainly could carry some humour. During the course of this voyage, I only wore underpants so my underwear through lack of laundry facilities had become decidedly grey. Planning ahead I took all I had with me to Melbourne with the intention of getting a proper laundering at my sister's. The results were definitely satisfactory being pristine in their whiteness again; however, when I returned to Auckland and put on clean underwear at the hotel and then ventured out to book the bus to Whangarei there was a definite discomfort in the nether regions with the sensation that my winkie was continually popping out, a most disconcerting state of affairs. On returning to the hotel the reason came to light; due to an excess of Nappy-San my sister had used to bring back the whiteness, and combined with the salt already residing in the fabric the crotch had rotted out. Fortunately only one pair had succumbed to this treatment.

There wasn't much for me to do while waiting for the coming week except potter around on the boat and make frequent pilgrimages to the supermarket to build up on sea stores for the next leg of the voyage and beyond. Although the run to Melbourne wasn't anticipated to be very long it made sense to make sure to be well supplied in case of emergencies, also it was anticipated that with family visiting the boat, there would not be any opportunity to store in Melbourne. As I had taken a particular liking to New Zealand beer this item received special attention on the basis of one beer a day to last as far as, if not beyond, Fremantle. Make hay while the sun shines as they say, and a satisfying stack of this beverage now resided under the forward berth.

During this waiting period the retaining battens for the windows were removed and the glass properly sealed around the edges, to prevent ingress of water in these areas. Before resetting the battens they were sanded to remove the old varnish, and provoked an irate marina Manager to express his displeasure at the dust drifting about. I did point out that the dust wasn't settling on any boats but drifting and falling on the river, but point taken. No more work that could cause displeasure to others would be carried out at this location.

On Monday, now that the town was operational once more, I crossed the bridge to the other side of the river and made my way first to the camera repairer leaving the camera there then proceeding along the river side to the contracted sail maker's Whangerai establishment where small jobs were handled, to make a deposit on my new sail. Much to my delight, immediately next door was a well stocked marine hardware store and here I ordered the wind generator so wantonly desired over the past few months. As this was to be ordered in I would have the intervening period to plan and anticipate a world with fully charged batteries. I enquired about of a sheet metal worker and much to my delight this artisan was just behind the sail maker's loft. Things really were looking up and starting to go my way.

The sheet metal worker I was to learn within minutes of explaining my needs, was a most outgoing person, and had recently bought the business from his former boss and was just starting out on his own. Hamish, as that was his name, Hamish Mead, had a most disconcerting manner when being spoken to of holding his head to one side and peering intently at my mouth. I soon realised that he was deaf and this was the way he supplemented the hearing aid out of immediate sight deep in the ear canal. Watch my lips as they say. They do say that if a person loses one of his senses then another sense is increased, and this certainly applied to Hamish because he was a most loquacious young man, intelligent, efficient and most helpful and friendly. Over the few days of our acquaintance I really got to like him. On explaining the need for bracing to stiffen up the rudder post he immediately grasped the situation and had my rudimentary sketch amended to a more practical arrangement. Impressed by this young man I made my way back to the boat confident that this job was in hand and taking priority. This young man could add integrity to his resume. Although I would have liked to add consideration to this impression of him by an offer of a lift back to the boat, that would have been nice, but then he was about to finish an outstanding job and then tackle mine so the chance of a ride was neither offered nor asked for. Rather this quality would surface at a later date.

On returning to the marina I was called into the marina office to take a call from the camera repair man. He had deduced that the reason the transport lever was jammed, was because the inside of the camera was seized solid with rust and beyond repair. The elation of the morning's events softened somewhat at this bad news, and glumly I resigned myself to this setback, adding it to the list of ill-starred events. The loss of the camera was sad but the loss of the photos taken at Venus Point was felt somewhat more strongly. After all it wasn't every day that memorable sight could be visited.

In the interim, while I had been ashore, the owner of the boat next door returned with his wife from touring the North Island over the recent weeks since my arrival. Like most boaters he was helpful and friendly, the people in the boating world being kindred spirits I suppose. However, this meeting proved to be fortuitous as the down haul for the radar reflector had for some time come adrift leaving the reflector stuck at the top of the mast. To retrieve this object required the efforts of two people, one to ascend the mast, and the other to winch him up there. Much to my secret delight, Roger, volunteered to go aloft. The offer was received with alacrity and I soon had him in the bosun's chair and making the ascent. There are a few reasons why I stand back when an offer is volunteered for mast climbing; principally, I like to be in control of an operation as I know my equipment the best and how it operates. Secondly, on a previous occasion, and previously mentioned, I was at the top of a mast when the boat was hit by a series of swells from a passing ferry causing a situation were the mast swung violently through a wide arc with me hanging on for dear life. Alarming though this experience was I have ascended masts since then, although not without a feeling of trepidation. Once Roger was back on deck with the operation successfully completed, the beer was brought out and a closer acquaintance established.

His wife, he told me, would only come on his boat when it was in port with not having any interest in being out on the ocean, so Roger had sailed from Montreal around Cape Horn, crossing the Pacific and, eventually ended up here in Whangerai. This truly impressed me as most people would transit the Panama Canal, but having done that on a previous adventure Roger decided on a different route. This particular day was Tuesday when beer was two for the price of one at the local watering hole and, with Roger's wife being in town, we repaired there for further discussions and to take advantage of a free beer.

After this pleasant interlude I only saw Roger at a distance as the following day I dropped down river to the boat yard for haul out and the fitting of a bigger through hull for the holding tank, the unreliable macerator pump having seized up once again. As there was no law against discharging effluence outside of territorial waters this pump had proved to be surplus to requirement anyway, and one of those unnecessary luxuries one acquires in ones enthusiasm when fitting out a boat. The discharge pump on the toilet was doing an excellent job of breaking up the solids so a macerator pump could be dispensed with. Also I did not have to siphon off the contents of the holding tank, a most disagreeable job, to remove the pump for maintenance. The topside paintwork also needed attention as due to the wave action over the past months the paint had come away in sheets again.

The boat yard had positioned my boat next to a boat that held a youngish couple. Much to my chagrin I was to listen to an almost continuous tirade of high pitched whining complaints of the female of the species against her male counterpart, whom I might add won my praise and admiration at not saying a word or for that matter not causing her demise and helping her out of this unsatisfactory world. To say she was a screeching harpy would be the understatement of the year. As Judy would have said they were having a domestic. But doesn't that take two? However, I was in mortal dread that she might try to strike up an acquaintance and involve me in her complaints. Still, as it happened I had my own problems to deal with and kept my own counsel.

The fitting of the through hull and the subsequent application of a coat of paint went well, although when I attempted to connect the hose to the tank it proved to be impossible, no matter what I tried. Even after softening the hose with boiling water it still would not go onto the tank connection. Obviously, the North American hose size is slightly, just slightly, larger than the local size. Now what? Although the holding tank was empty it would need to be washed out before drilling for another tank connection, and there was no way that could be carried out in the boatyard. This matter, (no pun intended), would have to be transferred to a bucket and disposed of at sea. Once again I was wondering what else could go wrong. For this there was no long wait.

The topside paintwork was proceeding nicely with the white sheer nearly completed. With the ladder placed against the pulpit rail, I was applying the last of the sheer painting to the forward port side. When suddenly I felt the ladder starting to slip and I immediately grabbed the rail to stop further movement towards disaster. Considering the predicament for a moment, I decided, as I was only about four feet above the ground it would be safe to jump. I let go of the rail and made the leap. Even the best laid plans can be fraught with anomalies and this was no exception. When the ladder and I parted company my right sandal came free leaving my foot naked, and I came down heavily with my right heel on a stone. Obviously this ruined my well thought out plan of landing safely. The ladder came down with a clatter and I rolled on the ground which brought people running. Commiserations all round didn't allay the agonising pain in the heel or for that matter my embarrassment. All I could say was only my dignity was hurt, to calm their concerns. As it transpired the lady that had rushed over from a boat across the yard was the wife of a doctor. As enough fuss had been generated by this unfortunate happening I was pleased that the good doctor had not become involved. There had been quite enough attention for the moment. Gritting my teeth against the pain I assured all these good people that I was fine, and that I didn't need to go to the hospital. Eventually they left to let me get back to my labours. Later though, Anne, the doctor's wife, came over and invited me for dinner aboard their boat that evening and it was then that I met Graham her husband the good doctor. He deduced the heel bone had been bruised and dispensed a pain killer. So I was reduced to hobbling around on my duties in the comfort of knowing that time heals (once again no pun intended) all wounds. In retrospect I was immensely pleased that the shrew next door hadn't been around when this happened. I cringed at the thought what might have transpired.

The following afternoon Hamish came to offer up the rudder stock brace, and found me sitting on the settee resting my gammy leg. With hobbling around on my duties the ankle had swollen and caused even more pain. On learning the circumstances of my incapacitation he very kindly went back into town for a bag of ice. The result of this kind gesture managed to reduce the swelling and also eased the pain a little and, added consideration to his overflowing resume of good qualities.

Over the next few days the blue topside painting was completed, bringing the boat up to its normal pristine loveliness. Graham and Anne's boat had already left and it was my turn to go back in the water. While I settled the account, Charlie the yard manager wanted to know why I had told him the boat was forty feet in length. This had me puzzled for a moment. "Because that is the length," I said, bringing to mind the building plans. "No, it's not," he said. "It's thirty-seven," and produced a conversion table pointing at eleven point one eight meters. "Thirty-seven feet." he repeated. There was no denying the fact; I had never taken to this metric thing, being comfortable with imperial measurements, obviously to my detriment. "Bloody, hell," I said. "To think that all these years, I have been going to marinas paying for an extra three feet." Much miffed at the thought, but most grateful to have been put on the right track, I thanked Charlie for pointing this out. Although the boat was forty feet on the plans, when it came to the survey for registration the measurement is from a vertical down from the top of the stem to the rudder post. Even at this late date one can learn something.

So it was then that I found myself back at the marina albeit tied up alongside another boat away from Roger's, waiting for the sail and making frequent peregrinations to the supermarket and other establishments for the necessities of making the boat operationally efficient. As matters on the money front were healthy I indulged in a few extras; the rain gear that had let me down (literally) was replaced with a more robust set. The tea caddy had succumbing to the elements rust wise, was replaced with a set of porcelain containers complete with clamped rubber sealed tops to hold coffee, sugar, as well as tea. A particular treat was a small compass that was placed on the rack in the saloon section above and behind my sleeping position on the settee this to facilitate easy reading during the hours of darkness of the course being steered was as it should be, the gyro compass still being out of commission. An early warning system, one might say, of whether the boat had caught me unawares while resting and decided to head on a reciprocal course. This would save a journey into the cockpit to check the main compass. This would be particularly useful should it be raining as I would not have to don the rain gear. It was a wonderful feeling of joy to finally, after all these months, get the boat back to a comfortable efficient unit again. The feeling of being able to carry on and complete the dream was becoming palpable. The high point of this elation was the long desired wind generator; the mast being fabricated and fitted with the good services of Hamish, with myself doing the wiring and the assembly of the unit. No longer would it be a worry whether the batteries were fully charged. There was just one anomaly to all this; there was no way I could get service for the autopilot as the service agent was just not interested. The electrician who made the tests on the batteries and checked for any leaks should they be discharging to sea, even he when contacting his sources could get no joy. A rather disappointing result I thought as it is not unreasonable to expect a manufacturer to back up his products through his appointed agents. The magnetic compass, in conjunction with the Hydrovane steering system, was doing justice to the problem of steering a course so the fact that the gyro compass was malfunctioning became academic and thus was considered to be a luxury item.

During these days of waiting for the new genoa I ran into Roger, of mast climbing fame, who told me he had overstayed his immigration six month visa and was returning to Montreal. This announcement had me perplexed for a moment; after-all I had an unrealistic picture of him sailing his boat, and one doesn't just sail a boat from New Zealand to Montreal just like that. Surely the statement should have been, 'I'll be leaving soon.' As it transpired he was leaving his boat here in Whangarei and flying out, to then return for another six months or so. What a wonderful approach I thought; why rush around when one can take a leisurely nomadic progress through life taking the time to smell the roses as they say. But then I had a mind set about these things, and it was fixed in my mind to do a circumnavigation and I was too rigid in my thinking to change at this stage of the game. Maybe next trip. Apart from that I was only just keeping ahead of the weather, the next concern being the cyclone season in the Indian Ocean.

Les Bissell, the sailing representative for NSA, turned up on my doorstep so to speak. He was in Whangarei for an interview with the local radio station in regard to his promotion of the National Stroke Foundation. Of course these also involved a get together at the local watering hole for a beer or two and talk about our experiences of our respective passages from Rarotonga. He also had been delayed by the adverse weather even though he had taken less time than Judy and I had, not that his boat was a faster sailer it was just that with leaving later he had missed the weather patterns that had delayed us in the early part of our passage and therefore made good time as a result. However, his experience of the sixty knot winds was somewhat different from ours. While we managed to motor the last few miles to sheltered waters, he was caught out in the open and while heading for the Bay of Islands only managed, after a rough night to get under the lee of one of them and shelter there until the wind abated and he could make the run into Opua. There had been another boat, incidentally of the same design as mine as previously mentioned, which left Rarotonga with Les but sailing single handed. Their different courses had left them out of sight of each other after a few days but still in touch by radio for a while. Then the silence came. One cannot but wonder what had been the cause of that silence and hope for the best. He was heading for Opua also but hadn't turned up by the time Les came down to Whangarei. Having met someone under these circumstances only brings home a greater awareness of the possible dangers he might have experienced, and make the desire for his safety that much stronger. Those sixty knot winds had come so suddenly.

Anne and Graham Evans and I crossed paths again; they had been having dinner at the same place as Les and I and on the way out invited us to visit their boat for a nightcap. They were due to leave the next day, heading south for the Bay of Plenty to lie there for a while. Graham had accepted a medical position at

Whangarei Hospital and they were filling in time cruising New Zealand until the appointment fell due. Anne, who was a radiologist by profession, hoped to secure a position also. Failing that, it was my opinion that she should become an interviewer as she was a delight to talk to and had with the utmost ease extracted opinions and circumstances of my life from me, something that with strangers I don't easily divulge. The new genoa had arrived earlier in the day and Anne had very kindly offered to help bend the sail. As I was expecting Hamish to return in the next day or two to finish up with the bracing of the rudder post, I had thought to prevail on his good services for this project while he was available. Still, the offer was much appreciated and I was once again made aware of how supportive the boating community is.

Shortly after breakfast the next day the Evans's passed by, heading down river with much in the way of shouted well wishes and jolly banter, to disappear forever from my acquaintance. A great pity as they were good people but, that's how it is; ships that pass in the night one might say. Les, having stayed onboard for the night, was the next one to leave, and remaining only long enough for a coffee then he took himself off for his interview and in the afternoon headed back to Opua.

Hamish came after lunch and finalised the rudder post bracing, a fine job he had made too, which left me well pleased. Thankfully no more worries with the post flapping about, creating a leak through the seal. The boat was now fully returned to operational efficiency, and what a joy that was. My elation was so great that now I could progress through the remainder of the voyage with the boat shipshape and Bristol fashion. Now I could finally leave Whangarei, broke, but happy in the thought that there would be time for the pension to accumulate before funds would be required again.

CHAPTER FOURTEEN
Whangarei to Melbourne

And the gates of Hell are opened and riven, and the winds of Hell are loosened and driven......

The Himalayan

The next day it was my turn to leave and first thing after breakfast I went over to the Office and settled the moorage bill, and then back to the boat to haul the dinghy on board, deflate and stow, and generally prepare for sea. While at the marina office the manager had arranged for me to meet 'Bruce the Immigration' at their Station at two-thirty for outward clearance, this appointment fell in nicely with my dropping down river to take on fuel prior to the rendezvous. The weather report for the Tasman Sea was excellent with two High Pressure Systems dominating the whole area, which promised a quick and easy passage to Melbourne. The situation really was on the up and up.

The arrangement for fuelling appeared to be based on an honesty system as there wasn't anyone to attend to the pump just a matter of getting self service, noting the amount taken then finding someone to take payment. Nice to be trusted, but no doubt there must have been some sort of check against thieving.

Well, what do you know; when I returned on board the engine wouldn't start. Here we go again, I thought, still staggering from one crisis to another engine-wise. All was not lost though as there was a mechanic at this establishment and sporting the logo of just the type of engine that I had. After a short delay while the mechanic changed one of the battery clamps, the engine was operational again. So simple when you know how to locate the cause of the problem Maybe one day I should take a course in small engine mechanics; the way piddling little things have gone wrong an achievement in that field would be an absolute boon.

Even with the hold up at the refuelling station I arrived at the Immigration dock on time, Bruce waiting to do the honours and with him a junior who was to take over Bruce's duties as he was about to retire. Nice helpful fellow was Bruce, but then with my limited experience of New Zealanders he was no exception. On our arrival at Whangarei at this dock, I had expressed to Bruce my intention of proceeding to Opua after leaving this port but, as the arrangement with Les and his sail had altered matters there would be no need to divert. Bruce needed reassurance that this was not now my intention as this would be highly illegal. Having being at sea all my life I was well aware of these procedures and assured him that should I have to divert to another New Zealand port I would clear inwards again. This stated understanding cleared the situation and I was allowed to proceed down river on my way to sea. The nearer I got to open water the stronger the wind became, finally blowing at about thirty knots from the south and right on the nose, driving spray the full length of the boat as I left the protective lee of the land. Well, I had my newly acquired rain gear on and when rounding Bream Head the wind would be on the port quarter so seeking shelter would not be necessary. Just chug along and dodge the spray. When I passed the oil refinery a ship was in the process of unmooring so that was something else to watch out for. When it came thundering past and so close the side of this ship seemed to be enormous but, thankfully with no concern, even the wash made no impact as the wind whipped-seas almost eliminated the effect.

Soon I was able to leave the channel and round Bream Head to set a course to the north. The wind was far too strong to attempt to hoist the mainsail so it was a case of boogying along nicely with just the new genoa, a sail gazed at with much pleasure and admiration, a strongly constructed sail that would last for quite some time. This had me thinking this enterprise certainly had taken an upward turn. Couldn't help wondering though how Graham and Anne were making out with this wind as they would be heading into it, probably sheltering somewhere I would think. So here we were getting along very nicely on the next leg of this pilgrimage, and time for a cup of tea.

Keeping a reasonable distance off the coast, as is my wont, to avoid any coastwise traffic, I made good time, passing the Bay of Islands at first light the following day and rounding North Cape at midnight meeting the one and only ship on this leg of the trip. As we were on reciprocal courses it was quite easy to keep out of his way and out of danger. It wouldn't do after all that had gone in the past months to be run down at this stage of the game.

The days passed easily in glorious weather crossing the Tasman Sea with the High Pressure Systems remaining steady over the whole area, truly a fabulous sail with all units functioning nicely. The wind generator was performing wonderfully, allaying any fears of the batteries quitting again, always a niggling worry now placed firmly to the back of my memory bank. All was not a picnic though, as during the night prior to entering the Bass Strait the boat decided to turn around and go back the way we had come. This had me scrambling on deck to sort out the problem; once again the boat head wouldn't come across the wind to come back to the correct course so it was case of starting the engine to assist this manoeuvre. Fine, it fired immediately but when it came to putting it into gear the gear lever wouldn't budge, immovable, seized solid it was. Well I wasn't about to try and sort out this problem in the middle of the night so I turned the engine off and I resorted to jibing the boat, bringing the wind around the stern. Not a preferred practice but needs must when the Devil drives as they say. However, I was back on course and I was left to lie down again and ponder the mysteries of why the engine didn't go into gear.

After breakfast I tackled the problem and found no logical answer, which proved to be academic anyway as the engine came out in sympathy and refused to start. Now this was a pretty pickle I found myself in as the engine was necessary to get through Port Phillip Heads into the bay, which would be the ideal method. The alternative was to sail through should the wind become favourable, which at the moment didn't look too promising. Failing this, I suppose I could call for a tow. Due to my pride this would not be the option that I would approach with alacrity. But, then again, after the number of tows I had this trip maybe, I could accept the indignity this time. All conjecture at this moment in time though, as there were still three more days to go.

The following night yet another matter had brought me out on deck; this was in the way of a bump. Not the running-into-something-type bump but coming from the deck above. What passed through my mind was that maybe a fish had landed there, rather a wild guess I know, but then what else could it be? On investigation there was nothing lying around; maybe it had gone over the side again. All these thoughts and the probable answers could well be the product of a tired mind, and the matter of being engineless was still uppermost. I had hove to the previous evening not wanting to get too far into the strait and too close to the many islands there during the hours of darkness, so the bump could not be a result of hard sailing, or any sailing for that matter. Somewhat puzzled, I lay down again with the resolve to investigate the matter in daylight. Strange how things happen during the hours of darkness on this boat. Well, they do say that things go bump in the night.

What with setting the sails before daylight and directing a course into the Strait when daylight did break, the matter had left my mind until I happened to look up the mast to find that the Radar dome had disappeared. Taking a deep breath and letting it out in forceful exasperation, with a muttered, 'Bloody hell', I wondered what else could go wrong on this trip. I found it hard to believe that an item bolted to a mast bracket could just fall off; after all it had been there for six years. Then I got to wondering if the mast rigger had used steel bolts as this would guarantee an electrolytic action with the aluminium which would eventually rot out. At the moment this could only be wondered at until the matter could be investigated, and left me wondering how much the new Radar would cost.

At least the day was proving to be absolutely gorgeous with a clear blue sky and a steady southerly breeze, which was something to be thankful for and progress was being made at a handsome rate of knots and as there was nothing that could be done about the recent problems, I resorted to enjoying the sunshine and the best way to navigate Port Phillip Heads *sans* engine. There were other chores to attend to, particularly finalising the caulking of the cabin deck. This job had been hanging on for long enough and it was only at Whangarei that caulking compound had come available. So just one more session, then once the compound had hardened it could be sanded and varnished. I must admit to feeling highly satisfied with the results so far and not a little smug at being so fortunate at acquiring the teak decking. The galley area had still to be done but that would have to wait until there was a possibility of the deck remaining dry long enough for the epoxy glue to take, which with the bilges taking water again didn't hold promise for the near future. Still, should I want to feel smug over teak decking I could always gaze at the cabin deck.

Lunch over and after a ten minute snooze, I went on deck again to enjoy a little more of the sunshine. The Hogan group of islands would be the next waypoint and these were expected to be cleared late evening. It was while pondering this event that I saw a white cloud on the horizon to the south. In a short while this cloud had spread the full width of the horizon and was making a steady progress north and to my locality. The unusual aspect of this was that it was perfectly white and fluffy, quite spectacular with the blue sky both before and behind. Having seen this type of cloud before some years previously off the coast of New South Wales I was well aware that it presented a Southerly Buster that would bring strong winds in its wake. With alacrity, therefore, I had the mainsail down again and lashed to the boom with the genoa rolled up to just a small 'v', in other words a heave-to situation again. Sure enough, within minutes of getting back to the cockpit the wind hit, building up in no time to forty knots. Indeed, fortunate was I to have had a previous experience with this type of phenomenon. On that occasion it was on a steam ship of five thousand tons which was somewhat different to my fourteen ton boat, a difference that wasn't long in presenting itself.

I hadn't been in the cabin very long, not even long enough to put the kettle on for a cup of tea even, when there was an almighty bang from out on deck. Of course this had me out on deck in no time to find with amazement that the genoa had unfurled to its full extent and was flapping wildly in the gale. It wasn't long before the reason presented itself; the haul-in line that controlled the amount of genoa to be let out had parted. Tying the two parts together as a temporary repair and then attempting to reduce the sail area once more proved impossible in such a wind and there was absolutely no movement at all that indicated the furling gear would take in the sail, so I suspected that the gearing could have jammed. There I was bouncing around on the plunging foredeck trying to control the sail, this thing possessed, with the sheets whipping and twisting themselves into a hopeless tangle. It dawned on me that in my haste to control this impossible situation I wasn't wearing a harness. Not a sensible situation under the circumstances and as the only possibility was to let the sail down and hope it wouldn't be lost, I went below to put on the harness and get the pliers to undo the shackle holding the lower end of the sail.

Satellite image of the storm over Victoria at 0225 UTC (1325 EDST) on 3rd February, 2005

The rapid deepening of the low pressure system resulted in wide spread gale force winds across most parts of the southern and central state of Victoria, with exposed coastal locations reaching storm force at times. Gusts of up to 148km/hr were recorded at Wilsons Promontory Lighthouse, while Fawkner Beacon, located on Port Phillip Bay, recorded the strongest gust in the Melbourne area with 104km/hr during the early hours of Thursday morning. The wind force was such that coastal waters, such as Point Nepean, recorded a peak wave height of 12.5 metres.

While engaged in this exercise the boat took on a violent shuddering. This shuddering didn't last more than a couple of seconds after which there was a terrific crashing sound. Expecting the worst, I was out on deck again to view a scene of absolute chaotic dismay. The mast had come down and was in the water over the starboard side, held on to the boat by the stays and shrouds. On its descent it had taken out all the starboard side stanchions. The rigging had decapitated the Hydrovane steering casting, and taken away the top half, complete with the wind vane, leaving a useless lower section. My beloved wind generator of just a few days had been knocked over, taking out most of the vanes. On viewing all the damage I must admit to a profound feeling of hopelessness at the way fortune had dealt all the wrong cards. I just plonked myself down on the cockpit seat and slumped. "Bloody hell! What next?" I asked myself. Matters had evolved far too quickly during the previous ten minutes for any great emotion to take over; I just sat staring at the latest misfortune until my brain dispelled the shock of it all and started functioning again.

"What's the next move?" I asked, always a good question under the circumstances. One reads about intrepid seafarers in similar circumstances rigging a jury mast and limping in to the nearest safe haven. Now that I was in the same circumstance, my mind of course mulled over the possibilities. First of all, something that would serve as a mast would be required, which apart from a boathook I didn't have. Not that a boathook would be suitable under the circumstances as it was too short to support a sail, which was over the side under the water, and could not provide sufficient propulsion to move a forty foot boat of fourteen tons. I have to admit at this moment I entertained doubts about the veracity of the stories one reads of man's determination to overcome misfortune.

While pondering, the question it came to mind that had I not been in the cabin when the mast came down, what would have been the consequences? It was not beyond the realms of possibility that with the wire shrouds and stays whizzing about causing such mayhem; I could have been seriously injured, decapitated even like the Hydrovane. At least I still had a head on my shoulders and the means to think of the next move so I could be grateful for that. Fate, it seems, still had some kindness.

Obviously, with not even an engine I wasn't going anywhere, just wallowing in a heavy swell with a gale whistling around my ears. At least the mast being in the water was acting as a steadying influence of sorts. The best thing to do would be to advise the Coast Guard of my situation and maybe get some advice from them. At least they would know I was out here and should the worst come to the worst should I perish, my family would know what had happened. These thoughts were not morbid considerations, rather a logical train of thought; after all wouldn't people like to know what had happened to me? As I didn't have the wherewithal to access the telephone number of the Coast Guard I phoned my sister in Melbourne and asked her to get it for me and I would phone back in an hour. Big mistake telling her that I was in a spot of bother as this upset her sufficiently for me to ask her to put my brother-in-law on instead. After the hour I phoned back, and in the interim my nephew had turned up and took over the enquiries, a situation that needed his clear thinking and firm hand.

By the time I had managed to call the Water Police, or to give them their full title the Victoria Police Air Wing, as the Coast Guard is called in Australia, it was evening. They gave me three alternatives; wait for the availability of a boat big enough to come out and tow me in; have them redirect a ship to enact a rescue; or be lifted off by helicopter. With the lateness of the hour, and needing time to think before making a decision I agreed that I would give my position each hour during the night and let them know in the morning what had been decided. Believe me it was a tough one. The thought of giving up didn't fill my heart with joy but, after a night of agonising over the alternatives between the hourly reporting in, common sense won the day on the basis of cost. Should I opt to be towed in, how much would a tow of forty miles to the nearest safe haven cost? Not to mention replacement of the Hydrovane, (I knew the cost of that and it wasn't cheap). Would a new mast be on the agenda? The wind generator I felt might be salvaged with replacement vanes and straightening of the post. Totalling up the possible cost and realising that my funds were limited, not to mention that from day one things had gone wrong as though there was a curse on the boat, who was to say that this would be the end of forever throwing money into this particular hole in the ocean? Although these thoughts where going round and round in my head throughout the night I think at the back of my mind it was a case of facing reality and be taken off by helicopter. There was no consideration given to being taken off by a passing ship. In this weather it would be a difficult and dangerous operation trying to get me up the side of a ship. Besides, who knows where I would end up? Back in Panama maybe, or some, God forbidden a place so far from anywhere that it would be well nigh impossible to return home? Morbid thoughts indeed. The only remaining option was to be taken off by helicopter. Being taken to Melbourne at least I would be with family. It was then that I began planning what to take with me. With wry humour I rejected the kitchen sink, and all other bulky objects. There were many items that would have been desirable but, considering the circumstances the only practical pieces were passports, credit and debit cards and most inconsequently a photograph of my dog. On reflection, I could only account for this oddity as subconsciously wanting to at least have something personal from my home of ten months. Whatever? Strangely the items that gave a twinge of regret were the cases of beer; all those lovely one-a-day treats I had planned for, going to the bottom of Bass Strait gave cause for heartache. Here I was planning to send my boat to the bottom and all the regret I had was losing a couple of cases of beer. Maybe it was time to get off while there was still some sanity left.

The wind hadn't decreased in volume during the night and it was still blowing a full gale. The mast which lay alongside had been acting as a steadying influence, lessening the violence of the waves, although the boat wallowed heavily, lurching from one side to the other. At full daylight I called the Water Police to inform them of my decision to be lifted off and suggested that when I saw the helicopter I would open the sea valves to sink the boat. This was met with a most vehement negative and told I was told in no uncertain terms to wait for the crewman to board and he would give instructions as to what procedures to follow. Well, I was aware of the rescue procedures. Only one authority should direct operations so as not to cause confusion, so it was then that I agreed, not without doubts though. It was imperative that the boat would have to be sunk, otherwise it would only be a danger to shipping, and with the boat bouncing around the way it was it didn't seem wise to hang around while any instructions were being issued. I was in the cockpit while this conversation was going on, and on conclusion of this the boat took a violent roll, jerk almost, which threw me off balance with enough force to smash the entry door with my elbow. Now the door was teak and although the door suffered so did my elbow, which bled profusely until a wood splinter was removed and the wound dressed with a tissue and I had applied pressure to stop the bleeding. The wind generator was bravely operating with the three remaining blades, bless it. However, as this might cause problems with the crewman I felt it wise to tie the blades to stop them spinning and prevent possible injury.

There was nothing left to do now but to get dressed in my go ashore gear, pull on the survival suit, and collect the relevant papers and documents in zip lock bags and place them in the pockets. On the off chance that it would be allowed, I collected my Journals and Notes of the voyage so far and placed them in a holdall. These were a record of my adventures and would be essential should I decide to write about the saga. As a sop to my regrets over the beer, I decided to open a can and have at least a taste of what was to be committed to the deep.

In due course the helicopter arrived and after doing a circuit, hovered to lower the crewman to land squarely into the cockpit, a manoeuvre that had my admiration for the professionalism of the pilot and his team. Immediately I was offered the harness but I suggested that first the sea valves had to be opened. To this he acquiesced with what seemed to be a hint of annoyance, although this had me puzzled, the moment wasn't for questioning, but it was a bit odd, though, that having been instructed to wait until the crewman boarded, everything seemed to be going pear shaped again.

Everything was ready for flooding the boat and it took no time at all for me to go below, open the ball valve and return to the cockpit. To my amazement the crewman had disappeared from the cockpit to be observed in the water some twenty feet away from the boat beckoning for me to join him. Much as this situation was displeasing to me and as it would mean the Journals getting soaked, it was not a situation to argue over. So over the rail I went and lowered myself into the waves to swim the short distance to my erstwhile dry saviour. A bit of a struggle as it turned out with the down draft from the helicopter blowing spray all over the place, not to mention twelve foot waves breaking over us both. However, the harness was quickly placed over my head and under my arms and the lift commenced. With the wave action the harness had slipped down around my waist and I found myself coming out of the water upside down with my legs around the crewman's neck, soon to be dropped down again, and fighting to get my head above water. In quick time, at least before I drowned, they had a very subdued survivor being winched up to the helicopter, wondering if it was possible to have any more indignities thrust upon him. I wasn't kept in the waiting too long as with the slow turn of our bodies in the ascent the last sight of the boat as it came up on a wave showed a considerable expanse of the bottom before our turning took us out of the view. I really thought that the bloody thing was mooning me. Not a comforting last sight to store in my memory of our shared time together. At least the bottom was clean with no sign of growth, which regenerated the thought of using Glidden's paint on any other future boat project.

EPILOGUE

I never saw the boat again. After the double dunking and being half drowned it was enough for me, after being hauled into the helicopter, to sit on the floor very subdued dripping water, with dejected thoughts over the loss and drained emotionally. The door had been pulled so the view was shut off. Had I been inclined to lean over for a last look at my home of the previous ten months, I would have felt no better.

I reflected on the events that led to me having to abandon my adventure, beginning with the parting of the control line for the genoa when only a small area of sail was exposed to the elements. It seemed very unfair, as I felt I could ride out the storm had the failure not occurred. I recall the saying; 'for the want of a nail the shoe was lost,' and so on, with the progression of events failing until the battle was lost, came to mind. Well it had happened, and there was nothing to be gained by playing "what if?"

The flight to the Air Wing Station took only a few minutes at least that is how it seemed at the time. It could have been fifteen, twenty. Clambering out of the helicopter I released a flood of sea water from down the legs of the survival suit to form puddles on the tarmac. Even in my dejected state I could find some humour in this. The crew member and I plodded over to the building to be met by a person of authority, no doubt, as he was reluctant to allow us inside. By this time I was shivering uncontrollably, wind and water producing a good combination for this effect. Maybe it was this or maybe the crewman's persuasiveness softened this person's heart for he finally allowed us in. The staff, however, proved to be most considerate and helpful as I was directed to the shower and given dry clothes. The underpants were not my usual choice having no fly and of a vivid red bikini style, but beggars can't be choosers and I was thankful for the consideration. A plastic garbage bag had also been supplied into which went my wet clothes, now all the possessions I had in the world. Well as they say, when at the bottom there is only one way to go and that is up.

The pleasant guys continued to be friendly after my welcome shower and had a cup of coffee ready on hand. He that had met us at the door continued to be off-hand, however, which had me wondering what his problem was. After all in this situation I could hardly be considered to be a bum asking for a handout. Even when I thanked him for the shower he only grunted. No matter, as after a short while we were back in the helicopter on our way to Essendon Airport, the main Air Wing Station to wait for the Immigration clearance and a taxi to take me to my sister's.

The train of events from the rescuer's side had been explained to me during the interim and it had transpired that they had tried to contact me via VHF to open the sea valves and be ready to be lifted off immediately the crewman had landed in the cockpit. Obviously with the radio antennae being at the top of the mast and the mast in the water, there was no way such a message could be received. Because of this, once again a sequence of events was brought into play; with me having to go below to open the sea valve. Even though it was such a short space of time it was sufficient for the boat to be hit by a wave and for the wind to catch the helicopter in a gust strong enough to push it off station, thus catapulting the crewman overboard into the sea to land some twenty feet away, thankfully unharmed. While in the water with the strop in place we were both forced under by wave action, causing the strop to slip down, with the result that I left the water upside down with the crewman frantically holding onto my leg. The winch man seeing this lowered us into the water again and this I was given to understand from a height of twenty to thirty feet. No wonder I felt subdued when I finally got into the helicopter.

The newspapers the following day reported how bad the weather had been; apart from many small craft dragged ashore from their moorings and suffering damage, the Melbourne to Tasmania ferry had suffered heavy structural damage, and passengers were injured making it necessary to put back into port. There was a little bit about my adventures, too, tucked away in the main article. Seems it had been quite a storm. There was a short radio interview with female reporter who due to her aggressive attitude and asinine questions I soon terminated. It was obvious she knew little or nothing of her subject while posing questions like: Why didn't I run for shelter behind one of the many islands in the strait. Now I ask in such a disabled condition: How could that be possible?

I didn't stay with my sister and family for more than a couple of days as they, with my brother-in-law's sister and her friend, were taking off for a tour of Tasmania. There was time, however, to purchase a limited wardrobe, limited in the sense that with having nothing and the realisation that one doesn't need very much, enough is enough. It was a just buy what is needed to live policy. Up to the time of writing I have followed that principle, realising that to accumulate goods and chattels for the sake of having them is only a drag on living. At least something of a tangible nature came out of the adventure.

From Melbourne I went to Fremantle to stay with my good friend Debbie for a couple of weeks, then to Kalbarri to stay with another good friend Norman, Both, with me are keen Endeavour Replica aficionados and we have joined up in different places in the world to be volunteer guides. I have to say how much I appreciated their generosity and understanding of my situation by not raising the questions that must have been at the forefront regarding my recent exploits. They gave me the time to sort myself out and adjust to the loss of my boat and the abrupt termination of a dream.

While in Fremantle as a result of shattering the cabin door with my elbow this had swollen to alarming proportions to the point I deemed it advisable to seek medical advice at the hospital. I mention this because the lady in Triage during our conversation mentioned that she and her husband had recently lost their boat in the Indian Ocean and had been taken off by a passing cargo ship. They both were working again with the intention of purchasing another boat to take another attempt at their dream. My effort in the light of this seemed like small potatoes.

From Australia it was a leisurely progress by way of England and then home to Canada bringing to mind and making notes of the adventure along the way. The loss of the journals I regretted as the picture would have been much fuller. However, on reflection might have made for a story bogged down in detail to the point of being tedious. It only remains for me to say that what has been related actually happened without resorting to flannel or too much detail.

I often think of the adventure and ask myself: Will I go again? Well, that would have to depend on resolving many, many logistical questions, which seem at this moment in time to be insurmountable. But, who knows?

The people I met in the boating community remain a fond memory as they seem unique in their outgoing friendly and kindly manner towards others in the same situation. Although, ship's that pass in the night, never to be seen again probably, I still hold their memory in high regard.

On a personal level I feel I have gained by the adventure. I left Pender with only my boat and my pension, and came back with only my pension. I'm happy and content in this situation, if with a twinge of regret, as now I don't have to worry about being tied down with the responsibility of material things. I'm free! To lose is to win.

While writing this account I have been advised that the helicopter crew have been given awards for bravery from both the Australian and Canadian Governments for their part in the rescue. Well, there is nothing like a couple of awards under the belt to enhance a career. Glad to have been of help, guys.

As for myself; my rewards were in the experiences of the whole adventure warts and all, and would I go again?

"Unquestionably! Yes."

Pender Island, BC.

14th June 2006.

CPSIA information can be obtained at www.ICGtesting.com
Printed in the USA
LVOW062043161211
259815LV00001B/10/P